A CRITICAL COMPANION TO
EARLY
CHILDHOOD

Education at SAGE

SAGE is a leading international publisher of journals, books, and electronic media for academic, educational, and professional markets.

Our education publishing includes:

- accessible and comprehensive texts for aspiring education professionals and practitioners looking to further their careers through continuing professional development

- inspirational advice and guidance for the classroom

- authoritative state of the art reference from the leading authors in the field.

Find out more at: **www.sagepub.co.uk/education**

A CRITICAL COMPANION TO
EARLY
CHILDHOOD

EDITED BY
MICHAEL REED & ROSIE WALKER

Los Angeles | London | New Delhi
Singapore | Washington DC

Los Angeles | London | New Delhi
Singapore | Washington DC

SAGE Publications Ltd
1 Oliver's Yard
55 City Road
London EC1Y 1SP

SAGE Publications Inc.
2455 Teller Road
Thousand Oaks, California 91320

SAGE Publications India Pvt Ltd
B 1/I 1 Mohan Cooperative Industrial Area
Mathura Road
New Delhi 110 044

SAGE Publications Asia-Pacific Pte Ltd
3 Church Street
#10-04 Samsung Hub
Singapore 049483

Commissioning Editor: Jude Bowen
Development editor: Amy Jarrold
Associate editor: Miriam Davey
Editorial assistant: George Knowles
Production editor: Katie Forsythe
Copyeditor: Christine Bitten
Proofreader: Thea Watson
Indexer: Charmian Parkin
Marketing manager: Lorna Patkai
Cover design: Wendy Scott
Typeset by: C&M Digitals (P) Ltd, Chennai, India
Printed and bound by
CPI Group (UK) Ltd, Croydon, CR0 4YY

Editorial arrangement © Michael Reed and Rosie Walker 2015

Chapter 1 © Michael Reed, Linda Tyler and Rosie Walker 2015
Chapter 2 © Karen Hanson and Karen Appleby 2015
Chapter 3 © Sue Callan 2015
Chapter 4 © Jennifer Worsley and Catherine Lamond 2015
Chapter 5 © Michelle Rogers 2015
Chapter 6 © Mary Benson McMullen 2015
Chapter 7 © Anna Popova 2015
Chapter 8 © Jackie Musgrave 2015
Chapter 9 © Frances Brett 2015
Chapter 10 © Anna Kilderry 2015
Chapter 11 © Robin Balbernie 2015
Chapter 12 © Aline Wendy Dunlop 2015
Chapter 13 © Claire M. Richards 2015
Chapter 14 © Caroline Jones 2015
Chapter 15 © Erica Brown 2015
Chapter 16 © Derval Carey-Jenkins 2015
Chapter 17 © Siân Wyn Siencyn 2015
Chapter 18 © Martin Needham and Dianne Jackson 2015
Chapter 19 © Josephine Bleach 2015
Chapter 20 © Sandra Hesterman 2015
Chapter 21 © Michael Gasper 2015
Chapter 22 © Alison Nicholas 2015
Chapter 23 © Victoria Cooper 2015
Chapter 24 © Alma Fleet, Catherine Patterson and Janet Robertson 2015
Chapter 25 © Carla Solvason 2015

First published 2015

Library of Congress Control Number: 2014954493

British Library Cataloguing in Publication data

A catalogue record for this book is available from the British Library

ISBN 978-1-4462-5926-9
ISBN 978-1-4462-5927-6 (pbk)

At SAGE we take sustainability seriously. Most of our products are printed in the UK using FSC papers and boards. When we print overseas we ensure sustainable papers are used as measured by the Egmont grading system. We undertake an annual audit to monitor our sustainability.

This book is dedicated to:

Anna, for all she taught us

Nick Johnson 1947–2014: a true companion

Oliver and Christopher
Rosie Walker

Ray and Barbara Reed, Tess, Juliette and Ellen
Michael Reed

To my grandmother Margaret Bleach and parents Thomas and Frances Bleach
Josephine Bleach

Michael and Jonathan – always my inspiration Sue Callan

To my wife Janet, our children Giles, Amy, Luke, Harry, and grandchildren Isabelle and Emily
Mike Gasper

Robert, David, Adam, Emily and Norman
Catherine Lamond

Beth and Imogen
Alison Nicholas

My dad
Anna Popova

My parents, Donal and Jo
Claire Richards

To D, N, G and UKb
Michelle Rogers

To Johsua and Jacob
Carla Solvason

Praise for the book

In this stimulating and provocative book Michael Reed and Rosie Walker have drawn together a diverse and international range of respected authors, each of whom has taken a critical approach to the contentious question of how you define and achieve quality early childhood services. It is a book designed to provoke and promote critical dialogue and discourse amongst practitioners and students through critical engagement with the position of the authors within the text, followed up with a set of Critical Learning Activities and carefully crafted follow up materials (supported with a very practical and extremely developmental website). Individually, each chapter provides an insight into reflective and dialogic practice, but collectively they stand as a model of critical thinking and professional praxis. As such this book should be required reading for all students engaged in early childhood studies, and all practitioner teams aiming to develop a learning community to support the development of excellence in their professional practice. I believe anyone who reads this book will be inspired and motivated to challenge and extend their thinking and professional practice, adopting the critical stance which lies at the heart of quality services for children and families.

Professor Chris Pascal, Director of Centre for Research in Early Childhood (CREC)

This book provides an interesting approach to a range of areas important to early years encouraging the reader to reflect on the issues with a critical awareness and consider different points of view. It provides a good grounding for those interested in early years. The book is strongly focused on quality in early years and what constitutes quality provision in terms of initiatives and policies and the role of the practitioner. As such, it touches on key areas for students and practitioners alike, encouraging critical thinking and an awareness of the historical journey and some of the debates about early years provision.

Rita Winstone, Senior Lecturer and Programme Leader, Early Childhood Studies, Teesside University

This book is aptly titled as it addresses the needs of those in the early stages of their professional journey in early childhood education and care. The group of respected contributors span the fields of education, health and social care introducing the reader to key themes, terms and issues through 25 accessible and wide ranging chapters. Vignettes, case studies and learning activities bring theory to life and encourage a critical approach to study and practice.

Linda Miller, Professor Emeritus of Early Years, The Open University

An invaluable aid to students of early years education and care, this book offers comprehensive, contemporary examination of critical issues surrounding working with young children, families and other professionals.

    The clear, user-friendly format and plentiful links to additional resources and learning activities, lead the reader to further explore and develop their own knowledge, making this a truly essential read!

Katrina Ivey, Sector Endorsed Foundation Degree in Early Years, University of Worcester

Within the current Early Childhood Education and Care (ECEC) climate, understanding, promoting and improving quality for children is a fundamental role of the practitioner. Using contributions from renowned sector experts, this book supports students to critically develop their personal, professional and ethical philosophy within the challenging ECEC environment.

Gaynor Corrick, Early Years Teacher, Sutton Seedlings, Herefordshire

Here is a treasure trove for the curious reader, inspiring a critical learning journey to challenge individuals and their early years practice. Each concise, relevant chapter, with Critical Learning Activities and Reflection Points, stimulates further exploration, guided conveniently by immediate further reading and references.

    This unique privilege is due to the range of inter-professional expertise honestly shared by the range of national and international authors, including from Australia, United States and Wales. All are actively engaged in practice, research or lecturing, with a refreshing variety of expression. Current experiences in Early Education and Childcare are compared and contrasted through different 'lenses', including transparent autobiographies, exemplars of child/student voice and active research. Case studies link theory to practice, modelling the expectation of engagement with babies, young children, families, colleagues and other professionals. The Editors have ensured connections can be made between topics, helpful for ongoing study.

    This 'Critical Companion' will support full-time undergraduates, experienced early years practitioners undertaking a Foundation Degree and BA 'top-up', plus all the 'reflective activists' that continually strive to improve care and learning opportunities with babies, young children and their families.

Jessica Johnson
Senior Lecturer Early Years, Kingston University

Table of Contents

List of figures and tables

Figures

Tables

List of abbreviations

ACARA	The Australian Curriculum, Assessment and Reporting Authority
ACECQA	Australian Children's Education and Care Quality Authority
ACT	Association for Children's Palliative Care
ADD	Attention Deficit Disorder
ADHD	Attention Deficit Hyperactive Disorder
ARACY	Australian Institute of Family Studies
CAF	Common Assessment Framework
CHAT	Cultural Historical and Activity Theory
CLA	Critical Learning Activity
CWDC	Children's Workforce Development Council
DAP	Developmentally appropriate practice
DEC	Division for Early Childhood
DEEWR	Department of Education, Employment and Workplace Relations
DfE	Department for Education
DfES	Department for Education and Skills
DH	Department of Health
ECE	Early Childhood Education
ECEC	Early Childhood Education and Care
ECERS	Early Childhood Environment Rating Scale
ELI	Early Learning Initiative
EPPE	Effective Provision on Pre-school Education
EYFS	Early Years Foundation Stage
EYLF	Early Years Learning Framework
MEEIFP	Monitoring and Evaluation of the Effective Implementation of the Foundation Phase
NAEYC	National Association for the Education of Young Children
NAPLAN	National Assessment Program – Literacy and Numeracy
NCCA	National Council for Curriculum and Assessment
NCSL	National College for School Leadership
NICE	National Institute for Clinical Excellence
NPQICL	National Post-qualification in Integrated Centre Leadership

NQF	National Quality Framework
OECD	Organisation for Economic Co-operation and Development
Ofsted	Office for Standards in Education Children's Services and Skills
PISA	Programme for International Student Assessments
PITC	Program for Infant Toddler Caregivers
PSLA	Pre-School Learning Alliance
QIRS	Quality Improvement Rating Systems
RIE	Resources for Infant Educarers
SEN	Special Educational Needs
SENCO	Special Educational Needs Co-ordinator
SENDA	Special Educational Needs and Disability Act
SENTW	Special Educational Needs Tribunal for Wales
SLD	Specific Learning Difficulties
SSTUWA	State School Teachers' Union of Western Australia
UNCRC	United Nations Convention on the Rights of the Child

About the editors

Michael Reed is a Senior Lecturer at the Centre for Early Childhood, within the Institute of Education at the University of Worcester. He teaches on undergraduate and postgraduate courses related to child development, practice-based research and leadership. He is a qualified teacher and holds advanced qualifications in Educational Inquiry, Educational Psychology and Special Education. He has been part of course development and writing teams at the Open University and is an experienced author. He has a particular interest in practice-based research carried out in collaboration with students and ways to explore the impact of training on practice. He has contributed chapters to a number of textbooks and co-edited books including *Reflective Practice in the Early Years* (2010), *Quality Improvement and Change in the Early Years* (2012) and *Work Based Research in the Early Years* (2012), all published by SAGE.

Rosie Walker co-ordinates a Foundation Degree with seven partner institutions. She is a Senior Lecturer at the Centre for Early Childhood, within the Institute of Education at the University of Worcester. She has supervised many research projects with Foundation Degree, BA and Top-up students as well as at Master's level. She has published book chapters and co-authored a textbook exploring practice-based research as well as journal articles. Professionally, she has managed two large children's centres and is a qualified Social Worker. She has worked in a variety of childcare settings including child protection teams. Rosie is also the author of *Success with your Early Years Research Project* (2014) with Carla Solvason, published by SAGE.

About the contributors

Karen Appleby is a Principal Lecturer within the Centre for Early Childhood, which is part of the Institute if Education at the University of Worcester. She teaches across a variety of early childhood programmes and is a University Learning and Teaching Fellow and a member of the Institute of Education Management Team. Her current responsibilities include leadership for learning, teaching and student experience. Previously she has held the position of Partnership Co-ordinator for the Foundation degree in Early Years, Course Leader for the BA (Hons) Integrated Early Childhood Studies and HND in Early Childhood. She is an experienced author writing on the subject of reflective practice and takes a particular interest in the way reflective learning is positioned within undergraduate study.

Robin Balbernie is clinical director of PIP UK, a charity dedicated to help establish infant mental health teams across the country. Previously he was consultant child psychotherapist in Gloucestershire. He also worked with Children's Centres as clinical lead of the team providing an infant mental health service, known locally and nationally as 'Secure Start'. He was involved with the Intensive Baby Care Unit at Gloucester Royal Hospital and ran supervision groups for Health Visitors for over 25 years. His interest in working with adopted children led him to the field of infant mental health and early preventative intervention, and this became his speciality following a Winston Churchill Memorial Trust Travelling Fellowship to look at related projects in America. He is an advisor to the Association of Infant Mental Health and the WAVE Trust and was a member of the Young Minds' Policy and Strategy Advisory Group.

Mary Benson McMullen is Professor of Early Childhood Education at Indiana University in Bloomington, Indiana (USA) where she has held appointments since 1993. Her recent scholarship focuses on well-being in caring systems, examining how elements throughout systems associated with physiological and psychological health and well-being directly impact young children and are supported and sustained by individuals, relationships, environments and policies. Her publications include works on practitioner beliefs and practices and the meaning of quality in differing contexts and cultures. Among many other positions, for the past ten years she has served as Research in Review editor of *Young Children*, a journal of the National Association for the Education of Young Children in the US.

Josephine Bleach has been Director of the Early Learning Initiative at the National College of Ireland since 2008. Prior to this, Josephine worked variously as a primary school teacher and a Home School Community Liaison Co-ordinator in Darndale, Dublin. She was involved in the development and delivery of the Early Start Pre-School Intervention Programme, and subsequently worked as a facilitator with the School Development Planning Support Service (Primary) of the Department of Education and Skills. Over the course of her career, she has worked with a wide range of early years services, schools and other educational stakeholders, community groups, voluntary and statutory agencies along with different initiatives. She has facilitated, motivated and mentored others in designing systems and structures that improve the quality of the service provided to children and their families. She has published widely and her book *Parental Involvement in Primary Education* is available from Liffey Press.

Frances Brett is a Senior Lecturer at the University of Worcester, UK. Her particular areas of interest are play and the nature of the play space, and the role of the expressive arts in supporting the child's self-revelation.

Erica Brown has class teacher experience in the early years and she has worked as a Senior Teacher, Head of Department and Headteacher in Special Schools. In the University Sector she has held posts as Senior Lecturer, Principal Lecturer, Head of Special Education and as a Principal Research Fellow in Children's and Young Peoples' Palliative Care. Most recently her work at the University of Worcester has focused on supporting children and families who are experiencing loss and she is committed to helping people of all ages and from all walks of life to develop resilience to sustain them through adverse life events. Erica has a wide-ranging portfolio of published books, book chapters and refereed journal articles. In 2008 her book *Palliative Care for South Asians* was launched in the House of Lords and in 2012 she was made a Fellow of The Royal Society of Arts in recognition of her work with life-limited children, young people and their families.

Sue Callan is a fellow of the Higher Education Academy and is currently an Associate Lecturer and consultant with the Open University. From a professional heritage of community-based education and pre-school provision, Sue has worked in further and higher education for over 25 years, supporting students in undergraduate and post-graduate courses. She now specialises in distance teaching and learning. In addition to contributing to the design, writing and development of Foundation Degree programmes for a number of universities, she is an experienced author for SAGE, editing and contributing to publications on reflective practice, work-based research, mentoring, play and management in the early years. She is currently part of a small-scale teaching and learning research project focusing on the role of feedback in promoting academic literacy.

Derval Carey-Jenkins is a Principal Lecturer and Course Leader for the Post Graduate Certificate in Education (PGCE) Early Years and Primary at the University of Worcester.She teaches across a range of subjects including the Master's Early Years Pedagogy and Management module, Special Educational Needs and Disability and Primary English. She is a Fellow of the Higher Education Academy. She spent 23 years teaching in primary schools including three years as a Deputy and eight as a Headteacher. She has developed a keen research interest in values, leadership, change, the early years and primary curriculum, policy and practice. In 2010 she was the recipient of the prestigious University Council for the Education of Teachers scholarship, travelling to Finland to research the extent to which Finnish education and teacher training are underpinned by key societal values. She is currently studying for her doctorate, focusing on Women in Leadership in Higher Education.

Victoria Cooper is a Senior Lecturer for the Faculty of Education and Language Studies at The Open University She currently chairs Children and Young People's Worlds: Developing Frameworks for Integrated Practice for postgraduate study and is extensively invloved in the production of a range of modules spanning early years education, research methods, chilhood and youth studies at postgraduate and undergraduate level. She has a background in early years teaching, research and professional development. Her research interests broadly fall into two areas: professional practice in education and identity development. Victoria has published on professional development in higher and early years education and children's developing identity.

Aline Wendy Dunlop is an Emeritus Professor at the University of Strathclyde in Scotland. Originally a pre-school and primary teacher, when she joined the University sector she built on the links between sectors she had developed as a Headteacher by studying the transition to school from early childhood settings in terms of policy and practice. This led to a 14 year longitudinal study of children's educational transitions from pre-school until school leaving. The study has informed her thinking on leadership, family engagement, children's agency and professional collaboration. Aline Wendy led a postgraduate diploma in which pairs of pre-school and primary teachers studied together over a two-year period during which they swapped sectors and then moved on to schools with their classes of pre-school children. She is currently part of an international research group looking at early childhood transitions in five countries. She was awarded an MBE in 2013.

Alma Fleet is an Associate Professor at the Institute of Early Childhood, Macquarie University, Sydney, Australia. She values particularly her work with Aboriginal and Torres Strait Islander early childhood educators. Alma teaches, researches and publishes in areas associated with educational change, the nature of teachers' work, and pedagogical documentation.

Michael Gasper MA (Ed) was a teacher for nine years and a Head for seventeen, between 1972 and 1998, with the majority of his experience in Early Years, in urban and rural settings. While a First School Head he promoted joint cross-curricular projects between First Schools in the same rural Middle School pyramid and as an Infant School Head developed interagency cooperation with Health, Community Mental Health and Social Services to establish early intervention with families 'at risk'. He joined the Centre for Research in Early Childhood (CREC) at the initial stages of the Early Excellence Centre (EEC) programme in 1998 and from 2000 he was coordinator of the EEC evaluation programme which CREC conducted for DfES.

Michael is currently an Early Years consultant and has worked over 9 years as a mentor, tutor and assessor on the NPQICL professional development programme for cohorts delivered by CREC, the universities of Lancaster, London (Institute of Education), Warwick , Wolverhampton, Worcester and SERCO; He is an assessor for Quality Assurance for the Effective and Baby Effective Early Learning (EEL and BEEL) programme and a tutor for the Accounting Early for Life Long Learning (AcE) programme and MA Leadership programmes run by CREC.

Michael contributed to *Early Years Policy: The Impact on Practice* by Zenna Kingdon and Jan Gourd and *The SAGE Handbook of Mentoring and Coaching* with Paul Watling. He is the author of *Multiagency Working in the Early Years: Challenges and Opportunities* published in January 2010 by SAGE.

Karen Hanson is the Head of the Centre for Early Childhood within the Institute of Education at the University of Worcester. The Centre provides an extensive range of undergraduate and postgraduate study routes, including Early Years Teacher. Staff at the Centre are active researchers and publish a range of textbooks and research papers. Karen has extensive professional experience which has included her role as a teacher, supporting parents and working in the wider community. She has experience of professional home-based early education as a registered childminder and worked for the Pre-school Play Association. This experience enabled her to see the significance of reflective practice in terms of meeting children's needs. Her Doctoral thesis and published research interests have encompassed the way reflective practice can be made visible to students as part of their academic and professional engagement with early education.

Sandra Hesterman is a highly committed educator who has taught extensively in early childhood and primary education prior to her appointment to Murdoch University in 2009. She is passionate about motivating students to learn in ways that have a sustained, substantial and positive influence on their future learning, and on

A Critical Companion to Early Childhood

their own quest for excellence. In 2013, Sandra received the Murdoch University Vice Chancellor's Teaching Excellence Award for developing a distinctive pedagogy of multiliteracies that stimulates student engagement and encourages independence in learning through the provision of authentic tasks in authentic contexts. Sandra's recent research, grounded in postmodern theory, examines the cultural interface of early childhood education and childcare, in particular, the impact of standardised testing in the context of advocacy work and the Australian National Quality Framework.

Dianne Jackson trained as an Early Childhood Teacher and taught in a broad range of community, early childhood and school settings. Dianne then became a lecturer in the School of Education at the University of Western Sydney where she completed a First Class Honours degree in Social Science. For almost 11 years Dianne has held the position of CEO of Connect Child and Family Services, an NGO in outer western Sydney that delivers a broad range of early childhood focused programmes with families. Dianne has recently been appointed CEO of the Australian Research Alliance for Children and Youth (ARACY), a national organisation focused on translating evidence into policy and practice. She is also the an EECERA country coordinator for Australia. Dianne holds an adjunct position at the University of Western Sydney where she completed her PhD in 2010 and her doctoral research won the 2010 European Early Childhood Research Association (EECERA) Best Practitioner Research Award. Dianne co-convenes an EECERA special interest research group with Pen Green in the UK and her organisation has recently opened an innovative parent and child meeting place, conceptually based on collaborative work she has done with her EECERA colleagues from the University of Ghent.

Caroline Jones is Course Director for the Sector-Endorsed Foundation Degree in Early Years (SEFDEY) at the University of Warwick. She started her career as a teacher in mainstream primary and special education, working across the Midlands area for 15 years. Caroline first joined the University of Warwick in 1994 as a part-time associate tutor on the undergraduate teacher-training programme (BA QTS). She taught on a variety of programmes and assumed responsibility for the Early Years Foundation Degree when it was introduced in 2001. She is a founder member of the National SEFDEY Network and Chair of the Midlands Region.

Anna Kilderry is a Senior Lecturer in Early Childhood Education at Deakin University, Melbourne, Australia. Previously, Anna has been a pre-school teacher, a lecturer and researcher in Australia and the UK, and managed the Early Years Professional Status (EYPS) at the University of Greenwich, London. It is through her involvement in teacher education that Anna has developed her research interests in early childhood curriculum, pedagogy and policy.

Catherine Lamond is a Senior Lecturer in Special Needs and Inclusion Studies within the School of Education at the University of Wolverhampton, teaching in the areas of inclusion, reflective practice and specific learning difficulties. Before working in Higher Education, she taught in primary schools in England and Ireland, developing a particular interest in supporting children with special needs. Her current area of research is looked-after children with a focus on aspirations for care-leavers. Catherine has published articles on hopes for the future of young people in care who are excluded from mainstream education; developing self-efficacy in HE students from non-traditional backgrounds; and how innovative forms of assessment can be used to support diverse student groups. In May 2012 she was awarded the first Academic Vice-President Award for Excellence at the Students' Union Teaching Awards ceremony. Catherine is a Fellow of the HEA.

Jackie Musgrave joined the Centre for Early Childhood as a Senior Lecturer at the University of Worcester in April 2012. She started off her working life as a nurse and she trained as a Registered Sick Children's Nurse at Birmingham Children's Hospital and worked in a range of paediatric and adult settings in hospital and in the community. In 1996, she started to teach Early Childhood Care and Education in a College of Further Education. In 2003, she began teaching in higher education to students on the Early Years Foundation Degree in partnership with Oxford Brookes University, where she managed the programme for four years before joining UW. Jackie also taught as an associate lecturer at Warwick University. She graduated with a Master's Degree in Early Childhood Education in 2010. Jackie successfully completed her doctorate studies in 2014. Her doctoral research brings together her interest in child health and young children's care and education. Her thesis is an exploratory case study which researches how practitioners in daycare settings create inclusive environments for young children with chronic health conditions.

Martin Needham trained and worked as an early years teacher in Nottinghamshire, London and Pakistan. This was followed by four years as an Early Years Development Officer for a local authority working on a range of initiatives including Early Years Development and Childcare Partnerships, and Children's Centres. During this time he worked regularly with one of the regional parent and child groups as part of the National Children's Bureau's Playing with Words project. He became a Senior Lecturer in Early Childhood Studies at the University of Wolverhampton in 2003 and a Principal Lecturer at Manchester Metropolitan University in 2014. Martin completed his PhD examining pedagogy and learning with children under the age of four at the Institute of Education, London University in 2011. Martin has two children with whom he attended parent and toddler groups. Martin is an experienced author and has published work on multi-agency working and applying theory to practice. Martin was the external examiner for the Peers Early Education Partnership (PEEP) which delivers practitioner training for those working with parents and children together from 2006–2010. Martin has also conducted research into leadership in early years settings.

Alison Nicholas is a Service Coordinator for Action for Children and manages two children's centres in Worcester City. Alison's career started in residential care in Gloucestershire working with Adults with Autism before moving to a job for 14 years working for Birmingham City Council, working with young people in care. Other roles have included working for the Youth Offending Service and within the voluntary sector, designing and implementing a programme to support isolated women living with depression.

Catherine Patterson has recently retired from her teaching position at the Institute of Early Childhood, Macquarie University (Sydney). She continues her research work exploring the realities of teaching and learning for early childhood practitioners. Her recent research has focused on teachers using practitioner enquiry in the early years of school.

Anna Popova is a Senior Lecturer at Australian Catholic University, working in the Early Childhood team. In the last 20 years she has worked as a school teacher, lecturer and researcher in Russia, the UK and Australia. She has studied, applied and developed socio–cultural–historical theory in a variety of practice and research contexts. She is interested in the ways education and early years professionalism gets constructed in particular cultural–historical contexts. Her particular interest is in historical aspects of practice formation and the ways in which social contradictions manifest themselves. She advocates for an increased focus on high quality early years provision and more emphasis on critical reflection in higher education for early years and education professionals.

Claire Majella Richards is Senior Lecturer of Early Childhood Studies within the Institute of Education at the University of Worcester. She has considerable experience of multi-agency partnership working, having been employed within the voluntary and statutory sectors. Her roles have varied in the fields of mental health, substance misuse and domestic abuse. As a non-practising barrister she remains a committed advocate for the rights of children and young people, and researches and writes extensively about aspects of the voice of the child in the context of safeguarding children, professional practice and integrated working. She is engaged with the activities of the Local Safeguarding Children Board and is a member of the British Association for the Study and Prevention of Child Abuse and Neglect (BASPCAN). At the time of publication Claire was also starting a year-long secondment at the National Centre for the Study and Prevention of Abuse and Neglect (NCSPVSA) at the University of Worcester.

Janet Robertson has a Master's in Early Childhood, and a specialisation in toddler education. She is also the outdoor teacher at Mia Mia (Child and Family Study centre at the Institute of Early Childhood, Macquarie University, Sydney).

Michelle Rogers has worked in higher education for the past 14 years, both in a FE College and as a Senior Lecturer at the University of Worcester where she is Course

Leader for the Foundation Degree in Early Years (Flexible and Distributed Learning). During her time at the University Michelle has been involved with curriculum development and designing online learning environments. More recently she has led the development of a flexible and distributed pathway for a Foundation Degree and is currently designing an online Top-up Degree. ELearning Co-ordinator for the Institute for Education, Michelle is leading the online development and design of international programmes for the Centre for Early Childhood in which she is based. Prior to working in higher education Michelle's interest lay in autism in early years and enhancing the learning environment. Her current research interests revolve around online learning, the student experience, online curriculum development and online communities of practice.

Carla Solvason is a Senior Lecturer within the Centre for Early Childhood, Institute of Education at the University of Worcester. Part of her role involves co-ordinating and managing student independent studies for the BA and Top-up degrees and in developing research within the centre and institute. Carla teaches on the BA, Top-up, Postgraduate Certificate of Education (PGCE) and Master's programmes and is a research degree supervisor. Prior to lecturing, Carla worked as a researcher, a consultant for schools looking to create communication-rich environments and a primary school teacher. Carla has published work relating to student research, the team around the student, school culture, educational equality, professionalism and ethicality.

Jenny Worsley is a Senior Lecturer in Childhood, Family and Community studies in the Faculty of Education, Health and Wellbeing at Wolverhampton University. She is also the course leader for the Foundation Degree Early Years services for part-time students. She is particularly interested in play and the learning experiences of young children and also widening participation in higher education. She is currently undertaking her doctoral research involving a longitudinal ethnographic study with mature part-time female students returning to higher education, examining their constructs of changes to their self-identity and factors which impact on their learning experience. She has published previous chapters on integrated working in a children's centre and developing an online learning community with part-time students.

Siân Wyn Siencyn is Dean of the Faculty of Social Sciences at the University of Wales Trinity Saint David and was previously the Head of School of Early Childhood. She has worked in both the voluntary and statutory sector in children's services. She was a member of the Minister of Education's advisory group on early education and more recently on the Welsh Government's working group on children's right to appeal. She has published, in both Welsh and English, on areas relating to children's rights, the UN Convention on the Rights of the Child and child citizenship and has edited two recent texts for students. Siân's specialist interests are child language development, early bilingualism, children's rights and ethical practice.

Acknowledgements

Amy Jarrold from SAGE for her patience and professionalism as SAGE Editor.

For help in the construction of professional case studies, Sarah Hancox and Lauren Belcher.

Companion Website

A Critical Companion to Early Childhood is supported by a companion website. Visit https://study.sagepub.com/reedandwalker to take advantage of the learning resources designed to accompany this book, including:

- Short **PowerPoint slides** written by the contributors of each chapter
- A complete **podcast series** to help you deepen your understanding
- Access to selected **SAGE Journal articles** for further reading
- Links to relevant **video links** across YouTube and Ted Talks on Early Years topics
- Free SAGE chapters on **Critical Reading**
- Selected **Critical Learning Activities** from the book

Introduction

Michael Reed and Rosie Walker

Welcome to *A Critical Companion to Early Childhood*. We hope you will enjoy reading the diverse and sometimes challenging views from a variety of eminent authors. The book is divided into five sections and each section contains five chapters. The chapters have the same broad structure starting with an overview of the main points that are covered and going on to articulate the position of the writer and involving you as the reader in considering the content and how you can extend your learning via Critical Learning Activities within the chapter or at the end of the chapter.

It is important that you see each section and the chapters as interrelated and not solely as 'stand alone' segments of information. This is because seeing an interrelationship between each chapter models the way early childhood studies encompass many facets of children's development and entails a critical examination of different viewpoints. This pattern of thinking is introduced in Chapter 1 where Michael Reed, Linda Tyler and Rosie Walker show the way you can consider which elements of the book interconnect. They suggest key critical questions you should ask when you read each chapter and we hope that this will allow a deeper interrogation of what you read and an aid to your studies. The editors assist in this learning process as they introduce each section and tease out some of the interrelated features between chapters. They focus upon the way each illustrates different writing styles as well as the way information is provided and how the authors position their views. The aim is to help you by acting as a critical companion as you progress through your studies and encourage you to see similarities and distinctions, reflect and learn, and challenge assumptions rather than accept one particular point of view.

The book is supported by a companion website (https://study.sagepub.com/reed-andwalker). The site contains:

- Printable hand-outs featuring key activities, checklists, diagrams and materials, mostly diagrammatic, taken from the book. These are for promoting in-class discussion and individual student study
- Critical Learning Activities organised by chapter
- Podcasts from the authors to expand on chapter themes and use as an aid to study
- Related journal articles (all are SAGE journal titles) to reinforce the chapter themes and to introduce and reinforce the importance of using journal articles when you engage in study and assignment writing
- Hyperlinks and extracts from other SAGE publications, for example on ethical research and practice-based research
- PowerPoint slides for each chapter that will allow students to prepare group seminar presentations and allow tutors to summarise points made within each chapter.

Key themes: quality, debate and challenge

Quality early childhood experiences underpin each chapter, because every author underlines the fact that those involved with children's learning aim to improve the quality of Early Childhood Education and Care (ECEC). However, determining what is meant by quality is a complex issue. It has been the subject of critical review resulting in a body of literature which provides evidence of an ongoing international debate that has considered how quality can be determined, evaluated and developed, see, for example, the work of Penn, 2011 and Moss, 2005, 2008. Indeed, quality can be viewed and interpreted from a number of interrelated perspectives. The first is the sheer range and scope of the evidence available about ways to measure and evaluate quality, for example, Mathers and colleagues (2012) produced a report for the Office for Planning Research and Evaluation (OPRE, 2009), which illustrates the array of measures available. There are literature reviews and reports exploring the range and scope of the subject, for example, Litjens and Taguma (2010). There are also international perspectives such as the work of Myers (2005) which remind researchers that the determinants of quality should not always be set within a European or North American context. In addition, there is research which considers the voice of the child and how this can be heard within the context of improving quality, for example the Department for Education (DfE) (2012a). What becomes clear is a recognition that quality ECEC improves the life chances of children, which is important both economically and socially – a point that a report from the Institute for Public Policy and Research (IPPR, 2013) considers as part of a wider project exploring a strategic approach to early years provision in the UK. It explores the literature surrounding quality, drawn from national and international sources, and arrives at ten lessons for policymakers that underpin and challenge existing practice and policy directives. It places a pronounced emphasis upon the value of training and how the role and actions of practitioners promote quality.

A second aspect involves the forms of research evidence used to determine quality. Feneche (2011) examined over 300 peer reviewed research papers which were concerned with quality and quality improvement. She suggests that a number of waves of research into quality have developed from the 1970s. These include a pronounced focus on care which was seen as underpinning quality, followed by a period when there was a prominence of rating scales such as the Early Childhood Environment Rating Scale (ECERS) to measure and interpret quality. Feneche suggests that the emergence of a predominately positivist discourse in early childhood research has limited how quality is thought about and valued and argues quality is a construct that is more complex and elusive than that encapsulated by measures. She sees a value in adopting both quantitative and qualitative research methods to explore quality, such as those used in longitudinal research projects such as the EPPE (Effective Provision on Pre-school Education) project (Sylva et al., 2004, 2011, 2012).

A third aspect involves how such evidence is used to consider national ECEC initiatives and policies. It is here a number of key drivers of quality emerge. For example, evidence from the Organisation for Economic Co-operation and Development, (OECD, 2006, 2011, 2012) recognises that definitions of quality differ across countries and stakeholders, but does suggest (OECD, 2012) five levers as key features to encourage quality. These involve:

- quality goals and regulation;
- curriculum design and standards;
- qualifications and training;
- engaging with families;
- data collection and research.

The report (OECD, 2012) explains how quality is also influenced by a structural tier of quality and process tiers (see Vandell and Wolfe, 2000; Litjens and Taguma, 2010). Structural quality can be described as those facets of ECEC which can be broadly regulated and encompasses child to adult ratio, curriculum design and establishes clearly monitored standards. It is sometimes also associated with orientation quality, meaning the emphasis given to early childhood policy, through national legislation, regulation and policy initiatives (CoRe, 2011). Process quality is viewed in terms of what goes on in and around an ECEC setting. It can be described as the interactions between those in a setting and what children and families actually experience. In effect, what happens on, in and for practice which has a direct impact on children's well-being and development.

The complexity of the issue is further underlined by a report into quality in ECEC from the New South Wales Government (2008). It cites Hwang and colleagues (1991: 117) who argue that quality is 'a slippery and multifaceted construct that requires careful measurement and interpretation'. It is also difficult to establish what drives forward quality as priorities, policies and actions on the ground vary considerably across countries (NESSE, 2009). In considering the impact of ECEC practitioners, a report from the European

Commission considered quality and competence requirements throughout Europe (CoRe, 2011: 23). It suggested that competency should be seen not just in terms of practitioner competencies, but in terms of a competent system that encourages integrated working and quality ECEC which should be seen in the wider socio-political context. It suggested that 'any discussion on quality in ECEC should be contextualised: it should encompass the regular review of understandings and practices'. The report goes on to say that 'quality needs to be considered as an ongoing process rather than as something that is achieved or not'.

To do this requires sophisticated professional skills, sound personal qualities and the necessity to respond to change and be an agent of change at a time where educational, economic and social reforms mean change is a constant that has to be managed. In practice this means being part of the professionalisation of the workforce as suggested by Maplethorpe et al., 2010; Miller and Cable, 2011; and DfE, 2012b. Added to this is the wider issue of cost, pay, service conditions and status in the workforce and its impact on quality as reported by Cooke and Lawton (2008). There is also the way practitioners are responding to developing and changing professional hierarchies and leadership as shown by a recent report which explored leadership within the early years sector (DfE, 2012b) – leadership which involves implementing quality improvement programmes as described by Mooney (2007) and encouraging reflection on practice in order to improve practice. This is rarely defined in terms of its impact on quality, though a report by the Office for Standards in Education (2011), which examined the way childminders enhanced quality, suggests the ability to reflect on practice was an essential component of improving quality. There are also the views of Appleby and Andrews (2012) who underline the importance of reflection on, in and for practice. They argue its value is because it asks practitioners to consider their values, beliefs and personal strengths and engage in a thoughtful and holistic view of practice and their own contribution to practice. This is something the book attempts to do in the way the chapters examine the critical role of parents, the way we should safeguard children's welfare, the importance of observing development and why this is important, the way we define the curriculum – its design and standards – and the issue of engaging with families and the value of practice-based research. The book takes these features and becomes a training companion as it actively encourages reflective critical awareness which is part of maintaining quality. It therefore has a focus upon the features identified by the OECD report mentioned earlier which were considered to make up the interrelated components of quality. Use the book to learn and challenge and we hope the chapters will make you think about:

- the views of others in relation to regulation, ratios, policy requirements, qualification requirements, health and safety, and physical resources;
- the importance of day-to-day interactions. For example, communicating with parents, implementing policies and forming relationships with children;
- the importance of considering theoretical positions about the way children learn;
- the way case studies can illustrate how views become much more visible when set in the context of actual practice;
- the critical importance of safeguarding processes to protect children;

- thinking about the way professionals work together, leading practice and the extent to which practitioners are actively encouraged to innovate, share expertise and generate an impact on practice;
- the value of curriculum design in and on practice;
- the value of self-evaluation and reflection.

The chapters are intended to be a catalyst to shape and form the features of quality and your own impact upon quality. Our view is that there are many structural features which influence quality but they are in themselves not a determinant of quality. It is when structural and process features are seen as interconnected that a deeper and wider view of quality takes shape. It is you who can see those interconnected strands and it is practitioners who are the glue that binds the two together.

References

Appleby, K. and Andrews, M. (2012) 'Reflective practice is the key to quality improvement', in M. Reed and N. Canning (eds), *Quality Improvement and Change in the Early Years*. London: SAGE.

Cooke, G. and Lawton, K. (2008) *For Love or Money: Pay, Progression and Professionalization in the Early Years Workforce*. London: Institute for Public Policy Research.

CoRe (2011) *Competence Requirements in Early Childhood Education and Care,* European Commission, Directorate-General for Education and Culture Final Report. University of East London, Cass School of Education and University of Ghent, Department for Social Welfare Studies, September 2011. Available from: www.vbjk.be/en/node/3559 (accessed 7 October 2014).

Department for Education (DfE) (2012a) *Listening to Children's Perspectives: Improving the Quality of Provision in Early Years Settings*. Part of the Longitudinal Study of Early Years Professional Status (Research Report DFE-RR239b by L. Coleyshaw, J. Whitmarsh, M. Jopling and M. Hadfield), CeDARE, University of Wolverhampton. Available at: www.education.gov.uk/publications/eOrderingDownload/DfE-RR239b%20report.pdf (accessed 11 November 2012).

Department for Education (DfE) (2012b) *Longitudinal Study of Early Years Professional Status: An Exploration of Progress, Leadership and Impact* (Final report, ref. DFE-RR239c, by M. Hadfield, M. Jopling, M. Needham, T. Waller, L. Coleyshaw, M. Emira and K. Royle), CeDARE, University of Wolverhampton.

Fenech, M. (2011) 'An analysis of the conceptualisation of "quality" in early childhood education and care empirical research: promoting "blind spots" as foci for future research', *Contemporary Issues in Early Childhood*, 12 (2): 102–117.

Institute of Public Policy and Research (IPPR) (2013) *Early Developments and Policy: Bridging the Gap Between Evidence and Policy* by I. Parker. Available from: www.ippr.org/publication/55/11073/early-developments-bridging-the-gap-between-evidence-and-policy (accessed 23 August 2013).

Litjens, I. and M. Taguma (2010) *Revised Literature Overview for the 7th Meeting of the Network on Early Childhood Education and Care*. Paris: OECD.

Maplethorpe, N., Chanfreau, J., Philo, D. and Tait, C. (2010) *Families with Children in Britain: Findings from the 2008 Families and Children Study (FACS)*. London: DWP and National Centre for Social Research.

Mathers, S., Singler, R. and Karemaker, A. (2012) *Improving Quality in the Early Years: A Comparison of Perspectives and Measures*. Research Brief. London: Daycare Trust and University of Oxford.

Miller, L. and Cable, C. (eds) (2011) *Professionalization, Leadership and Management in the Early Years*. London: SAGE.

Mooney, A. (2007) *Effectiveness of Quality Improvement Programmes*. London: Thomas Coram Research Unit and Institute of Education, University of London.

Moss, P. (2005) *Learning from Other Countries* (Policy Papers. No 4). London: Day Care Trust.

Moss, P. (2008) 'The democratic and reflective professional: rethinking and reforming the early years workforce', in L. Miller and C. Cable (eds), *Professionalism in the Early Years* (pp. 121–130). London: Hodder.

Myers, R.G. (2005) *In Search of Quality in Programmes of Early Childhood Care and Education*. Paper prepared for the 2005 EFA Global Monitoring Report: Early Childhood Care and Education (ECCE). Available from: unesdoc.unesco.org/images/0014/001466/146677e.pdf (accessed 11 November 2012).

NESSE (2009) *Early Childhood Education and Care. Key Lessons from Research for Policy Makers*. Available from: www.nesse.fr/activities/reports (accessed 7 October 2014).

New South Wales Government (2008) *Determinants of Quality in Child Care: A Review of the Research Evidence*. Huntsman L. Centre for Parenting and Research Service System Development Division, NSW Department of Community Services. Available from: www.community.nsw.gov.au/docswr/_assets/main/documents/research_qualitychildcare.pdf (accessed 10 August 2013).

OECD (2006) *Starting Strong II: Early Childhood Education and Care*. Paris: OECD.

OECD (2011) *PISA in Focus Nr. 10: What Can Parents do to Help their Children Succeed in School?* Paris: OECD.

OECD (2012) *Quality Matters in Early Childhood Education and Care: United Kingdom (England)*. Paris: OECD.

OPRE (Office for Planning Research and Evaluation) (2009) *Multiple Purposes for Measuring Quality in Early Childhood Settings: Implications for Collecting and Communicating Information on Quality*. Issue Brief 2, Child Trends by M. Zaslow, K. Tout, T. Halle and N. Forry. Washington, DC. Available from: www.childtrends.com (accessed 10 June 2013).

Penn, H. (2011) *Quality in Early Childhood Services: An International Perspective*. Maidenhead: McGraw-Hill/Open University Press.

Sylva, K., Mehuish, E.C., Sammons, P., Siraj-Blatchford, I. and Taggart, B. (2004) *The Effective Provision of Pre-school Education (EPPE) Project: Findings from Preschool to the End of Key Stage 1*. London: DfES/Institute of Education, University of London.

Sylva, K., Melhuish, E.C., Sammons, P., Siraj-Blatchford, I. and Taggart, B. (2011) 'Pre-school quality and educational outcomes at age 11: Low quality has little benefit', *Journal of Early Childhood Research*, 9: 109.

Sylva, K., Melhuish, E.C., Sammons, P., Siraj-Blatchford, I. and Taggart, B. (2012) *Effective Pre-school, Primary and Secondary Education 3–14 Project (EPPSE 3–14)*. Final Report from the Key Stage 3 Phase: Influences on Students' Development From Age 11–14. Department of Education/Institute of Education, University of London; Birkbeck, University of London; University of Oxford. Research Report: DFE-RR202.

Vandell, D.L. and Wolfe, B. (2000) *Child Care Quality: Does it Matter and Does it Need to be Improved?* (Special Report No. 78). Madison, WI: University of Wisconsin-Madison Institute for Research on Poverty.

Section 1

DEVELOPING CRITICAL REFLECTION

This section of the book considers a number of key interrelated themes. These include the way that a contemporary professional practitioner in ECEC needs to adopt a reflective stance in order to support children and families. In order to illustrate the interrelated themes, we have taken an unusual approach of presenting two case studies of student journeys through higher education so the reader can clearly see how their critical reflective thinking has developed over the course of their study and the impact this has had on their practice with children and families.

The section begins with a view of the importance of critically reflective study and considers how a developing practitioner engaged in study needs to see features of ECEC as interconnected and part of a whole rather than separate aspects of professional working. This can be seen clearly in Chapter 1 from Michael Reed, Rosie Walker and Linda Tyler. They ask the reader to consider ways of examining the chapters in the book critically and provide a framework to help you do this as you read through the book. The authors suggest this will reveal interconnected issues that can be used as part of your studies and in assignments.

The section moves on to present a chapter from Karen Hanson and Karen Appleby, which attempts to define and unpack the term reflective practice and underline its importance to the practitioner. They suggest that reflection aids their thinking and practice. The next chapter by Sue Callan builds on the need for reflection and introduces the concept of the ethical practitioner and provides a deconstruction of what this means. It also provides a theoretical position which suggests ethical reflection is an essential component of critical thinking. The chapter by Jennifer Worsley and Catherine Lamond that follows underpins the need to view critical thinking as a process that develops as you progress through your studies. They suggest it is a process which is valuable when used in collaboration with others – an important part of critical thinking. The final chapter by Michelle Rogers introduces the need to engage purposefully when using and learning from new digital technologies. She argues this too is part of reflective practice and has an essential part to play in the way you study and view the digital world that will inevitably change over the period of time you are engaged in study.

A collective position

The collective position or argument contained in this section is quite clear. Critical reflection on practice leads to critical awareness. When this is seen in the context of being an ethical practitioner it leads naturally towards the way practice-based research should encompass these elements as it shapes an evaluation of practice which is able to explore and even determine what quality looks like. The key questions are, do these facets of critical engagement make a difference and have an impact upon practice? Can they and have they actually been adopted by those engaged in a programme of study leading to a degree or professional qualification?

Figure S1.1 shows the key questions which are discussed with students as they prepare and engage in work-based inquiry. It is a model underpinned by the premise that a student who engages in practice-based inquiry considers what they are researching and why this is important in order to develop their thinking and knowledge. They should integrate ethical protocols into all aspects of practice and ensure that any form of inquiry has a defined purpose that should be valuable to the setting, children and families. In addition, the process should actively engage the setting in what goes on. It should recognise sound practice but go beyond simply accepting the information presented and consider ways to explore and critically examine practice. As a consequence of these actions it is possible to argue that they are shaping the practice environments that they inhabit. The aim is to develop research processes so that students are involved in real world collaborative inquiry as a means to elicit views on what is happening and what works on the ground (Reed, 2011). However, to make this work and meaningful in practice requires personal and professional characteristics (Potter and Quill, 2006; Messenger, 2010). For example, a recognition that they (as persons who are an integral part of the ECEC setting and therefore insiders) are accountable to others in the workplace and are motivated to engage ethically and rigorously in their investigations. To look at what works as well as issues that need attention, where appropriate through an appreciative form of inquiry (Cooperrider, 2005), they must also be able to share the findings of their inquiry honestly with others and reflect and learn from the process. Such characteristics which form an essential component of the researcher in practice resonate with the established discourse on leadership and practice-based research. Hallet (2013), for example, provides a perceptive view of the strategic and pedagogical leadership role in improving and shaping practice. She argues this involves leadership and learning by establishing a learning

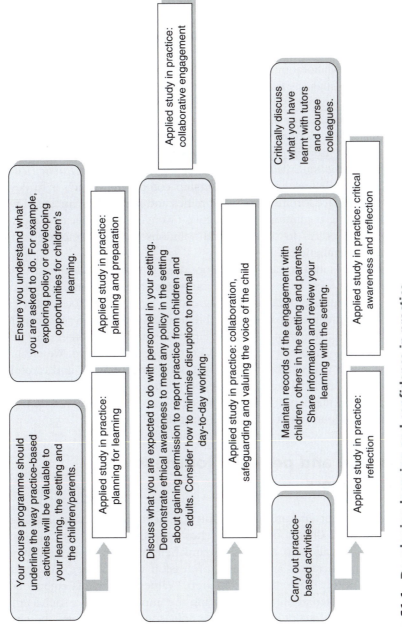

Your course programme should underline the way practice-based activities will be valuable to your learning, the setting and the children/parents.

Applied study in practice: planning for learning

Ensure you understand what you are asked to do. For example, exploring policy or developing opportunities for children's learning.

Applied study in practice: planning and preparation

Discuss what you are expected to do with personnel in your setting. Demonstrate ethical awareness to meet any policy in the setting about gaining permission to report practice from children and adults. Consider how to minimise disruption to normal day-to-day working.

Applied study in practice: collaboration, safeguarding and valuing the voice of the child

Applied study in practice: collaborative engagement

Carry out practice-based activities.

Applied study in practice: reflection

Maintain records of the engagement with children, others in the setting and parents. Share information and review your learning with the setting.

Applied study in practice: critical awareness and reflection

Critically discuss what you have learnt with tutors and course colleagues.

Figure S1.1 Developing learning and confidence in practice

culture in which learning, knowledge and pedagogy are highly visible within an organisation. This feature was also identified as an essential component of leadership in the *Effective Leadership in the Early Years Sector (ELEYS) Study* (Siraj-Blatchford and Manni, 2007). This study investigated leadership in the early years sector (ECEC), identifying fundamental requirements for leadership for learning which included an understanding of the context within which any impact of change would take place, a commitment to collaboration and a purposeful desire to improve quality. The work of Rodd (2006) also suggests that the research process can clarify and initiate issues for change. Similarly a paper by Raelin (2011) contends that the role of the researcher is to provide tools to encourage the observed to be part of the research dialogue and part of the inquiry itself. Moreover, the researcher should recognise and share the results of their practice-based inquiries with others in the setting. In effect doing what a report from *Developing Excellence in Practice-based Research in Public Health* (Potter and Quill, 2006: 17) sees as a key leadership component, which is to develop and encourage interactive forums across disciplines and institutions; an action which may be seen as forging communities of practice (Wenger, 1998) because the researcher is working with others in order to find solutions to issues relevant to their own settings and communities.

To develop this idea we ask you to consider the words and actions of two professional colleagues who have made this journey of reflection and critical awareness. Both are recent former students who agreed to become the focus of a case study designed to illustrate the impact of critical reflection on their own practice. Their views underpin why the chapters in this particular section and within other parts of the book should be seen as important facets of ECEC quality and practice. We are grateful for their co-operation and indebted to the way they have honestly and carefully shared their views and ideas. Making the journey through higher education is a process that, as developing practitioners, it is important to embrace and trust, even though at times, like all important journeys, it can seem a struggle.

The professional and personal journeys of two practitioners

Both entered higher education to complete a degree programme leading to a BA (Honours) in Early Childhood Studies. They can be described as capable and conscientious individuals who held values and beliefs which motivated them to gain professional qualifications and enter a profession which values children's learning and seeks to protect the welfare of children. (Values and beliefs embedded into the chapter by Sue Callan about understanding the importance of a sound ethical position are transposed into practice by Carla Solvason (Ch. 25) when she suggests the need to hold such values as part of a desire to engage in purposeful research in practice.)

Both colleagues engaged enthusiastically in their studies and were introduced to the idea of developing reflective and critical thinking via lectures, seminars and directed reading. (Something that the Editors see as fundamentally important, which is why the chapter on reflective practice by Karen Hanson and Karen Appleby is placed early on in this book.)

They were encouraged to reflect about their feelings as 'student practitioners on placement' as they experienced being part of a good quality early childhood setting. They reflected on what they had learnt, what key questions emerged and what they might use to enhance future placement opportunities. (A sign that professional development and being a developing professional is important, which is taken up in the chapter by Mike Gasper later in the book.) They both felt this allowed them to develop a view about the value of reflective practice, as one remarked: 'it took some time to actually get it', and went on to explain how it was important to develop a means of reflecting on practice, for practice and in practice. They both indicated how it was necessary to draw together facets of ECEC practice and reflect upon the non-visible features such as taking an ethical stance, being part of a professional community and developing the ability to view children and families holistically. They explained this view in terms of the way their course had asked them to see children and families in the context of their own social world, their community, their culture, heritage and family. They needed to accept difference and diversity and to accept that society and the way we view children's development may change and become refined through research and knowledge. This is not to say that they were accepting of everything they were exposed to as part of their training. They were challenging what they were reading and learning and seeing in practice. They described this ability to challenge as a process that required support and help from tutors and they said how they needed help to critically reflect. This process mirrors the issues that Jennifer Worsley and Catherine Lamond describe in their chapter. Importantly, they felt that this allowed them to see the importance of a less visible feature, which was responding positively to change. Not just change in curriculum design or changes in policy and regulatory aspects of practice, but also the way they were able to recognise changes in their own values, beliefs and competencies. An example was the way they both reported how they perceived themselves as advocates for children in terms of safeguarding their welfare and in practical terms about the way they developed expertise in using information technology and how they were embracing new technology. Indeed, they were keen to point out how online learning had enhanced their studies and felt that they had developed 'a positive ICT attitude' which meant feeling comfortable with the way technology aided communication and the way families were using technology with their children. This is a point that Michelle Rogers underlines in her chapter exploring the world of ICT and practitioner learning.

This positive responsiveness to change is illustrated in the way their degree programme spanned a time when there was considerable change being proposed and enacted by the UK Government about professional qualifications in ECEC. In particular, this was reflected in the need to 'professionalise' and enhance the quality of ECEC practitioner training. The result was a new Government initiative (in England) which encouraged practitioners to gain Early Years Professional Status (EYPS). This status required substantial evidence of practice ability across the 0–5 age range in terms of meeting required standards evidenced through a number of means including a portfolio of evidence, written tasks, observation of practice and witness statements from fellow professionals. (This has recently been replaced by a qualification to become an Early Years Teacher, which is closely allied to National Teaching Standards.) Both colleagues decided to enrol on the EYPS programme which was integrated into the final part of their degree programme and required them to think critically about leading and developing ECEC practice and how to promote quality in an early years setting. It is interesting that they both were quite clear about the way this was not just about developing professional competencies but as developing the qualities necessary to engage with families and importantly others in the ECEC field, such as health, social work and education. They were therefore progressing their thinking and practice and taking with them their established view of professional work that saw the child and family as part of a whole and not solely residing within an early childhood setting.

As they reached the conclusion of their studies, both completed a dissertation which involved engaging in practice-based research as 'insiders' within an early childhood setting. The focus of their investigations was discussed with the setting and was therefore professionally collaborative and they had time to share the results of their inquiries with others. Both used ICT to aid their research and demonstrated reflection and critical thinking in their assignments. Both emerged from their studies with degree classifications at a high level. They have since moved on to complete Post Graduate Certificates in Education, which means they can enter the teaching profession in the United Kingdom as qualified teachers.

What can we deduce from this?

We recognise this is a brief report of a series of interviews with our professional colleagues, but it is useful to examine some key points: both practitioners indicated how the course and its focus on reflection and critical thinking had aided their studies and both felt that embracing ICT was important. Both felt the process was transformative and that it had an impact on practice; for example, making an ethical practitioner, ethical researcher and leader visible. The case study illustrates the importance of leading practice and responding to change. Importantly, the practitioners in the case study identified many of the features of quality that can be seen in the introduction to this book. They also encompass the component parts of this section and sometimes beyond into other sections of the book. Their 'stories' illustrate how professional development is about gaining recognised qualifications, and what helps this to happen is becoming a reflective, critical practitioner and seeing the value of such reflection on practice, in practice and for practice.

References

Cooperrider, D. (2005) *Appreciative Inquiry: A Positive Revolution in Change*. San Francisco, CA: Berrett-Koehler.

Hallet, E. (2013) 'We all share a common vision and passion: Early years professionals reflect upon their leadership of practice role', *Journal of Early Childhood Research*, 11(3): 12.

Messenger, W. (2010) 'Managing multi-agency working', in M. Reed and N. Canning (eds), *Reflective Practice in the Early Years*. London: SAGE.

Potter, M.A. and Quill, B.E. (2006) *Demonstrating Excellence in Practice-based Research for Public Health*. Texas: Association of Schools in Public Health.

Raelin, J. (2011) 'From leadership-as-practice to leaderful practice', *Leadership*, 7: 195.

Reed, M. (2011) 'Reflective practice and professional development', in A. Page-Smith and A. Craft (eds), *Developing Reflective Practice in the Early Years*, 2nd edn. Milton Keynes: Open University Press. pp. 146–155.

Rodd, J. (2006) *Leadership in Early Childhood*. Maidenhead: Open University Press.

Siraj-Blatchford, I. and Manni, L. (2007) *Effective Leadership in the Early Years Sector*. London: Institute of Education.

Wenger, E. (1998) *Communities of Practice: Learning, Meaning and Identity*. Cambridge: Cambridge University Press.

1

The undergraduate journey

Michael Reed, Linda Tyler and Rosie Walker

Chapter overview

The chapter explores the professional and personal expectations of someone studying an ECEC (early childhood education and care) degree programme. It suggests that when using this book (or other study material) you recognise the interconnectedness between chapter content. It provides strategies for examining such interconnection as well as advice on developing your critical writing.

Introduction

It is generally acknowledged that there are two types of student that access ECEC programmes at higher education level in the UK. There are those who have journeyed through A levels (who tend to enrol for a BA Honours degree, with a minimum of three years study) and those who enrol for a vocational route (a Foundation Degree over two or three years). They then have the option of enrolling (or what is called 'topping up' this qualification) to gain a BA Honours degree. In other countries around the world such progression routes may be different, though there is little doubt that a graduate professional is beneficial to young children's development, because of the professional understanding and ability to reflect on practice that such training brings (OECD, 2006, 2012). Whatever the journey, each pathway to graduate status will require different teaching approaches in order to develop the critical reflection required. Supporting students through their transition into higher education is also a key focus of the tutors leading each programme. Degree students experience changes in environments, both physical and emotional, due to their level of practical experience and they must embrace different academic expectations.

When students are able to self-actualise, then critical thinking and hence critical reflection can be developed. This move from the transition phase to the critical thinking phase is shown in the pyramid in Figure 1.1.

Figure 1.1 illustrates how the process involves entering new places, developing new ideas and embracing new friends, and is often accompanied by the uncertainty of what is expected of an undergraduate in terms of their study and academic performance. Much of the material you read says things like: *the programme you have enrolled for intends to support you in becoming a reflective practitioner with the qualities necessary to support children and families.* This is useful, but begs the question: what exactly does this mean in practice? Is there some end point to your studies when you suddenly arrive at a place where you receive a badge saying 'reflective practitioner'? This is unlikely to be the case because you gradually develop, grow and transform your thinking and practice into a meaningful pattern of thought

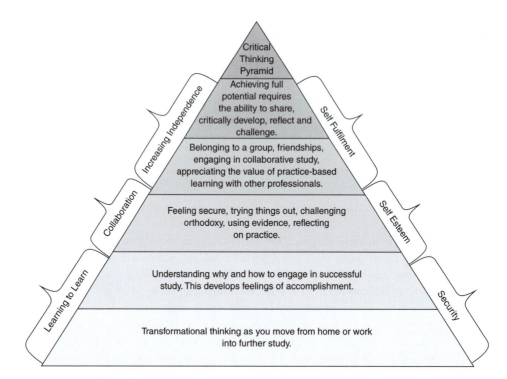

Figure 1.1 The different needs of each programme have been developed from Maslow's Hierarchy of Needs (1943)

which allows you to understand and question concepts and ideas. Study will also be transformative in that it will change your mind, your views, question your judgement and sometimes call into question your values and beliefs.

Measurement of the skills and qualities needed to be a competent early years professional

You may have completed previous qualifications where success is determined by meeting 'standards' and 'competencies' seen in practice. These competencies may represent an ideal state between having particular *skills* as a practitioner and the necessary *qualities* to engage purposefully with young children and their families. But are these so easily separated? Are they not interrelated? Indeed, a useful way of articulating the relationship between both aspects comes from a report on the subject from the European Commission in 2011. It suggests:

> '…being competent' (a fully human attribute) is often reduced to 'competencies' – a series of skills and pieces of knowledge that individuals need to 'possess' in order to perform a particular task. A key finding of CoRe is that 'competence' in the early childhood education and care context has to be understood as a characteristic of the entire early childhood system. The *competent system* develops in reciprocal relationships between individuals, teams, institutions and the wider socio-political context. (CoRe, 2011: 21)

The position taken by CoRe underlines the need for those in training to become part of a competent system and encourages students and tutors to engage in joint initiatives to promote learning and critical reflection. This involves collaborations between individuals and teams (online and face to face) as well as universities and ECEC settings (pre-schools; schools; support services for children and families). It also requires a positive engagement in developing the position that the CoRe report suggests is a competent system. In essence this means having the ability to both engage and stand back simultaneously when involved in academic or practice aspects of your course. It means reflecting on your own values and attitudes which we see as essential and should accompany reflection on wider issues of practice. In this way, you can contribute to making meaningful and positive changes in early childhood learning environments. Of course, this means deepening your understanding of your own and others' value base.

Initially developing a value base will require some type of guidance. For example working with and seeing others' reflections and how they are linked to improvements in practice. This is a framework which should be embedded as part of normal day to day practices when learning in practice. It may occur when you are working with others in an ECEC setting either employed or as a student on placement. It is therefore crucial that reflection is integral to this part of your learning and is often best achieved through use of a learning log, diary or journal which should be kept throughout any placement undertaken. Alternatively, you may be asked to consider recording critical incidents (to you and your learning) which in turn form descriptive and reflective questions in respect of a particular learning moment. Learning logs, diaries or journals are where you can record your experiences as a learner and can be hard copies and/ or online. They are often used to underpin the reflective thinking process and may form part of the academic assessment for a module or programme of study. The reason is quite simple – they capture the moment and your thoughts. Entries are not retrospective and clouded in a vague memory of what went on – as learning is immediate and there is sometimes an emotional response as you are able to capture the emotion and reflection of the moment. The evidence gathered in this way can be shared with others, sometimes through a virtual learning (online) environment. Asking questions, testing hypotheses and finding ways forward by applying theory to/in practical situations underpins this skills development. Such an approach will cause you to consider your own position about ways to solve problems and engage purposefully in situations where collaborating with others is the key to improving your learning over a period of time. This can be directed by a tutor or self-directed within a study group. It can also involve active study with others – an example would be a student explaining to a fellow group of students a situation which is problematic and to which no obvious solution is evident. The group of participants asks questions and, together, they analyse the situation and formulate a possible solution.

Communicating in writing

Reflective writing can be seen as the natural relationship between learning and language (Hilsdon, 2006). It is the way you are most likely to articulate theory you are learning and applying in practice. It can be described as standing back or developing a wide view of the early childhood landscape. It can be seeing the familiar as if it is new, or seeing the unfamiliar from the perspective of a child or parent. Sometimes the outcome is not only about your knowledge of child development or an interpretation of a child's learning, it is what you have learned from the process. You are developing the ability to use words to express complex issues. It means using *evidence, information, explanation, interpretation* and a consideration of sometimes wide ranging *outcomes*. This of course forms the initials E-I-E-I-O which we hope for those who have ever sung a children's song about a farmyard makes this list a little easier to remember. In practice this means attempting to develop a clear and confident argument which may or may not accept the conclusions of other writers but will have attempted to evaluate the arguments and evidence they provide. It may suggest why the conclusions of other writers may need to be treated with caution – to just dismiss arguments is not reflecting critically. It means taking a position and sometimes defending that position, which is sometimes challenging and risky. It is then essential to identify how best they can be woven into the argument that you are developing. This involves what Wellington et al. (2005) see as involving healthy scepticism: confidence but not arrogance; avoiding unsubstantiated arguments and a careful evaluation of published work. Of course, this is easy to say and difficult to do. There is a need to capture the narrative of what happened and use this to exemplify an aspect of practice and by the same token create an intellectual response that will gain marks for its critical reflection.

It is therefore important to develop your own academic voice but understand how this is best represented as you are assessed on a particular programme of study. Some tutors readily accept the use of 'I' and see this as a natural progression when articulating a reflective stance. There may be others that ask for different styles of interpretation that require a less personalised approach and a format which conveys objectivity. You may therefore need to develop a combination of the academic and the personal and consequently your arguments need to be quite clear about what constitutes the personal and professional aspects of your writing. Our advice is to check with tutors and be clear about the challenges and expectations placed upon any assessment requirements. In this way you are applying professional skills and behaviours and critically addressing the academic audience in the preferred style of your University or College. Such professionalism also incorporates your attitude and ability to write about what Bolton (2001) suggests are sensitive issues you may encounter when writing about practice. What you 'see' has to be represented in a way that is ethical and demonstrates professional propriety and not unsubstantiated criticism. Such sensitivity also extends to feedback on your own work because when you produce academic work you 'own' the subject and the process and it becomes personal to you. As a consequence tutor comments in your feedback can seem like criticism rather than the constructive support it is meant to offer. You can practise your planning and writing and we suggest that practice (or if you prefer careful planning and drafting of an assignment) is indeed an essential precursor to developing critical thinking and writing.

Critical Learning Activities

Here are three Critical Learning Activities (CLAs) which can be completed alone or with others, focusing on a particular theme, or focusing on a theme which is directed by a tutor. The first asks you to look at the chapter headings in this book. How will you use the chapters in your study? Will you interrogate the content so that when you come to use the content in an assignment you can provide a cohesive argument and perhaps show how one chapter theme can be seen as interconnected to another and in what way? For example, after reading a chapter (make notes, if you prefer, as you read), ask yourself the questions shown in Table 1.1.

(Continued)

(Continued)

Table 1.1   Critical Learning Activity

Question	Notes
Did the author make their professional experience and position clear?	
Was the writing accessible to you?	
Was there a balance between descriptive and critical writing? Were you able to tease out these features?	
Was the theoretical position of the chapter clear and was any 'conclusion' trailed and supported sufficiently by preceding evidence, analysis and argument?	
Are there elements in the content which you consider as interconnected to positions taken in other chapters?	
Did the chapter reflect on practice?	
Did anything in the content make you think and perhaps extend or change your views? If so, why?	

This process moves your thinking away from 'knowledge transfer' and much more into a critical view of what the chapter had to say and a critique on why and how it was said. In essence, learning how to learn. We hope that by doing so you will revisit and engage with the content and arrive at arguments to support your education and the content of your assignments. It will be interesting to consider what features you felt important in a chapter. It may be that you clearly saw the interconnectedness between the theoretical perspectives on ethical practice from Sue Callan in Chapter 3 and the way ethicality is part of a professional stance when safeguarding children's well-being in Chapter 13 by Claire Richards. It might be the way Carla Solvason in Chapter 25 advocates the importance of being a purposeful ethical researcher. Importantly, the exercise may have caused you to consider carefully which particular words have potency when you attempt to write critically and underlined the importance of drawing upon resources at your University or College which assist in developing writing skills.

To help in identifying the interrelationship between chapters, look at Table 1.2 which takes each of the chapters and asks you to consider how they are interconnected. When you do this consider if the chapters share particular key issues which when taken together form a pattern which we hope you see as spanning many of the critical features about quality ECEC and what constitutes quality, as set out in the introduction to this book. Of course, you may engage in the exercise alone or with a small study group. It may be that you will be directed to the exercise via a study workshop as part of your course if the tutor thinks the activity suitable.

Table1.2   Connecting chapters

Selected chapters	Key issues, ideas, concerns or questions	Full academic reference and page number, which you will need if you use a quote	How are issues interconnected with another chapter? The course or module you are studying?	Further reading to follow up
Chapter 1				
Chapter 2				
....				

Critical writing

Introducing an issue, reinforcing a point with evidence and raising questions are things which may be done a number of times in an assignment. The process should inform the reader, demonstrate your critical thinking and arrive at a well-argued position. Below is ONE example of engaging in critical writing presented as a template. It is a way of practising and refining your writing style. As you do this, you may find you adapt, change or refine aspects of the template. In effect, practising and refining how to formulate a written argument.

> Smith (2010) published research or wrote or edited a review, or explored *(description of the evidence)*. She suggests ... *(Make a specific point – provide a page reference if use is made of a direct quote)*. This is similar/contradicts/supports/is developed further by jones (2011), when he explored ... *(Description of the evidence)*. He argues that ... *(make a specific point – provide a page reference if use is made of direct quote)*. Both views are interesting as they are contradictory/similar/support/allow a reconsideration of ... *(present the argument)*. When seen/considered/related/ to evidence in practice, for example... *(present evidence, discussion/analysis of what was seen in practice)*. When taken together the evidence indicates ... *(present your own ideas, views and thoughts)*.

writing about a particular theme or component part of an assignment

The theme may be one of a number of component parts identified within an assignment. These can be drawn together to show how they may be interconnected and how one aspect interacts with another. This shows the ability to critically reflect, transform and synthesise information. When writing, words are important – think about the words you might use (see Table 1.3).

(Continued)

(Continued)

Table 1.3   Words to use when writing

Phase of writing	Words you might use
Knowledge of a subject	arrange, define, duplicate, label, list, name, recognise, relate, recall, repeat, reproduce or state
Application of what you have learned or read	apply, choose, demonstrate, employ, illustrate, interpret, operate, practise, interrogate, solve, use, write
Analysis of practice	analyse, appraise, calculate, categorise, compare, contrast, criticise, differentiate, discriminate, distinguish, examine, question, test
Develop your own argument	demonstrate, refine, change, adjust, review
Comprehension of an area of study or practice	classify, describe, discuss, explain, express, identify, indicate, locate, recognise, report, select, interpret
Imitation of something that you have read or practice that can be replicated	copy, follow, adhere, construct, co-ordinate, develop, modify, adapt, change, reflect, consider, re-arrange, apply
Evaluation	appraise, argue, assess, attach, choose, compare, defend, estimate, judge, predict, rate, score, select, support, value, evaluate
To draw issues together and provide synthesis	re-assemble, collect, compose, construct, create, design, develop, formulate, reflect, organise, plan, prepare, propose, set up, draw together

We hope these CLAs will assist you in developing your study skills and direct you to use the book as a critical companion. In conclusion we think it is important to say how critical thinking, reflection and representation through writing are all important and interconnected. To paraphrase our own words, you need to develop the ability to both engage and stand back simultaneously when involved in academic or practice aspects of your course. Therefore, do not read this chapter and put it to one side. As you progress in your studies, using Tables 1.1 and 1.2 to reflect and consider your own changing viewpoints. Finally, do practise your writing. Undergraduate study relies heavily on the written form as a way of representing your knowledge and understanding even though you may be asked to use other forms of representation, for example, verbal presentations, debates, position papers, online discussion, posters, video diaries, literature compendiums and academic reports. All require you to consider which information to report, offer some explanation about why these were chosen, consider if they reveal common features and critically explore their relevance to practice. The degree of accuracy, attention to detail and analysis matters.

Further reading, especially about enhancing your study skills as well as other materials to help your studies, is below.

Useful websites

- http://youtu.be/nWqMQ26Gqi4

Essay writing, ten minute video on YouTube. Quite instructive and useful to watch.

- http://youtu.be/tAmgEa1B1vI

Useful ten minute guide to essay writing and presenting an argument, on YouTube.

- http://youtu.be/-HutuMqTAPw

Ten minute video on sequencing language – for essay writing – quite useful for novice writers.

Further reading

Biggs, J. (1999) *Teaching for Quality Learning at University*. Buckingham: Open University.
Bolton, G. (2010) *Reflective Practice: Writing and Professional Development*. London: SAGE.
Cottrell, S. (2013) *The Study Skills Handbook,* 4th edn. Basingstoke: Macmillan Press.
Smale, R. and Fowlie, J. (2009) *How to Succeed at University: An Essential Guide to Academic Skills and Personal Development*. London: SAGE.
Wellington, J., Bathmaker, A., Hunt, C., McCulloch, G. and Sikes, P. (2005) *Succeeding with your Doctorate*. London: SAGE. This offers some suggestions for distinguishing between the academic and the non-academic voice (p.84).

References

Bolton, G. (2001) *Reflective Practice: Writing and Professional Development*. London: Paul Chapman Publishing.

CoRe (2011) *Competence Requirements in Early Childhood Education and Care*. European Commission, Directorate-General for Education and Culture Final Report, University of East London, Cass School of Education and University of Ghent, Department for Social Welfare Studies. Available from: www.vbjk.be/en/node/3559 (accessed 7 October 2014).

Hilsdon, J. (2006) 'Re-thinking reflection', *The Journal of Practice Teaching in Health and Social Work*, 6 (1): 57–70.

Maslow, A.H. (1943) 'A theory of human motivation', *Psychological Review*, 50(4): 370–96. Available at: http://psychclassics.yorku.ca/Maslow/motivation.htm (accessed 5 January 2013).

OECD (2006) *Starting Strong II: Early Childhood Education and Care*. Paris: OECD.

OECD (2012) *Quality Matters in Early Childhood Education and Care: United Kingdom (England)*. Paris: OECD.

Wellington, J., Bathmaker, A., Hunt, C., McCulloch, G. and Sikes, P. (2005) *Succeeding with your Doctorate*. London: SAGE.

Want to learn more about this chapter?

Visit the companion website at **https://study.sagepub.com/reedandwalker** to access podcasts from the author and additional reading to further help you with your studies.

2

Reflective practice

Karen Hanson and Karen Appleby

Chapter overview

The purpose of this chapter is to introduce a definition of reflective practice and discuss its relevance for those developing their professionalism within ECEC and other caring professions. There are few textbook answers to most of the diverse and complex situations you will be asked to deal with when working with young children, families and colleagues. Therefore it is essential that you develop strategies to enable you to feel confident and assured that your decisions have been informed by a critical, objective and multiple perspective inquiry. This approach to reflective practice has the potential to transform your thinking and encourage personal growth and knowledge which can be used to inform action in practice. We ask that you see your role as a 'reflective activist', which can be explained as a way of being in practice and a means of building your confidence and ability to advocate for those you work with and the children you support.

Introduction

Reflective practice has been written about extensively (Dewey, 1910, 1933; Schön, 1983, 1987; Brookfield, 1995; Boud and Walker, 1998; Mezirow, 1998; Moon, 2004; Bolton, 2010). It is therefore important to establish our position as authors whose current thinking about this subject has been influenced by those others who have theorised before us. The very nature of reflective practice means that theories on this subject are continually evolving in relation to ongoing research; it is therefore essential that we engage with a range of different perspectives to inform and develop our own 'theory of action' (Argyris, 1995). We therefore support the argument that a theoretical interpretation of critical reflective practice is essential if we are to avoid simplifying practice (Thompson and Pascal, 2012). This position reflects our belief that effective reflective practitioners need to engage in a similar process and become agents of their own change. Therefore, we ask you to consider our ideas and use them to question and develop your role in enhancing the quality of provision of care and education for children and families.

Our own research has highlighted some confusion in the terminology used to discuss reflective practice. It is often discussed in terms of 'the practice of reflecting' on evidence and experience; a process of thinking and learning. In common with others, we believe reflective practice also includes the application of knowledge within the workplace to inform action, what Thompson and Pascal (2012: 322) describe as 'reflection-for-practice'. Further to this we argue that all aspects of reflective practice should be examined and understood in relation to wider socio-cultural and political perspectives; that reflective thinking, learning and action involve a complex interaction between the individual and context. We would therefore ask you to consider the following definition of reflective practice that we will be examining within this chapter:

> Reflective practice is an active engagement in continual review and repositioning of assumptions, values and practice in light of evaluation of multiple perspectives, including the wider socio-cultural perspectives influencing the context; transforming and transcending self and practice in order to effect change and improvement. (Hanson, 2012: 144)

This focus on what we describe as 'reflective activism' (explored further within this chapter) has evolved from our experience of using reflection to inform our practice over many years. Discovering the concept of reflective practice was a liberating experience because it provided a clearly defined framework for evaluative thinking, learning and action. However, through personal experience, research and evaluation of our own reflective processes, we realised the limitations of the formulaic approach we used early in our careers to examine and develop our practice. Prescriptive models of reflective practice such as Kolb (1984) and Ghaye and Ghaye (1998), whilst providing a framework at the time, did not support a deeply critical, holistic and multi-perspective approach to informed decision making and improvement in practice. These early experiences did however stimulate an interest in developing our understanding of its potential. We both passionately believe, from an extensive study of the subject with students, that reflective practice has the potential to transform and empower individuals and professional communities (Appleby, 2010; Hanson, 2012). As a consequence we have deepened our understanding of what is involved and the potential impact on quality provision for children and families. This has reinforced our belief in the commitment and motivation of those engaging in reflective practice; for us it has always involved a pro-active stance in all aspects of reflective thinking, learning and action (Appleby, 2010).

Therefore the definition examined within this chapter is offered as a stimulus for further thinking about what it means to be a reflective practitioner; a tool for evaluation and personal theorisation of identity, role and responsibilities within professional contexts. The intention is that the process of 'coming to know' will further empower practitioners as change agents engaged in improving quality (Appleby and Andrews, 2012). The significance of reflective practice across professional boundaries (Thompson and Pascal, 2012) reinforces its relevance as a common language; a process of collaborative meaning making and knowledge creation which has the potential to inform evidence-based practice within the context of integrated and inter-professional working.

How do we become reflective practitioners?

The question is not so much about how we become reflective practitioners; it is about how we rekindle the 'natural resources' we already have to support further development of our existing reflective potential. Dewey (1910: 34) determined that there are three natural resources in the creation of a reflective thinker: curiosity, suggestion and depth. He argued that curiosity is the 'most significant and vital', and most young children possess this. Unfortunately if this resource is not nurtured in childhood then as adults we may struggle to adopt an exploratory approach to practice. However, working with young children enables us to recognise this characteristic in reflective learners and to nurture our own disposition to be curious about experience. The example of reflective thinking below demonstrates firstly the child's curiosity to explore an unfamiliar object, secondly the adult's curiosity to see what this new exploration will bring and thirdly how both adult and child are using reflective thinking interdependently to develop learning.

> I showed Bella (my 18-month-old granddaughter) my set of hand painted Russian Dolls. A colleague had brought them for me from her home in Russia so they are not intended as a toy but Bella was curious and had pointed to them in the display cabinet. We explored them together and built each individual doll. She was completely actively engaged, she had never seen such objects before yet she ordered them by size and named the largest doll 'mommy' and the second largest 'daddy'. Fascinating – this child is reflecting upon her existing knowledge and experience of the world to relate to these objects and use them as a symbolic representation.
>
> Reflective thought from an observation made by Karen Hanson (Bella's Nana), October 2010.
>
> (Hanson, 2012: 40)

Dewey (1910: 31) states that 'The curious mind is constantly alert and exploring, seeking material for thought, as a vigorous and healthy body is on the qui vive for nutriment'. Both adult and child demonstrate this human capacity to be curious, ask questions and to investigate. However, as adults this natural resource is sometimes dampened through experience; as practitioners, external factors such as prescriptive inspection frameworks are unlikely to encourage a curious mind. Brookfield (1995: 249) recognises the impact of cultural barriers when encouraging a reflective disposition and community, including how the 'education' profession can have a 'silencing' effect on practitioners. In response to these factors, practitioners need to actively nurture their own and others' curiosity. This will stimulate their reflective disposition; their thinking and learning, which will in turn inform their actions. It will nurture creative responses to complex issues and situations.

Reflective activism

A 'curious mind' (Dewey, 1910: 31) stimulates a process of learning that involves the ability to make personal sense and meaning through critical reflection on experience and evidence. Likewise, reflecting upon our professional practice should be equally critical and meaningful. It should avoid a narrow interpretation that views reflective practice as a tool to self-evaluate or evaluate practice in response to externally enforced rules (Moss, 2008). In contrast with this narrow and instrumental perspective, the definition of reflective practice as 'reflective activism' draws in part on Freire's (1970) argument for critical consciousness of the world. Further to this, Wood's (2011) concept of the 'activist educator' who engages critically with the political and ethical dimensions of practice informs a pro-active stance whereby practitioners question, examine and challenge different positions, including their own. Early childhood practitioners require this activist stance to recognise and understand the 'wider socio-cultural perspectives influencing the context' (Hanson, 2012: 144) including the impact on you and your practice. Knowledge gained from critically examining the 'material reality' (Bradbury et al., 2010: 3) in which you work, provides a strong foundation for change that is purposeful and relevant. It can give you the confidence to transform practice in a way that you know will make a positive difference for those involved. As Reed (2011: 147–8) identifies, this goes beyond the early childhood professional being the 'implementer of policies, competences and technical skills'.

Effective reflective practice also requires 'active engagement in continual review and repositioning of assumptions, values and practice' (Hanson, 2012: 144). This is by no means easy and as Dewey (1910: 13) reminds us, 'it involves willingness to endure a condition of mental unrest and disturbance.' Leitch and Day (2000: 181) propose that in addition to knowledge of the context in which we work, what defines an 'effective reflective practitioner' is a thorough understanding of oneself, the values and 'moral purpose' that underpin practice. Clearly articulated beliefs, values and principles provide a strong and necessary philosophy for practice; practice which is in danger of being 'blown about by the winds of cultural and pedagogic preference' (Brookfield, 1995: 265). In our experience of working with students, the examination of self can be challenging, particularly for practitioners who are used to focusing on the needs of children and families. Also for some, the transition from 'knowing' there is a 'right' answer to trusting a process of 'continual review' is unsettling. Our experience of supporting students and practitioners to engage in critical reflective practice includes a journey of self discovery, a process revealed by the research of Hanson (2012: 144), which demonstrated (within students) the potential for 'transforming and transcending self and practice in order to effect change and improvement'. Importantly it was found that the process must be seen as purposeful by the individuals involved and that the focus and direction of the reflective journey must therefore involve choice and personal ownership. All professionals involved in nurturing and facilitating reflective practice in this sense must recognise and be sensitive to the emotional dimension of learning.

Learning through critical reflection

Critically reflective thinking (i.e. critical reflection) is nurtured by our 'curiosity' but also involves a deeper level of thinking and learning which can only be gained from engagement with different perspectives and sources of knowledge. It may involve self-evaluation, research (our own and others') and dialogue with colleagues. For the 'reflective activist' this learning will inform and transform personal professional values and practice; insights gained from this learning can and should challenge and transform our identity as practitioners, our beliefs, values, principles and attitudes, and consequently our practice. It enables us to transcend 'self and practice in order to effect change and improvement' (Hanson, 2012: 144).

Developing your identity as a reflective practitioner

Developing our knowledge of self and our identity as reflective practitioners supports the ability to think and act objectively; not only to challenge assumptions and knowledge based on personal experience but also recognise that this is what you are doing. For ourselves and in our experience of working with students and practitioners, this process of articulating who you are and what is important to you as a practitioner is empowering. The examination of identity from different perspectives informs a 'way of being' in practice that inspires confidence (Appleby and Andrews, 2012) – a confidence gained from knowing that your decisions have a moral foundation. Lahav (2008: 20) asks us 'as philosophical practitioners, to embark upon the ambitious project of cultivating our ways of being and learning to understand from deeper parts of ourselves'. An aspect of this involves a commitment to ongoing examination of what you do and the improvement of practice for the benefit of others. This in turn empowers us to actively participate and make a contribution to improving quality (Appleby and Andrews, 2012).

Your role in 'theorising practice'

Your role and identity as reflective practitioners who engage critically with different perspectives is supported by the process of 'theorising practice'. This involves active engagement with and between practice and reflection (Brockbank and McGill, 2007). It identifies practitioners as creators of 'knowledge' which is relevant to specific contexts and the individuals involved. As Edwards and Thomas (2010: 412) argue, the problems emerging within practice are 'locally determined by an immersion in the social practice of which the participant is an extension', and therefore it is not possible to give a generic instruction to act as a formula for solving these problems. In this sense, 'theorising' your practice suggests a capacity for creating new meanings and consequently exploring different possibilities and solutions. This might be described as creative reflective practice. Thompson and Pascal (2012: 312) critically examine the concept of 'technical rationality', which in their view 'demeans professional practitioners, by relegating them to the status of unthinking followers of instructions and procedures'. They argue for 'artistry in practice' – a 'fluid approach in which there is a greater emphasis on integrating theory and practice' and in which the practitioner becomes a 'knowledgeable doer' (Thompson and Pascal, 2012: 313–14).

Becoming a 'knowledgeable doer'

In our experience, a theoretical perspective which has supported a questioning, creative and exploratory approach to knowledge (and self-knowledge) and consequently the transformation for many practitioners is Brookfield's (1995) four lenses theory. He asks that we apply different perspectives to what is known or assumed to stimulate informed critical reflection and learning, and see things through a variety of lenses. He suggests that we need to be conscious of using our own interpretive filters and states: 'to some extent we are all prisoners trapped within the perceptual frameworks that determine how we view our experiences' (1995: n28).

1. The 'autobiographical lens'

    When faced with a situation, issue, concern or problem, which makes us question our personal and professional practice, the first perspective used to evaluate is often from a personal viewpoint. This lens is framed by our life experiences as learners and practitioners and as such can be restrictive and may not consider other 'blind spots'.

2. The 'students' lens'

   Insight into the child's 'voice' can reveal how assumptions regarding our practice can be viewed and perceived very differently by those most closely and significantly affected by our practice.

3. The 'colleagues'/peers' lens'

   This lens involves participating in critical discussion and debate with others. It can highlight how colleagues who experience very similar situations may use alternative approaches and see things differently to ourselves. This enables us to gain an empathic perspective to enrich our knowledge of practice; it can also help us to develop a reflexive approach where we view ourselves and our practice from the position of others. Dialogue, as Freire (1973: 127) believed, has the potential to 'awaken awareness'. He found that discussion groups enabled his students to become more 'conscious' of it to gain a greater awareness of the power of their own ability to change it through their critical reflections. Brockbank and McGill (2007: 65) describe this as dialogue that 'engages the person at the edge of their current understanding and the sense of meaning they give to and with the world'. Engagement with this process can stimulate the development of new concepts, theories and practices for all involved.

4. The 'theoretical/literature lens'

   Most issues we problematise have been studied, researched, theorised and represented in some form by others. Therefore researching literature can provide informed interpretations of familiar circumstances and experiences.

In addition to these four lenses proposed by Brookfield (1995), Hanson (2012) engaged in research which identified an additional 'fifth' lens (see Figure 2.1). This is seen as the 'peripheral socio-cultural lens' which allows an objective view of the contextual matters influencing and impacting upon the situation. This view emerged as Hanson became conscious of her own socio-cultural frames of reference which limited her view of the wider socio-cultural influences surrounding her research. In particular, neglecting some technological evolutionary factors that belonged outside her own experience but played a significant part in the lives of those she was researching. Hanson (2012: 136) states that the peripheral socio-cultural lens,

> … can illuminate reflective evaluations further, and is determined by two aspects – the socio-cultural influence of the person engaged in reflection, and the socio-cultural influences of the particular context in which the reflection takes place.

Figure 2.1 illustrates the 'fifth lens' and bringing together or 'synthesising' the insights gained from the different lenses to inform and transform your understanding. It can

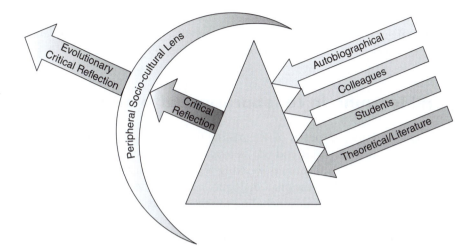

Figure 2.1   Evolutionary critical reflection

be likened to the workings of a kaleidoscope – as you turn it a different image or perspective is created, one that you have not seen before.

Reflective activism in context

Despite focusing significantly on the role and identity of the individual practitioner as a critically reflective practitioner we locate all aspects discussed thus far within a socio-cultural context. Schön (1987: 3) reminds us of the 'messy, confusing' problems that lie outside technical rationality:

> In the varied topography of professional practice, there is a high hard ground overlooking a swamp. On the high ground, manageable problems lend themselves to solution through the application of research-based theory and technique. In the swampy lowland, 'messy, confusing' problems defy technical solution.

The range of issues, concerns, problems and dilemmas occurring within Early Childhood practice require the efforts of a reflective activist who has the capacity to understand this complexity and to explore and learn about these issues to inform potential solutions and creative responses. This complexity includes understanding your own role as a participant and the impact you have on the setting and everyone involved; a process sometimes described as reflexivity. As Appleby and Andrews (2012) remind us, we are all individuals with different professional identities and qualities. Recognising, valuing and enabling this diversity can support the best use of available resources, thereby enhancing the possibility of positive outcomes, but this must be understood within the context of working with others. Reflective activism should not involve individuals imposing their will on others; rather it should enable participation and collaboration.

Working and learning in collaboration with others

We have engaged in a process of theorising reflective practice which has been informed by our own identities and our personal experience of the world, including our professional lives as practitioners working with children, students and practitioners. Our experience of professional dialogue has informed and transformed our perspectives on a range of issues including the themes presented in this chapter. We recognise that further research and dialogue will challenge our thinking in the future but feel comfortable with this because we are reflective practitioners who are 'curious' about this 'way of being'. Also as reflective activists we can identify the impact on our practice. We have benefitted from learning with others, including students and practitioners who share our interests within what Wenger and colleagues (2002: 4) define as a community of practice:

> ... groups of people who share a concern, a set of problems or a passion about a topic and who deepen their knowledge and expertise in this area by interacting on an ongoing basis.

Our experience as members of a stimulating community of reflective practitioners has informed the way we teach others, particularly in terms of creating a safe environment for discussion and debate. Hanson's (2012) research identifies the use of focus discussion forums and other peer discussion opportunities within Early Childhood undergraduate programmes of study for enabling the formation of communities of practice. This is affirmed by Tsang (2011: 17) whose research concluded that:

> Reflective group discussion offers different benefits to student learning compared to individual reflective writing, in particular, collaborative multi perspective learning and professional development through a support 'community of practice' engaging in critical dialogue.

Reflective activism therefore reflects a 'way of being' as a community as well as an individual practitioner. Consequently all aspects of the definition of reflective practice introduced at the beginning of the chapter apply equally to individuals and communities. Further to this, leaders of practice have a significant role in nurturing and developing a community of reflective activists who work together for the benefit of children and families as well as each other. The nature of communities will vary and the challenges may be significant for some but a shared commitment to improving practice as reflective activists provides the means as well as a purpose.

Conclusion

The themes examined in this chapter are presented with the purpose of provoking further critical reflection and learning. This reflects our belief in the significance of personal and shared ownership of the reflective process and a responsibility for making a contribution to discourses about reflective practice. The concept of reflective activism encapsulates our current theory of reflective practice; the significance of curiosity as the driver for critically reflective thinking and learning about practice and self for individuals as well as communities of practice; the role of this process in enabling us as 'knowledgeable doers' working together creatively for the benefit of children and families.

Reflective activism:

- is perceived as a 'way of being' for individuals and communities of practice. It builds on a strong value base that assumes personal/professional responsibility for improving the quality of provision for children and families;
- involves a complex interaction between the individual and context;
- involves a pro-active stance in all aspects of reflective thinking, learning and action whereby practitioners question, examine and challenge different positions including their own;
- should be equally critical and meaningful and avoid a narrow interpretation that views reflective practice for external demands;
- is stimulated by a natural disposition to be 'curious';
- involves actively engaging with the complexities and challenges within a diverse profession;
- recognises the significance of a reflexive approach which involves critical examination and 'theorisation' of what you do and why in relation to the impact this has on self and others;
- requires a full critical evaluation of evidence gained from multi-dimensional reflections including the fifth 'socio-cultural' lens (Hanson, 2012).

Critical Learning Activity

Identify the key themes presented in this chapter.

Apply Hanson's (2012) model of Evolutionary Critical Reflection (Figure 2.1) to critically reflect on your identity as a reflective practitioner and the nature of your professional community.

- Your autobiographical lens;
- The lenses of the children you work with;
- Your peers/colleagues lenses;

(Continued)

(Continued)

- Theoretical/literature lenses;
- The socio-cultural fifth lens.

Analyse the evidence from the different perspectives.
What have you learned about your identity as a reflective practitioner?
Has your perspective changed? If it has, how and what are the implications for your practice?

References

Appleby, K. (2010) 'Reflective thinking; reflective practice', in M. Reed and N. Canning (eds), *Reflective Practice in the Early Years*. London: SAGE.

Appleby, K. and Andrews, M. (2012) 'Reflective practice is the key to quality improvement', in M. Reed and N. Canning (eds), *Implementing Quality Improvement and Change in the Early Years*. London: SAGE.

Argyris, C. (1995) 'Action science and organizational learning', *Journal of Managerial Psychology*, 10 (6): 20–26.

Bolton, G. (2010) *Reflective Practice: Writing and Professional Development*. London: SAGE.

Boud, D. and Walker, D. (1998) 'Promoting reflection in professional courses: the challenge of context', *Studies in Higher Education*, 23 (2): 191–207.

Bradbury, H., Frost, N., Kilminster, S. and Zukas, M. (eds) (2010) *Beyond Reflective Practice: New Approaches to Professional Lifelong Learning*. Abingdon: Routledge.

Brockbank, A. and McGill, I. (2007) *Facilitating Reflective Learning in Higher Education* (Society for Research into Higher Education), 2nd edn. Berkshire: Open University Press.

Brookfield, S. (1995) *Becoming a Critically Reflective Teacher*. San Francisco, CA: Jossey-Bass.

Dewey, J. (1910) *How We Think*. Boston/New York/Chicago: D.C. Heath & Co.

Dewey, J. (1933) *How We Think: A Restatement of the Relation of Reflective Thinking to the Educative Process*. Chicago: Henry Regnery.

Edwards, G. and Thomas, G. (2010) 'Can reflective practice be taught?', *Educational Studies*, 36 (4): 403–414.

Freire, P. (1970) *Pedagogy of the Oppressed*. London: Penguin.

Freire, P. (1973) *Education for Critical Consciousness*. London: Sheed and Ward.

Ghaye, A. and Ghaye, K. (1998) *Teaching and Learning through Critical Reflective Practice*. London: David Fulton Press.

Hanson, K. (2012) *How Can I Support Early Childhood Studies Undergraduate Students To Develop Reflective Dispositions?* EdD thesis, Exeter University. Available from: http://hdl.handle.net/10036/3866.

Kolb, D. (1984) *Experiential Learning: Experience as a Source of Learning and Development*. London: Prentice Hall.

Lahav, R. (2008) 'Philosophical practice: have we gone far enough?', *Practical Philosophy*, 9 (2): 13–20.

Leitch, R. and Day, C. (2000) 'Action research and reflective practice: towards a holistic view', *Educational Action Research*, 8 (1): 179–193.

Mezirow, J. (1998) 'On critical reflection', *Adult Education Quarterly*, 48: 185–198.

Moon, J. (2004) *A Handbook of Reflective and Experiential Learning: Theory and Practice.* Abingdon, Oxon: Routledge.

Moss, P. (2008) 'Foreword', in A. Paige-Smith and A. Craft (eds), *Developing Reflective Practice in the Early Years*. Berkshire, England: Open University Press.

Reed, M. (2011) 'Professional development and reflective practice', in A. Paige-Smith and A. Craft (eds), *Developing Reflective Practice in the Early Years*. Berkshire, England: Open University Press.

Schön, D.A. (1983) *The Reflective Practitioner*. London: Ashgate Publishing Ltd.

Schön, D.A. (1987) *Educating the Reflective Practitioner*. San Francisco, CA: Jossey Bass.

Thompson, N. and Pascal, J. (2012) 'Developing critically reflective practice', *Reflective Practice: International and Multidisciplinary Perspectives*, 13 (2): 311–325.

Tsang, A.K.T. (2011) 'In-class reflective group discussion as a strategy for the development of students as evolving professionals', *International Journal for the Scholarship of Teaching and Learning*, 5 (1): 1–17.

Wenger, E., McDermott, R.A. and Snyder, W. (2002) *Cultivating Communities of Practice: a Guide to Managing Knowledge*. Boston, MA: Harvard Business School Press.

Wood, E. (2011) 'Listening to young children: multiple voices, meanings and understandings', in A. Paige-Smith and A. Craft (eds), *Developing Reflective Practice in the Early Years*, 2nd edn. Berkshire, England: Open University Press.

Want to learn more about this chapter?

Visit the companion website at **https://study.sagepub.com/reedandwalker** to access podcasts from the author and additional reading to further help you with your studies.

3

The ethical practitioner with children and families

Sue Callan

Chapter overview

Ethical behaviour is part of personal professional responsibility for service delivery and research. This chapter explores the social, political and historical discourse underpinning notions of ethical practice, professional interactions and relationships. Reflective questions are posed throughout the chapter in a critical appraisal of key issues which underpin collaborative work with others. It is recognised (Etherington, 2007) that critical reflection requires an understanding of the personal values and beliefs underpinning work-based roles and dynamics. This chapter draws on a range of literature to illustrate and explore the discourse of early childhood and contemporary research. It also gives indicative links to forthcoming chapters so that the reader can identify examples of the interrelationship between practice, policy and values.

By unpacking assumptions and concepts relating to ethical practice and the nature of the democratic approaches which underpin this, the chapter scrutinises the extent to which competing ideologies influence the potential for a genuinely collaborative partnership between practitioners, children and families. It demonstrates the necessity of establishing a grounded personal professional perspective through critical reflection, in a sector which is characterised by constant change.

Towards a critical understanding of ethical practice

There is every opportunity to think about an ethical approach to 'being' in the twenty-first century. National and international media continually debate the possibilities of ethical banking, investment and business practices. Individuals can chose to engage in ethical shopping through Fairtrade schemes – or source clothes produced without use of child labour. In a further example, conservation and wildlife organisations, both domestic and international, encourage the concept of ethical farming and sustainable land use for the benefit of animals, local populations and the longer term health of the planet. In general terms, most of us are aware of conforming to social expectations of 'decency', whilst people of faith will be conscious of explicit codes of behaviour towards others.

Can we possibly agree a specific definition of ethical social behaviour from such a diverse base? In our daily lives, perhaps this simply boils down to an intuitive recognition of social and cultural expectations and the moral codes that these represent.

Critical thinking about ethics will 'complicate' this intuitive personal understanding. By taking specific examples from the above, it is possible to see that the notion of ethical behaviour in one area sometimes conflicts with others. In terms of faith, schism is often the result of debates about truth, values and behaviours. Thus, a critical approach to ethics will reveal a socio-economic and political dimension to the discourse. Whilst it may be possible to find a specific dictionary definition, this will generally be focused to a notion of universal meanings and 'truth' whereas, as Dahlberg and Moss have shown (2005), applied ethics is generally dependent on social context and purpose. In seeking to simplify a highly complex area of meta-philosophy, Mortari and Harcourt (2012) suggest that we consider two core strands: an 'ethics of justice' based on universal principles and rules as part of a normative framework; and an 'ethics of care' which prioritises the well-being of those 'towards whom an agency is directed' (2012: 240). In other words, a distinction is made between codes and rules (the 'what' of practice); and their application in a personal professional role and codes of conduct in distinct contexts (the 'how' of practice). This helpful model supports the exploration of wider issues in the chapter. To understand this dynamic, practitioners need to critically examine and understand the historical emergence of ethical practice for the sector.

For those entering the childhood services sector, the plethora of standards, requirements, focus on quality, inspection, regulation and the substantial local policies to be read and digested (recognised from the definitions above as the 'what' of practice in a 'normative' framework) may come as quite a shock. From an external viewpoint, the world of children and early childhood is often perceived as a fairly straightforward, safe and joyful environment to inhabit. Yet this world view is constantly challenged – either through high profile individual tragedies and evidence of institutional abuse; or where there is environmental trauma or conflict. These events challenge our thinking and disturb the 'intuitive' understanding of what constitutes a commitment to working ethically with children and families, because they confront assumptions about 'basic' principles and a world view of what is 'normal'.

As a specific example, focusing on child safeguarding, the detailed framework for service provision in education, welfare and health is understood as a basic code of conduct for a range of interventions and interactions encountered in daily contact with children as well as other professionals, which we can relate to in terms of ethics as 'protection' (Mortari and Harcourt, 2012).

This is centralised, highly codified and prescribed, and grounded in social concern for children's safety. However, as an example of applied ethics, local policies on behaviour in settings will offer for children and adults a way of navigating through conflicting needs in an emotionally charged environment, as they are based in interpretations of the needs of a specific community.

To go beyond an acceptance of established frameworks (the 'what' of practice), to question and consider underpinning issues and perspectives (the 'why' of practice) and to emerge with a personal position informed by theory and experience (the 'how' of personal professionalism) is the real stuff of critical reflective practice – and should be continually informed by critical questioning of assumptions and values. Such an approach requires the professional practitioner to know what they feel about practice as well as understanding its requirements (Rawlings, 2008) – to be conscious of personal values and beliefs in interpreting the external national policy drivers to daily conduct in the workplace.

The technical application of an ethics of justice approach (Mortari and Harcourt, 2012) is apparent in all four nations of the United Kingdom (UK). The UK early childhood frameworks stress the uniqueness of each child, a commitment to equality of opportunity in education and welfare, partnership with families and trans-agency working focused on the need to support children to achieve positive outcomes through which they make a contribution to the wider society. These principles seem to be a 'core' ethical underpinning for practice, reinforced by the acceptance of the human rights agenda, specifically the United Nations Convention on the Rights of the Child (UNCRC) (UNICEF, 1989). However, the complexity of the national legislation and policy process as it is interpreted across service provision also serves to remind us that each of the four nations sets its priorities in the application of ethics of care based on values specific to that community. Similarly, whilst there has been some useful international comparison of models of children's provision based on stated 'universal' principles (CfBT, 2010), differences in implementation within national borders can be best understood if we apply the model of the two strands of ethical practice.

Ethically informed practice

How can we proceed from this understanding of the contextual nature of ethical childhood practice to establish a way of working in a personal professional role within international pedagogic discourse? The following section explores and examines the development of the commitment to ethically informed practice. It is useful to pause and summarise what experienced practitioners will bring to this discussion. Experienced practitioners will recognise in policy and practice frameworks a strong model of normative ethical behaviours. This emphasises the individuality of the child, the expertise and contribution of the family – however that family is constituted (including respect for gender and sexual orientation) – as part of the 'team around the child' (Siraj-Blatchford et al., 2007). It values language, faith and cultural communities from all social classes and recognises the strengths and potential of those with complex health or welfare issues through a commitment to promote inclusion. The principles of confidentiality and care in the use of records and personal data are also part of this approach, as are the expectations that those undertaking work-based research will seek permissions and show sensitivity to participants (Flewitt, 2005; Callan, 2011). Such is the 'known' of ethical codes underpinning practice. The ethical practitioner is required to have basic qualities of empathy and commitment in order to be effective in understanding and interpreting the professional responsibilities of the role. These features sit well with the motivation of most individuals to act with 'decency' in their relationships with others and particularly the emotional commitment to working positively for children, a value set which combines normative and applied models of ethical practice (a commitment to justice and care).

The critically reflective practitioner should however be keen to fully understand the values underpinning the codes for working with children and families and to question assumptions and values relating to their particular context for practice. Leaders and managers in the sector are required to be 'theoretically informed' – so the need to recognise and engage with theory and research is crucial to graduate qualities of thinking and emerging professionalism. Participation in such reflection and study provides an opportunity to consider the nature of democratic practice in the professional role (Moss, 2012) beyond the boundaries of distinct settings.

Unpacking ethical practice in early childhood contexts

Why does a commitment to ethical practice involve the recognition of power dynamics in relationships with children and their families? In constructing three strands of the professional role – carer, technician and reflective researcher/professional – Moss (2008) shows that critical reflection through research involves outcomes and change as part of conscious leadership practice. Thinking about leadership in the context of working within communities has engaged researchers (Lee, 2008; Dalli and Te One, 2012; Dockett et al., 2012) in a critical view of why we should be concerned about impacting on the child in his or her world when we study children's experiences.

The concern to be sensitive to the experiences of children, to research children's lives, and to consider the impact of decisions about provision on the child and on his or her world is relatively recent. Historical events and changing attitudes to children and childhood have played a part in driving this concern which involves the recognition of 'agency' – the child's ability to express a view on matters that concern him/her and of the right to do so (Mishna et al., 2004; Dockett et al., 2012). More specifically, a focus on practitioner ethical literacy also recognises the increasing complexity of the relationship between agencies concerned with the child and family (Wenger et al., 2002; Whitmarsh, 2007) and the way that the ethical models within different professions (early years, social work, nursing, teaching) interact in consideration of the needs of the child, but also limit the possibilities for engaging collaboratively with children and families.

Just as important as these strands are the wide ranging social changes that characterise community experiences in the twenty-first century – particularly the diversity of children and families represented in many settings as a result of movement of peoples across national/international borders. The uniqueness of the child and each family is more apparent now than ever before (Rhedding-Jones, 2005), and the diversity of language groups within small communities is an obvious example of the need to research and work with children and families in order to include and promote their active participation in a sector representing wider social, educational and cultural institutions. This social change also has an impact on the evolving understanding of what now constitutes 'community' – so that practitioners need to be aware that they must look beyond their own class, sexuality (Gunn, 2011), language and cultural group in order to understand the multi-layered nature of children's environments, experiences and spaces (Raittila, 2012). In short, all assumptions about the world as we may previously have seen it are challenged. The notion that one model of 'children' and 'childhood' prevails is challenged as are assumptions about what is 'normal' in terms of behaviours and development. Researching in practice is now focused on promoting and enabling child-centred narratives to emerge so that the postmodern concept of the child as 'a co-constructor of knowledge, identity and culture' (Dahlberg et al., 1999: 48) is not only recognisable in the contemporary framework for children's services, but gives a clear indication of an ethical approach to working with them – ideally an approach that will continue to promote participation in sensitively constructed research and democratic practice.

The idea that there is no definite 'truth' often alarms students and emerging professionals who hope through study to find distinct models for practice and guidance for their role in negotiating the challenges of a complex sector. This generates dependence on codified frameworks and practice guidance. For this reason, inexperienced practitioners often strive to work within the 'letter of the law' when applying framework documents and procedures since this offers some security that they are doing things 'right' – as Moss (2008) notes, there is a focus on the 'technical' aspects of practice which disempower those who work daily with children. Whitmarsh (2007) supports this view and argues that codified models for practice undermine the ability of practitioners to develop individual, professional, ethical behaviours. In deconstructing the concept of prescribed *ethical practice* within the perspective of contextualised *ethics of care*, Mortari and Harcourt (2012) show the liberating effect of postmodern perspectives for leading practice, particularly with regard to collaborative and co-operative working with children and families in local communities.

It is vital to recognise and understand the significance of power dynamics to interpretations of human relationships and the emergence of a focus on Human Rights since the mid-twentieth century. Much of the historical debate is highlighted in later chapters through exploration of specific features of the practitioner role. In the context of power relations, the continued drive by successive governments in the UK to standardise curriculums and approaches to practice regardless of specific contexts can be regarded as very much in the mould of a social, cultural, economic and scientific focus on 'order' – or 'disciplinary power' (Foucault, cited in Dahlberg and Moss, 2005). In a world where the speed of social and technological change is so unrelenting, it was proposed as early as 1916 (Dewey, 1916) that a vital part of educational practice is professionals questioning the conceptual framework underpinning provision and research. For example, such reflection continues with the work of Lee (2008), who emphasises the localised relationships at the heart of pedagogy which must be sustained in good research practice.

It is hard to negotiate the range of professional role responsibilities without a critical appreciation of these apparently opposing positions: the aspirations and values of practitioners who recognise that settings are 'capable of many purposes' (Moss, 2012: 94) as part of a pioneering tradition for child-focused family services; contrasting with the continuation of a market driven, diverse sector and the need for centralised regulation (Lloyd, 2012). In establishing a personal professional ethical position, practitioners should recognise that this tension of competing ideologies is grounded in the dynamic of 'democratic practice' – the extent to which leaders can share and distribute power as part of their interactions and experience in the community (Lee, 2008) and where their main responsibilities lie.

How does rights-based practice impact on our understanding of 'the ethical practitioner'?

In recognising the need to share power with parents, children and colleagues, it is possible to understand the contribution of researchers such as Clark (2005) and Cullen et al. (2009) who have striven to integrate the child's voice and community perspectives into the study of children's experiences as part of an 'ethics of care' approach. Such practice is based on valuing a model of rights and participation which is grounded in the belief that members of the community are 'experts' in their own lives and which results in a distinct change in perception of the position of the researcher/lead practitioner in terms of balance of power in studying and leading provision. This is an example of the movement for democratic practice most usually identifiable in international models of early childhood provision – in the Nordic countries, the Reggio Emilia schools in Italy and the pedagogy of the Te Whāriki curriculum in New Zealand. That these curriculum philosophies have contributed to underpinning principles for practice, and focus on 'quality', in the nations of the United Kingdom will be recognised by established practitioners, but there is a crucial difference. Moss cautions that in the UK, 'these [principles] are not folded into the larger political concept of democracy; they risk instead becoming parts in management's toolkit, a box to tick as evidence of having done some market research and having checked out "customer satisfaction"' (2012: 103), and he urges practitioners to remain vigilant about the restrictive influences of normative approaches on the potential for a genuinely collaborative partnership between practitioners and communities.

This difference between the two models of ethics is most apparent if we look at the concept of advocacy, an underpinning principle for radical educators in the continuum of principles for democratic education from Dewey (1916), through Foucault (1977) to Paulo Freire (1970, 1972, 2004). In the international models noted, a key part of the conceptualisation of the practitioner role – particularly the social pedagogue – is the responsibility to promote and create 'spaces that reflect and support educational values, including democracy' (Moss, 2012: 103). The role of the early childhood educator is therefore to promote participation of children and families in democratic processes that will extend beyond the immediate world of the setting, and to act as an advocate for collective social well-being grounded in the framework of human rights and social justice. It may be that such an argument confronts the practitioner's personal world view and this indicates a key outcome of critical reflection – the consideration and formulation of a developed personal perspective as the result of a reflexive struggle with ideas and beliefs, which then informs an enhanced professional identity.

In a normative model, the principles of good practice identified by national frameworks in the UK are inextricably linked to notions of service 'quality' and workforce professionalism in moves to standardise provision across sector and professional boundaries and in attempts to promote children's inclusion, welfare and educational attainment. It is worth pausing to consider the way in which the model of the ethical practitioner has so far been presented. It has been argued that an understanding of the ethics of care is bound up with ensuring that children, families and colleagues are given due respect as partners in co-constructing both provision and research, a position often undermined in prescriptive frameworks. Those entering the workforce are supported through training to identify strategies for implementing statutory requirements, but are not always encouraged to critically appraise the sometimes conflicting values, interests and assumptions of the policy and practice infrastructure. This requires us to 'problematise' the whole notion of ethical practice and be concerned with the concept of power in social relationships: to consider a broader construct of democratic practice in the international context of history and ideas and, specifically, to recognise that social accountability to the community of the setting goes far beyond responding to statutory inspection and regulation regimes. Ethical, democratic practice is therefore understood as focused on individual and collective needs of the broader community (informed by research and the 'voices' of the community). Such an understanding gives renewed meaning to the importance of integrated working, the concept of 'quality' in provision and the role of the lead practitioner. Practitioners who have recognised that professionalism includes participation in the wider community, acting as an advocate for the sector alongside the children and families within it, are integrating the various role responsibilities contained within the internationalist, historical tradition of philosophy in education.

How might this impact on the nature of personal conduct for the way forward?

Reflexivity involves a willingness to examine values and beliefs in the light of experience and theoretical knowledge, together with a commitment to change in response. This is the nature of 'conscious' practice which is quite distinct from the intuitive ethical behaviours explored in the earlier part of the chapter. A confident practitioner recognises and adopts a professional identity which is informed by knowledge and understanding of the traditions and discourse within the sector. This identity is developed through reflection and research to embrace a professional 'position' in terms of enduring values and beliefs in the context of shifting statutory frameworks. The established practitioner is able to engage in professional dialogue as a pre-requisite for integrated working as well as democratic partnership with children and families. Such a dialogue is only possible within a listening culture facilitated by open communication and work-based research tools that enable representation and interpretation of all the voices concerned (Gabb, 2010). Indeed, dialogue would be impossible without a commitment to work-based investigation and research as part of professional practice. The professional disposition enables an established practitioner to explore and explain the 'why' and 'how' of personal practice, whilst implementing the 'what' of specific requirements which are common to all but can be interpreted and applied for distinct communities. Thus, critical reflection generates 'conscious' practice and abilities that define a democratic, ethical professional. Moss (2008: 125) has outlined these qualities as:

- The ability to participate in meaningful dialogue and be proactive in researching the experiences and work of others;
- The ability to maintain an internal dialogue as part of curiosity and critical thinking about experience in the setting;

- The ability to listen and to value different interpretations of practice – accepting uncertainty as part of a continuous process of change;
- The ability to recognise that there is no objective viewpoint – multiple perspectives are embraced to construct and develop discourse with others.

Working in this manner represents the aspirations of the sector in embracing a 'relational pedagogy' (Papatheodorou and Moyles, 2009). It places the quality of relationships in the centre of provision and gives value to the contribution of parents, children and colleagues in co-constructing the local pedagogy. Such an approach demands trust, which is the foundation of open interactions, inclusion and honest, respectful communication at the heart of participation – whether participation is 'formal' or 'informal'. Formal situations will include the implementation of codified processes for inclusion, assessment requirements, staff appraisal procedures and research ethics. Informal interactions will involve the day to day relationships within a setting and which constitute a caring partnership with adults as well as communication for teaching and learning.

How can I sustain an ethical focus in my practice?

Rowson (2006) has proposed a framework to facilitate ethical thinking in the professions in order to work effectively within 'culturally complex democracies' (2006: 14) – in other words to demonstrate ethical literacy by interpreting the responsibilities of the professional role. Rowson's framework is adapted by Rawlings (2008: 64) to offer core principles with which to appraise the quality of personal behaviour and professional practice – the 'ethics of care'. Using the FAIR mnemonic, practitioners can carry these commitments in mind as part of practical daily actions centred on

- Fairness – the commitment to treat individuals justly and fairly
- Autonomy – the commitment to respect the autonomy of adults and children
- Integrity – the commitment to act with integrity
- Results – the commitment to seek the 'best results'; those which will be fair, beneficial and have the least harmful consequences for individuals, the setting and the diverse groups within it.

These commitments are applicable to both elements of ethical practice – in fact all areas through which practitioners adopt a way of professional 'being'. Rawlings' model addresses the concern expressed by Whitmarsh (2007) that prescriptive, distinct templates undermine interpretative practice. It also sits more comfortably with the work of Cullen and colleagues (2009) which is focused on democratic practice, transcending professional disciplines and international boundaries by placing children and families at the heart of research-informed provision. This is what constitutes ethical practice in settings and serves to impact positively on children's lives.

As a feature of ethical practice arising from the review of literature and perspectives, it would seem appropriate to argue that Advocacy should be added as a further commitment to this model – a notion that is explored as part of inter-professional transactions in Chapter 13. Through advocacy and involvement at local and national levels, practitioners can challenge governments to fulfil the articles of the UNCRC (UNICEF, 1989) across local/national and international boundaries. The significant legislation for equal opportunities would not have emerged without co-operative campaigning across communities in order to achieve progress. Thus, advocacy as part of practitioner ethical behaviour involves challenging ideas and viewpoints within and beyond the immediate setting and engaging in the continued struggle for social justice. This final commitment can be presented as a challenge to emerging practitioners in a final reflective question: by unpacking assumptions and concepts relating to ethical practice, and the nature of democratic approaches which underpin this, in what ways can I make a difference to children's lives?

Critical Learning Activity

This chapter has focused primarily on the 'tensions' within constructs of ethical practice. You may like to go to your curriculum framework and see where ethical perspectives are apparent or can be clearly identified. Reflect on the following questions and discuss your responses with your peers in study and practice.

- Are ethical values explicitly identified in the framework? To what extent do you agree with the contention that normative frameworks result in a 'tick-box' approach to managing practice?
- How far do you recognise yourself as being ethically literate? Consider how your developing knowledge and professional experience could enable you to develop this skill for future practice.
- To what extent does awareness of ethical practice promote your professional identity as a social pedagogue?

Further reading

Albon, D. (2010) 'Postmodern and post-structuralist perspectives on early childhood education', in L. Miller and L. Pound (eds), *Theories and Approaches to Learning in the Early Years*. London: SAGE. This helpful text offers further reading on the historical development of critical approaches to practice.

Callan, S. (2011) 'Ethical positioning in work-based investigations', in S. Callan and M. Reed (eds), *Work-Based Research in the Early Years*. London: SAGE. Reflexivity includes a degree of self-appraisal so that new insight can be applied to developing engagement with colleagues, children and families. The case studies featured in this chapter, and throughout the book, show that by relinquishing the role of 'expert', practitioners improved confidence in participation and quality of experiences for all involved in their settings.

Hoyuelos, A. (2013) *The Ethics in Loris Malaguzzi's Philosophy*. Reykjavik: Isalda. This is a detailed and scholarly exploration of the nature of ethics underpinning the influential practice in Reggio Emilia schools. It brings together all of the themes raised in this chapter and has a particular focus on empowerment.

Pre-School Learning Alliance (2011) *Changing Lives, Changing Life: The Pedagogical Perspectives of the Pre-School Learning Alliance*. London: PSLA. Practitioners working in England as part of the Pre-School Learning Alliance will be very much aware of the fact that the organisation has a long history of commitment to parent-led, community-based provision (PSLA, 2011), valuing and nurturing the participation rights of all involved in establishing the unique pedagogy of each setting. This book celebrates that tradition and the values embraced.

References

Callan, S. (2011) 'Ethical positioning in work-based investigations', in S. Callan and M. Reed (eds), *Work-Based Research in the Early Years*. London: SAGE.

CfBT Education Trust (2010) *Research Report: An International Perspective on Integrated Children's Services*. Reading, CFBT. Available from: www.cfbt.com/evidenceforeducation/ourresearch/evidenceforgovernment/internationalpolicyreforms/publishedresearchreports/integratedchildrensse (accessed 23 August 2012).

Clark, A. (2005) 'Ways of seeing: using the Mosaic approach to listen to young children's perspectives', in A. Clark and P. Moss (eds), *Beyond Listening*. London: National Children's Bureau and Joseph Rowntree Foundation.

Cullen, J., Hedges, H. and Bone, J. (2009) 'Planning, undertaking and disseminating research in early childhood settings: an ethical framework', *New Zealand Research in Early Childhood Education*, 12: 109–118.

Dahlberg, G. and Moss, P. (2005) *Ethics and Politics in Early Childhood Education*. Abingdon: Routledge and Falmer.

Dahlberg, G., Moss, P. and Pence, A. (1999) *Beyond Quality in Early Childhood Education and Care: Postmodern Perspectives*. London: Routledge Falmer.

Dalli, C. and Te One, S. (2012) 'Involving children in educational research: researcher reflections on challenges', *International Journal of Early Years Education*, 20 (3): 224–233. Available from: http://dx.doi.org/10.1080/09669760.2012.715408 (accessed 29 October 2012).

Dewey, J. (1916) *Democracy and Education: An Introduction to the Philosophy of Education*. New York: Macmillan.

Dockett, S., Einarsdóttir, J. and Perry, B. (2012) 'Young children's decisions about research participation: opting out', *International Journal of Early Years Education*, 20 (3): 244–256. Available from: http://dx.doi.org/10.1080/09669760.2012.715405 (accessed 29 October 2012).

Etherington, K. (2007) 'Ethical research in reflexive relationships', *Qualitative Inquiry*, 13 (5): 599–616.

Flewitt, R. (2005) 'Conducting research with young children: some ethical considerations', *Early Childhood Development and Care*, 175 (6): 553–565.

Foucault, M. (1977) *Discipline and Punishment: The Birth of the Prison*. London: Penguin.

Freire, P. (1970) *Cultural Action for Freedom*, trans. Myra Bergman Ramos. Middlesex: Penguin.

Freire, P. (1972) *Pedagogy of the Oppressed*, trans. Myra Bergman Ramos. Middlesex: Penguin.

Freire, P. (2004) *Pedagogy of Hope: Reliving Pedagogy of the Oppressed*. London: Continuum.

Gabb, J. (2010) 'Home truths: ethical issues in family research', *Qualitative Research*, 10 (4): 461–478.

Gunn, A. (2011) 'Even if you say it three ways it still doesn't mean it's true: The pervasiveness of heteronormativity in early childhood education', *Journal of Early Childhood Research*, 9 (3): 280–290.

Lee, W. (2008) 'ELP: empowering the leadership in professional development communities', *European Early Childhood Education Research Journal*, 16 (1): 95–106. Available from: http://dx.doi.org/10.1080/13502930801897087 (accessed 29 October 2012).

Lloyd, E. (2012) 'The marketisation of early years education and childcare in England', in L. Miller and D. Hevey (eds), *Policy Issues in the Early Years*. London: SAGE.

Mishna, F., Antle, B.J. and Regehr, C. (2004) 'Tapping the perspectives of children: emerging ethical issues in qualitative research', *Qualitative Social Work*, 3 (4): 449–468.

Mortari, L. and Harcourt, D. (2012) '"Living" ethical dilemmas for researchers when researching with children', *International Journal of Early Years Education*, 20 (3): 234–243. Available from: http://dx.doi.org/10.1080/09669760.2012.715409 (accessed 29 October 2012).

Moss, P. (2008) 'The democratic and reflective professional: rethinking and reforming the early years workforce' in L. Millerand and C. Cable (eds), *Professionalism in the Early Years*. London: Hodder Education.

Moss, P. (2012) 'Making democracy a fundamental value: meaning what exactly?', in L. Miller and D. Hevey (eds), *Policy Issues in the Early Years*. London: SAGE.

Papatheodorou, T. and Moyles, J. (2009) (eds) *Learning Together in the Early Years: Exploring Relational Pedagogy*. London: Routledge.

Pre-School Learning Alliance (2011) *Changing Lives, Changing Life: The Pedagogical Perspectives of the Pre-School Learning Alliance*. London: PSLA.

Raittila, R. (2012) 'With children in their lived place: children's action as research data', *International Journal of Early Years Education*, 20 (3): 270–279. Available from: http://dx.doi.org/10.1080/09669760.2012.718124 (accessed 29 October 2012).

Rawlings, A. (2008) 'Ethics, beliefs and values in early years', in *Studying Early Years: A Guide to Work-Based Learning*. Maidenhead: OUP/McGraw-Hill.

Rhedding-Jones, J. (2005) 'Questioning diversity', in N. Yelland (ed.), *Critical Issues in Early Childhood*. Buckingham: Open University Press.

Rowson, R. (2006) *The Framework for Ethical Thinking in the Professions*. London: Jessica Kingsley.

Siraj-Blatchford, I., Clarke, K. and Needham, M. (2007) (eds) *The Team Around the Child: Multi-Agency Working in the Early Years*. Stoke on Trent: Trentham Books.

UNICEF (1989) *Convention on the Rights of the Child*. New York: United Nations.

Wenger, E., McDermott, R. and Snyder, W. (2002) *Cultivating Communities of Practice*. Boston: Harvard Business School.

Whitmarsh, J. (2007) 'Negotiating the moral maze: developing ethical literacy in multi-agency settings', in I. Siraj-Blatchford, K. Clarke and M. Needham (eds), *The Team Around the Child: Multi-Agency Working in the Early Years*. Stoke on Trent: Trentham Books.

Want to learn more about this chapter?

Visit the companion website at **https://study.sagepub.com/reedandwalker** to access podcasts from the author and additional reading to further help you with your studies.

4

Critical thinking

Jennifer Worsley and Catherine Lamond

Chapter overview

This chapter focuses upon critical thinking. This is a term which can be simply defined as forming and articulating a position about what we do and what we think. It is something (as tutors in higher education) that we seek to encourage within our own teaching and we believe that such thinking is a vital skill for students. We see the process as an examination of values and developing a challenging evaluation of practice. Thus, in the context of ECEC, it develops a culture of questioning what goes on and asking why and how this enhances quality for children and families. This we see as being represented in a variety of different forms as students engage in study, for example, verbal presentations, written assignments, poster presentations, online blogs, collaborative online discussions and personal reflective journals. As to how such critical reflection can be encouraged as part of study is a wider question. We argue this is best done via the use of open-ended practice-based tasks, in real-world or 'authentic' problem contexts. Something which requires students to go beyond recalling or restating previously learned information.

Introduction

Brookfield (2011) and Moon (2008) discuss how critical thinking can be described and defined. They suggest it relies on interdependence between theory and practice and requires an engagement in a process which provides meaning, but is itself also actively meaningful. Our approach to developing critical thinking with students underpins this viewpoint and is rooted in teaching and learning processes which provide students with the opportunities to learn to think, and specifically 'how to think' rather than 'what to think'. It is a framework for learning and teaching which Thomas (2009: 245) views as 'intellectual sustainability' which can be interpreted as a process which encompasses the development of professional and personal features, such as academic rigour, personal capacity to learn, the ability to collaborate with others, effective communication and ethical propriety. Features which when taken together represent what we might call a set of transferable skills, because they can also be seen as essential and effective strategies in enhancing the way practitioners are able to engage purposefully with children, young people and families. Such transferability is important and an essential component of ECEC as these skills encourage a practitioner to actively question and challenge assumptions and accepted values (Dryden et al., 2005). It is also a process which can enhance critical engagement with practice and develops behaviours which can positively affect outcomes for children and young people. These include confidence in one's own abilities, a sustainable open-minded approach, reflective thinking and flexibility (Murphy, 2012). Moreover, in terms of study, critical thinking develops an interrelationship and interconnectedness between what is studied, how it is studied and the range of opportunities to share and learn with others.

In this chapter we supply examples of what this looks like and these examples stem from our teaching at a University in England, but they could equally be applied to the United States, many countries in Western Europe, Australasia, Ireland or Wales. This is because critical thinking crosses international boundaries and actively seeks out new ideas which include exploring what goes on in other countries and learning from others, which is itself part of criticality.

A useful starting point to examine the subject further is itself an underlying concept of critical thinking, namely formulating questions:

- Can we arrive at a meaningful working definition of the term critical thinking in relation to undergraduate study?
- Is criticality encouraging people to challenge their previously held assumptions?
- Is writing part of critical thinking?
- How important is dialogue, sharing the views of others (including the use of contemporary online strategies), and how is it part of the process?
- Are there examples you can think of which illustrate critical thinking and its impact on the person, their practice, their studies and work with children and families?

What is critical thinking?

Moon (2008), in writing about critical thinking, regards it as an integral goal of learning in higher forms of education. A view which resonates with Murphy (2012: 68) who suggests 'students find they must synthesise their theoretical and practice knowledge within a challenging environment, promoting the growth of critical thinking behaviours.' However there are misunderstandings as to what is meant by critical thinking and what it involves. It is often regarded as a form of reflective thinking, which Moon (2008) argues provides depth and adds another dimension to reflection. This tells us it is more than simply evaluating what happened and thinking of different solutions, as Willingham (2007) argues, it is not just about the surface structure of problems or superficial aspects of tasks. To become a critical thinker a learner must look more deeply at situations and events and take multiple perspectives on a problem. For Brookfield (1987: 5–7) the characteristics of critical thinking involve engaging in productive and positive activity; considering process as well as outcome; understanding that what occurs may vary according to the context in which it occurs; they are triggered by positive as well as negative events; and can be emotive as well as rational. These are interesting descriptors and start to establish a definition of criticality and reflection to which Cottrell (2011) adds the use of mental dispositions such as attention, categorisation, reasoning and judgement. Dispositions, which can be seen as attitudes or habits of mind, include open- and fair-mindedness, inquisitiveness, flexibility, a propensity to seek reason, a desire to be well-informed, and a respect for and willingness to entertain diverse viewpoints. Cottrell (2011: 2) goes on to present a useful overview of critical thinking as a process of thoughtful consideration, involving personal skills such as:

- identifying other people's positions, arguments and conclusions;
- evaluating the evidence for alternative points of view;
- weighing up opposing arguments and evidence fairly;
- being able to read between the lines, seeing behind surfaces, and identifying false and unfair assumptions;
- recognising techniques used to make certain positions more appealing than others such as false logic and persuasive devices;
- reflecting on issues in a structured way, bringing logic and insight to bear;
- drawing conclusions about whether arguments are valid and justifiable based on good evidence and sensible assumptions;
- synthesising information by drawing together judgements of evidence to form a new position;
- presenting a point of view in a structured, clear and well-reasoned way that convinces others.

When taken together these characteristics should be seen again as interdependent rather than separate aspects. Critical thinking is perhaps a multi-dimensional skill; it evolves and is a developmental process. It includes both critical thinking skills but also the dispositions to develop and use these skills. For Brookfield (1987: 12–13) it involves also 'emancipatory learning' and is part of 'recognizing the assumptions underlying our beliefs and behaviours.' This entails the ability to see such interrelated and connected relationships and to adopt a 'healthy scepticism' (Wellington et al., 2005). These are not easy tasks for a novice practitioner or researcher and it requires them to develop self-confidence in their ability to make their own judgements. What is more, as Bensley and Murtagh (2012) suggest, they also need support from others and opportunities in practice to use the skills appropriately. We therefore contend that critical thinking is the ability to practise and learn how to evaluate and challenge what goes on, as well as recognising the benefits of an environment that offers support and encourages self-reflection in practice, on practice and is aimed at improving practice.

Illustrating critical reflection in practice

This example comes from our work with undergraduate students who are also employed in ECEC settings. Our aim was to 'hone their critical skills, cultivate a critical character, understand the nature of critical thinking, including the standards for judging its quality and understand the subject matter they are thinking about' (Golding, 2011: 357). The issue then became how it was possible to do this within a learning and teaching approach where they could learn, challenge and interpret aspects of practice. A starting point was to form small student study groups who would create online blogs and engage in a 'web quest' exploring theories and interpretations of critical thinking and reflection which were introduced online by tutors. Each group was encouraged to discuss these theories with another group and reflect on their relevance to ECEC practice. The aim was not to seek a 'right answer' but to establish active involvement with a varied range of materials to encourage ways to think critically and apply information in different ways (Richmond and Hagan, 2011). We also used what Golding (2011) refers to as a thinking–encouraging approach where the use of questioning would support students to think for themselves and understand there was a body of knowledge which itself promoted ways of making critical judgements – an approach which involved collaborating with and constructively responding to others, taking responsibility for their own learning and importantly evaluating the credibility of their views and defending those views. As the process moved forward there was a gradual realisation that effective critical communication required the use of appropriate language, providing evidence to support assertions, not making unsubstantiated assumptions, having due regard for ethical propriety and building a balanced argument – features expected as part of academic writing. There was also a need (in order to engage effectively) to provide constructive feedback to others and respond professionally to comments from others – the very features identified by Cottrell (2011) thought to encourage students to engage in learning at several levels. In particular, a level which integrated theory and practice: for example, how practice differs in a variety of ECEC arenas; why this might be the case and what they were learning from making such comparisons. An analysis of their responses showed they were demonstrating:

Interconnected features	Application to professional practice
Ethicality	Negotiated professional protocols and an ethical sensitivity within and beyond the group context.
Purpose	Open-ended tasks encouraging students to solve real life problems in the context of their own ECEC arenas.
Challenge without cynicism	Comparing and contrasting experiences with others in a non-judgemental way. Providing praise as well as constructive criticism.
Positionality	Valuing their own perspectives, but also those of others. Defending a position.
Exploring a landscape of practice	Thinking was grounded in a professional body of knowledge, progressively developed via dialogue and study.
Transformative	Transforming information to make it meaningful in practice and developing the skills necessary to engage in study at undergraduate level.

The transformational nature of the process was important and warrants a little more explanation. The responses revealed the transfer of ethical knowledge into ethical action as suggested by Sternberg (2011). This includes a perceptive awareness of not only the actions required to meet professional standards of propriety but an awareness of the ethical dimension and individual responsibility required as a professional when taking action in practice. This requires taking a step back from just reporting everyday experiences and critically reflecting on those experiences. For example let us look at a student we shall call Claire and how she reflects and critically considers her work with parents. She says:

> It is important to remember that although the feelings of parents/carers are important the ultimate goal for all concerned is enabling the individual child to reach his or her full potential through whatever path is needed.

Another example comes from a student we shall call Sophie who illustrates ethicality, purpose and academic reflection. We can see here that theory is not an abstract idea to be learnt, but rather something to be applied to practice to deepen understanding (from an online discussion, which is why references are at this point excluded).

> Bandura's cognitive social learning theory extends Skinner's idea of operant conditioning by demonstrating that people learn by observing others. Bandura claimed that children are continually learning both desirable and undesirable behaviours by observing, remembering and then imitating. In particular, he showed that people tend to imitate models who are rewarded for their behaviour, rather than those who are punished ... Bandura's ideas highlight the importance of using an approach where practitioners are positive role

models, displaying desired behaviours in their interactions with others and rewarding instances of desirable behaviours that they observe.

Additionally, Jennifer demonstrates challenge without cynicism as she 'talks back' to theory:

> I think you misunderstood my blog. What I was saying was why is it that if a person is not learning or grasping information is it about them having a particular style of learning. On the other side of the coin as I stated before could it not be that the teacher for example lacks the skills in feeding the information over to her students in a coherent way and so the students fail to receive or grasp that information. I am not saying I disagreed with Kolb's learning styles I'm just saying it doesn't always have to be about the person receiving the information it could be about how the information is given.

Her views are important as they illustrate what Montgomery and Walker (2012: 95) consider as 'self-awareness of ethical and moral professional decisions and actions' and 'maintaining a high level of professional competence and integrity.' Jennifer is evaluating theories rather than accepting them as given, and relating concepts to broader issues from her own professional experiences. This helped Jennifer acknowledge her understanding that others may not think in the same way. We found, as the students become comfortable with each other, that they were prepared to disagree and they began to justify their points of view while at the same time being aware that others may disagree. From this we assert that Jennifer was demonstrating positionality, which was non-judgemental, when responding to a query and using her reflections based upon previous experiences. Such examination of one's own position is valuable because it encourages different voices to be heard within the academic community and to engage at a personal level about what being part of that community means. For example, Jennifer said:

> Reflecting back on the feedback I received for my assignment was very interesting in answering a lot of questions about myself and getting an evaluation. In this assignment it allowed me a re-evaluation of myself. It showed my strengths and weaknesses. My strengths are the passion for learning, ideas, and interaction with others. My weaknesses are time management and putting my thoughts and ideas down on paper in a consistent manner. I start things off fine and then my mind goes off the subject completely.

As a consequence of this comment she was encouraged to maintain a reflective journal, as suggested by Moon (2008) to help her to organise her thoughts. Interestingly, another student, Yasmien considered this strategy and prompted further reflection when she said:

> Whilst I agree with Moon's reflection theory (journal use), it has to be carried out over a certain length of time to get any satisfactory results. My question to you: how will you control this and motivate yourself since you have mentioned that you have difficulty in concentrating and 'your mind goes off the subject completely'?

As to whether these examples demonstrate what Dencev and Collister (2010) suggest is a shift in consciousness or just a form of debate is perhaps an interesting question. We explored this aspect and considered that students showed an appreciation of how their positionality was being shaped (Sletto, 2010). For example, Sophie's comment:

> A more in depth knowledge and discussion with other practitioners does make you reflect on the way you work and makes you more open to trying new approaches and considering other viewpoints. I have found the blog very useful in discussing and reflecting together. But for me the university experience as a whole and not just this module has helped me to become a more reflective practitioner, not content to stay the same but to keep learning and developing.

This transformation was also evident when a 'step back' reflection was examined and Alex said:

> I am back on Monday and have therefore been reflecting on a few things that happened last term, while I have been making sure all my work things are together ready for the mad dash Monday morning. I have also looked through my diary to see what is planned for this month. I then looked back at the last few weeks of term to remind myself of things that had happened. Twenty minutes later I realised I was making notes about past events including; what had happened, how I'd managed it, the outcome, how I'd felt during and after, any follow up work needed and what I'd do differently in future. This made me smile as without even thinking I'd began reflecting in two different ways – Gibbs' 'model of reflection' and Moon's 'reflective writing'.

This account resonates with the work of Brookfield (2011) who suggests critical thinking is more easily understood when it is grounded in specific events or a personal dilemma. This was the case for Alex but, more than this, she is showing how her thinking had a value to her and also a purpose.

★ Reflection point

We have discussed the features of critical thinking and how these emerge as part of student learning. There is no easy definition but there is perhaps a way of revealing critical reflection in practice, not only for practice but as an integral part of practice. For this to happen it requires an engagement with real-life ECEC issues and dilemmas that stem from practice. We say this because it is nurtured through thoughtful debate about challenges in professional practice. This layered approach enables students to present and defend their own position while respecting others', and use expert opinion and wider reading, thus becoming actively engaged in building an academic community. The process of developing critical thinking can truly be said to be transformative as it promotes personal and professional development: as

Sophie says, this develops practitioners who are 'not content to stay the same but [who want] to keep learning and developing'.

We have provided our perspective on a complex area of study. There are many other ways of considering criticality and a growing body of knowledge on the subject. This becomes apparent when you read Chapter 2 by Karen Hanson and Karen Appleby and you may recognise similarities in what they say and what we say. Sue Callan in Chapter 3 underlines the essentiality of being an ethical practitioner which again reinforces our position. We can add Michelle Rogers in Chapter 5 and her advocacy for digital communication – an approach we support and have used in our work and consider it to have significant benefits for learning. Likewise, we agree with Reed, Tyler and Walker in Chapter 1 who advocate the value of reflective thinking and study. Therefore let us return to an earlier point in this chapter and say that critical thinking is not one single strand or point of view, it is an interrelationship between a variety of views and approaches. Understanding and seeing that interconnectedness is the important point and from our perspective – through active, collaborative learning with others – it enhances practice.

Critical Learning Activity

When you engage in undergraduate study you are usually presented with what are called key support materials, source materials or key readings. These underpin and extend your learning on a course of study. These and other materials you engage with as part of your studies, need to be examined and the results collated. This will help you to demonstrate critical engagement with a subject or course theme. One strategy for doing this is shown below.

Ask yourself: What sort of material is available? Is it a research article in a journal? Is it a Government report or a report from an international organisation? Is it a video presentation or a webinar or digital platform? Is it an online presentation taken from a University website or a chapter in a book? Did the source material (or the materials cited by those engaged in an online discussion) have relevance to the theme of the discussion or course of study? It is important to recognise material which has some authority. A bright and colourful website which supplies little academic evidence to support its view needs to be used with caution.

The type, range and scope of material determine its authority. However, when critically examined and taken together it is possible to identify issues, similarities, different academic positions and implications for practice.

- Was the significance of the material to your studies apparent? Is it appropriate to use this work for a course project or assignment?
- Was the theoretical position and or argument or relevance to practice made clear?

(Continued)

(Continued)

- If the material was a report of research in practice, was the construction explained, the findings clear and any discussion informative? (including tables, charts or figures)
- Did the material relate to professional practice? In what way?
- Did the material enhance your knowledge? In what way?
- Did anything in the content make you think and perhaps change or refine your view?
- Overall, was the material easy to follow and did it have a gradual focus towards key issues?
- Carefully, consider its relevance to the assignment and the course/module you are following.
- Will the material underpin/support/enhance/inform discussion between groups of students or individual students expressing their views about a theme or area of study online or as part of face to face discussion?

When you have done this, organise the materials into a grid such as the one shown below.

Full reference and page numbers.	What was the main focus?	Compare or contrast the key points from one piece with another.
Smith (2003) etc. (full reference)	Four well explained definitions of play ...	The definitions of play are useful, but they focus on a developmental approach and promote activity-based learning rather than promoting play opportunities.
Jones (2003) etc. (full reference)	Play describes what children do. Playing is a child's way of being	This challenges the views of Smith (2003) and illustrates the debate about play and learning in practice. A child-focused, opportunity-based, playful approach is suggested.

The grid allows you to compare and contrast ideas and viewpoints and forms a useful way of presenting an argument within an assignment or presentation. Remember this is ONE way of interrogating information and is a starting point for study. Other strategies can be explored (see Chapter 1).

Further reading

Brock, A. (2012) 'Building a model of early years professionalism from practitioners' perspectives', *Journal of Early Childhood Research*, 11 (1): 27–44.

Chalke, J. (2010) *What's Critical about Critical Thinking? Understanding Academic Terminology on a Foundation Degree in Early Years*. Available from: www.foundation-stage.info/articles.

Rose, J. and Rogers, S. (2012) *The Role of the Adult in Early Years Settings*. Maidenhead: Open University Press.

References

Bensley, A. and Murtagh, M.P. (2012) 'Guidelines for a scientific approach to critical thinking assessment', *Teaching of Psychology*, 39 (1): 5–16.

Brookfield, S.D. (1987) *Developing Critical Thinkers: Challenging Adults to Explore Alternative Ways of Thinking and Acting*. San Francisco, CA: Jossey Bass.

Brookfield, S.D. (2011) *Teaching for Critical Thinking: Tools and Techniques to Help Students to Question their Assumptions*. San Francisco, CA: Jossey Bass.

Cottrell, S. (2011) *Critical Thinking Skills: Developing Effective Analysis and Argument*. London: Palgrave McMillan.

Dencev, H. and Collister, R. (2010) 'Authentic ways of knowing, authentic ways of being: nurturing a professional community of learning and praxis', *Journal of Transformative Education*, 8 (3): 178–196.

Dryden, L., Forbes, R. Mukherji, P. and Pound, L. (2005) (eds) *Essential Early Years*. London: Hodder Arnold.

Golding, C. (2011) 'Educating for critical thinking: thought-encouraging questions in a community of inquiry', *Higher Education Research & Development*, 30 (3): 357–370.

Montgomery, D. and Walker, M. (2012) 'Enhancing ethical awareness', *Gifted Child Today*, 35 (2): 95–101.

Moon, J. (2008) *Critical Thinking: An Exploration of Theory and Practice*. Oxon: Routledge.

Murphy, J.A. (2012) 'Home health care: a place to grow students' critical thinking behaviours', *Home Health Care Management and Practice*, 24 (2): 67–72.

Richmond, A.S. and Hagan, L.K. (2011) 'Promoting higher level thinking in psychology: is active learning the answer?', *Teaching of Psychology*, 38 (2): 102–105.

Sletto, B. (2010) 'Educating reflective practitioners: learning to embrace the unexpected through service learning', *Journal of Planning Education and Research*, 29 (4): 403–415.

Sternberg, R.J. (2011) 'Ethics from thought to action', *Educational Leadership*, 68 (6): 34–39.

Thomas, I. (2009) 'Critical thinking, transformative learning, sustainable education and problem-based learning in universities', *Journal of Transformative Education*, 7 (3): 245–264.

Wellington, J., Bathmaker, A., Hunt, C., McCulloch, G. and Sikes, P. (2005) *Succeeding with your Doctorate*. London: SAGE.

Willingham, D.T. (2007) 'Critical thinking: why is it so hard to teach?', *American Educator*, Summer: 8–19.

Want to learn more about this chapter?

Visit the companion website at **https://study.sagepub.com/reedandwalker** to access podcasts from the author and additional reading to further help you with your studies.

5

ICT and learning for students: a new way of thinking

Michelle Rogers

Chapter overview

This chapter explores student engagement in undergraduate study using digital technology. It underscores how technology may enhance not only what we learn but how we learn. It assumes a student in today's world will increasingly be developing their confidence in using various technologies and is motivated to explore new and exciting technological innovations. It argues that learning though digital technology is now an integral part of that developing confidence and a contemporary aspect of learning in Higher Education. It should be seen not as an alternative to classroom learning but as a complement to classroom engagement. The chapter concludes with a suggestion that digital technology is part of a social learning experience for children as well as students and why an early years practitioner should recognise that digital learning is now part of the child's world and the world of their parents.

The context

The twenty-first century learning landscape recognises that technology is synonymous with change and innovation and is now part of the student experience. In the last few years, it is likely there have been at least four upgrades to the average mobile/cellphone. Many people will have changed/upgraded a computer and various operating systems may have been installed automatically on digital devices. Technological enhancement and change is therefore inevitable, although some changes are so subtle because they are now part of our daily landscape. For example, apps are now part of our everyday experience. In view of this, it is essential to consider the pedagogical implication of using such technology and incorporating this into professional life. For example, we have at our disposal a global library of information, which reflects knowledge that allows views, research, argument and critical thinking to be available almost instantly. Students studying Early Childhood Education and Care (ECEC) can search materials outside the confines of a library. Classrooms are no longer confined to a physical building or lectures and debates in seminar rooms. Students can participate in learning from their home, via online blended learning (a mode of study by which individuals have both face to face and online learning sessions) or distance learning, which is delivered remotely and does not have a requirement for face to face meetings with tutors.

We are all part of a digital world (a Critical Learning Activity)

Take a few moments to look at Table 5.1. It considers how you currently engage with technology and positions this within the context of ECEC, for example, what this means in terms of your own digital learning, communication with parents, ethical and professional behaviour and issues that may need addressing in the future. You may decide to post it online and engage in discussion with others under the direction of a student study group theme or as directed by a tutor who may use it as part of a course of study. It is meant to raise issues, not provide easy answers.

Table 5.1   We are all part of a digital world

What you do now	How is this part of learning in Higher Education?	Study skills/ learning as a student?	Professional application	Ethical implications	Wider implications and issues
Use technology in a variety of forms to communicate, find information, travel and shop.	It shows that you have an existing digital footprint in using technology, thus preparing you and giving you confidence for digital study.	Online interaction encourages access and sharing of online materials.	Communication with parents' via technology. Access professional reports, information and study materials.	Who sees what, how and where? What is personal and what should be shared?	Recognise that not everybody engages in the digital world.

(Continued)

Table 5.1   (Continued)

What you do now	How is this part of learning in Higher Education?	Study skills/ learning as a student?	Professional application	Ethical implications	Wider implications and issues
Use social media.	Underpins the use of professional networks at College and University.	Online dialogue with others.	Understanding the value of sharing information quickly.	Professional boundaries when considering using social networks. Do you really want parents viewing your online digital footprint?	How does a leader and those involved in an ECEC setting establish protocols for social media use?
Write emails, communicate with others.	Share ideas, communicate with clarity, and take a stance on issues.	Communication sometimes requires more than short, sharp information giving. It also needs purpose and critical reflection.	Practising critical and focused writing and communicating with others for a specific audience.	What information to share? What information is authoritative? How to communicate in a way that respects the views of others.	How to use digital communication and respond to an ever-increasing range of digital communication platforms dependent upon the audience.

The grid may have alerted you to how much you already know about technology and how much of this knowledge you can transfer to study and practice. You are therefore what Weiler (2005) describes as 'e-ready'. This is because today there are people who have become immersed in the use of technology from an early age. They are the generation who reside in the developed world who are well versed in using smartphones and touchscreen digital tablets as well as the internet. These persons are now entering higher education and researchers such as Taylor (2011) argue that students learn equally well from digital texts as from written materials. Furthermore, Buzzard and colleagues (2011) suggest that although students and tutors are sometimes reticent to engage fully with technology, they are willing to experiment with digital media, especially if the opportunity is provided alongside professional support from tutors and higher education establishments. There is also research from Schwier (2012) and Belliveau (2013) who confirm the expectation that new digital technology can be transferable between private and professional lives and can therefore impact upon study. It is therefore not unusual to find that in order to optimise the learning experiences of their students, universities are now considering the implications of this movement and developing programmes of study which directly integrate the use of digital learning.

Active learning, issues and concerns

Many of the learning experiences of students in higher education consist of a blend between online learning and face-to-face teaching. The approach may differ greatly from course to course. For example, many Universities and Colleges use a Virtual Learning Environment (VLE). This is a teaching and learning medium designed to enhance a student's learning experience by including computers and the internet in the learning process. The principal components of a VLE package include curriculum mapping (breaking the curriculum into sections that can be assigned and assessed), student tracking, online support for both tutor and student, electronic communication (e-mail; threaded discussions; chat; web publishing) and internet links to outside curriculum resources. It can also include online learning spaces where students write and post written reflections within an online journal. Within many VLEs there are additional tools which support both synchronous (real-time) and asynchronous (posting of information and interaction whenever is convenient) interactions. This contemporary way of learning is a positive approach to learning which can actively engage students, because they like the more personalised approach that the use of the VLE affords (Dutton, 2010) – a process which can parallel levels of personal engagement and critical reflection and discussion expected for undergraduates. Buckley et al. (2010) researched such learning and online forums and showed how students developed a deeper and strategic understanding of the learning outcomes associated with their taught modules of study. This may be because of the careful design and planning of the teaching and learning process and the careful development of an online learning community – an important issue because without such careful consideration, there is a danger of non-engagement from a student which could lead to 'digital exclusion' (Eynon and Helsper, 2010). It is therefore important for tutors and students to recognise how some participants may have limited digital learning experience, or lack confidence. This is because sharing views online can be a 'learning leap' both emotionally and in terms of developing writing skills. It is therefore important to build student confidence through positive responses via the digital community and perhaps through the use of e-mentors (a more digitally experienced e-buddy). These strategies help to support technological advancement, self-sufficiency and subject knowledge and online discussion forums provide opportunities for shared learning (Heaton-Shrestha et al., 2009). As a result of such initiatives students are likely to gain a sense of control and become more proactive about the use of the VLE. This is a view supported by Means et al. (2010) and Glance et al. (2013) who see the benefits of online learning in recognising the improved performance of students within online environments. This is not to suggest blind faith in the pursuit of digital learning but to underscore its value in complementing traditional methods of learning. As Dutton (2010) explains, good teaching is just as important within the online environment as within traditional methods. Just as with traditional methods, online or digital learning requires careful planning so that online engagement is valuable. This includes creating an open dialogue and a shared understanding and ability to protect individuals online (Ziegler et al., 2006).

Therefore, the virtual learning space provides many opportunities for students to work together. McCabe and Meuter (2011) analysed the effectiveness of such spaces using seven principles of good practice as a framework. These include encouragement of contact between the University and students; reciprocity and co-operation among students; active learning; prompt feedback; time on task; having high expectations; and respecting diverse talents and ways of learning. It was found that an online learning facility can aid students who find face-to-face discussion difficult. Students can connect with each other outside the classroom and discussions can develop and expand learning. Students can take charge of their own learning through the VLE resources and opportunities. Discussions allow for more prompt feedback to be given and for this to be ongoing. From a personal perspective, as a tutor, I share this enthusiasm for digital learning and can see positive results with students. The collaborative element of the digital space allows it to work effectively. What is also required is a realisation that we are learning new ways of working, some of which may be going beyond the functional use of digital learning. We have to be conscious of developing a digitally responsible generation that understands the need for an ethical framework or protocol when collaborating digitally, in order to provide a safe environment to enable individuals to become more proficient and engaged. With this final point in mind consider the following wider personal and social perspectives about using digital learning and the VLE.

Critical Learning Activity

Investment from the outset of your engagement

Identify and explore how best you think and learn in a digital space.

Consider the purposefulness of the digital areas you visit on the VLE and what they are used for. How best can you use them?

Consider how your ethicality and digital identity will evolve and change as the dynamics of the online community evolve in response to factors: for example members of the group leaving; change in expectations of engagement being poorly communicated.

Clear commitment, expectation and principles of engagement

Consider if there are principles and expectations for all online communication and outcomes expected from learning activities.

Facilitating spaces to learn online requires the tutor to establish clear guidance and develop this in collaboration with students.

Ethical protocols for online use

Within social spaces it is imperative that ethical awareness is understood, for example issues of confidentiality and recognition of the appropriate membership of the space.

Ethicality is the heart of the online experience, within the learning space and social space. Without the facial communication, or the intonation of voice, communication is sometimes misconstrued and the implications for this can be destructive. A clear, collaboratively agreed protocol is essential from the outset for a productive, responsible and professional community. This awareness is transferable into any other online environment and supports the comments made in Table 5.1 in promoting individual online responsibility.

Implications for early childhood and early education practice

A technologically aware student who is actively engaged in practice can bring a range of experience and positive interaction to an ECEC setting. They are in a position to recognise that children are growing up with technology. As Tyler (2012: 94) asserts, children are using technology in the home as part of their everyday life and this raises questions about how early years settings are supporting this and how inconsistencies in their experience may impact on their learning and development. As she argues 'We cannot merely consider ICT as a learning benefit: we have to consider it as part of children's "digital" nativity. We cannot predict what a digital future may look like but we can respond to it'. She has coined the phrase 'digizens' (digital citizens) for those who use technology to travel physically and virtually wherever they want to go.

These students are aware, responsive and capable when using technology and see its use as part of who they are, and they are indeed developing a digital identity. They see their sibling's videos and pictures of themselves uploaded onto social media almost every day. Even young children are adept at using the latest technology, leaving adults in awe of their capabilities and distraught by the widening gap of technological confidence, awareness and skills. Of course, this view of digital nativity and technologies can be challenged but we have to engage with technology and recognise its pedagogical value as well. A point that Stephen and Plowman (2008) identified and suggested was the need for adults to support children when using technology with appropriate knowledge – something which cannot be undertaken where there are shortfalls of confidence and skills. Simon et al. (2013) completed a detailed survey of technology in use within ECEC: they identified that 51% of individuals who worked in ECEC were shown how to use technology by colleagues, and 20% of teachers had no professional development in using educational technology. More concerning was the reason given for using technology was that it was 'fun', with no apparent recognition of its value to children's learning – an issue which is thrown into sharp relief by considering this short extract from practice:

> Emma, a second year degree student, found herself actively engaged with a VLE for study and the exposure to the benefit of using different forms of representation. For example using a collaborative package within the VLE allowed Emma to attend tutorials online, but still have the face to face real-time discussions with her lecturer and also her peers. For a required group presentation, some members of the group were unable to attend the presentation, so Emma suggested their presentation be presented using the collaborative facility. This allowed the group to present within their own home, a recording of the presentation was captured which ensured that Emma and her group could individually review the presentation and reflect on the content and the delivery skills when it was convenient to them. The presentation was accessible to the lecturer to grade and give feedback either individually or to the group, via the same media or email.
>
> Emma felt this allowed her to be as critically aware and bring issues together in much the same way as essay writing but she felt innovative and it allowed her to express herself using a digital environment. Consequently she became more confident in addressing staff and parents and realised that for the first time she actually heard her own voice and how it transmitted to others.

These skills were transferable into the wider practice-based arena and resulted in Emma engaging in a publically accessible face to face conferencing package for parents who found it difficult to come into the setting, or stay for any length of time at pick-up or drop-off times. This had a benefit for parents and children as they were able to communicate directly to staff who were working with their children at mutually convenient times, thus feeling part of their child's experiences at the setting.

The use of technology promoted a discussion about the appropriateness of using technology in practice and the necessity to widen the setting communication routes to parents and to network with other settings in the pursuit of training and development for the staff; an issue which is worth considering at the end of this chapter – not as an afterthought, but to underline how digital learning and communication is becoming an integral part of professional development. This is being used to promote training and professional development via self-help groups, local communities, and parent forums and as part of Government policy consultation documents. There are extensive training materials available online via such diverse digital platforms as self-posted video sites, authoritative video presentation lecture sites and Government training materials such as those from Australia, all of which require reflection and critical examination to ensure the information we seek and find is appropriate.

Conclusion

This chapter has charted a route through what I would term a digital landscape. It began with a view of digital learning within Higher Education which a prospective early education practitioner will use. It asked how digitally aware you might be, suggesting how even a broad level of digital awareness – using the internet, email and social media – means you too are part of a digital nation. It has touched upon wider issues that impact on ECEC practice and your own learning, such as ethical awareness and collaborative learning. It went on to consider how your digital literacy can become an essential part of your studies via Virtual Learning Environments and collaborative online learning platforms. Your attitude, an effective VLE and an innovative course design within the ECEC undergraduate arena is important. The position is clear: you will undoubtedly use technology as part of your learning journey in Higher Education, and children will use technology as part of their learning journey at home.

Further reading

Hague, C. (2009) *A Review of the Current Landscapes of Adult Informal Learning Using Digital Technologies.* FutureLab, Bristol: Becta.

References

Belliveau, V. (2013) 'Re-imagine learning', in 15th Conference on Learning Technologies and Skills, London, 29–30 Jan. London: Learning and Skills. pp. 32–34.

Buckley, A., Pitt, E., Norton, B. and Owens, T. (2010) 'Students' approaches to study, conceptions of learning and judgments about the value of networked technologies', *Active Learning in Higher Education,* 11: 55–65. Available at: http://alh.sagepub.com/content/11/1/55 (accessed 2 March 2014).

Buzzard, C., Crittenden, V.L., Crittenden, W.F. and McCarty, P. (2011) 'The use of digital technologies in the classroom: a teaching and learning perspective', *Journal of Marketing Education,* 33: 131. Available at: http://jmd.sagepub.com/content/33/2/131 (accessed 2 March 2014).

Dutton, S. (2010) *Online Learning: The Impact on Students' Self-Esteem and Academic Progress.* Available at: www.nfer.ac.uk/nfer/PRE_PDF_Files/10_43_12.pdf.

Eynon, R. and Helsper, E. (2010) 'Adults learning online: digital choice and/or digital exclusion?', *New Media Society,* 13: 534. Available at: http://nms.sagepub.com/content/13/4/534 (accessed 2 March 2014).

Glance, D., Forsey, M. and Riley, M. (2013) 'The pedagogical foundations of massive open online courses', *First Monday,* 18: 5. Available at: http://firstmonday.org/ojs/index.php/fm/article/view/4350/3673 (accessed 2 March 2014).

Heaton-Shrestha, C., May, S. and Burke, L. (2009) 'Student retention in higher education: what roles for virtual learning environments', *Journal of Further and Higher Education,* 33 (1): 83, 92. Available at: www.tandfonline.com/doi/pdf/10.1080/03098770802645189#.UxMrmOBTEqY (accessed 2 March 2014).

McCabe, D.B. and Meuter, M.L. (2011) 'A student view of technology in the classroom: does it enhance the seven principles of good undergraduate education?', *Journal of Marketing Education,* 33: 149–159.

Means, B., Toyama, Y., Murphy, R., Bakia, M. and Jones, K. (2010) *Evaluation of Evidence-based Practices in Online Learning: A Meta-Analysis and Review of Online Learning Studies.* US

Department of Education. Available at: http://aed.sagepub.com/content/early/2014/01/23/0 004944113517828 (accessed 2 March 2014).

Schwier, R.A. (2012) 'Comparing formal, non-formal, and informal online learning environments', in L. Moller and J.B. Huett (eds), *The Next Generation of Distance Education Unconstrained Learning*. New York, NY: Springer Science and Business.

Simon, F., Nemeth, K. and Macmanis, D. (2013) *Technology in ECE Classrooms: Result of a New Survey and Implications for the Field*. Available at: www.hatchearlylearning.com/?wpfb_dl=275 (accessed 24 January 2014).

Stephen, C. and Plowman, L. (2008) 'Enhancing learning with information and communication technologies in pre-school', *Early Child Development and Care,* 178 (6): 637–654.

Taylor, A.K. (2011) 'Students learn equally well from digital as from paperbound texts', *Teaching of Psychology,* 38: 278.

Tyler, L. (2012) 'Evaluating the quality impact of technology in the early years', in M. Reed and N. Canning (eds), *Implementing Quality Improvement and Change in the Early Years*. London: SAGE.

Weiler, A. (2005) 'Information seeking behaviors in Generation Y students: motivation, critical thinking and learning theory', *The Journal of Academic Librarianship*, 31: 46–53.

Ziegler, M., Paulus, T. and Woodside, M. (2006) 'Creating a climate of engagement in a blended learning environment', *Journal of Interactive Learning Research,* 17 (3): 295–318. Available at: www.editlib.org/p/6286 (accessed 2 March 2014).

Want to learn more about this chapter?

Visit the companion website at **https://study.sagepub.com/reedandwalker** to access podcasts from the author and additional reading to further help you with your studies.

Section 2
THE DEVELOPING CHILD

This section invites you to explore the development of your own professional identity through considering and applying the authors' perspectives and interpretations of theory to practice. Each author shares with you their own reflective personal journey and the impact this has had in shaping their thinking and professional practice.

Each chapter explores a number of interrelated features that are necessary when considering quality ECEC provision. There are five chapters, all of which take a particular position and encourage the reader to reflect on that position and critically examine the content from a number of perspectives. In particular the necessity to link theory with practice and expose key issues rather than arrive at conclusions or an answer. For example you may consider the way children learn and mature as following sequences or stages of development and therefore see things from a developmentalist perspective. When you observe a child or children you may have this in mind and link this view to what you see in practice. You might observe children using negative words or phrases to another child and demonstrate what poststructural theorists consider to be the power of words to include or exclude others. There are also theories which underline a socio-cultural viewpoint and the importance of the social world of the child to their learning and the way they learn with and from others. Other examples within practice include where you are giving praise and rewards to reinforce good behaviour and therefore using a behaviourist approach which is underlined by behavioural theory. Of course, these are quite simplistic examples and any theory related to practice should not be seen in isolation from another theory or without detailed explanation and analysis. Indeed, theoretical positions are often debated and shown to be interconnected because one theory rarely falls neatly into an easily observed aspect of practice. (At the end of this introduction you will find some further reading on this subject which may be useful to understand the concept of theory and practice.)

It is therefore important to see the possibility of linking theory and practice as a foundation for debate and indeed argument. This is important because critical reflection does not have to emerge with a conclusion and may well raise issues, shed light on a feature that requires illumination or offer a viewpoint that for many people is new or even innovative. In essence, something that makes you think.

In this section the process begins with a chapter from Mary Benson McMullen who describes some key features of ECEC based on her own experiences of early childhood training and her considerable experience reviewing practice in the USA. It is clear that Mary holds particular views and shares these without imposing a particular stance but by proposing arguments and presenting practice-based evidence to support her views.

This is followed by a chapter from Anna Popova which again presents a position or viewpoint emanating from the work of Lev Vygotsky which leads the reader to an examination of views based upon her own experience and the use of research reports as well as a consideration of practice. She illustrates something which is often asked of students, namely: take a theory or examine the views (usually of one person) who is a proponent of a particular theory or view. Link their theoretical position to practice. Not an easy task and one which is rarely modelled for a student audience.

Jackie Musgrave presents a different form of critical engagement but still follows the pattern of linking her position to theory and practice. She asks us to consider children's well-being and what impacts upon well-being in the economically developed and developing world. This is followed by a chapter exploring play and once again Frances Brett provides a position and challenges the orthodoxy surrounding this feature of children's engagement with learning. She asks difficult questions (for us as practitioners) and suggests that we must look at the purpose of what we do and that play and learning should be driven by the needs of children rather than the need to observe and assess their development. She argues that play comes first. The final chapter comes from Anna Kilderry who critically examines the idea of always using developmentalist approaches when considering children's maturation and raises key questions that make us think and perhaps reconsider what we do as early years practitioners.

What each of the chapters has in common is the way they present an argument and the way that argument is defined, explained, looked at from different perspectives and the opinion underpinned by theory. In most cases this is done using a first person writing style that uses phrases such as: *I think that ... it is my view ... I have looked at ... my experience is ...* This could equally be a third person writing style using phrases such as: *the view of the writer is ... what becomes clear from the evidence ... the writer has determined ...* Both have their place and in this case the writers are providing their own views and therefore do so using a style that gives such personal opinion weight. The important aspect to consider is the way the argument is constructed and for the reader the way they can deconstruct the argument and see the potential of using what is said as part of their own learning journey and as part of evidence for assignments and when underpinning practice-based research. It is also important to see the argument as a starting point rather than an end point in your learning. This is why each of the authors have been asked to provide Critical Learning Activities as part of their chapter content. These act as a way of allowing you to explore theory and practice alongside case studies that are presented in the chapters. These are intended to again provide a link between theory and practice. There are also examples of further reading to encourage you to look beyond the chapter and take on board other views. Do use those recommendations as they will offer different perspectives and extend the range and scope of your learning.

Pointers from practice

As part of your studies you will be engaged in what is called practice placement. This means joining an ECEC setting as a 'student practitioner' for a period of time. When you do this it is most valuable to observe children and from these observations consider what you can learn about children's well-being, the way they learn and how you can best observe practice. Look at some of the questions you could ask in the table below on practice-based critical questions.

Table P2.1   Practice-based critical questions

Consider your recent practice experience with children. Here are some 'nudge points' in order to:

- reflect on the professional landscape you experienced;
- refine your views and opinions about children's development;
- reconsider what you did. For example, needing to find out more; improving the way you observe and reflect upon practice;
- revisit these experiences as part of an assignment or seminar group discussion.

Nudge points

- What age phase did the setting support? For example, the education of babies, toddlers or other age groups?
- What was happening in the setting? What made up a day's routine?
- Was the setting inclusive? Were children allowed to 'be' themselves and see themselves and see their culture and language represented in the setting?
- Were they helped to access all of the opportunities to learn?
- How did you observe and consider children's development? Did you stand back and observe what they did? Did you look and listen as an active participant in what was going on? Did you speak to practitioners and/or parents? Which helped you to consider what children were 'doing, saying and thinking'? Or indeed did all of these?
- Did this help you to consider what the children felt about their daily experiences?
- What decisions were the children involved with? How were they invited to participate and contribute?
- Give one example of something or someone in the setting who influenced the experiences of children? What did they do?
- What opportunities were there for families to communicate about their children, so that they shared how children were learning and became involved in decisions about their children's learning? Did that include sharing their culture and beliefs to the extent that suited them?
- Is there one thing you did on placement that you were very pleased about? Why?
- What did you see which helped children to develop secure, consistent relationships with parents and carers? (This aspect is relevant to Chapter 11 from Robin Balbernie.)

Reminder:

When considering your practice experience, speaking with others or at a seminar at University or College, the name of the setting, children, parents and names of staff should not be used or written. A professional attitude towards describing the setting and the actions of all those involved should prevail at all times.

You may wish to add more 'nudge points' after reflecting on your experience. We say this because these are starting point prompts to make you think and reflect about what occurred in practice. You can use the questions to plan for practice experience, when in practice or post practice.

Critically reflect on the 'weight' you give to the answers taken from one way of observing and another approach. Look for the interconnectedness between what was observed, between and within approaches. This allows you to take a position on what factors promoted learning and the relative importance of each. It also prompts you to consider if there are theoretical positions that can be illustrated in your work with children. For example: were your views driven by a predominately developmentalist perspective? Were they driven by the views of Vygotsky? Are you seeing the whole child? Was the way you observed the children fair, honest, rigorous and underlined by the theoretical stance set by Sue Callan and Carla Solvason in Sections 1 and 5? Was the information gained with the consent and assent of the children? Did you read about and consider your own ethical position about ways to observe children? Was the thinking and creative development of the children shaped by activities or opportunities? Were the observations consistent with the position taken by Alma Fleet and colleagues in their chapter in Section 5? These are all questions which ask for a reflection on practice and an ability to link theory with practice. Thinking around these issues will take you on your own journey of developing your own theories and becoming the 'Deliberate Practitioner' who works from a strong philosophical and theoretical framework, personal values, capabilities and talents.

6

Deliberating on practices with young children in the United States

Mary Benson McMullen

Chapter overview

This chapter explores the context of Early Childhood Education and Care (ECEC) and resulting issues, as well as dominant philosophies and models of practice and what they mean for American children, families and practitioners. Like the US itself, American ECEC can best be portrayed as complicated and diverse. There is no national system of childcare; instead, regulations, standards and the distribution of federal funds (e.g. for families with disabilities and/or in poverty) occur within and at the discretion of individual state systems. The resulting diversity benefits some families. However, lack of coherent oversight has also contributed to the so-called 'trilemma' of care – the highly interconnected elements of affordability, availability and the quality of ECEC programs. The diversity also requires practitioners to adopt a strong personal philosophy of practice to rely on in the decisions they make in their work with young children and families to ensure children's physical and psychological health, development, learning and well-being, now and in the future.

Introduction

The US is a large nation of tremendous diversity. It has long been idealised as a place of hope and opportunity. Most citizens emigrated or descended from immigrants who came from all corners of the globe seeking a new life or personal freedoms. Less than 1% of US citizens identify with one of many indigenous tribes; and many of the approximately 12% of African Americans are descendants of slaves who were brought to the country unwillingly. Americans are recognised for their fierce independence, rugged individualism and adventurous spirit, and for being highly creative. Many of them believe rights '…for life, liberty and the pursuit of happiness' have been divinely bestowed, as stated in the US Declaration of Independence of 1776. Recognising characteristics and fundamental values of Americans may aid in understanding the context of policies and practices related to Early Childhood Education and Care (ECEC). This chapter is presented to explore the context of ECEC and resulting issues, as well as dominant philosophies and models of practice and what they mean for American children, families and practitioners, and to invite readers to deliberate on what these ideas mean in their own practice.

Unlike most nations, the US has no nationwide system for childcare or education, birth to age 18. Although its 50 states are 'united', the principle of 'states' rights', upholds individual state governance, guaranteeing as little national interference as possible. This governance structure trickles down to counties within states, then cities and towns, and eventually to families and individuals; and of course, individuals elect representatives at each level – school, city, county, state and federal. Although federal statutes exist, most of what happens in US ECEC is determined within each individual state and then local municipalities. Individual state laws determine, for instance, the level of education required for practitioners and how/if childcare centres and family childcare homes will be regulated (Barnett et al., 2010; Child Care Aware of America, 2013). Federal funding for government-mandated programmes for children with disabilities and/or in poverty are given to states which design and implement their own systems for supporting children and families, contributing greatly to diversity in services provided to children and families.

The most far-reaching nationally supported programmes are: tax breaks for families with dependent children, support for children with disabilities, the nutrition programs WIC (Women, Infants and Children) and Food Stamps, welfare programmes for children and families in poverty including Temporary Assistance for Needy Families (TANF) and childcare for children in poverty through Early Head Start (birth–age 3) and Head Start (ages 3–5). Overall, the US spends approximately $10 billion annually (€8/£7 billion) for free and reduced childcare for low income families, funded by taxpayers; funding usually cut significantly at times of economic decline.

Overall, ECEC in the US can best be portrayed as complicated and diverse, much like the country itself. The value for independence, lack of centralised governance and inconsistency within state regulatory systems combine to result in wide variance in beliefs about the role of ECEC, how quality is defined, and how states maintain records and report outcomes. The remainder of this chapter has two main sections: the first provides an overview of the context of childcare and the second presents dominant perspectives influencing ECEC in the US.

Context of ECEC

As in most modern nations, childcare is a fact of life for most American families, a necessity in an economy in which women are essential in the workforce. Approximately 67% (11 million) American children under the age of 6 spend an average of 35 hours per week in non-parental care, and it is estimated an additional 1.2 million children need childcare but either cannot find it or afford it (US Census Bureau, 2011). A family fortunate enough to find affordable childcare is likely to find a 'mediocre' program, the average quality rating for childcare in the US (Child Care Aware of America, 2012). The US faces three major challenges in ECEC – availability, affordability and quality – comprising what has been called the 'trilemma' of childcare (Lash and McMullen, 2008).

Availability

Nearly a third of American families who need care for their children use a combination of arrangements involving professional caregiving programs, family members and friends, making it difficult to provide a fully accurate picture of childcare in the US. Estimates are that 33% of children under the age of 6 are cared for primarily by a parent, 27% by relatives, and 40% by non-family members in full-time childcare centres or family childcare homes. The most popular arrangement for 3–5 year-olds is centre-based childcare. Families with infants and toddlers do utilise centres, but tend to prefer family childcare homes, as well as so-called FFN (Family, Friend and Neighbour) care.

Affordability

Families pay 90% of the cost of childcare in the US (Child Care Aware of America, 2012). Average cost varies by location, with everything being much more expensive in coastal regions and relatively less in the middle and southern states. Everywhere, it is expensive. A year of childcare costs more than a year at a publically supported American University! Recent figures reveal the average cost of childcare is $9100 (€7000/£6000) compared to $8244 USD (€6300/£5400) for a year at University (US Census Bureau, 2011). In general, family childcare homes cost about 20% less than centre-based care.

Only 10% of families (13–14% of American children) are eligible for free or reduced childcare through a federally subsidised program, either because they have children with diagnosed disabilities or their family lives at or near poverty level. Families are typically referred to programmes by health care professionals and social service providers, or self-refer in response to outreach done within their communities by the programmes themselves. The wide variability in how states distribute and fund programmes for families results in differing definitions of 'level of poverty' and whether or not a child is 'at risk', and subsequent unevenness in the number of children served and quality of service provision (Annie E. Casey Foundation, 2012; Child Care Aware of America, 2012).

Quality

Everyone benefits from high quality childcare – children, families, communities and society as a whole. The quality of childcare impacts the overall healthy growth, development, learning and well-being of children in the present and for a lifetime (Bowman et al., 2001; Halle and Vick, 2007; O'Connor and McCartney, 2007). Increasingly, Americans have recognised the benefits and sought to identify and define expectations for quality childcare and hold programmes accountable, if not by national mandate, then in other ways. For instance, most states have instituted Quality Improvement Rating Systems (QIRS) targeting continuous improvement of environments and promoting professional development of programme staff. Also, the largest and most influential professional organisation for ECEC in the US, the National Association for the Education of Young Children (NAEYC), administers a rigorous and expensive voluntary national accreditation system, currently accrediting over 6,500 programs (NAEYC, 2013). The highest rating on state QIRS is typically tied to NAEYC accreditation criteria.

Quality ECEC in the US is built upon and then assessed through structural and process factors (Halle and Vick, 2007; Burchinal, 2010). Structural elements of ECEC are generally easier to observe and measure, such as square footage per child, ratios of adult to child and group sizes. For example those illustrated in Table 6.1.

Process variables tend to be more difficult to assess, but are considered ultimately more important to children's overall well-being; these include subjective evaluations of practitioner effectiveness, highly relational factors such as sensitivity of interactions, and family engagement.

Table 6.1 Recommended ratios and group sizes

Category	Recommendation
Adult to child ratios and group size	
Infants	1:3 or 4 infants; maximum 6–8
Toddlers	1:5 toddlers; maximum 10
Twos	1:5 twos; maximum 10
Mixed-age 0–3 years	1:4 or 5, based upon age of youngest child
3–5 year-olds	1:10; maximum 20

Practitioner qualifications and compensation

The practitioner is considered the biggest determinant of overall quality in a childcare programme (Halle and Vick, 2007; Burchinal, 2010; Pianta et al., 2012). Awareness of the impact of quality on outcomes for children and pressure from advocates has resulted in increased qualifications for practitioners in programmes receiving state or federal funding. Twenty years ago, most states either had no requirements or only very basic educational requirements for practitioners. As of 2010, 36 states required a bachelor's degree or higher for ECEC practitioners in programmes receiving subsidies, although 15 of them did not require that degree to be in early childhood education or child development. Among other states, 16% required two-year associate degrees, 13% 'CDAs' (a practitioner-based certificate equivalent to about a year of College), and in 4%, practitioners needed no more than a high school diploma or its equivalent (known as a 'GED') (Barnett et al., 2010; Child Care Aware of America, 2013).

Wages, however, have not increased simultaneously with educational requirements and remain woefully low (Ackerman, 2006; US Census Bureau, 2013). A comparison of wages for the average ECEC practitioner with selected 'unskilled' labour and 'caring' or 'helping' positions is shown in Table 6.2, demonstrating average ECEC practitioner wages aligning more closely with those in the mid-range of the selected unskilled workers. Implications for building and retaining a high quality practitioner workforce seem clear. Students wishing to better the lives of children and families, possessing strong caring dispositions, and working on a bachelor's degree may be compelled to think carefully about a career choice in ECEC versus elementary school teaching or social work, for instance.

Table 6.2 Comparison of average annual wages of childcare practitioners and other selected members of the US workforce in 2010

UNSKILLED WORKERS		'CARING' PROFESSIONALS
Delivery truck drivers $29,390 (£19,439/£22,487)		Registered nurse $69,950 (£46,946/£54,466)
Factory workers $28,360 (£19,030/£22,082)		Police officer $55,270 (£37,086/£43,035)
Parking lot attendants $23,710 (£15,683/£18,141) ←	**Childcare practitioners** $25,700 (£17,244/£20,011) →	Elementary school teacher $51,380 (£34,476 /£40,006)
Day labour/dock workers $22,560 (£15,138/£17,566)		Religious clergy $44,060 (£29,143/£33,711)
Janitor, cleaner and maids $22,320 (£14,763/£17,077)		Social worker $42,480 (£28,503/£33,076)

Source: data compiled from US Bureau of Labor Statistics, 2010

★   **Reflection point**

In a large country, state and municipal control over decisions that impact local communities is a good thing, in theory. Local authorities in a large and diverse country
are more aware of the needs, sensibilities, etc. of those in their communities. But
what is the down side when it comes to addressing the needs of the trilemma of
care – availability, affordability and quality? How might decisions related to the
trilemma be considered 'moral' or 'ethical' concerns for a society?

Dominant perspectives on practice

The absence of unified national government standards and oversight and the indi-
vidualistic nature of American society contribute to diversity in US ECEC and the types
of programmes offered. This affords those families with access to and who can afford
the choices offered the opportunity to select childcare that may best reflect their needs
and values. The diversity also means practitioners must understand who they are,
what they believe, and what path they wish to follow as professionals in the field of
ECEC.

Philosophy of practice

A coherent and ethical philosophy of practice provides a firm foundation for making
decisions and undergirds practitioner behaviours that support the growth, development, learning and well-being of young children. Philosophies provide a way to think
about, or conceptualise practice, but not a recipe or 'how to' list of exactly what to do
and when. Program models and standards more often specify behaviours and expectations, but how a practitioner interprets these specifications should be filtered
through the lens of highly individualised, internalised philosophies of practice.

Developmentally appropriate practice (DAP) is a philosophy articulated by NAEYC, a
professional organisation of practitioners, scholars and policymakers (Copple and
Bredekamp, 2010). DAP has dominated conceptualisations of recommended practice and
informed notions of quality in the US for over 30 years. Constant critique has resulted in
frequent, continuous revision of DAP (Ryan and Grieshaber, 2004; Kim and McMullen,
2012). At its core, DAP is informed by the work of Piaget, Erikson, Dewey, Vygotsky and
Montessori, and more recently, research on how the brain works (Shore, 2003; Mooney,
2006). DAP has three guiding principles: (1) focus on the whole child including physical
and psychological health, development, learning and well-being; (2) focus on all
children regardless of ability, exceptionality or circumstance; and (3) recognition of
children as part of families, communities and larger cultures/societies (DEC and

NAEYC, 2009; Copple and Bredekamp, 2010). Although DAP does not prescribe practice, it does lead to implications for respectful practices with children and families, responsive practitioner behaviours, the organisation of environments, and the purposes of assessment.

Program models

Few US ECEC programs follow any one program model, although they may say, for instance, they are: 'doing Reggio', 'following Bank Street' or 'just like Montessori', etc. Usually such claims mean they are inspired by and incorporate elements from these models into planning environments and experiences. Exceptions are true Montessori, Waldorf and High/Scope programmes which require specialised training for practitioners and strict interpretation of their models in practice. Thus, typical US practitioners are influenced by ideas from multiple models of practice. Popular US models highlighted below, organised around implications for practice that arise from DAP, include: High/Scope, Bank Street, the Creative Curriculum, Reggio Emilia, Montessori, Waldorf, the Project Approach, the Program for Infant Toddler Caregivers (PITC) and Resources for Infant Educarers (RIE). (See Related links.)

Respecting children

Bank Street and the Project Approach are child-centred models in which practitioners and children decide on goals that are real and meaningful. In both programs, children are given large blocks of uninterrupted time to work/play and can make choices about what they do and how they do it. High/Scope and Reggio Emilia also stress shared decision-making between children and practitioners and fostering agency in children, although there is more adult scaffolding in these models.

Practitioners support autonomy by providing opportunities for children to be independent and self-sufficient and support agency by sharing power and decision-making. Providing children opportunities to feel a sense of control through choice-making and to learn from natural consequences allows them to be agents of their own lives. Autonomy and agency are considered human rights and children's rights (Tobin, 2005; UNICEF, 2005), sufficient enough reason to embed them in practice, but they are also linked to multiple positive outcomes for young children in literacy, problem-solving and social development (Bowman et al., 2001; O'Connor and McCartney, 2007), and understanding democratic principles (Gartrell, 2012).

Reggio Emilia, Waldorf and Montessori are known for honouring children as capable and valued members of their groups. This is demonstrated in practitioner behaviours as well as in their aesthetically pleasing work/play environments. Children who believe they are valued will come to understand they are worthy individuals and in turn how to care for and value others, critical aspects of social-emotional development (Eisenberg and Musson, 1997).

Partnering with families

High/Scope, Reggio Emilia and Waldorf models influence US notions of family-centredness in ECEC. The field has moved toward understanding family-centredness as more than mere family participation or involvement related to holding conferences, or inviting parents to luncheon, teas, fetes or fairs. Family-centredness requires full and complete partnership with families in decision-making, goal-setting and the assessment of and planning for children in programmes (DEC and NAEYC, 2009; Pianta et al., 2012). When families are partners, not clients or recipients of care, relationships of mutuality and trust form in which both family and practitioner expertise is recognised and valued, ideas are shared and beneficial goals are defined for children (McMullen, 2013).

Responding sensitively

The Program for Infant Toddler Care (PITC) and Resources for Infant Educarers (RIE) stress caring, respectful relationships in ECEC environments, as well as sensitive responsiveness in communicating with and addressing the needs of young children. PITC and RIE are based on relational systems theories (Bronfenbrenner and Morris, 2006) which stress that all relationships with and surrounding children matter to overall physical and psychological development and well-being (Shore, 2003; NSCDC, 2004). Practitioners create cultures of respectful caring by promoting positive relationships throughout childcare systems – child/practitioner, child/peers, colleagues, practitioners/families, practitioners/managers and managers/outsiders (McMullen and Dixon, 2009).

Central to PITC and RIE are practitioner behaviours that are sensitive to the needs of children and directly, promptly and respectfully respond to their verbal and nonverbal communications (Lally et al., 2004). Relationship-based practices are founded largely on principles from Emmi Pikler and her student Magda Gerber, and are supported by attachment theories, for example, John Bowlby, Mary Ainsworth, and more recently T. Berry Brazelton (Mooney, 2010). Sensitive responsive care and the formation of trusting relationships are considered central to the formation of secure attachments, and key to positive development and learning (O'Connor and McCartney, 2007). Lessons from PITC and RIE have led to widespread support in the US for assignment of primary (key person) practitioners and continuity of care (requiring teams of practitioners and groups of children to remain together over multiple years).

Planning organised environments

Creative Curriculum and High/Scope are models that promote well-planned environments with interest areas based upon specific objectives for both individual children and groups. Practitioners define objectives related to goals for all areas of development (social and emotional, physical, etc.) and curriculum (literacy/communication, numeracy, science/nature, etc.). Practitioners carefully prepare environments and plan experiences in which children can assimilate knowledge into existing schemas, and be challenged sufficiently to accommodate new knowledge by creating more complex mental structures. These models are informed by Jean Piaget's Cognitive Developmental Theory, the social constructivism of Lev Vygotsky and learning theorist Jerome Bruner. Similarly, Reggio Emilia and the Project Approach structure environments and practices based upon principles of constructivism and learning theories, scaffolding children as they engage in work/play with peers, practitioners, and appropriately challenging materials (Katz et al., 2014).

Assessing children's strengths

The enduring legacy of the Bank Street model, now nearly a century old, is an understanding that to address the needs of individual children, practitioners must know them thoroughly and deeply. Child growth and development involves multiple interacting domains (e.g. physical, social/emotional, communication, etc.), all of which impact and are impacted by each other. Further, child development occurs within the context of numerous socio-cultural and environmental factors (McMullen, 2013). Bank Street, among other models popular today, encourages a 'capabilities' perspective (focus on what children can do), rather than on perceived deficits or unachieved benchmarks (DEC and NAEYC, 2009).

Reggio Emilia and the Project Approach advanced the field's understanding of the amazing capabilities of young children and provided methods for documenting their work. High/Scope and Creative Curriculum offer invaluable tools for helping practitioners become keen observers of children, document children's accomplishments and collect their work, and efficiently keep records to share with families. Documenting and keeping records of children should be part of practitioners' daily practice, and include multiple sources of data and different types of information. Most importantly, the primary purpose of such careful observation and documentation of children is to have information to reflect upon in order to know how to best meet their needs and those of their family (Elicker and McMullen, 2013).

Conclusion

Each individual must take a deliberate approach in determining how and in what way different philosophies, perspectives and models of practice 'fit' who they are and wish to be as practitioners. The deliberate practitioner always proceeds from a strong philosophical frame, one built upon experience, knowledge and beliefs, shaped over years, as well as their unique capabilities and talents. The beliefs that guide their professional decisions are reasoned beliefs, ones that have come from years of purposeful thought on the interconnectedness of theory, research and practice. These guiding beliefs should not be clouded by personal outside issues or lingering prejudices from youth, nor should they be formed out of convenient habit or based on unexamined assumptions. A philosophical frame is not a solid, static structure, but rather organic, allowing room for growth and change. As the elements of the frame become frayed or faded, old ideas, practices and beliefs should be revisited and re-examined; old no longer useful beliefs or elements of the structure may need to be pulled from the frame, others may need to be strengthened, or entirely new ones may need to be woven in. In all ways, all beliefs supporting the philosophical framework must be defensible and stand the test of scrutiny as they are articulated to others and lived out in practice.

The deliberate practitioner is intelligent, flexible and ethical in thinking about all they do; sensitive, respectful, caring and compassionate in interactions with children, families and colleagues; deliberate, reflective life-long learners willing to grow and change as they gain new knowledge and experience. These characteristics and dispositions are necessary for ECEC practitioners who support healthy growth, development and learning outcomes for young children, one of the most important and exciting jobs in the world!

Critical Learning Activity

All practitioners bring deeply held beliefs, early experiences, talents and special abilities, informed by our educations and inspired by the mentors who shape us throughout our educations and careers with young children and families. Decisions about 'who we are (will be)' and 'how we (will) practice', should be made deliberately, knowing that what we do impacts the overall physical and psychological growth, development, learning and well-being of the children with whom we work, now and in the future.

Now it is your turn: Reflect on the question, 'who am I as an ECEC practitioner?' Put your own knowledge, experiences and beliefs together to outline your own 'Philosophy of Practice with Young Children and Families'.

Further reading

Brazelton, T. Berry and Greenspan, S.I. (2001) *The Irreducible Needs of Children: What Every Child Must Have to Grow, Learn, and Flourish*. Cambridge, MA: Da Capo Press. Written by a paediatrician (Brazelton) and child psychiatrist (Greenspan), renowned and trusted in the US, this important book speaks to families, practitioners and society at large about policies and practices needed to succeed, and provides a strong critique about what is lacking.

Cadwell, L.B. and Rinaldi, C. (2002) *Bringing Learning to Life: A Reggio Approach to Early Childhood Education*. New York: Teachers College Press. There is so much appealing about the Italian Reggio Emilia model, but many American practitioners have struggled to implement this approach in a culture that values individualism over socialism; these authors provide vivid portrayals of how this can be done.

File, N., Mueller, J.J. and Wisneski, D.B. (eds) (2012) *Curriculum in Early Childhood Education: Re-examined, Rediscovered, Renewed*. New York: Routledge. In this edited volume, authors reconceptualise existing ECEC curriculum, models and practices through research and powerful stories from early childhood environments from around the world, providing real-life examples for practitioners and new directions for scholars and policymakers.

Related links

American Montessori Society: www.amshq.org/
Association Montessori International USA: www.amiusa.org/
Bank Street Developmental-Interaction Approach: http://bankstreet.edu/theory-practice/
Creative Curriculum for Early Childhood: www.creativecurriculum.net/
High/Scope: www.highscope.org/
North American Reggio Emilia Alliance: www.reggioalliance.org/
Program for Infant Toddler Care: www.pitc.org/pub/pitc_docs/home.csp
Project Approach: www.projectapproach.org/
Resources for Infant Educarers: www.rie.org/
Waldorf Education in North America: www.whywaldorfworks.org/

References

Ackerman, D. (2006) 'The costs of being a child care teacher: Revisiting the problem of low wages', *Educational Policy*, 20 (1): 85–112.

Annie E. Casey Foundation (2012) *Kids Count Data Book: State Trends in Children's Well-being*. Available at: www.aecf.org/KnowledgeCenter/Publications.aspx?pubguid=%7B68E8B294-EDCD-444D-85E4-D1C1576830FF%7D (accessed 29 August 2014).

Barnett, S., Epstein, D.J., Carolan, M.E., Fitzgerald, J., Ackerman, D.J. and Friedman, A.H. (2010) *The State of Preschool 2010: State Preschool Yearbook*. Washington, DC: The National Institute for Early Education Research.

Bowman, B.T., Donovan, M.S. and Burns, M.S. (eds) (2001) *Eager to Learn: Educating our Preschoolers*. Washington, DC: National Academies Press.

Bronfenbrenner, U. and Morris, P.A. (2006) 'The bioecological model of human development', in W. Damon and R.M. Lerner (eds), *Handbook of Child Psychology*, 6th edn, Vol. 1. Hoboken, NJ: Wiley. pp. 793–828.

Burchinal, M. (2010) *Differentiating among Measures of Quality: Key Characteristics and their Coverage in Existing Measures*. Washington, DC: US Department of Health and Human Services.

Child Care Aware of America (2012) *Leaving Children to Chance: Ranking of State Standards and Oversight of Small Family Child Care Homes*. Available at: www.childcareaware.org (accessed 7 October 2014).

Child Care Aware of America (2013) *We Can Do Better: Child Care Aware of America's Ranking of State Child Care Center Regulations and Oversight.* Available at: www.naccrra.org/sites/default/files/default_site_pages/2013/wcdb_2013_final_april_11_0.pdf (accessed 29 August 2014).

Copple, C. and Bredekamp, S. (2010) *Developmentally Appropriate Practices in Early Childhood Programmes Serving Children from Birth through Age 8.* Washington, DC: NAEYC.

DEC and NAEYC (2009) *Early Childhood Inclusion: A Joint Position Statement of the Division for Early Childhood (DEC) and the National Association for the Education of Young Children (NAEYC).* Available at: http://npdci.fpg.unc.edu/resources/articles/Early_Childhood_Inclusion (accessed 29 August 2014).

Elicker, J. and McMullen, M. (2013) 'Appropriate and meaningful assessment in family-centred infant toddler programs', *Young Children,* 68 (3): 22–27.

Eisenberg, N. and Musson, P.H. (1997) *The Roots of Prosocial Behavior in Children.* Cambridge, MA: Cambridge University Press.

Gartrell, D. (2012) *Education for a Civil Society: How Guidance Teaches Young Children Democratic Life Skills.* Washington, DC: NAEYC.

Halle, T. and Vick, J. (2007) *Quality in Early Childhood Care and Education Settings: A Compendium of Measures,* report for the Administration for Children and Families, US Department of Health and Human Services. Washington, DC: Child Trends.

Katz, L., Chard, S. and Kogan, Y. (2014) *Engaging Children's Minds: The Project Approach,* 3rd edn. Santa Barbara, CA: Praeger.

Kim, Y.H. and McMullen, M.B. (2012) 'Evolving conceptions of the child in early childhood education: Challenging dominant assumptions about "best" practice', *Sophist's Bane,* 6 (1): 14–21.

Lally, J.R., Griffin, A., Fenichel, E., Segal, M., Szanton, E. and Weissbourd, B. (2004) *Caring for Infants and Toddlers in Groups: Developmentally Appropriate Practice.* San Francisco, CA: WestEd.

Lash, M. and McMullen, M.B. (2008) 'The child care trilemma: How moral orientations influence the field', *Contemporary Issues in Early Childhood Education,* 9 (1): 36–48.

McMullen, M.B. (2013) 'Development in the first three years of life', in C. Copple, S. Bredekamp, D. Koraleck and K. Charner (eds), *Developmentally Appropriate Practice: Focus on Infants and Toddlers.* Washington, DC: NAEYC. pp. 23–50.

McMullen, M.B. and Dixon, S. (2009) 'In support of a relationship-based approach to practice with infants and toddlers in the United States', in J. Brownlee (ed.), *Participatory Learning and the Early Years.* London: Routledge. pp. 109–128.

Mooney, C.G. (2006) *Theories of Childhood: An Introduction to Dewey, Montessori, Erikson, Piaget and Vygotsky.* Upper Saddle River, NJ: Pearson Education, Inc.

Mooney, C.G. (2010) *Theories of Childhood: An Introduction to Bowlby, Ainsworth, Gerber, Brazelton, Kennell & Klaus.* St. Paul, MN: Readleaf Press.

National Association for the Education of Young Children (NAEYC) (2013) *Why NAEYC Accreditation?* Available at: www.naeyc.org/academy/interested/whyaccreditation (accessed 29 August 2014).

National Scientific Council on the Developing Child (NSCDC) (2004) *Young Children Develop in an Environment of Relationships.* Available at: http://developingchild.harvard.edu/ (accessed 29 August 2014).

O'Connor, E. and McCartney, K. (2007) 'Examining teacher-child relationships and achievement as part of an ecological model of development', *American Educational Research Journal,* 44 (2): 340–369.

Pianta, R.C., Barnett, W.S. and Justice, L.M. (eds) (2012) *Handbook on Early Childhood Education*. New York: Guilford Press.

Ryan, S. and Grieshaber, S. (2004) 'It's more than child development: critical theories, research, and teaching young children', *Young Children*, 59 (6): 44–52.

Shore, R. (2003) *Rethinking the Brain: New Insights into Early Development*, rev. edn. New York: Families and Work Institute.

Tobin, J. (2005) 'A right to be no longer dismissed or ignored: children's voices in pedagogy & policy-making', *International Journal of Equity and Innovation in Early Childhood*, 3 (2): 4–18.

UNICEF (2005) *Convention on the Rights of the Child*. Available at: www.unicef.org/crc/ (accessed 29 August 2014).

US Bureau of Labor Statistics (2010) *Current Employment Statistics*. Available at: www.bls.gov/ces/ (accessed 29 August 2014).

US Census Bureau (2011) *Who's Minding the Kids? Childcare Arrangements: Spring 2010*. Available at: www.census.gov/hhes/childcare/data/sipp/2010/tables.html (accessed 29 August 2014).

US Census Bureau (2013) *United States Census 2010*. Available at: www.census.gov/2010census/ (accessed 29 August 2014).

Want to learn more about this chapter?

Visit the companion website at **https://study.sagepub.com/reedandwalker** to access podcasts from the author and additional reading to further help you with your studies.

7

'Vygotsky Rocks'! An argument that helps use Lev Vygotsky's ideas in early years practice

Anna Popova

Chapter overview

When you begin to study child development, observe children and try to understand what guides their development, you will be developing your own theories of why things are the way they are. In addition, you will be reading about other people's perspectives and their interpretations of children's development, and you will be applying these different ideas to practice. In this chapter, I am offering the argument that concepts developed by Lev Vygotsky appear to be more appropriate in unpacking the intricacies of child development today. I will argue that other concepts of child development in psychology and sociology are very important but that Vygotsky's framework incorporates them in a way that allows a more modern and culturally appropriate explanation of what guides children's development. I do not insist that my view is the most appropriate but I am trying to show how I, as a former teacher, have built this perspective, and my argument is just an example of the kind of thinking you might generate while learning about child development. In this chapter, I will be referring to other development theories, and it is from their perspectives that I will critically evaluate Vygotsky's concepts. It is important to note that Vygotsky's ideas were developed by many other researchers, and currently the research in this theoretical framework is referred to as Cultural Historical and Activity Theory, often abbreviated as CHAT.

Introduction

Through my experience of teaching in primary schools, and also teaching child development courses in higher education in Russia, the UK and Australia, I have identified a number of debates in child development that seem to re-occur. It seems practitioners and students are curious about the dominant factors in human development (whether our genes play the dominant role or whether it is the social environment that dominates). They also want to understand whether the way we develop has some consistency about it or whether it is easy for us to change. When my students and I work on trying to understand what children need for their development, we discuss how it is best to study child development and what needs to be taken into account. In other words, we discuss the best way to research child development. And whatever discussions we have we always try to apply them in the practice of working with children; we test and critique their usefulness. In this chapter I will discuss how Vygotsky's concepts can help understand these issues. In order to present this argument to you, I have selected the texts that have influenced me in the last 20 years while I was practising and learning Vygostky's theory.

It is not just about nature vs. nurture

In your child development course you might encounter a popular debate of what guides children's development: nature or nurture. For example, in textbooks by Lindon (2010) and Berk (2009), this debate is introduced as a way for students to think about what factors are more dominant: children's own physical and mental capacities or influences from the environment. This debate still exists even today because child development textbooks consider maturation theories (Geselle, 1954 cited in Lindon, 2010) seriously. These theories emphasise the self-guided nature of child development, whereby a child's body is actively interacting with the environment, and it is the genetic predisposition, e.g. brain capacity, that is responsible for the way in which the child interacts with the environment.

In my experience, the nature vs. nurture debate is usually concluded with the idea that both nature and nurture are important, and yet, it is the interaction between the two that I find most intriguing. It is not so important what dominates, nature or nurture, but the complexities of a child's interaction with the world in which she or he grows up. It has been proven through a number of studies of feral children (children who have been deprived of human contact for a substantial amount of time) that they acquire the behaviour and manners of the animals they interact with. Basically, humans are mammals, and if left without the society of other humans, they will behave like other animals (dogs or wolves, for example). A vivid example is presented in the film about Oksana, a Ukrainian girl who was left with dogs and who acquired all the physical and vocal habits of the dogs (YouTube, 2010), and yet because she had some contact with humans, she managed to develop some skills of communicating in her native language. So, now she can do both, bark like a dog and speak (still in a limited way) like a human.

Lev Vygotsky (1978, 1986) did not engage in the nature vs. nurture debate. It was clear to him that it is only through human interaction that a human becomes a human. He argued that what really separates us from other mammals is our interaction with cultural tools, and the most important cultural tool is language. This is Vygotsky's most important contribution to our understanding of human development. It is not a direct interaction with the environment; the interaction occurs through cultural mediation. For example, what images do you have in your mind if you come across a word 'soldier'? Perhaps, you might think of an adult man or woman in military uniform. This is the notion that we develop by acquiring the word 'soldier' in the culture where we grow up. Yet, in some African countries, the word 'soldier' does not necessarily conjure up an image of an adult person; often it is children who become soldiers. The word may be the same as in the West but the meaning mediated within a culture is different. Roth (2010: 49) comments:

> In much of the educational literature, thinking is taken to be the result of conceptual/cognitive frameworks that generate thought; speaking is taken to be the process by means of which thought is made available to others. Lev Vygotsky, however, conceives of thinking and speaking as two mutually constitutive processes that continuously evolve at microgenetic, ontogenetic and cultural-historical levels.

Usually, when discussing children's development with a societal framework, it is the work of Bronfrenbrenner (e.g. 1994) that is referred to most often. He acknowledged that the development of the child occurs in one particular context, and that context can be seen as a complex structure of micro elements and factors (developing within a family and local community) and macro factors (economic structure; political situation). His contribution was very important, but he failed to explain how these different factors are linked in the development of one child. Vygostky suggested that the development of the child first happens outside of the child's body and mind, in the interaction of the child and other people, and only then do internal changes occur. These people use cultural tools to mediate notions that are deemed appropriate in their culture. I remember growing up in Soviet Russia which in political terms was under dictatorship. I knew the things that I was allowed to say as being appropriate at that time, and not to say the words that my family might have been punished for because they were deemed politically inappropriate. As a child I did not have an understanding that the political situation in Russia was severe, but through communication with the adults in my family I had an 'invisible' connection with macro elements of Russian society.

Holland and Lave (2001) and Valsiner (2007), who continued to work on Vygotsky's concepts, suggest that a child develops through a dialogue. This two-directional communication is enacted within a socio-cultural context in which the child is placed, within a particular linguistic reality (which is often multi-lingual) and within an established set of practices. Children are negotiating their place in the socio-cultural situation through acquiring the language, ways of behaviour and values needed to negotiate their reality in the way that is suitable to their unique way of being. Thus, although I understood what I was allowed and not allowed to say when growing up in Soviet Russia, I also developed my own view of the political situation of the time. I disliked the fact that people around me were not free and that we were restricted in what we wanted to say publicly. If my situation were considered from a point of view of maturation theories that expect children to develop certain capabilities by a certain age, by nature pushing the development in one predictable direction, then it would be difficult to explain how a five year-old child may develop the skills to interpret a political situation. Vygostky's concept of the development being mediated by cultural tools allows us to understand how this may be possible.

Enduring nature of the context

Another debate that you might join during your course in early childhood and within your practice, is how much children's development depends on the context in which they happen to be. You will hear arguments that 'depending on a situation, the child's behaviour may be different'. Doherty and Hughes (2014) suggest that 'most psychologists take the view that development has both elements of continuity (gradual and unbroken) and discontinuity (separate stages marked by major changes)' (p. 22). In contrast, Vygotsky did not consider continuity vs. discontinuity, instead he argued that a child develops by participating in socio-cultural and historical activities, or practices which have a long history. Activity and individual development are interconnected. Leontiev (2006) points out:

> [...] consciousness cannot be understood in any other way than as a product of activity. Functionally, they are interconnected: activity is 'directed by consciousness' and at the same time, in a certain sense, it is activity that directs consciousness. (p. 33)

Contexts are episodes where particular practices reveal themselves. Thus, a day in a nursery or school is part of the long tradition of educating children. What happens today in a school is not an accident, it is an expression of cultural practice. For example, you hear that a child in your room or class makes a racist comment. What will be your interpretation of their behaviour? Will you blame the family? Or will you examine the practice in your own setting? I have been in early years settings in rural communities in the UK where practitioners did not think it was necessary to introduce children to cultures other than the ones represented in their small community. If a child has not acquired a concept that 'it is OK to be different', can she or he be necessarily blamed for making a racist comment? Perhaps it is the practice itself that needs reconsidering. Valsiner (1998) states that

> collective culture is person-anchored and not a 'property' of social units. It is of no use to speak of 'American collective culture' or 'the collective culture of high school No 4', but it is possible to speak of the collective culture that organises the life of John or Sally who studies in high school in a town in the United States. (p. 31)

Overall, CHAT (Cultural Historical and Activity Theory) promotes the idea that the development of the child occurs within practices which are prone to internal conflicts. It is acknowledged that although we think that it is the child that might be in the driving seat of his or her development, it is important to unpack and examine that 'collective culture' Valsiner refers to above. Engeström (1999) proposed that it is important to find out who is in the centre of the cultural practice and who may be a dependent actor. For example, it is often said that children are active in their learning, but is it really true in all the contexts? When a teacher constructs the lesson based on curriculum guidelines that have to be implemented at this time of the year because it will help prepare children for exams, is she really letting children drive their own development? Yet, prescribed curricula are an accepted educational practice in many countries. According to CHAT, this is due to the enduring nature of socio-cultural activities and unresolved systemic contradictions.

Vygotsky's ideas in early years research

During your studies of child development in the early years, you will be asked to observe the children you are working with. There is a long tradition of using observations as the main method of collecting data about the ways in which children develop. Most of the literature on observations of young children describes observation as a research method that originates from psychology research (Boem and Weinberg, 1997; Smidt, 2005). By this I mean that it is required of early years practitioners that observations should be as 'objective' as possible; students and practitioners are warned of a possible 'bias' in interpreting the observations. Hence, it is recommended that the observers themselves try to focus on what is observed, i.e. just the children or the child. This view is challenged in CHAT research.

In CHAT, because it is argued that the child develops by participating in socio-cultural activities, and by acquiring cultural tools in collaboration with others, the others who are with the child are as important as the child herself. The most important contribution to understanding research in early years from a socio-cultural perspective has been made by Hedegaard and Fleer (2008). They argue that 'A methodology for studying children's development in everyday settings has to use methods that are different from those of natural science and medicine, where the research is often on human functioning' (p. 5). They add that 'the aim is to research the conditions as well as how children participate in activities. This allows the conditions and the child's development to be conceptualised as a whole (p. 35).

Because the language is the most important cultural tool that mediates children's development, Hedegaard and Fleer (2008) focus on collecting and analysing narratives that children are involved in. These are conversations between adults and children, and children's conversations with each other. The analysis focuses not only on what children do, or only on what they say; it tries to unpack what children accomplish together with others, or as a result of communication with others. A very famous concept created by Vygotsky, the Zone of Proximal Development (Vygotsky, 1978), happens to be in the centre of research. CHAT researchers want to know how the child can change if offered adequate support at the right time. That is why the research that helps determine developmental milestones (see Lindon, 2010) is not supported by CHAT. Although CHAT researchers do not deny some maturation and ethological principles of human development, their interest is not to find out how children develop on average; they want to know what can be done in particular socio-cultural contexts so that the child can reach their potential (a potential which is not based upon an established norm).

You can find an excellent example of such research in the article by Hjorne and Saljo (2004) called 'There is something about Julia...'. The article tells us a story about Julia, who is considered to have a hyperactive disorder. Usually, in order to identify if a child has a hyperactive disorder, their own behaviour is assessed (what they do and how often, how they react to certain situations). In this research, however, the focus has been on conversations about Julia in different professional meetings. Conversations during meetings have been recorded every time Julia's name has come up. It has been found that every time Julia did something that the teachers and other professionals did not think 'normal', they suggested that 'there was something about her' that reminded them of hyperactive disorder. Hjorne and Saljo conclude that it is the people around Julia who have labelled her as having hyperactive disorder, instead of analysing the contexts in which she behaved in an unusual manner. The focus of the professionals was on Julia, and not on her interactions, or what she would have done had the situation around her been changed.

Implications for early years practice

As a former practitioner and currently a researcher, I keep reflecting on the impact of the CHAT concepts on my everyday practice. It seems that if we accept the usefulness of CHAT concepts, we need to move away from the idea that we can expect children of a certain age to perform as expected. We also can no longer think that today's situation at our place of work is very temporary and has no history or repercussions for the future. CHAT concepts encourage us to think about the socio-cultural context where we are interacting with the children, about our own role in that context; we need to think whether we are free to act in the best interests of the child or whether there are some rules that prevent us from doing so. Hedegaard and Fleer (2008) emphasise that in early years research (and I will add 'in practice') 'the research problem becomes connected to how well the researcher in his or her conceptualisation can handle the different perspectives. In order to catch the child's perspective, the researcher has to enter into the everyday activities of the child' (p. 35). If we take CHAT concepts seriously, we can no longer remove ourselves from the trajectory of the child's development. What we say and do in response to the child's action, or as an attempt to prompt an action, makes us part of the child's development.

An interesting example of how early years practice can be constructed with the help of CHAT concepts is the Australian Early Years Learning Framework (EYLF) (Department of Education, Employment and Workplace Relations, 2009). Its creation was based on the CHAT concepts. The result was a document that equipped early years professionals with thinking tools that could support them in unpacking particular situations that they came across in practice. It avoided direct guidelines and rules, and instead encouraged professionals to think deeply about the history of their practice, the child's socio-cultural environment and their interactions with the children. EYLF offers a socio-cultural view of the child, whereby each cultural context is co-constructed by professionals, children and communities. Professionals, therefore, are offered a framework, which emphasises analytical activities they should engage in, i.e. to learn, analyse and reflect, rather than following a set of principles and achieving a certain number of standards. The EYFL views professionalism as an autonomous, fluid and reflective process and a community of practice which is trustworthy and capable of analytical thinking.

At the end of this chapter I need to caution you against accepting CHAT concepts blindly. They may be and have been perceived to be idealistic. For example, Roth and Lee (2007: 186) comment that it is difficult to find research recommendations concerned with knowing and learning in and out of schools and across the life span that take into account the kind of holistic integration that Vygotsky had originally championed. Now, as then, we are confronted with a number of conundrums in educational research and practice, which advances in modern psychology have not fully overcome.

Holzman (2009) also raises this concern. She made a huge contribution to practising Vygotsky's concepts outside academia. She stated that 'cultural-performatory activity – a participatory process in which people exercise their collective power to create new environments, new social-emotional-intellectual growth, and new forms of social relational life' (p. 111), thus claiming that CHAT concepts need to be practised. However, she emphasises that to achieve this in social life, we need an enormous social upheaval both in everyday practices and values.

So, to be true to the CHAT tradition, I suggest that in and through your everyday work with children, you can 'try out' the concepts presented above and make your own conclusion as to whether they are what you need. In order to succeed, you need to examine the context in which you are working and reflect honestly on your own personal/professional history. This will help you understand how the practice should be transformed to help children who are in your care develop further. If you have to work within certain government guidelines, analyse them in connection with what happens in your context and adapt them. On an everyday basis ask yourself:

- What do I know about this child? Is it enough to make decisions about his or her development?
- Am I taking into account where the child comes from and what the child experiences every day?
- In which ways is the child connected to these different activities? How can I bring them into my relationship with the child?
- Do I give direct answers or provide prompts?
- Do I know how I speak to each child? Is it the same way?
- Who is in my community and how do they construct the child's reality?

You might have gleaned from the argument above that to study and use Vygotsky's concepts is not a simple process of applying theory to practice. In my experience, these concepts have become part of the way I think about life, my practice and my relationships. In her recent lecture, a leading post-Vygotskian Irina Verenikina, stated:

> I feel I have been very lucky to have been introduced to the cultural-historical theory in my life. I find that a lot of my colleagues struggle with educational dilemmas, and I feel that I have better tools to resolve them than they do, because this theory is part of who I am and how I live my life. (Verenikina, 2012)

Critical Learning Activity

In this chapter I have tried to argue that Vygotsky's ideas have helped me understand child development and shape my thinking around the ways in which I can help children in their development. Can you find examples in this chapter of when I developed arguments to persuade you that my point of view has weight?

Further reading

Gray, C. and MacBlain, S. (2012) *Learning Theories in Early Childhood*. London: SAGE. Chapter 5 – Vygotsky: Learning in a Social Matrix.

References

Berk, L.E. (2009) *Child Development*, 8th edn. Boston, MA: Allyn & Bacon.

Boem, A.E. and Weinberg, R.A. (1997) *The Classroom Observer: Developing Observation Skills in Early Childhood Settings,* 3rd edn. New York: Teachers College Press.

Bronfenbrenner, U. (1994) 'Ecological models of human development' in T. Husen and T.N. Postlethwaite (eds), *International Encyclopedia of Education*, 2nd edn, Vol. 3. Oxford, UK: Pergamon Press. pp. 1643–1647.

Department of Education, Employment and Workplace Relations (2009) *The Early Years Learning Framework*. Australia: Department of Education, Employment and Workplace Relations.

Doherty, J. and Hughes, M. (2014) *Child Development: Theory and Practice 0–11*, 2nd edn. Harlow: Pearson.

Engeström, Y. (1999) 'Activity theory and individual and social formation' in Y. Engeström, R. Miettinen and R. Punamäki (eds), *Perspectives on Activity Theory*. Cambridge: Cambridge University Press. pp. 19–39.

Hedegaard, M. and Fleer, M. (2008) *Studying Children. A Cultural-Historical Approach*. Maidenhead: Open University Press.

Hjorne, E. and Saljo, R. (2004) '"There is something about Julia": symptoms, categories, and the process of invoking attention deficit hyperactivity disorder in the Swedish school: a case study', *Journal of Language, Identity & Education*, 3 (1): 1–24.

Holland, D. and Lave, J. (2001) 'History in person: an introduction' in D. Holland and J. Lave (eds), *History in Person: Enduring Struggles, Contentious Practice, Intimate Identities*. Sante Fe: School of American Research Press. pp. 3–33.

Holzman, L. (2009) *Vygotsky at Work and Play*. New York: Routledge.

Leontiev, A.A. (2006) '"Units" and levels of activity', *Journal of Russian and East European Psychology*, 44 (3): 30–46.

Lindon, J. (2010) *Understanding Child Development: Linking Theory and Practice*. London: Hodder Arnold.

Roth, W.-M. (2010) 'Vygotsky's dynamic conception of the thinking-speaking relationship', *Pedagogies*, 5 (1): 49–60.

Roth, W.-M. and Lee, Y.-J. (2007) '"Vygotsky's neglected legacy": cultural-historical activity theory', *Review of Educational Research*, 77 (2): 186–232.

Smidt, S. (2005) *Observing, Assessing and Planning for Children in the Early Years*. London: Routledge Falmer.

Teaching Agency (2012) *Early Years Professional Status, from September 2012*. UK: Department of Education.

Valsiner, J. (1998) *The Guided Mind. A Sociogenetic Approach to Personality*. Cambridge, MA: Harvard University Press.

Valsiner, J. (2007) *Culture in Minds and Societies: Foundations of Cultural Psychology*. Los Angeles, CA: SAGE.

Verenikina, I. (2012) 'Scientific and everyday concepts: Theory and practice for quality practice', open lecture, Asia-Pacific Australian group of the International Society for Cultural and Activity Research (ISCAR), December, Monash University, Melbourne, Victoria, Australia.

Vygotsky, L.S. (1986) *Thought and Language* (A. Kozulin, ed. and trans.). Cambridge, MA: The MIT Press. (Original work published in 1934.)

Vygotsky, L.S. (1978) *Mind in Society* (M. Cole, V. John-Steiner, S. Scribner and E. Souberman, eds). Cambridge: Harvard University Press.

YouTube (2010) Ukrainian Girl Raised by Dogs. www.youtube.com/watch?v=UkX47t2QaRs (accessed 6 June 2012).

Want to learn more about this chapter?

Visit the companion website at **https://study.sagepub.com/reedandwalker** to access podcasts from the author and additional reading to further help you with your studies.

8

Child health and wellbeing: exploring implications for practice

Jackie Musgrave

Chapter overview

Children's health and well-being are two concepts frequently considered together and whilst they are interrelated, it should be remembered there is growing literature about each area. Consequently each will be given its own place within the chapter and contemporary issues relating to these concepts will be examined. The chapter also encourages you as early years practitioners to examine your role in promoting and maintaining the health of children. Again, these are two interrelated and important aspects of child health and well-being. The chapter stems from my professional experience and interest as a nurse and teacher working with early years practitioners within the UK, however, I feel it is important to think more widely than national frontiers and consider health and well-being from an international and national perspective. This is because we live in a global world and it is important that we have an understanding of how socio-cultural factors may influence health and well-being within developed and developing contexts.

Current views of the importance of well-being mean that the developed countries of the world are making significant attempts to promote good well-being. Good health is a factor that contributes to good well-being and investments are being made globally to improve children's health. In developed areas of the world, the role of early years practitioners is seen as key to implementing the policies aimed at improving health and well-being.

The concepts of health and well-being for children are not only interrelated but they are influenced by features that are visible, for instance the symptoms of some diseases, such as an infectious disease. However, there are also invisible features that influence health and well-being. An example of this is the qualities that practitioners are required to develop in order to gain the trust of parents. Trust between a setting and parents may mean that practitioners will be better positioned to engage in preventative approaches to promoting and educating parents about child health. It is important that practitioners are aware of the complexities of how these factors influence each other because there are implications for practice.

Children's well-being

In many developed regions of the world there has been a significant government input aimed at improving children's well-being. This is because there is growing awareness of the importance of good well-being in earlier life leading to higher achievement educationally and in turn, greater economic success. A recent publication in the UK by the National Institute for Clinical Excellence (NICE, 2012) describes well-being as 'good' or 'poor'. However, there is often a lack of clarity about what is meant by 'good well-being' and this is not helped by the lack of a universal definition. In which case, I suggest we consider a useful definition offered by Statham and Chase (2010: 2). In their *Childhood Well-being* review of recent UK and international research in this subject, they describe well-being as:

> the quality of people's lives. It is a dynamic state that is enhanced when people can fulfil their personal and social goals. It is understood both in relation to objective measures such as household income, educational resources and health status; and subjective indicators such as happiness, perceptions of quality of life and life satisfaction.

This description is a little like a cooking recipe because there is a range of ingredients (or factors) that contribute to what is meant by well-being. In a similar way to many recipes, depending on which recipe you look at, ingredients and proportions of ingredients can vary. This analogy is used to describe how the concept of children's well-being may differ if examined from a global perspective as it would appear that factors that contribute to either poor or good well-being can depend on which part of the world a child lives. For instance, in parts of the developing (or majority) world where many children live in absolute poverty, good well-being is often linked to acquiring basic needs of life such as adequate nutrition, clean water and sanitation – these visible factors are closely linked to good health. However, if children live in relative poverty, usually in the developing world (defined as living in a family where household income is less than 60% of the median disposable income for the country concerned), it would appear that the factors that are a challenge to individuals feeling as if they have good well-being are different.

This can be illustrated by a study carried out to investigate child well-being in Kazakhstan (Roelen and Gassman, 2012). Kazakhstan has an emerging economy and as it has become a richer country, there are less children living in absolute poverty. The study found that children who lived in areas of the country where absolute poverty prevailed identified lack of access to nutrition, water and sanitation as factors that contributed to their poor well-being. However, in the areas where the economic situation had improved and people were emerging from poverty, lack of education for children in Kazakhstan was a factor that contributed to poor well-being. This possibly reflects that if humans are nourished – and as Maslow (1943) suggested, in a seminal work on the subject of well-being, which he called a 'hierarchy of needs', if our physiological and visible needs are met – we are then able to consider higher level factors that contribute to good well-being, such as accessing education, which can help us meet our cognitive needs.

In the developed areas of the world, the concept of good well-being in relation to children is linked to positive emotional and social development. If we return to the report by NICE we can see the authors profess a view of emotional well-being. The following illustrates a developing view on the subject which asks us to recognise that well-being is much more than physical welfare.

> Emotional well-being – this includes being happy and confident and not anxious or depressed
>
> Psychological well-being – this includes the ability to be autonomous, problem-solve, manage emotions, experience empathy, be resilient and attentive
>
> Social well-being – has good relationships with others and does not have behavioural problems, that is, they are not disruptive, violent or a bully. (NICE, 2012: 33)

The NICE report is complemented by an Australian study of children aged 8–15 years of age, which concluded that children's definition of good well-being included factors related to positive emotional and relational well-being (Fattore et al., 2007). These findings are based on older children's views. However as research has informed us, for example Bowlby's (1969) work on attachment theory, the foundations of our ability as humans to make positive relationships starts in the early period of life. This view has implications for practitioners working with young children and parents to develop positive relationships. However, not all children have the advantage of positive relationships with their parents or carers and this can mean that children are less able to develop good well-being. There are factors that contribute to children developing 'poor social and emotional capabilities' (NICE, 2012: 18). Children who live with disadvantage are more likely to be vulnerable to poor well-being and the factors that make children vulnerable to poor well-being include:

- children with parents who have drug, alcohol and mental health problems;
- difficult family relationships, especially if domestic violence and criminality are features of family relationships.

In the UK there has been an ongoing commitment from government over the last 15 years to improve children's lives, which has included considerable investment in state-funded pre-school education. Therefore, reports of decreasing levels of well-being and as a result, increasing levels of depression reported in UK children (de Braal, 2009) are of concern to society as well as to professionals working with children. Layard and Dunne (2009) conducted the Good Childhood inquiry in order to explore the state of contemporary childhood. They drew upon the work of leading experts as well as giving children's views of childhood. The report concluded that there are more children reporting anxieties about emotional difficulties as a result of several factors which include: children living in relative poverty; family break-up and the sometimes negative influence of the internet.

Critical Learning Activity

Having read this summary, what are your thoughts about your role in promoting good social and emotional well-being in children? What considerations should you bear in mind in relation to the influence of social and cultural influences on children's well-being? Consider the concept of well-being from a global perspective and think about children living in harsh conditions without access to education or adequate nutrition and without access to the internet, or perhaps living in war-torn countries. Are there barriers for children in your setting to developing good well-being?

Children's health

The health of a nation's children is viewed as an indicator of a country's economic success and level of civilisation. As globalisation has increased over the last two decades, so has the interest in improving and promoting children's health. The United Nations Convention on the Rights of the Child (UNCRC, 1989) initiated a global interest in children's health. Article 24 states that children have a right to the best possible health and health services. The right to health needs to be viewed in the context of each country and its progress in policy related to improving child health. There are wide variations in the level of health care as well as the challenges to child health, especially between the developing and developed world. It is also important to be aware that there are inequalities in access to health care and levels of care within developed countries in the minority world, for example the UK. We live in a global world where children are immigrants and emigrants and may experience different approaches to health depending on the country in which they reside – this will be explored below. Before we explore implications for practice about health in the early years, let us consider what we mean by the concept of 'health'.

Defining health

Definitions of health lack a common terminology. Health is a nebulous concept and what health means to an individual is often only considered when we are feeling unwell because of lack of good health. The World Health Organisation (1986: 29) offers this definition:

> The extent to which an individual or group is able on the one hand to realise aspirations and satisfy needs; and, on the other hand, to change or cope with the environment. Health is, therefore, seen as a resource for everyday life, not the objective of living; it is a positive concept emphasising social and personal resources, as well as physical capacities.

This definition implies that health is not just absence of disease or ill health, but the changes that may be needed in order to achieve good health. These may include taking medication, for example insulin injections to restore normal blood sugar levels to an individual with diabetes. A change to the environment could be reducing the level of dust in the setting of a child with asthma. Equally, changes to the environment can include prevention of disease as a result of improving sanitation to minimise the spread of micro-organisms that breed in dirty water and can cause infectious diseases. Or in malaria zones of the world, changes may be required to environments such as school buildings in order to reduce infestations of mosquitoes.

Global perspectives of child health

The United Nations Convention on the Rights of the Child (UNCRC, 1989) is a powerful global tool for helping to make positive changes in children's lives. Article 24 is the right to the best possible health and health services. However, there are major inequalities in child health across the world. The highest rates of child mortality are in Sub-Saharan Africa, a part of the developing world where one in eight children dies before the age of five. The most common causes of death in the developing world include pneumonia, diarrhoea, birth complications and lack of oxygen at birth. These causes of death in children under five continue to be problems because of lack of access to clean water, antibiotics, ante-natal and midwifery services. All of these services are widely available in the developed world and this is reflected in the much lower mortality rate of young children. However, the Millennium Development Goals is an initiative by the United Nations (2000) and goal four is aimed at reducing child mortality. The interventions that have been put in place are having a positive effect on the mortality rates of many countries. An example of how this is being achieved includes successful measles immunisation programmes, notably in Africa, which has had the effect of reducing cases of this potentially fatal disease.

Reducing the mortality rates in young children is important, but it is also important to improve the health of children. The effect of poor health on developmental outcomes is under-recognised (Grantham-McGregor et al., 2007). It is estimated that 200 million children under 5 in developing areas of the world fail to reach their potential because of the effects of poor health, poverty and malnourishment. The impact of these factors is not any different on children in developed areas of the world, but what is different is the level and type of poverty experienced in developing regions of the world, which can result in inadequate nutrition and poor hygiene. This in turn can lead to stunting of growth and increased infections; these factors combined with a lack of health services makes the situation for children's health less optimistic and in turn magnifies the problem of loss of potential for individuals. The economic implications for countries where there are large numbers of children who do not reach their potential development are that they are less likely to make a positive contribution in adult life, thus reducing the possibility of earning money and increasing the level of national poverty.

★ **Reflection point**

What are the messages about child health from developing countries of the world? Consider your own settings – were all children born in the country where you work? How might early experiences impact on their health?

National perspective on child health in a developed country

In recent years there has been recognition that health can impact on developmental outcomes. This is reflected in England's Revised Early Years Foundation Stage (EYFS) (Department for Education, 2012: 13) which makes the statement that 'children learn best when they are healthy, safe and secure'. Indeed, the statutory guidance to the EYFS requires practitioners to promote good health for children and it is now a formal requirement that practitioners review the progress of children at the age of two. The aim of the two year-old progress check is to summarise children's areas of strength as well as identifying any areas where the 'child's progress is less than expected' (2012: 11). Another purpose of the two year-old check is to provide information for the Healthy Child Programme health and development review that is conducted by health visitors. This initiative is evidence of policies that complement each other and reflects joined-up thinking. It is a positive move towards recognising that early years practitioners are well placed to work with parents to assess children's development and inform health reviews. However, this will require practitioners to have in-depth understanding of not only child development, but also a range of the complex factors, including health, which can impact on developmental outcomes.

The UK's Healthy Child Programme is an example of a national health service aimed at preventing conditions in children that can cause ill-health and consequent developmental delay with possible lack of potential development. Ill-health prevention can be achieved by health promotion and health education interventions; activities where practitioners can play a key role. The next section examines what is meant by health promotion and education and then considers implications for practice.

Prevention of ill health: health promotion and health education

The medical advances that occurred during the twentieth century meant that there was increased understanding of the epidemiology (how diseases are caused, distributed and controlled) of diseases. As research revealed the causes of diseases, there was greater understanding about how they could be prevented and consequently, there was a shift from disease cure to disease prevention. This was partly initiated when the World Health Organisation was established in 1948 and programmes for health education and health promotion have contributed to improving children's health.

Health education is an area where many practitioners play an active role in promoting positive health and passing on positive messages about healthy choices. Blair (2010) claims that knowledge about health is an important factor in maintaining and promoting good standards of health. On the other hand, lack of knowledge is disempowering. An example of a successful health education campaign is the Back to Sleep campaign in the 1990s. Davies (1985) noted that in Hong Kong it was the usual practice for parents to adopt the Chinese practice of putting new-born babies to sleep on their backs rather than on their front, which was the more common western practice. He made the connection that sudden infant death syndrome (SIDS) occurred less in Hong Kong compared to the western world. The Back to Sleep campaign health education approach is still proving to be successful because numbers of babies who die unexpectedly as a result of SIDS has reduced significantly. However, not all health education is as successful, for instance health education and health promotion relating to healthy eating. We know that unhealthy eating can impact on health, but the strategies to improve eating habits may not be working because we are seeing increased obesity, anaemia and rickets as well as heart disease, type 2 diabetes and high blood pressure in young children. These conditions will be returned to below in the section relating to contemporary child health issues.

★ **Reflection point**

- Why do you think the Back to Sleep health education campaign was received positively and implemented globally?
- Can you think of any other health education messages that have also been successful?
- Consider the children and parents in your setting – what are the health needs relevant to promoting health and education and what interventions would be helpful to achieve these objectives?

Contemporary issues in child health

Despite the investment in efforts to promote child health, there remain serious challenges to children's health in the UK. Paradoxically, the legacy of improved ante-natal and neonatal medicine is resulting in increased levels of disability, and conditions that leave a legacy of complex medical needs amongst children, which are discussed in Chapter 15. The following conditions are some of the main concerns that negatively affect children's health in the developed world:

- concerns about the effect of obesity on children and healthy eating;
- mental health;
- the impact of poverty on health;
- dental decay;
- control of infection;
- chronic health conditions: allergy, anaphylaxis, asthma, diabetes mellitus, eczema, sickle cell anaemia and thalassemia;
- rickets.

These are all very important features of child welfare and health and are recognised as such, but for the purposes of this chapter I will concentrate on one particular facet in order to illustrate contemporary issues and reflect on the notion of prevention.

Promoting and educating healthy eating in early years settings

Over the last 20 years sociological changes mean that children have spent less time playing outdoors and more time engaged with sedentary activities. Therefore, children have become less active. These changes, combined with diets that are higher in calories, have resulted in an epidemic of obesity (Hall and Elliman, 2006). A policy approach to try and reverse the growing levels of obesity is England's Early Years Foundation Stage (2012) statutory guidance which states that: 'meals … must be healthy, balanced and nutritious' (DfE, 2012: 22). This advice is not new – healthy eating for children has been an issue that has been a source of government policy, medical research and media attention for over 100 years (see Albon and Mukherjee, 2008: 16 for a summary). However, there is a continuing tension between the rhetoric of what foods are healthy and the reality of what children are given to eat and what they like to eat. Consider the following scenario in order to illustrate this point:

> Charlotte and Sharon manage a daycare setting in an area of high deprivation. They noticed that some of the children were not eating all of their food at mealtimes and were concerned about the waste. They decided to look at ways to improve their provision of food and as a starting point they surveyed the parents and children to research their food preferences. The favourite foods were: burgers from a fast food outlet; chips, sausage and pizza. An example of healthy foods included faggots and mash.

★ **Reflection point**

- How do you think Charlotte and Sharon can take the healthy eating message forward in order to educate parents and children about this aspect of health promotion?
- Do you think that there are ethical issues in relation to promoting this aspect of health?
- How can they realistically try to meet the statutory requirements for providing healthy food that children will eat?

Charlotte and Sharon's experience may reflect your experience of implementing a healthy eating policy with the reality of children's food choices. The difference between the success of the Back to Sleep campaign and healthy eating education is striking. In your reflections related to both these examples, you may have wondered why parents have been willing to respond with enthusiasm to ensuring their babies have an increased chance of life, but the response to education and promoting healthy eating is not having a similar impact on people's behaviour (Hall and Elliman, 2006). This may seem surprising when we consider the negative impact of obesity on children's health and self-esteem. Clearly, food and eating is a complex issue and there are many influences that make it difficult for some people to make healthy eating choices.

Recent research by Anderson and Anderson in Canada explored the impact that pre-school television shows may have on the development of eating habits leading to obesity in children. The research suggests that young children are influenced by 'the "rule" of getting rid of hunger with sugary foods' (2010: 1333) that is conveyed by the characters in pre-school television programmes. Such research is helpful in enabling us to understand more about the complexities surrounding food and human behaviour. However, it also suggests that the benefits of healthy eating may continue to be a difficult message to convey and more importantly, to turn into reality.

⭐ **Reflection point**

- Do you consider that you have a role in promoting health and educating children and parents about health in your setting/placement? What are the challenges associated with health education and health promotion?

Preventing infectious diseases

Over the last 100 years, our understanding of infectious diseases has increased and a major development in preventing infectious diseases is by giving immunisations to children in order to reduce the risk of dying, or becoming disabled from a range of infectious diseases. All children in the UK are entitled to receive a programme of immunisations against a wide range of infectious disease (see current guidelines on the Department of Health website). This is a free service for children in the UK, however not all parents take up the offer of immunisations and if this service, which is part of the Healthy Child Programme, is not taken up, there is no legislation to enforce the uptake. This can mean that children who cannot receive immunisations for genuine medical reasons, may be vulnerable to infection that is potentially avoidable. In the United States, immunisations must be given to children before they enter school and this is enforceable by law.

However, immunisations are not the only way of reducing infectious diseases and there are many infections that can impact on children's health. Health education and the promotion of hygienic practices in preventing infectious diseases is a vital part of maintaining the health of all children. Infectious diseases are caused by bacteria, viruses and fungi which are inhaled into the lungs, ingested into the stomach or inoculated through the skin. A major factor in spreading these organisms is cross contamination on our hands. As a young student nurse on placement in an operating theatre, I remember being taught by a fierce theatre sister (as she demonstrated the correct hand-washing technique to me) that the single most important way of reducing the risk of cross infection is by using a good hand washing technique.

Early years practitioners have responsibilities in preventing and minimising the spread of infection in the following ways:

- Understanding how diseases are spread: awareness of the causes and transmission of infection;
- Developing policies;
- Modelling good practice;
- Educating staff, children and parents.

⭐ **Reflection point**

There is no room for complacency in tackling infection, especially as there are reports of the resistance of some bacteria to antibiotics, which could previously be relied upon to treat infections. What are your thoughts about your role in preventing infectious diseases in your setting? What tensions could there be in working with parents in preventing infection?

Conclusion

Health and well-being must be viewed in a global, economic, political and socio-cultural context because these factors influence how individuals access, engage with and respond to services.

Some of the factors that contribute to good health and well-being can be sensitive issues to address and promoting health can be a difficult message to convey. It is important that training needs are identified in order to ensure that practitioners are equipped with up-to-date knowledge. This clearly has cost and time implications. The success of achieving, or attempting to achieve, good health and well-being requires the co-operation and motivation of parents.

Useful websites

Department of Health: www.dh.gov.uk
Department for Education: www.education.gov.uk
Health Protection Agency: www.hpa.org.uk

References

Albon, D. and Mukherji, P. (2008) *Food and Health in Early Childhood*. London: SAGE.

Anderson, L.M. and Anderson, J. (2010) 'Barney and breakfast: messages about food and eating in pre-school television shows and how they may impact the development of eating behaviours in children', *Early Child Development and Care*, 180 (10): 1323–1336.

Blair, M. (2010) *Child Public Health*, 2nd edn. Oxford: Oxford University Press.

Bowlby, J. (1969) *Attachment and Loss: Volume 1*. New York: Basic Books.

Davies, D.P. (1985) 'Cot death in Hong Kong: a rare problem', *The Lancet*, 2 (8468): 1346–1349.

de Braal, B. (2009) 'Depression in childhood – is there an epidemic?', *School Health Journal*, 5 (2): 18–20.

Department for Education (2012) *Statutory Framework for the Early Years Foundation Stage: Setting the Standards for Learning, Development and Care for Children from Birth to Five*.

Available at http://media.education.gov.uk/assets/files/pdf/s/eyfs%20statutory%20frame-work%20march%202012.pdf (accessed 4 January 2013).

Fattore, T., Mason, J. and Watson, E. (2007) 'Children's conceptualisations of their well-being', *Social Indicators Research*, 80 (1): 5–29.

Grantham-McGregor, S., Cheung, Y.B., Cueta, S. Glewwe, P., Richter, L. and Strupp, B. (2007) 'Child development in developing countries 1: developmental potential in the first five years for children in developing countries', *The Lancet*. 369: 60–70.

Hall, D. and Elliman, D. (2006) *Health for All Children*, rev. 4th edn. Oxford: Oxford University Press.

Layard, R. and Dunn, J. (2009) *A Good Childhood: Searching for Values in a Competitive Age*. London: Penguin.

Maslow, A.H. (1943) 'A theory of human motivation', *Psychological Review*, 50 (4): 370–96. Available at: http://psychclassics.yorku.ca/Maslow/motivation.htm (accessed 5 January 2013).

NICE (National Institute for Health and Clinical Excellence) (2012) *Social and Emotional Well-being: Early Years*. NICE public health guidance 40 available at: www.nice.org.uk/nicemedia/live/13941/61149/61149.pdf (accessed 23 November 2013).

Roelen, K. and Galsmann, F. (2012) *Study on Child Well-being in Kazakhstan*. Institute of Development Studies. Available at: www.ids.ac.uk/publication/child-well-being-in-kazakhstan (accessed 10 January 2013).

Statham, J. and Chase, E. (2010) *Childhood Well-being: A Brief Overview*, Childhood Well-being Research Centre Briefing Paper 1, August. Available at: www.education.gov.uk/publications/eOrderingDownload/Child-Wellbeing-Brief.pdf (accessed 3 January 2013).

United Nations (2000) *Millennium Development Goals*. Available from: www.un.org/millenniumgoals/ (accessed 28 March 2014).

United Nations Convention on the Rights of the Child (1989) Available at www.unicef.org.uk/Documents/Publication-pdfs/UNCRC_PRESS200910web.pdf (accessed 29 June 214).

World Health Organisation (1986) *Definition of Terms*. Available at: www.who.int/hac/about/definitions/en/ (accessed 13 January 2013).

9

Play and creativity: how important is this in terms of the developing child?

Frances Brett

Chapter overview

This chapter explores the nature of play as a vehicle for a child's holistic development and argues that play has a significant place in developing quality ECEC practice. The author sees play as incorporating the range of environments that the child experiences, enabling interactivity between the individual and their world so that play itself becomes a creative journey in which the child leads their own development. In many ways this parallels creative journeys fostered by professional artists working in the expressive arts. The chapter raises questions about how we (as ECEC practitioners) view play and is apprehensive about the way play can be developed as a framework for assessment rather than articulating the creative voice of the child.

Introduction

Any discussion of play begs the question, what do we mean by play? How do we define this? Our personal definitions are inevitably influenced by how we value play in relation to learning and development – whether we even see these as separate elements to begin with – and the recognition we actively afford play in terms of time, space and resources. But perhaps the more compelling question is, what value do children themselves place upon play? In asking this question, other questions are implied regarding how the practitioner views and responds to children's play, and their own role within the play environment: is play a means to monitor children's progress or to provide meaningful opportunities for holistic development? In effect: Who is play for? Is it for the benefit of the practitioners or the child and do we sometimes model play and play spaces to reflect what we want to observe rather than offering a canvas upon which the child can express their capability? Therefore let us explore play from the child's perspective and ask what the significance of play is to a child's own experience of their development.

Play is essential to the development of the young child. Playfulness, arguably, is the child's prime mode of being. Prime in the sense of offering (for the majority of children) a first response to examining the world around them but also prime in that it is the optimum state in which children can most fully be themselves and so best meet and interpret the world. For this reason, play can be seen as the means by which children engage most effectively with learning, both as individuals and within social groups. As such, play is integral to the child's holistic development; it allows a view of development which is about what children learn and also how they learn. It values play as their strength and (it could be argued) an entitlement. Indeed, play should perhaps be seen in terms of what Appleby (2011) asserts in considering some perceptions of play in early education. She offers a critical dimension on the subject in her book chapter and argues that play should not be seen solely as a word used to describe what goes on or what children do, but to describe *children's way of being* and thus a natural part of their social world. This is something to reflect upon carefully as you move though this chapter and I hope this opening segment might have started you thinking about how play is a complex and complicated part of a child's world, a world that it is a privilege to occasionally be allowed to join. It is therefore possible to contend that many academic commentators and researchers agree on the primacy of play in relation to children's learning and well-being. For example (and there are other examples, which will be introduced later) a review of the literature by Evangelou and colleagues (2009: 4) presents a key finding from their extensive review, namely: 'Play is a prime context for development … but there are now studies on different kinds of play, especially the ways it can be enriched by guiding, planning and resourcing on the part of the staff in settings.' It is therefore fair to assert that it is not just play itself that is of importance in terms of social, emotional and cognitive development but of equal importance are the day-to-day interactions between professionals and children that *promote and sustain play and establish a play space: in effect, those who design and maintain the physical and emotional context in which children enact their play.*

Play and creativity

Today there are myriad research studies and commentators who have contributed to the discourse about play and learning. Some of the most recent literature reviews in the field (McLellan et al., 2012; Davies et al., 2013) continue to underline the holistic value of play in children's development but there is also an increasing emphasis on the role of play in supporting creativity and the conditions that enable this to flourish. Exploring this from the child's perspective, however, it is perhaps more useful to think of the continuum of the child's play – across all the different contexts for play which the child experiences – as where the creativity actually lies. What are the connections the child is making, within their play and across their play – and why? This is important because there is a danger that although play is a prime focus for learning it can also be perceived as a vehicle for assessment. This is a view which inevitably drives practitioners towards the provision of activities that promote play and that allows children at play to be assessed, rather than the provision of opportunities that fuel creativity, choice and recognise the child's voice. A report by CeDARE (2012) gives weight to this view. A counter choice for practitioners might be to see play as much more like a creative journey that does not fall neatly into a developmental assessment of the child. (A point that you will find explored further in Chapter 10 by Anna Kilderry.) Such a creative journey of play is echoed in the working practice of artists (in all forms) who consciously play – in their own words – as a means to finding their voice, their own 'destination'. Here two artists – one a playwright, one a musician – examine their creative process as 'playing' towards something they were trying to understand and express:

> You know – feel – where you want to go but it's not knowing what the path is to get there ... it's being very alert and exploring in whatever ways you can what's in your head... . You hang on to the bits that do work; you discover things through trying ... and when you're there you will know it's right. You don't rest until you find it's right. You start off here – explore, explore, explore – and then you're there – but you can't get there otherwise – without going through the journey between.
>
> (Sheila Hall, Playwright, 2011)
>
> The best state of mind to be in, that's an interesting thing: it's a combination of deep concentration and being very relaxed. Very free. Starting somewhere and following to see where it goes ... but somehow suddenly you've got a sense of something in there – like Michelangelo saying he just had to chip away at the stone to find the form – as if you know the tune, but don't know the notes – as if you're finding your way to them, to the tune.
>
> (Richard Jones, Musician, 2011)

Seen in this way it becomes possible to argue that the child is on a meaningful journey that they themselves are capable of directing, a journey that is towards something felt or intuited, just as the creative artists have described above. It also becomes apparent that in appropriating evidence of children's play and attaching this to developmental descriptors we are manipulating their play to meet a spurious goal. Yes, it is important to enable children to play, and to observe that play: but what are we actually looking for when we observe, and in whose interest? The developmental narrative can be restrictive as it tells one aspect of the child's whole story – the observable 'development'. It is, if you like, simply one layer of the story. In looking for these discrete developments we can miss the child's own developing narrative, which involves the whole self.

The fluent self

As practitioners, can we trust that the child, driven by a desire to make meaning, creates their own developmental learning journey, and that play is their vehicle to make this quest? Bronfenbrenner – particularly in his revised bio-ecological view of childhood (Bronfenbrenner and Ceci, 1994) – promotes a consideration of the child as ecologically bound, an inhabitant of not just one context but many, whilst Lemke (2002) notes the importance – in fact the necessity – of the child making meaningful connections across these different contexts in order to make sense of, and for, themselves. This remains true for us as adults, of course. In a new situation, we use the evidence around us – the environment that we experience as being made up of people, places, textures, sounds, smells, colours, events – to find some confirmation of our previous understanding and make sense of the new in relation to this. And gradually we build some consistency – a fluency – across the different versions of ourselves that we encounter. Perhaps this could be described as the fluent self, the identity that is in some way a developing response to the question 'Who am I?'.

Putting the matter in this way makes it harder to distinguish adulthood from childhood and to view them as separate stages within a scale of development over a human life span. Instead, trying to answer that same question is the act which unifies the individual across time and place, even if we become more adept at answering it, synthesising our previous and current realities ever more fluently. At times of greatest change – new job, relationship, house move, an unexpected event – the question may be just as loud, raw and unanswered as during our first steps away from the known that is represented by our parent or main carer when we are children.

Play: the perfect vehicle!

At a straightforward level, play in its many forms is capable of providing a connection across different environments and experiences. It is a mode of being and as such, is a means of making the risky journey away from the known and familiar, into the new and strange, until this is assimilated and a new status quo – a place of safety – is established. So play is capable of locating the child within a particular environment – a specific time and context – and at the same time of connecting them to 'elsewhere' and carrying them from place to place. It is, if you like, a vehicle for the journey! These illustrations may help to understand what this means in practice.

CASE STUDY

Louis

Louis, aged 3, is a superhero. He lives with his mother and his grandmother, attends a local pre-school setting three mornings a week and a childminder one day a week. He is part of a large extended family and at weekends often stays a whole day and sometimes overnight with his aunt and uncle and cousins. But in all these places he is still a superhero. He has special powers that allow him to be invisible and to freeze people into statues; he wears a blue cloak to show when his powers are 'active'. Over time, Louis' family, his childminder and pre-school staff have all begun to share their recognition that when Louis wears his blue cloak, he is 'powerful', and that this helps him to cope with transitions, both small and large, and change.

More than this, though, this shared understanding of something that could be simply described as role play offers Louis *actual* power; knowing that he is recognised as a superhero in all these places gains Louis some fluency of self across the separate parts of his life, but also confidence to engage in many other acts of play, different in kind, but which enable him to reveal his strengthening dispositions, and emotional and physical capabilities. In other words, through the character play he can begin to find and express his own powerful self in the real world. By being accepted at his own definition, he can more fully be his actual self. And the more he is able to operate at his highest level, actualising his full self, the more he is able to develop.

This outcome is made possible by all those involved in Louis' care, from family to practitioners, honouring Louis' play and recognising its value *to him* in supporting a consistent view of himself. He makes sense of himself, for himself, and this meaning is reflected back to him consistently.

Play: a creative learning journey

Louis' superhero play is a means of making connections across a range of contexts. Now, let's turn the telescope around, and, looking through the other end, consider play as a child's means of making connections across their inner landscape.

CASE STUDY

Joe

Aged 4 years and 6 months, Joe rarely speaks and does not engage in play or inter-action with other children to any great degree. He tends to observe or simply copy others, or just run around by himself. He lives on a large farm and spends much of his time outdoors with two older brothers. His parents – very busy farmers – are often unaware of how he is spending his time.

Recently, during his setting's visits to the local river, he has begun to build a pile of sticks and stones; each time he returns to this, he dismantles it and creates it again in a slightly different way: different materials, different con-struction. He has begun to tolerate other children offering materials although he does not want them to actively help build. He begins to mime hammering, sawing; occasionally he issues an instruction to another child: 'stick'; 'flat'; 'here'. Back in the setting, he has begun to draw large outlines on paper, a little like chimneys, and his key worker notes that he is climbing all the time – particularly to the top of the slide.

All of these separate developmental steps forward are carefully post-it noted, but it is when Joe steps back from his latest (and tallest) pile of sticks, leaves and stones, and announces 'castle' that setting staff are able to make the connection that has presumably been there for Joe the whole time. And when his mother collects him that day she says, with some surprise, yes, they'd had a picnic at a castle – ooh ages ago now – but Joe had loved it.

A child's play is made up of many separate play 'acts' – different kinds of play, as well as playful approaches to activity. Sand play, water play, block play, games with rules and without, indoor, outdoor, symbolic, representational, there is no single act of play; even if a child 'always plays with the dolls' house', each time is a different play act, for the child, even if it may appear to be very similar to what has been seen before. What, then, is the connection between each play act? The child themselves; the line of their thinking. For Joe, enacting his idea of 'cas-tle' through different play elements has created a personal learning journey that has not only refined his idea of what a castle represents to him, over a period of several months, but has also provided opportunities that both trigger and reveal development. The importance of him putting these acts together in a way that was personally meaningful is key. As Duffy (1998: 18) has noted, creativity is concerned with 'connecting the previously unconnected', so constructing mean-ing for the self, and it is clear that Joe has taken whatever is available – in terms of experiences, opportunities and materials – to map his own route to under-standing and development. This has been further supported by the practitioners around him being prepared to be in a state of unknowing: not making simple assumptions about Joe's play but allowing his ideas to unfold, over time, and enabling other children to be the key protagonists who, through their play, could support Joe's evolving expression. The practitioners had to risk not knowing until they understood the connections that Joe was trying to make and could then sup-port and strengthen these.

So as well as being the vehicle, is play also a creative journey that the child maps for themselves? As in any journey there is a destination, whether known, sensed or imagined, and the process of undertaking the journey allows a connection to be made between one place and another, one idea and another. The creativity lies in the way the journey is made; how it is put together. Play in all its forms provides opportunities that both trigger and respond to development, as well as reveal it, thus it could be described as the perfect vehicle for the developmental journey. And it is a perfect vehicle in another way: it offers a creative journey, in which creativity is defined as the opportunity to examine the same thing in many different ways, in order to really know and understand the matter in question. In this sense it offers the personal *spiritual* fulfilment described by Craft (2005) that has its own intrinsic value, as opposed to a mechanistic usage of personal creativity to simply innovate. From this standpoint, the environment is the context in which the child reveals themselves through play; play is the vehicle – their mode of being; and creativity is the nature of the journey.

Play in practice?

What then are the elements that we as practitioners can provide to support the child's creative journey of play? Returning to the two examples above, certain aspects stand out: a recognition that there is a connection across all of a child's play, wherever this takes place and the differing types of play this may consist of; allowing space – physical and temporal – for play to unfold and so discern the developing narrative that the child's play expresses; offering open-ended materials in a variety of contexts and noting what the child does with these; being prepared to be open-minded – *un*knowing – about what the child's inner narrative might be, rather than rushing to impose a narrative of our own.

Looking closer still, what are the key questions that practitioners might ask of the environment that they are offering for play? Table 9.1 offers a means (via a series of key questions that practitioners can pose about practice) to examine the

Table 9.1 Promoting a creative journey

Key questions (you as a practitioner) might imagine children would ask	Key questions for practitioners *Opportunities*	Key questions for practitioners *Spaces*	Key questions for practitioners *Time*	Key questions for practitioners *Materials*	Key questions for practitioners *Records*
What do you know about me? My likes, dislikes, attitudes, dispositions, who are my friends, what do I like to play with and explore?	When and how do I find out about the other contexts that this child is part of? – Before they begin at the setting? – While they are at the setting?	Where is the child's life beyond the setting walls represented *within* the setting? How do I welcome this child's family/carers? How do I make connections with the other people that work with this child?	How often do I enable/provide opportunities for children to make connections to other play experiences/opportunities that they experience?	Are the resources that I offer open-ended enough to support a wide range of interpretation? Do they reflect the other contexts of which this child is part?	Where do I record information about this child's other experiences? How do I share this with the child?
Where can I find myself in this setting?	Does each child have a personal space – a place to represent themselves? Where can this child find reminders of where they come from (places, people, gender, faith, heritage, culture) as well as where they want to be (imaginative worlds, current preoccupations)?	Do I offer empty space that can be transformed and reconfigured? Where new connections can be made?	Can the child retrace their thinking each day because their play can continue where it left off the day before?	What do I offer that is familiar? That is new and surprising?	How am I recording and reflecting back the child's journeys in terms of wall displays?
Who can help me recognise connections? How can I be helped and encouraged to re-connect to something I did yesterday or last week?	Do I provide opportunities which interconnect visual, auditory and physical resources, indoors and outdoors? Can materials be taken from place to place and recombined?	Have I offered flexible spaces where 'work in progress' can be left and returned to until 'finished'? Do I display the child's ongoing narratives within the setting, to reflect back connections made?	Can I enable this child's explorations to take as long as they need?	How do I support children in their negotiation with each other regarding use of spaces and materials?	How do I record connections and re-connections? Can I look, listen, stand back, observe and consider the play space environment as part of planning? Is there surprise and unconnectedness?

play context and so evaluate how this is supporting the child's creative play journey. The questions ask that we not only see the play space in terms of resources, but also consider the play environment and how the child relates this to what else they know; as well as recognising that surprise and *unconnectedness* might be as valuable as logical next steps to enhance play and learning. How many times have you carefully observed a child's interests and offered something that you think might extend these, only to find these materials completely ignored? Instead, it may be a case of understanding how what the child is doing *now* connects with what they were doing before ... What is the connection in *their* minds? If you introduce something unrelated, what do they do with this? How does this connect with what has gone before *for that child*? Another way of looking at this is to say that materials are less important in themselves than observing how the child uses them and the connections they are making across all their current experience. In essence, critically examining if we as practitioners are effectively using space, materials and ourselves to engage children at their highest level of creativity, as they enact themselves.

Conclusion

This chapter has endorsed the primacy of play in a child's life and its potential to support the child's self-directed developmental journey. It has argued that opportunities rather than activities, offered within a listening environment, enable the child to make meaningful connections across all the contexts within which they play.

Carla Rinaldi (2009) goes to the heart of the child's playful journey towards themselves, speaking here from their point of view:

> I don't want to be recognised as a person who doesn't make meaning, who makes mistakes; I want to be recognised as someone who is the best expression of humanity.

In order, then, to reflect the child's development it seems important to offer an environment that is a canvas on which the child can express their capability, through which it is possible to capture a picture of their development that reflects the child's own view of their play journey, not simply the developmental outcomes – though these will be evident too. It could be argued that this picture forms a record of their creative play journey and so offers a true 'learning journey'.

Play is a creative journey, one that the child makes to their own understanding of themselves within the context of themselves – and we, as external observers, cannot construct the conclusion, nor decide where this should fall. By standing back but listening closely, we can walk hand in hand with the child, making meaning *with* them, allowing them to be the best expression of themselves.

Critical Learning Activity

1. Using the play space key questions grid (Table 9.1), analyse a play space. This can be any existing play space or a space that you and others are planning to introduce indoors, outdoors or both.

   o   How does a consideration of the play space environment help to answer the key questions?
   o   How is the play space supporting children in making connections? How will you support children to make such connections?

2. How do your preferred methods of recording what children do in your setting map children's questions, and the way that they are answering them? Do you consider how to record the connections being made? Importantly, how do you record and respond to these connections?

Further reading

Kelly-Vance, L. and Ryalls, B.O. (2005) 'A systematic, reliable approach to play assessment in pre-schoolers', *Social Psychology International*, 26: 398.

Kington, A., Gates, P. and Sammons, P. (2013) 'Development of social relationships, interactions and behaviours in early education settings', *Journal of Early Childhood Research*, 11: 292.

Lifter, K., Mason, E.J. and Barton, E. (2011) 'Children's play: where we have been and where we could go', *Journal of Early Intervention*, 33: 281.

References

Appleby, K. (2011) 'Playing and learning: ways of being in action', in N. Canning (ed.), *Play and Practice in the Early Years*. London: SAGE.

Bronfenbrenner, U. and Ceci, S.J. (1994) 'Nature-nurture reconceptualized in developmental perspective: a bioecological model', *Psychological Review*, 101 (4): 568–586.

CeDARE (University of Wolverhampton: Coleyshaw, L., Whitmarsh, J., Jopling, M. and Hadfield, M.) (2012) *Listening to Children's Perspectives: Improving the Quality of Provision in Early Years Settings*, part of the Longitudinal Study of Early Years Professional Status. DfE Research Report DFE-RR239b.

Craft, A. (2005) 'Creativity in schools: tensions and dilemmas', Keynote paper presented at *Creativity: Using it Wisely?*, Cambridge.

Davies, D., Jindal-Snape, D., Collier, C., Digby, R., Hay, P. and Howe, A. (2013) 'Creative learning environments in education – a systematic literature review', *Thinking Skills and Creativity*, 8 (April): 80–91.

Duffy, B. (1998) *Supporting Creativity and Imagination in the Early Years*. Open University Press.

Evangelou, M., Sylva, K., Kyriacou, M., Wild, M. and Glenny, G. (2009) *Early Years Development and Learning Literature Review*. Available at: www.gov.uk/government/uploads/system/uploads/attachment_data/file/222003/DCSF-RR176.pdf (accessed 30 March 2014)

Hall, S. (2011) Personal communication.

Jones, R. (2011) Personal communication.

Lemke, J. (2002) 'Becoming the village: education across lives', in G. Wells and G. Claxton (eds), *Learning for Life in the 21st Century: Sociocultural Perspectives on the Future of Education*. London: Blackwell. pp. 34–45.

McLellan, R., Galton, M., Steward, S. and Page, C. (2012) *The Impact of Creative Initiatives on Wellbeing: A Literature Review*. Available at: www.creativitycultureeducation.org/the-impact-of-creative-partnerships-on-the-wellbeing-of-children-and-young-people (accessed 30 March 2014).

Rinaldi, C. (2009) Lecture given during Reggio Preschools UK Study Week, 21 April.

Want to learn more about this chapter?

Visit the companion website at **https://study.sagepub.com/reedandwalker** to access podcasts from the author and additional reading to further help you with your studies.

10

Repositioning developmentalism

Anna Kilderry

Chapter overview

This chapter looks at the notion of the 'developing child'. It commences with a discussion about critical thinking and questioning. Next, it provides an overview of what child development and developmentalism are in the ECEC context, and it critiques the way developmentalism is relied upon to inform practice in ECEC. In the final section readers are introduced to the concept of postdevelopmentalism (Blaise, 2005; Edwards, 2009) and how a postdevelopmental framework (Nolan and Kilderry, 2010) can reposition developmentalism.

Introduction

The 'developing child' is a notion that is very familiar with those who work in Early Childhood Education and Care (ECEC). The notion of the developing child in ECEC stems from child development theory. What we know as child development theory in ECEC draws from theories generated by Rousseau, Montessori, Erikson, Freud, Gesell, Vygotsky, Bruner, and in particular theories developed by Piaget (Cannella, 1997; MacNaughton, 2003; Grieshaber, 2008; Berk, 2012). Child development theories operate as a significant source of knowledge guiding ECEC practice in the UK (Walkerdine, 1998; Walsh et al., 2010), Australia and New Zealand (Farquhar and Fleer, 2007; Edwards, 2009) and the USA (Lubeck, 1996, 1998a, 1998b; Graue, 2008). Child development theory has had a century-long domination shaping ECEC curriculum frameworks and pedagogy in westernised countries (Bloch, 1992; Zimiles, 2000; Krieg, 2010). Due to its prominence guiding ECEC practice in an Australian pre-school context (children birth to five years), I maintain that child development theory requires some critique before applying it to practice (Kilderry, 2012). The reason being so that we can better understand how child development theories shape and guide practice, and to provide space for other theories and perspectives to emerge. Viewing the child as 'developing' and by default, 'not-yet-developed', affects the way adults interact with children, children's disposition as learners, and children's emerging identity. The process of critique enables us to better understand how theory operates, and it provides intellectual space for us to consider other possibilities for practice.

Critical thinking and questioning

Critical thinking and questioning are helpful processes as they enable us to ask critical questions about theories and practices we know so well, and this can give rise to uncovering issues that may not have come to our attention unless our common-sense understandings are challenged. Each author in this book has a slightly different approach to being critical, whether thinking and questioning critically, or practising critically. Critical theory (Marcuse 1964; Adorno, 1973; Adorno and Horkheimer, 1979) is used in this chapter, to question the 'status quo' or the way things are usually done and who is advantaged or disadvantaged by this. In the ECEC context, it pertains to everyday theories that lie beneath our practice decisions. In addition to using critical theory as a form of critique, this chapter draws on poststructural notions to consider what possibilities lie beyond a particular way of thinking and practising.

Child development

What we know as child development theory in ECEC stems from various theorists (for example Rousseau, Montessori, Erikson, Freud, Gesell, Piaget, Vygotsky and Bruner). These diverse theories have come together to form what is recognised as *child development* in ECEC (Cannella, 1997; MacNaughton, 2003; Grieshaber, 2008; Berk, 2012). Child development operates as a sub-discipline of developmental psychology (Edwards and Fleer, 2003). Developmental psychology is concerned with psychological and biological changes that take place as humans progress through different stages of physical and cognitive growth and development (Muir, 1999). It includes changes that occur across the life span and are affected by the specific context. Child development is concerned with the development of children, including their biological, social, emotional and cognitive growth through the life cycle (Berk, 2012). Early work within child development was undertaken by Gesell (1950), who followed laws and sequences of maturation. Within this perspective, a developmental view involves an:

examiner who is truly imbued with a developmental point of view [and] is keenly sensitive to the past history of the child, and looks upon the psychological examination, not as a series of proving tests, but as a device or stage for evoking the ways in which this particular child characteristically meets life situations. (Gesell, 1950: 18)

Child development is a key concept in this chapter and is recognisable in ECEC through two main underlying principles: (i) children develop in individual ways and (ii) children's development can be categorised into emotional, social, physical and cognitive domains (Bowman and Stott, 1994). These two principles assist practitioners in understanding children's learning and behaviour and inform their work with young children (Bowman and Stott, 1994).

Developmentalism

In this chapter I have used the term *developmentalism* to encompass theories and social practices that stem from child development theory and are applied to ECEC. Developmentalism in ECEC is a set of ideas and practices that are particular to the sector and have unique meanings associated with them, largely shaped by Piaget (1953, 1959), Gesell (1950), Vygotsky (1987) and Erikson (1950). In many contexts, being educated as an ECEC practitioner, one is immersed in 'developmentalism', and learns about how children develop through various stages, and how important child development theory is for practice. In some contexts, developmentalism informs how children are observed, how learning experiences are planned, the type of curriculum content introduced, and it shapes pedagogy. Illustrating such a point, 'developmentally appropriate practice' (DAP) (Bredekamp, 1987; Bredekamp and Copple, 1997; Copple and Bredekamp, 2009) in the USA has been described as the 'field's signature pedagogy' (Ryan and Goffin, 2008: 386). DAP is one example of how dominant developmentalism can be in ECEC. In practice, DAP is where practitioners assess children in terms of developmental domains (physical, cognitive, social and emotional) and plan learning experiences accordingly (Copple and Bredekamp, 2009). Furthermore, by using the DAP approach, the type of educational experiences offered to children depends on the developmental ability of individual children (Farquhar and Fleer, 2007; Graue, 2008). In curricular terms, the task of ECEC practitioners in DAP is to match curricular content in the form of activities to the child's developmental level and introduce more complex materials and learning when the child is deemed to have the cognitive ability for mastery (Elkind, 1989). This can limit the repertoire of educational experiences offered for children if educators are to gauge and match children's developmental abilities. Knowledge and practices stemming from child development theories are unique to the way developmentalism has been constructed in ECEC. Social practices stemming from developmentalism, such as recording developmental observations of children and planning learning experiences based on an assessment of children's developmental abilities can potentially restrict practitioners' pedagogical approach (Blaise and Nuttall, 2011; Kilderry, 2012). Therefore, this chapter aims to reposition developmentalism and see what practice can look like when a developmental view is not central to practice.

Critiquing developmentalism

Critiquing knowledge allows us to question and reframe current ways of thinking about practice and allows us to ensure that the theories we rely on are fit for purpose. For example, critiquing theory underpinning practice allows us a space to reconsider ideas, knowledge and associated practices. Theories underpinning ECEC have been critiqued by numerous people. For example, Cannella critiqued the way the field of ECEC relies on developmental theories; Burman (2008) deconstructed developmental psychology and the way it frames thinking; Lubeck (1998a, 1998b) has extensively critiqued DAP; and Blaise and Nuttall (2011) have more recently explained the link between power and pedagogy in ECEC. These theories provide a repertoire of pedagogical approaches outside of the developmental frame.

The intention of critiquing developmentalism is not meant to dismiss child development theories used in ECEC built up over the years that provide useful insights into children and their learning. Instead, the purpose of the critique is to see what the educational landscape could look like when developmentalism is repositioned, allowing other perspectives to emerge. Moreover, it has been argued that 'without multiple forms of critique, our field can only foster dominant perspectives; the field thus functions to silence the voices of diverse others' (Cannella, 1997: 17).

It must be noted that in some contexts developmentalism is seen as a form of protection against an outcomes-based and standards-driven curricula, where expectations of pre-school children are overly academic. The purpose of this critique is *not* to replace developmental theories and associated practices with a standards-driven and overly academic curriculum in ECEC, but rather it is an opportunity to revitalise practice through careful consideration of the underpinning theories guiding practice.

Critical theory (Marcuse 1964; Gramsci, 1971; Adorno, 1973; Adorno and Horkheimer, 1979) is used as a useful theoretical framework in this chapter as it has the ability to question taken-for-granted understandings within ECEC. Critical theory can assist with understanding how developmentalism operates in ECEC, bringing awareness to the less obvious ways it positions children and affects practice. Critical theory is one way of uncovering forms of power, for example, who or what is privileged by certain knowledge, and who or what might be disadvantaged. It provides a systematic way of asking critical questions, such as, what or whose knowledge, values and practices are privileged? Such an approach can be applied to other forms of dominant knowledge or theories that require critiquing.

Table 10.1 has used critical theory to critique developmentalism in ECEC. It illustrates how theory can challenge commonly held assumptions and generates a list of useful critical insights and questions. Each of these critical questions can be asked in different contexts with different responses generated.

Table 10.1　A critique of developmentalism in Early Childhood Education and Care

Developmentalism	Using critical theory to critique ECEC practice	Using critical theory to critique developmentalism
Broad definition	*Purpose*	*Purpose*
Developmentalism in Early Childhood Education and Care (ECEC) includes all the ideas and social practices inspired by child development theories.	To better understand how ECEC practice functions.	To find out how developmentalism might overshadow and exclude other ways of thinking about ECEC practice.
Key ideas	To consider and challenge who is advantaged and disadvantaged in this situation.	*Assumptions to challenge*
Each child is unique and develops individually. Children develop in predictable ways.	*Critical questions*	Children are constructed as either 'developed' or 'not-yet developed' by adults.
Theory guiding practice	What theories and practices are dominant and privileged in ECEC? Why is that?	Individual children are measured to a 'normal development' range, indicating there is also an 'abnormal' range.
Individual children's development is categorised into emotional, social, physical and cognitive domains. Individual children's development is observed and measured in each developmental domain.	What everyday understandings about practice are left unchallenged?	The better understanding practitioners have of child development theory, the better the educational and development outcomes will be for children.
There is a 'normal development range' for children. Children have developmental needs and strengths, assessed by adults.	How do we view young children? For example, as 'developing', as 'capable', or as empowered people with rights? How does practice look different in each of these situations?	*Critical questions*
Adults match activities and learning experiences to individual children's developmental abilities.	Who decides what will happen in ECEC?	Is the categorisation of children being 'developed' or 'not-yet-developed' a useful way to view children? Are there more respectful and equitable ways to view and assess children's learning?
The better the understanding practitioners have of child development theory, the more 'developmentally appropriate' practice will be. Thus, the better the educational and development outcomes will be for children.	Which decisions about their day can children have input into?	Who determines what normal (child) development is? In which contexts does 'normal' apply?
	What aspects of the curriculum and practice are inequitable for some children and families?	How is the developed/not-yet-development perspective limiting our view of young children, their abilities and their potential learning?
	How does early childhood policy position children, practitioners and families?	

Critical theory enables us to disrupt the way developmentalism operates in ECEC, and ask questions such as, 'is there such a concept as a *normal* development age range for children?' and 'how is viewing a child as *developing normally* useful, or harmful?' For example, some have argued that a hierarchical categorisation of children's maturation both generalises and oversimplifies children's capabilities and it can orientate practitioners to think about children in deficit terms (Lubeck, 1996, 1998a; Burman, 2008). Analysis and critique such as this can inspire new ways of thinking and give rise to different sets of practices, practices that were previously not considered. Postdevelopmentalism is another way to reposition developmentalism and generate new ways of thinking about practice. The next section outlines what postdevelopmentalism is and how it can be applied in this context.

Postdevelopmentalism

Postdevelopmentalism (Blaise, 2005; Edwards, 2009; Nolan and Kilderry, 2010), is a term coined to describe theories and practices located outside of developmentalism, or those relying on child development theories. Postdevelopmentalism refers to 'post' or 'beyond' a developmental era, an era in ECEC that has been characterised by practices dominated by developmental theories. To hold a postdevelopmental view, one would *not* think about children as 'developing', but rather in terms of all of their capabilities as active citizens in democratic society, drawing on a wide range of theories and perspectives. It is not to say that child development theories are not considered at all, but they are not at the forefront of thinking about children and guiding practice. Postdevelopmentalism draws on poststructural ideas where the concepts of 'truth, knowledge, power and identity' are questioned (Appelrouth and Edles, 2012: 611). Poststructuralism itself is not one theory, but rather an assemblage of ideas stemming from a critique of structuralism by mid-twentieth century French theorists such as Foucault, Baudrillard, Derrida, Lacan, Deleuze and Guattari (Appelrouth and Edles, 2012).

Table 10.2 provides guidance to how one might go about conducting a critique informed by poststructural notions. It takes the basic tenets of child development theories and practices relied upon in ECEC, and it uses key concepts from poststructuralism, where 'truth', power and knowledge are questioned, to scrutinise developmentalism. Similar to the way critical theory was used to critique developmentalism in Table 10.1, the aim of Table 10.2 is to show how central child development theories are in practice and if required, reposition developmentalism.

Table 10.2   Repositioning developmentalism in Early Childhood Education and Care

Developmentalism	A poststructural critique	A postdevelopmental framework for ECEC (adapted from Nolan and Kilderry, 2010)
Broad definition	*Purpose*	*Purpose*
Developmentalism in Early Childhood Education and Care (ECEC) includes all the ideas and social practices inspired by child development theories.	Questions power, knowledge and 'truth'. Challenges and destabilises traditional assumptions about concepts, identities and theories.	To consider other ways to think about ECEC practice.
Key ideas	*Critical questions*	*Postdevelopmental framework*
Each child is unique and develops individually. Children develop in predictable ways.	What is (the notion of) the 'developing child'? According to whom?	*Repositioning* Practitioners move from the position of planning for young children in developmental terms and reposition children in terms of capabilities.
Theory guiding practice	What are the multiple understandings of the 'developing child'? What does this mean for children's learning?	
Individual children's development is categorised into emotional, social, physical and cognitive domains. Individual children's development is observed and measured in each developmental domain.	Do children all pass through the same developmental stages? Is this a useful way to view children and their learning? How do developmental identities affect children, practitioners and families?	*Reframing* Children's learning and growth is viewed through a range of theoretical lenses – perspectives other than those offered by developmentalism. *Engaging learners* Recognising the varied and diverse ways in which children and adults learn.
There is a 'normal development range' for children. Children have developmental needs and strengths, assessed by adults.	What multiple roles and identities are possible for children and practitioners beyond developmentalism? For example, what are other ways to conceptualise practice?	*Empowering* Children as rights' holders able to express their views and to have their opinions heard and acted upon.
Adults match activities and learning experiences to individual children's developmental abilities.	Can developmental and postdevelopmental roles and identities co-exist together?	*Critical reflection* Practitioners critically reflect on practice, and devise equitable and ethical ways of working with young children.
The better the understanding practitioners have of child development theory, the more 'developmentally appropriate' practice will be. Thus, the better the educational and development outcomes will be for children.		

Noticing common characteristics operating in postdevelopmental thinking and practice, Nolan and Kilderry (2010) named these features with the intention of providing one way to reframe pedagogy in ECEC. The five characteristics of postdevelopmental pedagogy are: i) repositioning, ii) reframing, iii) engaging learners, iv) empowering and v) critical reflection. The five characteristics of postdevelopmental pedagogy are explained in more detail in column 3, Table 10.2. Each of these characteristics enables early childhood practitioners to work with children in ways other than those influenced (and sometimes) dominated by developmentalism. The postdevelopmental framework is not intended to make developmental theories redundant, but rather to broaden the type of theories ECEC practitioners can draw from and create an awareness of how to critique dominant theories informing practice.

Conclusion

This chapter has described the concept of developmentalism, and how child development theories can operate as prevailing sources of knowledge in ECEC. It has illustrated how developmentalism in ECEC can be critiqued and repositioned using critical theory and poststructural concepts. The purpose of critiquing developmentalism in ECEC is to bring awareness to how particular theories might be relied upon in practice, and how other perspectives and views might be relegated to the sidelines, or even silenced. Through the process of critique, dominant theories and practices can be illuminated, critiqued and repositioned, with the aim of making practice as inclusive and equitable as possible.

Critical Learning Activity

The first Critical Learning Activity involves using the questions outlined in Columns 2 and 3 in Table 10.1. It is an exercise which may challenge existing knowledge and practices through what is best termed critical questioning. It asks that you consider the underlying theories you rely on when working with young children. Are these theories ethical, empowering and equitable? If they are, then this is affirming for your practice; if not, some repositioning and reframing of theory could occur to revitalise practice. The critical theory inspired questions (Column 2) can be used to see who is advantaged and disadvantaged in a particular context, and to critique the way developmentalism informs practice in ECEC. The critical questions listed in Column 3 of Table 10.1 can be asked about practice.

The second Critical Learning Activity draws from insights generated from the poststructural critique illustrated in Table 10.2. If practice is already as ethical, inclusive and equitable as it can be, then this type of questioning can be carried out to validate practices. Column 2 of Table 10.2 asks some critical questions inspired by poststructural ideas. These can be asked in relation to your ECEC setting. In addition, the following questions, inspired by the postdevelopmental framework, can be used to reposition and reframe practice:

(Continued)

(Continued)

- Reposition – what theories are used in your setting to observe and plan learning experiences for young children? How can children be re/positioned as 'children with capabilities'?
- Reframe – what theories other than those offered by child development can be used to view children's achievements through?
- Engage learners – how can you recognise the varied and diverse ways in which children learn? What are the many ways this can be represented?
- Empower – how can practice encompass a view where children are viewed as rights' holders, able to express their views and to have their opinions heard and acted upon? What do you need to change to enable children to be positioned this way?
- Critical reflection – in what ways can practitioners critically reflect on practice, and devise equitable and ethical ways of working with young children?

Further reading

Burman, E. (2008) *Deconstructing Developmental Psychology*, 2nd edn. Hove, East Sussex: Routledge.

Blaise, M. and Nuttall, J. (2011) *Learning to Teach in the Early Years Classroom*. Melbourne: Oxford University Press. pp. 110–133.

Cannella, G.S. (1997) *Deconstructing Early Childhood Education: Social Justice and Revolution*. New York: Peter Lang.

Dahlberg, G., Moss, P. and Pence, A. (2007) *Beyond Quality in Early Childhood Education and Care: Languages of Evaluation,* 2nd edn. Abingdon, Oxon: Routledge.

References

Adorno, T. (1973) *Negative Dialectics*. London: Routledge & Kegan Paul.

Adorno, T. and Horkheimer, M. (1979) *Dialectic of Enlightenment*. London: Verso.

Appelrouth, S. and Edles, L. (2012) *Classical and Contemporary Sociological Theory,* 2nd edn. London: SAGE.

Berk, L.E. (2012) *Child Development,* 9th edn. Boston, MA: Pearson.

Blaise, M. (2005) *Playing It Straight! Uncovering Gender Discourses in the Early Childhood Classroom*. New York: Routledge Press.

Blaise, M. and Nuttall, J. (2011) *Learning to Teach in the Early Years Classroom*. Melbourne: Oxford University Press.

Bloch, M.N. (1992) 'Critical perspectives on the historical relationship between child development and early childhood educational research', in S.A. Kessler and B.B. Swadener (eds), *Reconceptualizing the Early Childhood Curriculum: Beginning the Dialogue*. New York: Teachers College Press. pp. 3–20.

Bowman, B.T. and Stott, F.M. (1994) 'Understanding development in a cultural context: the challenge for teachers', in B.L. Mallory and R.S. New (eds), *Diversity and Developmental Appropriate Practices: Challenges for Early Childhood Education*. New York: Teachers College Press. pp. 119–133.

Bredekamp, S. (ed.) (1987) *Developmentally Appropriate Practice in Early Childhood Programs: Serving Children from Birth through Age 8*, expanded edn. Washington, DC: National Association for the Education of Young Children.

Bredekamp, S. and Copple, C. (eds) (1997) *Developmentally Appropriate Practice in Early Childhood Programs: Serving Children from Birth through Age 8*, revised edn. Washington, DC: National Association for the Education of Young Children.

Burman, E. (2008) *Deconstructing Developmental Psychology*, 2nd edn. Hove, East Sussex: Routledge.

Cannella, G.S. (1997) *Deconstructing Early Childhood Education: Social Justice and Revolution.* New York: Peter Lang.

Copple, C. and Bredekamp, S. (eds) (2009) *Developmentally Appropriate Practice in Early Childhood Programs: Serving Children from Birth through to Age Eight*, 3rd edn. Washington, DC: National Association for the Education of Young Children.

Edwards, S. (2009) 'Beyond developmentalism: interfacing professional learning and teachers' conceptions of sociocultural theory', in S. Edwards and J. Nuttall (eds), *Professional Learning in Early Childhood Settings*. Rotterdam: Sense Publishers. pp. 81–95.

Edwards, S. and Fleer, M. (2003) *The Theoretical Informants of the Early Childhood Curriculum: A Historical Review*, paper presented at the Australian Research in Early Childhood Education conference, January, Monash University, Melbourne.

Elkind, D. (1989) 'Developmentally appropriate practice: Philosophical and practical implications', *Phi Delta Kappa,* Oct.: 113–117.

Erikson, E.H. (1950) *Childhood and Society*. New York: Norton.

Farquhar, S. and Fleer, M. (2007) 'Developmental colonisation of early childhood education in Aotearoa/New Zealand and Australia', in L. Keesing-Styles and H. Hedges (eds), *Theorising Early Childhood Practice: Emerging Dialogues*. Sydney: Pademelon Press. pp. 27–49.

Gesell, A. (1950) *The First Five Years of Life: A Guide to the Study of the Preschool Child*. London: Methuen & Co.

Gramsci, A. (1971) *Selections from the Prison Notebooks*. London: Lawrence and Wishart.

Graue, E. (2008) 'Teaching and learning in a post-DAP world', *Early Education and Development,* 19 (3): 441–447.

Grieshaber, S. (2008) 'Interrupting stereotypes: Teaching and the education of young children', *Early Education and Development,* 19 (3): 505–518.

Kilderry, A. (2012) *Teacher Decision Making in Early Childhood Education*, unpublished PhD thesis, QUT, Brisbane, Australia.

Krieg, S. (2010) 'The professional knowledge that counts in Australian contemporary early childhood teacher education', *Contemporary Issues in Early Childhood,* 11 (2): 144–155.

Lubeck, S. (1996) 'Deconstructing "child development knowledge" and "teacher preparation"', *Early Childhood Research Quarterly,* 11: 147–167.

Lubeck, S. (1998a) 'Is developmentally appropriate practice for everyone?', *Childhood Education,* 74(5): 283–298.

Lubeck, S. (1998b) 'Is DAP for everyone? A response', *Childhood Education,* 74 (5): 299–301.

MacNaughton, G. (2003) *Shaping Early Childhood: Learners, Curriculum and Contexts*. Maidenhead: Open University Press.

Marcuse, H. (1964) *One-Dimensional Man: Studies in the Ideology of Advanced Industrial Society*. London: Routledge and Kegan Paul.

Muir, D. (1999) 'Theories and methods in developmental psychology', in A. Slater and D. Muir (eds), *The Blackwell Reader in Developmental Psychology*. Oxford: Blackwell. pp. 3–16.

Nolan, A. and Kilderry, A. (2010) 'Postdevelopmentalism and professional learning: implications for understanding the relationship between play and pedagogy', in E. Brooker and S. Edwards (eds), *Engaging Play*. Maidenhead: Open University Press. pp. 108–121.

Piaget, J. (1953) *The Origin of Intelligence in the Child*. London: Routledge and Kegan Paul.

Piaget, J. (1959) *The Language and Thought of the Child*, 3rd edn. London: Routledge and Kegan Paul.

Ryan, S. and Goffin, S. (2008) 'Missing in action: Teaching in early care and education', *Early Education and Development,* 19 (3): 385–395.

Vygotsky, L.S. (1987) *The Collected Works of Vygotsky: Volume 1: Problems with General Psychology* (trans. Norman Minik). New York: Plenum Press.

Walkerdine, V. (1998) 'Developmental psychology and the child-centred pedagogy: The insertion of Piaget into early education', in J. Henriques, W. Holloway, C. Urwin, C. Venn and V. Walkerdine (eds), *Changing the Subject: Psychology, Social Regulations and Subjectivity* (reissued edn). London: Routledge. pp. 153–202.

Walsh, G., McGuinness, C., Sproule, L. and Trew, K. (2010) 'Implementing a play-based and developmentally appropriate curriculum in Northern Ireland primary schools: What lessons have we learned?', *Early Years*, 30 (1): 53–66.

Zimiles, H. (2000) 'On reassessing the relevance of the child development knowledge base to education', *Human Development*, 43: 235–245.

Want to learn more about this chapter?

Visit the companion website at **https://study.sagepub.com/reedandwalker** to access podcasts from the author and additional reading to further help you with your studies.

Section 3
TAKING A HOLISTIC VIEW

This section is underpinned by a view that is held by the editors and shared by all the contributors to this book. It is that reflection and critical thinking can improve quality; however, quality is only meaningful if it is accessible to all. We therefore argue for a need to see quality as requiring an understanding of issues that reflect critical incidents in children's lives as they move through the education sector as well as dealing with issues that surround disability, health and child protection. They are less reliant on the work of one person and usually take a range of professionals to manage. In practice they require patience, concern for children, specialist training and a positive attitude towards meeting the needs of others: features which certainly apply to Chapter 15 from Erica Brown who considers professional support for families of children with life limiting illness. When you read her chapter consider your emotional response and the need to take a professional and supportive approach to caring for young children with such complex needs. An approach that may seem less apparent is covered within Chapter 12 by Aline Wendy Dunlop who considers the support necessary to respond to the way children make transitions as they move through the education sector. However, both chapters emphasise the need for a careful observational record and developing a proactive response to children's needs. Transitions may well include leaving a parent for the first time and ensuring that any individual or special needs are considered by all concerned in the process. These include physical disability or sensory loss as well as learning disability and the difference a positive and supportive attitude makes to the lives of children. These issues are taken up in Chapter 14 by Caroline Jones where she describes positive practice-based approaches to meet the individual needs of children.

This section also deals with an essential component of work in ECEC and confronts the complex subject of safeguarding the welfare of children. This is addressed in Chapter 13 written by Claire M. Richards who uses her considerable experience to underline the importance of critically appraising our own actions and the actions of others. The first chapter (Chapter 11) by Robin Balbernie deals with another complex issue. It challenges the way we perceive young children become attached to a significant other in their early lives and the importance of understanding what this means as well as challenging some assumptions about how attachment theory is interpreted.

All of the chapters require you to consider issues which we refer to as complex and complicated. They do however explore facets of ECEC which are important and we feel the authors have provided information sensitively so the subject is understood, explanation in terms of how it is seen in practice and a level of interpretation. This allows the position taken by the author to be revealed and explored and shared with the reader. They strive to provide balance and attempt to extend and develop your understanding by developing Critical Learning Activities and further reading.

The chapters share a common theme. They all seek to illustrate and explore the diversity found in young children's lives. They profile the different ways childhood is understood and experienced and encourage us to see the world through the eyes of the child. The chapters encompass modern perspectives about child development which emphasise individualism and the value of the child in society. They provide a collective recognition that all children are valuable in society and that community engagement in shaping early childhood services is essential as safeguarding and understanding the vulnerable child is (Lomas and Johnson, 2012). The chapters also recognise the importance of parenting and the need for the child to form positive relationships with caregivers and have the right to be cared for, given warmth and attention, and protected from harm. A common position which also underlines the chapters in this section is how children are significantly influenced by the social, cultural world within which they reside and the humans with which they form close relationships. These include parents, brothers, sisters, the extended family, friends and the professionals who offer support. All influence how the child views the world and shapes their experience of the world. The chapters reinforce this view and also tell us that we can adopt positions and use strategies that will be part of that influence and shaping of the world. Therefore, what we think and what we do is important. It is not about linking theory to practice as we are part of the theory and an integral part of practice. Finally, the message of this section is to take care of your needs as a professional dealing with potentially emotionally demanding and complex situations.

Returning to our initial thoughts about quality it is clear that the chapters represent issues that reach beyond those we can consider as meeting developmental learning goals. But it is also true that structural tiers such as regulatory requirements to develop inclusive policies and child protection policies and practices provide a vehicle for collaborative planning. We know that quality is enhanced when practitioners collaborate and work together; in particular, when this is within and between core services for children. This process requires the practitioner to demonstrate qualities which allow a positive engagement with parents. The reason for this is clear and the chapters show how theoretical positions which advocate the value of parental professional collaboration can be applied in practice. This is because such contact is reassuring for the child and allows the practitioner to see and sometimes prevent problems because communication is part of establishing trust between parents and practitioners. This does not just mean a desire to be liked or an acceptance of what a parent says or does. On the contrary, it means understanding that children need to form close relationships with their caregivers and parents and that they need to be supported in the life changes they experience.

Recommended related chapters

The chapters in this section are not able to encompass all of the issues and features associated with meeting diverse needs. It is therefore necessary to look within other chapters to consider complementary theoretical positions about social and cultural contexts which influence children's development. For example, the views of Anna Popova in Chapter 7 where she explores Vygotsky's social constructivist theory or the views of Martin Needham and Dianne Jackson in Chapter 18 about collaboration with parents.

References

Lomas, G.I. and Johnson, H.A. (2012) 'Overlooked and unheard: abuse of children who are deaf or hard of hearing and their experience with CPS and foster care', *The Family Journal*, 20 (4): 376–383.

11

Security and attachment

Robin Balbernie

Chapter overview

During the first few years of life a child requires a warm secure relationship (attachment) with a caregiver, which contributes to their emotional well-being and future life chances. For example, parents fall in love with their babies and in so doing securely anchor their children's development in positive relationships. This chapter explores the implications for the child and parent when a secure relationship is less visible. It explains that this may be hard to distinguish from the effects of other adverse life experiences children can face within their early life, and attachment is one indicator of the quality of family life. The chapter therefore cautions against oversimplifying the subject and accepts the difficulty of being professionally aware of all the nuances of attachment behaviour and intervention strategies to support children and families. Nonetheless, it is important to unpick the nature of attachment and raise some important critical issues for discussion within the context of early intervention strategies.

CASE STUDY

Emily is two years old has been attending nursery for the past three months. She is what can be described as 'clingy' with staff and seems to constantly ask to be lifted up, carried and cuddled. She is always hungry even after meals but seems

(Continued)

(Continued)

to be growing according to typical physical developmental norms. She is demanding of adult attention to the detriment of engaging in play with other children alongside them. She has a tendency to want to be close to and in close proximity to adults and sometimes becomes distressed for no obvious reason. She easily cries and is distressed when asked to make transitions between learning and play activities and opportunities provided within the nursery session. When her mother collects her from nursery Emily can change from engagement in an activity to being inconsolable almost instantly, and is still crying when her mother has put her in her car seat. Her mother finds this very hard to deal with and gets upset about Emily's reaction. Her key worker at the nursery (a practitioner with particular responsibility for Emily and a number of other children) has spoken to Emily's parents and learnt that Emily was born very prematurely. She was in intensive care for several weeks and had surgery for a suspected heart condition. Her parents were warned that she might not have lived and consequently her mother describes times she detached her emotions from Emily to prepare for the potential pain of loss while she also became intensely involved in trying to understand the medical aspects of her condition and her care in the Intensive Care facility. It has been difficult for her mother to regain consistent close feelings for Emily as she finds herself watching closely for any sign of a medical emergency and, when describing her day, she realises that she tends to respond to Emily's emotional signals only when they match her anxieties. At the same time she has been finding Emily's constant clingy behaviour difficult to manage and describes this as not allowing her any space to think. This seems to reinforce the feeling of not being easily able to become close to Emily and she feels she is in a cycle of behaviour that she is struggling to change. Emily's father works long hours and finds difficulty arranging time to be with Emily as she is often in bed when he returns home. Weekends are a busy time for him as he is always trying to catch up on paperwork.

As a practitioner you may recognise that Emily and her parents are likely to need ongoing support and attention from the key worker in providing advice about developing and maintaining secure attachment for Emily. It may well be that the nursery has a role in referring the family to a specialist agency as part of their responsibility to the child and family and seeing the issue as best responded to with the support of a multidisciplinary team of professionals.

What issues may underpin Emily's situation? What do we mean by 'attachment'?

Attachment theory was initially developed by Bowlby (1969, 1973, 1981, 1988), a psychoanalyst and child psychiatrist. He began by attempting to unravel the traumatising effects of maternal deprivation by studying the normal course of attachment relationships. His work within a Child Guidance Clinic with what was termed at the time of his original research 'damaged and delinquent children' led him to recognise the crucial importance of early relationships for the later development of the child. Bowlby (1988: 26) defined attachment as 'any form of behaviour that results in a person attaining or maintaining a proximity to some other clearly identified individual, who is conceived as better able to cope with the world'. This nearness to a protective figure is the key to attachment, but in humans who have the ability to be self-reflective this proximity implies an intersubjective overlap between child and parent (Balbernie, 2007), where the closeness powered by the attachment dynamic sculpts the growing mind. From the small child's point of view an attachment figure provides a sense of felt security, while fulfilling the role of a 'safe haven' to return to in times of fear and a 'secure base' that holds the emotional supplies needed to set out and explore the world. The function of attachment behaviour, common to all mammals, is to ensure that the relatively helpless child remains safe by being protected, nurtured and educated by his or her parents. As development proceeds, the automatic pull into the growing child's immediate group ensures that they become dynamically embedded within those significant family relationships that structure both the internal and interpersonal worlds; and after that into their particular society (Small, 1998: 40). Therefore, the quality of a child's early parenting may put the child on a pathway to different destinations. Attachment theory and research into attachment – especially its integration with neuroscience (Hruby et al., 2011) – provide insights into the importance of everyday intimate relationships and how these mediate between universal human biology and individual psychology; the way caregiving relationships influence the structure of the early developing brain and the effects of internalised early experiences on behaviour later on in life (Shonkoff and Phillips, 2000). Such research has added to, and in some cases altered, Bowlby's initial formulations. The practical importance of attachment theory lies in the creation of a common vocabulary and scientific understanding of the patterns of relationships that may affect us all from the beginning to the end of life. It can be used to describe the two-way traffic between the outer world of behaviour and the internal world of feelings, thoughts, attitudes, mental representations and emotional regulation. 'What happens between an infant and her caregiver is vitally important. It is important not only for the way the infant will come to relate to herself and to other people, but also for her developing capacity to think' (Hobson, 2002: 180). This is a point that an early years practitioner needs to consider as they care for the cognitive and emotional development and well-being of a child.

Research

The initial emphasis of attachment research on observed behaviour inspired longitudinal studies where the life path of children has been recorded and studied from before birth to their late twenties and early thirties (e.g. Grossmann et al., 2005.; Sroufe et al., 2005). Following the creation by Ainsworth and colleagues (1978) of a laboratory method for differentiating different patterns of attachment, called the Strange Situation Procedure, attachment behaviour was initially split into three *observable* categories. The Strange Situation is a graded series of separations and reunions between caregiver and toddler with the occasional presence and departure of a stranger. This standardised paradigm demonstrates within a comparatively short period of time how small children expect and accept comfort as well as their preferred strategy for regulating their own emotions, with or without the help of their caregiver, when under mild stress. The majority of children demonstrate secure attachment, to be contrasted with anxious-avoidant, anxious-ambivalent and, a later conceptualisation, disorganised - controlling or disoriented patterns of attachment. (This last category is the most worrying and such children are the least likely to have a well-developed capacity for self-control and most likely to become involved with social care.) The Strange Situation reveals a child's particular stratagem, not a quantified score. The different categories of attachment, once in place, demonstrate how the child has acclimatised to immediate parenting and gained the skills for negotiating their likely future (Hinde and Stevenson-Hinde, 1991; Belsky, 1999).

Table 11.1 summarises the types of attachment and the typical behaviours attached to these. They are a brief snapshot and should be taken as a starting point to further reading and understanding.

Table 11.1 Types of attachment

Type of attachment	Some typical behaviours
Secure attachment	Attachment behaviour is usually only observed if the child is worried and the attachment system should lie dormant until activated by threat. When attachment behaviour has not been switched on children can leave parents and check out their wider environment through investigation, mischief and play. *Secure* children show exploratory, not attachment, behaviour and this is mostly a matter of curiosity and creative play. Security can be experienced in the company of parents or some trusted alternative caregiver.
Insecure attachments 1) Anxious avoidant	*Avoidant* children tend to avoid showing their emotional needs, keeping their distance from adults when distressed. They unconsciously assume that caregivers will reject their advances when they are upset. The parents of avoidant children often go for the 'stiff upper lip' approach with an inability to show sympathy when their child is upset or needy. Such children suppress awareness of their emotional needs, de-activating attachment behaviours. When distressed they do not seek closeness or ask for help, but instead mask worry and fear (which are physiologically present) and engage in self-comforting behaviour that feigns independence. The strategy of switching off, not asking for help, continues in other settings, such as school or peer group. This may then make them further isolated and new caregivers may feel dissatisfied and emotionally withdraw.

Type of attachment	Some typical behaviours
2) Anxious ambivalent or resistant	*Ambivalent* children hyper-activate the attachment system from a fear that the attachment figure(s) may either fail to respond or be over intrusive. They have habituated to caregivers who often worked from their own agenda rather than an accurate appraisal of the child's internal state. They may be responsively tuned in to their child's mind almost by accident, when the state is shared or is one that the parent tends to dwell on, and at other times they are psychologically unavailable or respond more on the basis of their emotional preoccupations than noticing what is really on the child's mind. These children are engulfed by feelings with no way of dealing with them, convinced that if there is to be any connection then they have to set it up and perpetually feel a victim. The same expectations will be pasted onto new relationships, so that they explode with exaggerated need and distress when feeling shaky. This may make any new caregiver feel that they are inadequate in soothing the child, leaving the adult exasperated, exhausted and dreading the next onslaught of demands. The caregiver may occasionally react with the threat of giving up on such a draining and unsatisfying relationship; thus the cycle is reinforced.
3) Disorganised, controlling or disoriented	*Disorganisation* is frequently a marker for some form of maltreatment, where closeness to a caregiver increases fear rather than reducing it. Longitudinal and retrospective studies have linked disorganised attachment to severe mental health problems in adulthood, such as borderline personality disorder (Fonagy et al., 1995), dissociative (multiple personality) disorder (Carlson, 1998; Liotti, 1999), and 'odd, intrusive controlling, or incompetent social behaviours' (Lyons-Ruth and Jacobvitz, 1999: 539). It needs to be taken seriously and an intervention arranged as soon as possible.

In the short term, disorganised attachment is predictive of the development of behavioural problems at preschool and school (Moss et al., 1999). Children may show an aggressive, disruptive behaviour pattern that is associated with disorganisation. Such difficulties may stem from neurobiological impairments of the stress response and the ability to regulate emotion. It has also been found that the rate of disorganised attachment associated with failure to thrive is extremely high (Wood et al., 2000). These children end up in foster or adoptive care, or a therapeutic community, and their unintegrated behaviour may lead to further rejection, the last thing they need. The new parents of such children must be given unlimited appropriate support (Cairns, 2006; Archer and Gordon, 2013). |
| 4) Reactive Attachment Disorder (RAD) | This is relatively rare, found in such extreme cases as early institutionalisation where children have suffered 'grossly pathogenic care' (American Psychiatric Association, 2000). RAD 'is a syndrome characterised by relative failure to develop committed intimate social relationships' (Rutter et al., 2009: 536). However, caution over this diagnosis is necessary, as its definition is controversial and not fully supported by research findings (O'Connor and Zeanah, 2005). It may be viewed as an evolved response to the loss of dedicated parents (Balbernie, 2010) and more an adaptation to disaster than pathology. However, these are unhappy children adrift in the world with no meaningful relationships, and they need all the help available. In the UK this condition may be met in children adopted from foreign orphanages. |

The quality of attachment should be seen as a pointer for family life, *not* as a diagnosis. To mix metaphors, secure attachment is a psychological asset; but it does not confer psychological immunity. The opinion that a child is in danger of developing an insecure attachment is hardly a reason for drastic intervention; and there is a danger that the findings of attachment research can get hijacked in a naïve way and then used to rationalise the unnecessary removal of a child from their primary caregiver – a traumatic experience even when this is an abusive relationship as strength and quality of attachment are not the same. Similarly, both avoidant and ambivalent strategies imply enough comparatively safe consistency for the child to create a useable internal working model that affords some prediction and some closeness. However, the internal working models of relationships and emotional regulation associated with insecure attachment are risk factors that will have an adverse effect on development when combined with other stresses, or outright traumas, that may be encountered in the course of life.

Emotional health from the outside in

A child has a sense of confidence and self-esteem, derived from internal (felt) security, if his parents appreciated how he felt and responded appropriately in a way that communicated a sense of being understood and thus 'held' or 'contained' in a safe way. (In many ways attachment, self-esteem and affect regulation are synonymous; you do not need 'specialists' to measure the former or observe the latter.) The development of secure attachment depends more upon parental attitudes, empathy and self-awareness than any catalogue of 'correct' behaviour. Internal working models of relationships are built upon the general quality of day-to-day emotional contact with all its usual ups and downs.

The foundations of a later secure attachment are laid down by sensitive and appropriately responsive parenting in the first six months of life (Sroufe, 1995). The dance of reciprocity at the beginning of life is one the baby is eager to join once they feel felt by their parents and become held in mind (Emde, 1989). This builds upon Winnicott's (1972: 43) concept of 'holding', the phase of relationship between mother and baby when the ego begins to integrate, which denotes 'the total environmental provision prior to the concept of *living with*'. The newborn will pull the parent in by mimicking facial expressions and even simple hand gestures, and in return the sensitive parent responds *as if* the baby had done this intentionally. These actions are known as proto-conversations based on mutual adoration and have a 'serve and respond' rhythm and structure when they are going well. In effect, an interaction between an adult and a baby includes words, sounds and gestures that attempt to convey meaning before the onset of language.

The connotations that the parent gives to all behaviours shown by their child, derived from their own childhood experiences, will largely determine their responses, and this is especially true for the demands of attachment. They impose a shared meaning and emotional tone within the interactions that will become the child's unconscious internal working model to be passed on down the line.

> The child is likely to be securely attached if *either* the parent's internal working model of relationships is benign, dominated by favourable experiences, *or* if the parent's reflective function is of sufficient quality to forestall the activation of working models based on adverse experiences inappropriate to the current state of the child and caregiver. (Fonagy et al., 1995: 258).

The degree to which infants experience attuned closeness with caregivers matches their subsequent ability to have an undefended awareness of their own and others' internal worlds; but this does not have to be perfect, recognising and sorting a glitch is what counts (Siegel, 2012: 20–23).

Sensitivity and responsiveness alone are not sufficient for secure attachment. A parent can be exquisitely sensitive to their baby's signals but respond in a totally inappropriate way; for example, the parent may shake a baby because crying is unbearable, which produces silences through shock, and then do this increasingly as the baby habituates and so ends up causing neurological trauma. Secure attachment relies upon a process of seeking an appropriate response, recognition of error or mis-attunement when this occurs and then repair, as much as getting it right in the first place. Similarly, a child's growing emotional vocabulary and how it becomes applied to relationships, or used to think about potential actions (i.e. conscious empathy, reflective function or 'mindsight') and be enlisted in the service of self-control, will build upon their parents' capacity to allocate and convey the appropriate words for internal states (Kobak, 1999).

It has been demonstrated that the 'mind-minded' comments made by a child's mother are a better predictor of security of attachment than sensitivity, with 'mind mindedness' defined as the caregiver's capacity to see their child as an individual with a mind, rather than merely as a creature with needs that must be satisfied (Meins et al., 2001: 638). Fonagy (2001: 167) argues that the mother's mental capacity to contain the baby and provide physical care, in a way that 'shows awareness of the child's mental state yet reflect[s] coping' is important. Containing refers to how the caregiver 'if she is receptive to the infant's state of mind and capable of allowing it to be evoked in herself, can process it in such a way that in an identifiable form she can attend to it in the infant' (Britton, 1998: 22). It is the parent's largely unconscious emotional software for acknowledging the minds of others that informs responsiveness and thus quality of attachment. Secure mothers consistently demonstrate more mind-mindedness (Meins et al., 1998). This is a necessary caregiver skill that enables the child to acquire a vocabulary for feelings, another internal resource that correlates with attachment status, whereas 'parents of insecurely attached children are not necessarily intentionally contradicting or attempting to distort children's attachment representations, but rather they are developing patterns of family emotion communication that fail to facilitate children's full understanding of all emotionally charged events' (Leibowitz et al., 2002: 57). A new language gets harder to learn the older you become.

Trauma and treatment

Early intervention holds out the best chance for helping many children, and by considering known risks this can be offered before a baby or toddler has suffered (WAVE

Trust and DfE, 2013). The importance of preventative work in the first years of life not only aims to improve immediate attachment/caregiving experiences but can also modify patterns of family interaction before they become well established. It is quicker, easier and cheaper to bring about therapeutic change when both the family system and the baby's developing neurological system are flexible (Moss et al., 2011). The language of shared emotional understanding is a major component of the relationship between caregiver and child, and it is this, as well as observed interaction, that infant mental health interventions target. However, it is never too late to promote change through the medium of positive relationships; it just takes progressively more effort as neuroplasticity declines.

Resilience and even morality can be traced back to pre-verbal experiences with sensitive, playful, caregivers who were capable of maintaining mutually satisfying reciprocal interactions with their babies (Emde, 1990). Reflective function or mind-mindedness locates the parent in an intersubjective overlap with their baby wherein sensitivity and apposite responsiveness to their infants' signals creates the positive relationship signalled by secure attachment. This has to be transformed into actions and words in order for children to take safety for granted and thus be able to explore the world about and within them. When a child has suffered trauma within relationships then the professional network needs to respond in a similar way, thinking rather than reacting, and in the most serious instances the child may need specialised relationship-based treatment such as psychotherapy. The child who hears and feels emotionally true responses from his or her parents as development proceeds will one day be able to listen and respond appropriately to the distress of others. This is what therapeutic intervention at any age aims to provide and promote.

Conclusion

Attachment theory is an important paradigm that integrates many branches of social and biological science with the insights of psychoanalysis. Every piece of research done under the mantle of attachment theory (even if not planned that way) has a tie into someone's relationships and their capacity to emotionally reflect and respond. This inherent compassionate stem has supported disparate branches of enquiry, from neurobiology to discourse analysis, and will continue to hold them together for the foreseeable future. It is no longer easy to ignore just how important relationships are throughout life, especially during the first few years, and this has implications on both a personal and social level. An attachment perspective on individual development, backed up by data from research, confirms what psychoanalysis has maintained – the events that occur between very young children and their carers in the context of intimate family life can have a lifelong influence.

Critical Learning Activity

Attachment is an essential area of study for those involved in ECEC and appears as a training pre-requisite for early years teachers in the UK and beyond. This chapter has introduced the subject and we now ask that you follow up with further reading and develop a wider view of the subject. In particular, understanding and identifying the development and interactions of children and their relationships with parents/carers. These you will find on the book companion web page, which includes links to an audio presentation by the author and further reading.

Further reading

Ayling, P. and Stringer, B. (2013) 'Supporting carer-child relationship through play: a model for teaching carers how to use play skills to strengthen attachment relationships', *Adoption and Fostering*, 37: 130.

Raby, K.L., Cicchetti, D., Carlson, E.A., Cutuli, J.J., Englund, M.M. and Egeland, B. (2012) 'Genetic and caregiving-based contributions to infant attachment: unique associations with distress reactivity and attachment security', *Psychological Science*, 23: 1016.

References

Ainsworth, M.D., Blehar, M.C., Waters, E. and Walls, S. (1978) *Patterns of Attachment: A Psychological Study of the Strange Situation*. Hillsdale, NJ: Erlbaum.

American Psychiatric Association (2000) *Diagnostic and Statistical Manual of Mental Disorders*, 4th edn. Washington DC: American Psychiatric Association.

Archer, C. and Gordon, C. (2013) *Reparenting the Child Who Hurts*. London: Jessica Kingsley.

Balbernie, R. (2007) 'The move to intersubjectivity: a clinical and conceptual shift of focus', *Journal of Child Psychotherapy*, 33 (3): 308–324.

Balbernie, R. (2010) 'Reactive attachment disorder as an evolutionary adaptation', *Attachment & Human Development,* 12 (3): 256–281.

Belsky, J. (1999) 'Modern evolutionary theory and patterns of attachment' in J. Cassidy and P.R. Shaver (eds), *Handbook of Attachment*. New York: The Guilford Press. pp. 141–161.

Bowlby, J. (1969) *Attachment*. London: The Hogarth Press and the Institute of Psychoanalysis.

Bowlby, J. (1973) *Separation*. London: The Hogarth Press and the Institute of Psychoanalysis.

Bowlby, J. (1981) *Loss*. London: The Hogarth Press and the Institute of Psychoanalysis.

Bowlby, J. (1988) *A Secure Base*. London: Routledge.

Britton, R. (1998) *Belief and Imagination*. London: Routledge.

Cairns, K. (2006) *Attachment, Trauma and Resilience*. London: BAAF.

Carlson, E.A. (1998) 'A prospective longitudinal study of attachment disorganization/disorientation', *Child Development*, 69: 1107–1129.

Emde, R.N. (1989) 'The infant's relationship experience: developmental and affective aspects', in A.J. Sameroff and R.N. Emde (eds), *Relationship Disturbances in Early Childhood*. New York: Basic Books. pp. 33–51.

Emde, R.N. (1990) 'Lessons from infancy: new beginnings in a changing world and a morality for health', *Infant Mental Health Journal*, 11 (2): 196–212.

Fonagy, P. (2001) *Attachment Theory and Psychoanalysis*. New York: Other Press.

Fonagy, P., Steele, M., Steele, H., Leigh, T., Kennedy, R., Mattoon, G. and Target, M. (1995) 'Attachment, the reflective self, and borderline states', in S. Goldberg, R. Muir and J. Kerr (eds), *Attachment Theory: Social, Developmental, and Clinical Perspectives*. Hillsdale NJ: The Analytic Press. pp. 233–278.

Grossmann, K.E., Grossmann, K. and Waters, E. (eds) (2005) *Attachment from Infancy to Adulthood: The Major Longitudinal Studies*. New York: The Guilford Press.

Hinde, R.A. and Stevenson-Hinde, J. (1991) 'Perspectives on attachment', in C.M. Parkes, J. Stevenson-Hinde and P. Marris (eds), *Attachment Across The Life Cycle*. London: Tavistock Publications. pp. 52–65.

Hobson, P. (2002) *The Cradle of Thought: Exploring the Origin of Thinking*. London: Macmillan.

Hruby, R., Hasto, J. and Minarik, P. (2011) 'Attachment in integrative neuroscientific perspective', *Activitas Nervosa Superior Rediviva*, 53 (2): 49–58.

Kobak, R. (1999) 'The emotional dynamics of disruptions in attachment relationships: implications for theory, research, and clinical intervention', in J. Cassidy and P.R. Shaver (eds), *Handbook of Attachment: Theory, Research, and Clinical Applications*. New York: The Guilford Press. pp. 21–43.

Leibowitz, J., Ramos-Marcuse, F. and Arsenio, W.F. (2002) 'Parent-child emotion communication, attachment, and affective narratives', *Attachment & Human Development*, 4 (1): 56–67.

Liotti, G. (1999) 'Disorganization of attachment as a model for understanding dissociative psychopathology', in J. Solomon and C. George (eds), *Attachment Disorganization*. New York: The Guilford Press. pp. 291–317.

Lyons-Ruth, K. and Jacobvitz, D. (1999) 'Attachment disorganization: unresolved loss, relational violence, and lapses in behavioural and attentional strategies', in J. Cassidy and P.R. Shaver (eds), *Handbook of Attachment: Theory, Research and Clinical Applications*. New York: The Guilford Press. pp. 520–554.

Meins, E., Fernyhough, C., Russell, J. and Clark-Carter, D. (1998) 'Security of attachment as a predictor of symbolic and mentalising abilities: a longitudinal study', *Social Development*, 7: 1–24.

Meins, E., Fernyhough, C., Fradley, E. and Tuckey, M. (2001) 'Rethinking maternal sensitivity: mothers' comments on infants' mental processes predict security of attachment at 12 months', *Journal of Child Psychology and Psychiatry*, 42: 637–648.

Moss, E., St-Laurent, D. and Parent, S. (1999) 'Disorganized attachment and developmental risk at school age'. pp. 160–186 in Solomon, J. and George, C. (eds), *Attachment Disorganization*. New York: The Guilford Press.

Moss, E., Dubois-Comtois, K., Cyr, C., Tarabulsy, G.M., St-Laurent, D. and Bernier, A. (2011) 'Efficacy of a home-visiting intervention aimed at improving maternal sensitivity, child attachment, and behavioral outcomes for maltreated children: a randomised control trial', *Development and Psychopathology*, 23: 195–210.

O'Connor, T.G. and Zeanah, C.H. (2005) 'Attachment disorders: assessment strategies and treatment approaches', *Attachment & Human Development*, 5 (3): 223–244.

Rutter, M., Kreppner, J. and Sonpuga-Barke, E. (2009) 'Emmanuel Miller lecture: attachment insecurity, disinhibited attachment, and attachment disorders: where do research findings leave the concepts?', *Journal of Child Psychology and Psychiatry*, 50 (5): 529–543.

Shonkoff, J.P. and Phillips, D.A. (2000) *From Neurons to Neighborhoods: The Science of Early Development*. Washington, DC: National Academy Press.

Siegel, D.J. (2012) *Pocket Guide to Interpersonal Neurobiology: An Integrative Handbook of the Mind*. New York: W. W. Norton & Company Inc.

Small, M.F. (1998) *Our Babies, Ourselves*. New York: Anchor Books.

Sroufe, L.A. (1995) *Emotional Development: The Organization of Emotional Life in the Early Years*. Cambridge: Cambridge University Press.

Sroufe, L.A., Egeland, B., Carlson, E. and Collins, W.A. (2005) *The Development of the Person: The Minnesota Study of Risk and Adaptation from Birth to Adulthood*. New York: The Guilford Press.

WAVE Trust and Department for Education (2013) *Conception to Age 2 – The Age of Opportunity*. Available at: www.wavetrust.org.

Winnicott, D.W. (1972) *The Maturational Process and the Facilitating Environment*. London: The Hogarth Press and the Institute of Psychoanalysis.

Wood, M.J., Lee, S.S. and Lipper, E.G. (2000) 'Failure-to-thrive is associated with disorganized infant–mother attachment and unresolved maternal attachment', *Infant Mental Health Journal*, 21 (6): 428–442.

Want to learn more about this chapter?

Visit the companion website at **https://study.sagepub.com/reedandwalker** to access podcasts from the author and additional reading to further help you with your studies.

12

The developing child in society: making transitions

Aline Wendy Dunlop

Chapter overview

In current early years educational practice there is a greater awareness of children's transitions than ever before. The knowledge base is increasingly well informed by research from a range of perspectives, including those of practitioners and the children and families with whom they work. Transitions studies may be grouped broadly into three paradigms – those that focus mainly on the individual development and readiness of the child for the 'next stage'; those that, on the other hand, look more at early years and early school contexts, systems and structures to find answers to ease transitions; and those that combine to consider development in context with a focus on the interpersonal and socio-cultural, thus creating 'transitions capital' (Dunlop, 2013). This chapter will support early years practitioners to heighten their awareness of the significance of transitions in children's lives, to evaluate their own transition practices and to interpret children's and families' experience through a more critical theoretical lens. It will consider why some children are vulnerable in transition and will propose that transitions can be turned around so they are no longer considered as problematic, but rather as vehicles for change that can equip children well so that they become 'transitions ready'. The chapter finishes with a focus on professional roles and responsibilities in supporting positive transitions for all.

Introduction: change and transition

This introduction aims to heighten awareness of the significance of transitions in young children's lives, ask how transitions may affect and/or be embraced by families and professionals surrounding the child and to show by illustration from relevant research literature how greater knowledge helps and is needed to improve awareness. Mutually embedding research and practice can help in this venture: intersections between children, families, practitioners, settings, evidence, policy and changing practices are shown through reference to an ecological model of transitions.

In contemporary society change can be understood to be part of everyday life, but changes are experienced differently, according to individual circumstances, the way people are positioned in society (Davies and Harré, 1990), how this affects what they do, why they do it and how they may feel (Harré et al., 2009), and through personal attitude to change. Some transitions are very common, such as the transition to parenthood, starting daycare, pre-school or school, undertaking a course of study, starting a new job, experiencing loss and bereavement: each new experience will make its own demands and provide particular opportunities. Increasingly we all manage change, including young children who may experience some or all of family, childcare, pre-school, school, after school, across a given day. Why then, when so many changes occur in daily life, do we describe some changes as transitions?

Change is easier to navigate when those involved are prepared, have confidence and experience or are given relevant support. Young children will benefit from others focusing on the changes happening in their lives: by attending well to such changes, well-being, positive interactions, learning, social opportunities and engagement with others will be developed and sustained. For some time now there has been a growing recognition that attending to change as a process, rather than an event, means thinking of changes, even everyday changes, as transitions that children and their families are moving through rather than one-off happenings. Using the term 'transition' brings a renewed emphasis to this change process.

While there is a healthy development in transitions research and publication (Keinig and Margetts, 2013; Perry et al., 2013), much of this research in recent years has focused on the educational transitions in young children's lives. The broad reach of early childhood services is becoming more integrated and as it does, and to promote this integration, it is essential that transitions research and practices widen to embrace the scope of professional practice and policy ambitions in the early years. For the purposes of this chapter the term 'early years practitioner' includes the diversity of titles given to those working with young children and their families from pre-birth right through to the early years of school, including teacher, educator and pedagogue. A raised profile of publication in this wider field of early childhood transitions and a growing emphasis on the contribution different disciplines can make to improving understanding of what works at times of transition, can only be positive.

A model for thinking about transitions

In order to take account of the transitions that can affect children it is useful to have a model to aid reflection – for many transitions researchers Bronfenbrenner's bio-ecological systems approach (Bronfenbrenner and Ceci, 1994) continues to prove helpful. It is not the only way of considering transitions, but it is a useful and practical approach as it lends itself to seeing the interrelationships between the different influences on child and family experience. We will look at how this approach can be used in practice and make use of my own interpretation of bio-ecological systems in that process.

Research into transitions

In the field of early childhood transitions researchers from across Europe and beyond have written on different aspects of the transition to school: promoting continuity, considering ways to support children through discontinuity, and placing an emphasis on improved relations and collaboration between sectors, sharing of knowledge across the home/early childhood and early childhood/school borders and developing shared approaches: always paying attention to the child in context. Many such researchers lean to an ecological model of transitions as such a model allows for children's development, the influence of the environment and the interrelatedness and interaction of the individual with the environment and with the people that populate the environments through which children, families and practitioners travel.

Bronfenbrenner proposes a bio-ecological systems model (1994) which addresses human development in context over time. This includes the dual analysis of material through looking at the influence of at least two micro-systems and those that populate them upon each other; integrating experiences in an interaction of interrelated elements. Within this ecological systems view it is interesting to embrace the work of others in order to understand early childhood transitions better, for example Corsaro and Molinari (2008) consider the whole of the pre-school experience is a priming for later learning; whereas the anthropologist van Gennep (1960) teaches about rites of passage – a concept that lends itself well to understanding transitions as a process; Campbell Clark (2000) writes of border crossing; and Bourdieu's work in sociology (1990) reminds us of the part played by rites of institution and social capital. In terms of children's daily experience and the challenges for children in functioning in new environments the situated nature of children's learning (Lave and Wenger 1991), their intent to participate (Rogoff et al., 2003) and the importance of learning in companionship (Trevarthen, 2002) have all been argued as important knowledge for participating adults in guiding and supporting children's transitions (Dunlop, 2013).

What ecological systems theory does very well in its many interpretations is straddle development and environmental contexts through bringing these together in an interrelated and dynamic systems approach. Other disciplines too have much to offer, for example anthropology, educational history, pedagogy, psychology and family studies. It can be argued that in order to ensure educationally successful children we also need competent systems (Urban et al., 2011) to ensure continuity and progression of educational, social and emotional experience for children, supported by transition aware professionals.

Figure 12.1 shows these interlocking systems with the child at the centre traversing systems and being influenced by the wider exo- and macro-systems, which in turn influence each other.

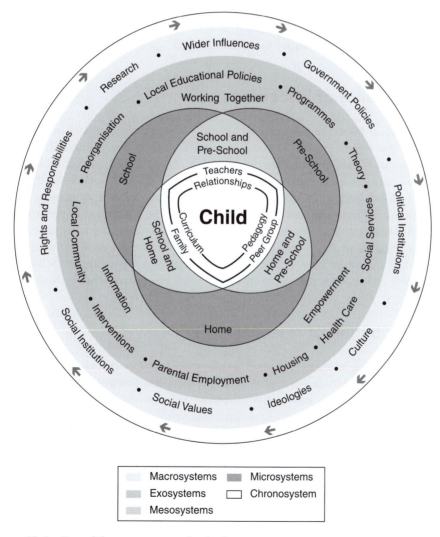

Figure 12.1 Transitions as an ecological system

© Aline Wendy Dunlop, 2012, adapted from Fabian and Dunlop 2002 version

Thinking about models of learning

A 2003 report by BERA focused on pedagogy, curriculum and adult roles, professional development, training and the workforce and promoted 'a proactive and interactive role for practitioners, which was more in tune with the socio-cultural theories of Vygotsky (1978: 15) than with the traditional laissez-faire ideologies of play.' Such a model of learning and teaching led to what has been called a negotiated curriculum – a model which takes account of the voice, interests and curiosities of the child by creating meaning together with others and matching and anticipating possible routes to learning. This continues to resonate as pedagogies of transition are considered. Seeing transitions as a proximal process helps to dilute negative child-deficit models and promote continuous learning across different settings.

The importance of leadership

The relationship between the early childhood sector and the school sector can be affected by the relative status afforded to each. Too often the younger the child the lower the status of the professional appears to be. This makes for unequal relationships between sectors and challenges in working together in the best interests of children. It calls for focused leadership in both sectors if the experiences and learning children have achieved at home and in the prior provision is to be built upon in pre-school and in school. Informed leadership can work towards continuity of teaching, learning, pedagogy, curriculum and relationships. Tied into such discussions is the role the early childhood world might play in leadership of change in early primary schooling by relating early childhood leadership to the early years of primary school (Dunlop, 2008).

The contribution of research

Research has brought about a greater awareness of childhood transitions than ever before. Current research explores a range of perspectives: children, families and practitioners, and is sensitive to new policy initiatives. How accessible are research findings to practitioners? It is possible to find *advice-literature* for all involved in childhood transitions, but to what extent is this backed by research generated knowledge or experience generated research? There are a number of examples of strong links between research findings and practical guidance for families and practitioners – writers such as Fabian (2002) and Dockett and Perry (2006, 2007) make strong connections through a research–practice cycle, and Hartley and colleagues (2012) co-construct understandings of transition locally though researcher- and educator-based enquiry and make recommendations based on real world examples such as using portfolios and developing 'mutually interesting projects' between stages.

Where practice meets local and national policy

The Transition to School Position Statement developed by the international Educational Transitions and Change Research Group (2011: 1) 'reconceptualises transition to school in the context of social justice, human rights (including children's rights), educational reform and ethical agendas'. The strengths of research, policy and practice working together to promote young children's opportunities, expectations, aspirations and entitlements at times of transition drives this statement.

In the same year the Council of the European Union was drawing conclusions on the future direction of Early Childhood Education and Care policy and included the following statement as a measure that could improve equitable access and the quality of provision by:

> Promoting cross-sectoral and integrated approaches to care and education services in order to meet all children's needs – cognitive, social, emotional, psychological and physical – in a holistic way, as well as to ensure close collaboration between the home and ECEC and a smooth transition between the different levels of education. (Council of the European Union, 2011: 5)

In the UK policy initiatives in relation to transition vary from country to country: in Scotland the strongest lever for educational change is the 3–18 curriculum's Early Level 3–6 (Scottish Government, 2007), matched by a rights-based approach to children from pre-birth to three (Scottish Government, 2010) which places an emphasis on the rights of the child, relationships, responsive care and respect. In wider social policy affecting children, *Getting it Right for Every Child* (Scottish Government, 2008) takes a holistic child world view approach. In England and Wales the EPPE study (Sylva et al., 2003) found the beneficial effects of having attended a pre-school between the ages of 3–5 remained evident at age 7, although some outcomes were not as strong as they had been at age 5 when children entered primary school: this trend to quantify the impact on early experience has generated economic models of early childhood provision, but it is not unreasonable to reflect on how the gains afforded by pre-school might be best sustained in the primary school through attention to transitions.

Siraj-Blatchford et al. (2011) help us to understand better how some children succeed against the odds: in considering 'protective' and 'at risk' factors related to the child, the home, and the pre-school and school environment they explore the influence of relationships with peers and friendships as well as relationships external to home and school, while Dockett et al.'s (2011) work on 'Complex Families' encourages us all to take a strengths-based approach: working from what both children and families do well, rather than positioning them in a deficit model based on weaknesses or what they can't do. Siraj-Blatchford et al. (2011) identify that children's motivation, learning dispositions, being seen in a positive light, effective emotional and practical support, encouragement from parents, sensitive, authoritative and interactive practitioners and good relationships with other children who have positive learning dispositions all provide protective factors for school success: these factors translate well in terms of supporting all children in transition.

Part of the responsibility of policymakers is to understand how policy is played out in communities (Press and Skattebol, 2007), while it is the responsibility of practitioners to have vision about the affordances policy offers them and to be aware of how their own local knowledge and experience intersect with what policy may propose.

Transitions themselves can be understood as intersections between prior and new experiences: combining this understanding with the idea of transitions as a process encourages a view of transitions as key opportunities to look again and to understand what is happening for all stakeholders – in this process points of similarity and difference become clearer and as a result spaces for action are opened up. Many authors have highlighted the importance of supporting young children through transitions by ensuring there is enough that is familiar and recognisable in the new situation, and yet avoiding 'more of the same'.

Transitions come in many guises – watching a baby who is strong enough to sit up for the very first time; taking the baby's perspective allows the observant adult the chance to understand this new view of the world, the quest for understanding and the need for encouragement and support that comes with each new physical transition the baby makes. The route from babyhood to school, from within the family to the community and wider culture, from home care to group daycare, from a few close familial relationships to many beyond the family as the child learns and develops – each challenge us to think more deeply about the processes that involve children in transition.

No transition happens in a vacuum: the family, cultural, community and social contexts of transition need to be properly understood: to do so we return to Bronfenbrenner's systems model which also provides context for understanding three paradigms that group transitions research – individual child development and readiness; the pre-school or school context; and development in context. This was Bronfenbrenner's journey and led him to look firmly at human development in context and to understand the mutual interaction and interrelatedness of development and context and the importance of interacting, intersecting systems.

Where the emphasis is on getting children ready for school, in isolation from the school making sure it is ready for the diversity of children in every entry group, the focus is on changing the child. Study of such approaches reveals the success and effectiveness of transition resting on the positioning of the child in terms of personal readiness which quickly labels children as successes or failures in the new system. Study of systems approaches allows us to focus on the nature of early childhood and school systems, curriculum, training of staff, policy influences and structures. Such findings argue for bringing together the knowledge about individuals with the knowledge generated about systems, in ways that inform the development of approaches able to adapt and change in order to respond to differences in children, their experience, their interests and their family cultures. From this we can focus on development in context, ensuring that attention is paid to both.

In the international research group currently studying pedagogies of transition we see strong and informing connections between child, systems, professionals, research, ethical approaches, expectation, entitlement, aspiration – now rather than thinking about school readiness my work is moving towards a concept of 'transitions ready' children. To equip children to make transitions with ease we need to ensure they have positive experiences of transition – that they are supported to bridge into new relationships, can navigate their way in different physical environments, have experienced the different mores and terminologies of a variety of situations, can articulate their prior experience and recognise enough that is familiar in the new environment in order to make use of their own strengths. These ideas work for all of us as we navigate change.

Key aspects of transitions

Outcomes of a longitudinal study of transitions emphasise ideas of professional collaboration, parental engagement and children's agency as key elements to take account of when working on/preparing for transitions/building transitions readiness. These elements have been discussed in more detail elsewhere (Dunlop, 2013). Here, using the lens of critical reflection, it is appropriate to look at professional collaboration across the borders that exist between systems. Early years practitioners need strengths in communication and dialogue, self-knowledge and a thorough knowledge of the new settings their charges will access. They can be mindful of helping children to feel familiar with the environment, encouraging adult:child talk with children, knowing the new setting properly – never using 'when you go the pre-school, reception, primary one you mustn't do that', but rather ensuring the relationships, handing over and following through all build on strengths as children move on (Dunlop, 2011).

Transitions in practice

What then is a 'good' transition and why are some children more vulnerable with change? Before answering that question certain values need to be considered. Consider the value you and your colleagues place on quality, ethical approaches, advocacy, partnership with parents and children's play, and then ask, as the Transitions Position Statement document suggests, what opportunities, aspirations, expectations and entitlements flow from your values base. Ask too how it is for children as they make transitions: try looking at the transition for children settling into your setting through the eye of the child and then think about what you are happy with and what you might want to change and why. For children some of the considerations include feeling familiar or feeling strange; recognising a familiar face or not knowing anyone; getting to know the new situation, environment, people, things they'll find there; understanding the way in which people speak. The 'new' ideally will seem interesting and different: how do you make your setting both interesting and accessible so children know quickly not only what to expect (in behaviour; contribution; taking part) as they make the transition into your setting, but also recognise the familiar?

By getting to know the situations or systems children occupy over the day and week, and what they move onto when they leave your charge, you can help them to build transitions readiness. Professional responsibility means more than adults making decisions, it means co-constructing experience with children through books, social story making together, play situations, practical firsthand experience, using photographs, making visits, taking time to link children who are going on to a new setting together, inviting the new adults in the next setting to visit, preparing parents similarly and knowing what goes on at the next stage yourself.

Conclusion

In reflecting on why we bring emphasis to normative changes by referring to them as transitions, this chapter has proposed that through critical reflection on what is meant by transitions in early childhood it is possible to turn away from seeing transitions as problematic and begin to view them as vehicles to equip children in a supported way to be able to handle change: being transitions-ready is a needed skill in our society where transitions have become part of day-to-day experience.

How we position both children and families at times of transition can be very influential on their subsequent experience. Sometimes children are positioned as the noisy child, the quiet child, the able child, or even 'the perfect daycare child' (Duncan, 2005). Practitioners may identify some children as competent and capable, others as creative and others yet as more vulnerable, slow or needing help. This active construction of children's identity may extend to the family – 'No wonder he's fretful, his mother's always late' when a child is positioned as anxious, the mother positioned as letting him down – rather than reaching out to find out if 'the late mother' needs help, has work issues, or needs extended hours.

As children and families build experiences of successful transitions they have more to draw on to make subsequent transitions into positive opportunities, the dips that may occur are soon dealt with and the process of transition can become much easier and better understood. The building of experience is like having tools to draw upon – I have called this 'transitions capital', but theorising does not stand still and so I have challenged the idea of 'school readiness' which so many writers make the focus of a successful start in school, in that we could argue like Corsaro and Molinari that the whole of life is a preparation for each next stage or phase. In replacing current concepts of school readiness with a concept of 'transitions ready' children and combining this with the growing idea of 'ready' early childhood settings and schools, we can build capacity for the significant transitions children make in terms of relationships, identity, role, status, curriculum, communication, learning and development, and also be ready for families whose child's move to day-care, pre-school or school means they are also in transition.

Critical Learning Activity

Think about your own experience of transitions – how positive are transitions for you? Now consider your workplace transitions practices:

- Arrange to meet with a colleague (if possible someone working in another setting) – compare and contrast your work-based approaches to the transitions children and families make into your settings – what can you learn from each other?
- What do you each see as important in preparing children for transition, in easing children's transitions and in building their capacity to gain positively from transitions in the future (transitions readiness, transitions capital and transitions ease)? The further reading below should help with this activity.

Further reading

Although the following texts have been referred to in this chapter, they appear here as accessible recommendations for further reading.

Dockett, S., Perry, B., Kearney, E., Hampshire, A., Mason, J. and Schmeid, V. (2011) *Facilitating Children's Transition to School from Families with Complex Support Needs*. Available at: www.csu.edu.au/__data/assets/pdf_file/0004/517036/Facilitating-Childrens-Trans-School.pdf (accessed 30 May 2014).

Educational Transitions and Change (ETC) Research Group (2011) *Transition to School: Position Statement*. Albury-Wodonga: Research Institute for Professional Practice, Learning and Education, Charles Stuart University.

Learning and Teaching Scotland (2010) *Preschool to Primary Transitions*. Available at: www.educationscotland.gov.uk/earlyyears/curriculum/transitions.asp (accessed 30 May 2014).

Siraj-Blatchford, I., Mayo, A., Melhuish, E., Taggart, B., Sammons, P. and Sylva, K. (2011) *Performing against the Odds: Developmental Trajectories of Children in the EPPSE 3–16 Study*. Research Report DFE-RR128, Institute of Education. London: Department for Education.

References

British Educational Research Association (BERA) (2003) *Special Interest Group Report on Early Years Research: Pedagogy, Curriculum and Adult Roles, Training and Professionalism*. Available at: www.bera.ac.uk/system/files/beraearlyyearsreview31may03.pdf (accessed 5 August 2013).

Bronfenbrenner, U. and Ceci, S.J. (1994) 'Nature–nurture reconceptualized in developmental perspective: a bioecological model', *Psychological Review*, 101 (4): 568–586.

Bourdieu, P. (1990) *Language and Symbolic Power*. Harvard University Press.

Campbell Clark, S. (2000) 'Work/family border theory: A new theory of work/family balance', *Human Relations*, 53 (6): 747–770.

Corsaro, W.A. and Molinari, L. (2008) 'Policy and practice in Italian children's transition from preschool to elementary school', *Research in Comparative and International Education*, 3 (3): 250–265.

Council of the European Union (2011) *Council Conclusions on Early Childhood Education and Care: Providing all our Children with the Best Start for the World of Tomorrow.* Available at: www.consilium.europa.eu/uedocs/cms_data/docs/pressdata/en/educ/122123.pdf (accessed 21 December 2013).

Davies, B. and Harré, R. (1990) 'Positioning: The discursive production of selves', *Journal for the Theory of Social Behaviour,* 20 (1): 43–63.

Dockett, S. and Perry, B. (2006) *Starting School: A Guide for Educators.* Sydney: Pademelon Press.

Dockett, S. and Perry, B. (2007) *Transitions to School: Perceptions, Experiences and Expectations.* Sydney: University of New South Wales Press.

Dockett, S., Perry, B., Kearney, E., Hampshire, A., Mason, J. and Schmeid, V. (2011) *Facilitating Children's Transition to School from Families with Complex Support Needs.* Available at: www.csu.edu.au/__data/assets/pdf_file/0004/517036/Facilitating-Childrens-Trans-School.pdf (accessed 30 May 2014).

Duncan, J.M. (2005) '"She's always been, what I would think, a perfect day-care child": Constructing the subjectivities of a New Zealand child', *European Early Childhood Education Research Journal,* 13 (2): 51–61.

Dunlop, A.-W. (2008) *A Literature Review on Leadership in the Early Years.* Glasgow: Education Scotland. Available at: www.educationscotland.gov.uk/publications/a/leadershipreview.asp (accessed 5 August 2013).

Dunlop, A.-W. (2011) 'Moving in, on, up and out: successful transitions', in J. Moyles, J. Georgeson and J. Payler, *Beginning Teaching, Beginning Learning: In Early Years and Primary Education,* 4th edn. Maidenhead: Open University McGraw-Hill.

Dunlop, A.-W. (2013) 'Thinking about transitions – one framework or many? Populating the theoretical model over time', in B. Perry, S. Dockett and A. Petriwskyj (eds), *Starting School: Research Policy and Practice.* Netherlands: Springer.

Educational Transitions and Change (ETC) Research Group (2011) *Transition to School: Position Statement.* Albury-Wodonga: Research Institute for Professional Practice, Learning and Education, Charles Stuart University.

Fabian, H. (2002) *Children Starting School: A Guide to Successful Transitions and Transfers for Teachers and Assistants.* Abingdon: David Fulton Publishers.

Fabian, H. and Dunlop, A.W. (eds) (2002) *Transitions in the Early Years.* London: Routledge Falmer.

Hartley, C., Smith, J., Carr, M., Rogers, P. and Peters, S. (2012) *Crossing the Border, A Community Negotiates the Transition from Early Childhood to Primary School.* Wellington: NZCER Press.

Harré, R., Moghaddam, F.M., Pilkerton Cairnie, T., Rothbart, D. and Sabat, S.R. (2009) 'Recent advances in positioning theory', *Theory and Psychology,* 19 (5): 5–31.

Keinig, A. and Margetts, K. (2013) *International Perspectives on Transitions to School: Reconceptualising Beliefs, Policy and Practice.* London: Routledge.

Lave, J. and Wenger, E. (1991) *Situated Learning. Legitimate Peripheral Participation.* Cambridge: Cambridge University Press.

Perry, B., Dockett, S. and Petriwskyj, A. (eds) (2013) *Starting School: Research Policy and Practice.* Netherlands: Springer.

Press, F. and Skattebol, J. (2007) 'Early childhood activism, minor politics and resuscitating vision: a tentative foray into the use of "intersections" to influence early childhood policy', *Contemporary Issues in Early Childhood,* 8 (3): 180–191.

Rogoff, B., Paradise, R., Arauz, R.M., Correa-Chávez, M. and Angelillo, C. (2003) 'Firsthand learning through intent participation', *Annual Review of Psychology,* 54: 175–203.

Scottish Government (2007) *Building the Curriculum 2 – Active Learning in the Early Years 3–6.* Edinburgh: The Scottish Government.

Scottish Government (2008) *Getting it Right for Every Child* (regularly updated). Available at: www.scotland.gov.uk/Topics/People/Young-People/gettingitright (accessed 30 May 2014).

Scottish Government (2010) *Pre-Birth to Three, Supporting our Youngest Children*. Glasgow: Education Scotland.

Siraj-Blatchford, I., Mayo, A., Melhuish, E., Taggart, B., Sammons, P. and Sylva, K. (2011) *Performing against the Odds: Developmental Trajectories of Children in the EPPSE 3–16 Study*. Research Report DFE-RR128, Institute of Education. London: Department for Education.

Sylva, K., Melhuish, E., Simmons, P., Siraj-Blatchford, I., Taggart, B. and Elliot, K. (2003) *The Effective Provision of Pre-School Education (EPPE) Project: Findings from the Pre-school Period, Summary of Findings*. London: Institute of Education, University of London.

Trevarthen, C. (2002) 'Learning in companionship', *Education in the North: The Journal of Scottish Education, New Series,* 10: 16–25.

Urban, M., Vandenbroek, M., Lazzari, A., Peeters, J. and van Laere, K. (2011) *Competence Requirements in Early Childhood Education and Care (CoRe)*. Project report, University of East London/University of Ghent, London and Ghent.

van Gennep, A. (1960) *The Rites of Passage*. London: Routledge and Kegan Paul.

Vygotsky, L.S. (1978) *Mind in Society*. Cambridge: Harvard University Press.

Want to learn more about this chapter?

Visit the companion website at **https://study.sagepub.com/reedandwalker** to access podcasts from the author and additional reading to further help you with your studies.

13

Taking a holistic view: critically examining complex professional issues

Clare M. Richards

Chapter overview

This chapter offers a perspective on the significance of professional assertiveness in the arena of child protection work and its merits within the evolving culture of Early Childhood Education and Care. A particular focus is given to the concept of the 'professional voice' in relation to challenging and difficult discussions between professionals who work with children and their families, when there is a concern about the safety and welfare of a child and where there are differences of opinion about assessed risk and the outcomes for the child. The commitment to promoting the voice of the child as a professional value is deeply embedded within the culture of early years practice; this value arguably has a strong place in the processes of assessment and decision making to protect a child, and in working with vulnerable families and abusive or neglectful parents.

Introduction

The right to be heard is critical in promoting the dignity and integrity of the human rights agenda; the right of the child to be heard is synergised with respect for the adult's right to be heard. If these beliefs are upheld within inter-professional communications, there is promotion of a culture of a shared understanding and value base of working together to safeguard children. Therefore no single agency or professional should have the monopoly of power or control in decision making and there is due regard for the knowledge or expertise of all professionals involved in the child protection process.

'Poor inter-agency communication is a major feature of child protection tragedies' (Davies and Ward, 2012: 132), and this factor is borne out in the UK experience from the evidence of former public inquiries, including the deaths of Victoria Climbié, (Laming, 2003), Peter Connelly (Laming, 2009) and Kyra Ishaq (Radford, 2010).

The twentieth century has seen an insidious promotion and development of the language of the rights of the child, enshrined within the United Nations Convention on the Rights of the Child 1989 which was adopted within UK (England and Wales) domestic law by means of the Children Act 1989. There are undoubtedly tensions among adults, parents and professionals in recognising the attributes of the competent child being involved in decision making which affects them, and to give voice to the child through meaningful engagement and consultation. Lansdown recognises the importance of listening to children and states that:

> respect for the right to be heard, and to exercise rights in accordance with evolving capacities, is integral to the obligation to promote children's best interests. (2011: 153)

She pointed to a concerning observation from evidence that there is a need to challenge the view that adults are always best placed to make decisions and judgements about children's welfare; there is a need to challenge complacency and to question whether all adults are best placed to adequately protect children. I intend to consider this assumption in the context of integrated services and professional communications, as the concept of professional assertiveness in being heard within professional discussion and challenge is perhaps a worthy subject to promote safe and good practice among professionals, especially within Early Childhood Education and Care.

Vive la Démocratie!

I often reflect on what I perceive to be the struggle and drive of the early years profession in being recognised in status, credibility and prestige amongst the municipality of professionals who work with children and families, particularly in the instance of this chapter, the field of child protection. My reflection on this point refers to the early years practitioner as 'a fledgling professional amongst the more established range of professionals' (Richards, 2010: 74) and it may be the case that this struggle will continue until there is a recognised professional body in the UK to advocate and promote the interests of this group, in addition to a Professional Code of Conduct and a salary that is commensurate and reflective of the complexities and importance of quality care for children, and equal to professional comparators involved in working with children and families. It is beyond the scope of the chapter to further discuss these issues, however, it is my intention to raise the issues of the political movement within this culture of early years and the democratisation of childhood and how this may be mirrored within the experiences of the early years practitioners.

Pascal (2003: 11) asserts that 'early childhood is political' and she refers to the potential of early years settings in developing an emancipatory and empowering role in promoting a real change across communities and cultures, in the context of participation and influencing their needs and lives: this begins with empowering children. This early education of children can be significant in removing obstacles of inequality and division and disabling constraints which immobilise and silence those who are excluded and disadvantaged. Participatory politics, as we see in the promotion of the voice of the child by early childhood practitioners, is powerful. Pascal affirms that 'empowered practitioners create empowered children' (2003: 11). But this concept of empowered practitioners is intriguing, perhaps idealised and may be at odds with the real or occasional experiences of practitioners in everyday practice in early childhood settings. Creative and empowering leadership may be stifled by a culture of managerialism (Thompson and Pascal, 2012: 320) at the behest of the scrutiny of legislation, policy and guidance which permeates so much of modern day early years service provision (DfE, 2012). There may be challenges to practitioners as to how to promote the principles of democracy to children while their own voices and experiences of professional participation and inclusion may be disregarded or undermined in multi-agency working.

The interesting perspective of a fly

Let me park this question for now and try to illustrate an appreciation of the likely emotional and rational aspect of professional challenge. If you ever had the occasion to call a waiter to tell him that there was a fly in your soup, you might recall that you were feeling totally justified in doing so. The appearance of the floating fly repelled you and gave you due cause for concern about food hygiene and your health. You perhaps have no qualms in telling the waiter how unacceptable and upsetting this experience has been as a customer, you are calm and confident and there is little doubt about the validity of your grievance. The waiter duly apologises, offers to replace the soup, but you decline and request an appropriate compensation. You depart from the restaurant with a complimentary voucher and you reciprocate, leaving the waiter with a flea in his ear. A brief analysis of this scenario depicts you, the consumer, in a powerful and confident position in articulating your concern and what you expect as an outcome. You have been reasonable and listened but remain uninfluenced by the excuses about being short staffed in the kitchen on a very hot day; you remain clear and assert your rights and are confident about the unacceptability of your experience and response.

If we translate the position of you in the restaurant to the Child Protection Conference described above and if we invite our friend the fly to offer a commentary of what he observes from the wall, it would be interesting to adapt the same confident and assertive position to the interchange between the early years practitioner and the social worker. The practitioner may feel uncomfortable and anxious in the face of professional challenge, but she is sure of her knowledge of the child and his compe-tence and ability to express his needs. Likewise she is sure of her expertise in promoting the needs of the child and the importance of her professional value in articulating their needs. The social worker can listen attentively and re-considers her position in response to the authority and expertise expressed by her early years col-league and has the humility to admit that they perhaps had not given full recognition to the voice of the young child. Indeed, the observant fly on the wall concurs that this is a favourable outcome despite the detected air of tension and slight rise in room temperature and bodily perspirations. The scenario is somewhat simplistic and may not typically represent a range of challenging professional discussions, however, it is important to consider the implications of not communicating information effectively or challenging professional viewpoints, particularly when the consequences of not doing so have significant consequences for the children in our care who may be in need of protection (Laming, 2003).

A perspective of the literature and lessons to be learnt

In the UK there have been many child abuse inquiries, which highlighted persistent themes of inadequate approaches to sharing information about the child; a lack of understanding about accountability and training among agency staff; poor communica-tion between agencies, including an unwillingness to challenge other professionals; and parents or carers who were experienced as hostile and evasive. Lord Laming (2009) has underlined the importance of respectful challenge among professionals and agen-cies, including parents, as an integral aspect of child protection practices. This point is also emphasised by Hingley-Jones and Allain (2011) and Powell and Uppal (2012) who stress the importance of the key messages from Serious Case Reviews following the death or serious abuse or neglect of a child; that agencies and professionals have to communicate and work together more effectively in their assessments and decision making affecting children. Powell and Uppal (2012) make specific reference to the early years practitioner in understanding the significance of their role in contributing to the collective multi-agency response in safeguarding and protecting children.

If we consider the complexities and challenges of working with children and families without the factor of child protection concerns, it is fair to say that there is undoubtedly a mixed bag of emotions to be experienced in terms of the realities of intimacy, fun, frustration, sadness or celebration. The added factor of worry about a child's safety or welfare can bring a flood of fear and anxieties about what to do for the child, the implications for the relationship with the parents or family, fear of get-ting it wrong in terms of sharing information and ultimately that the consequences for the child could be catastrophic. Being emotionally aware and sensitive is a posi-tive attribute of any competent early years practitioner and Hingley-Jones and Allain

(2011: 50) refer to how this alertness of 'human factors' can be 'informative' to child protection work.

It is the essence of these human factors and emotionality that inform and impact upon experiences of professional discussion and challenge that can further impact on the outcomes for a child. The position of Feng et al. (2010: 1484) perhaps is poignant here as they explain that:

> The advantages of working together as a group to protect children include anxiety reduction and a reduced burden of caring, reduced risk of becoming a target of angry family members, and improved quality of care and communication.

The authors highlight the benefits of a commitment to collaborative working within a team and this is perhaps a key element of assurance but not complacency, that team members are mutually supportive and effective in their safeguarding responsibilities. The authors also refer to the concept of 'power struggles' (p. 1484) between professionals as a barrier to effective child protection work, describing experiences of disrespect, arrogance, distrust and reluctance to share information among professional groups. Payne (2000: 143) considers the significance of power within teams and how its misuse can perpetuate experiences of inequality and oppression among staff and service users. He discusses two types of power; the first is political power, which he attributes to the capacity to achieve one's goals or wishes because of an association with organisational and social structures. A particular feature of political power is that its formation is based on coercion and legitimacy and perpetuated by customs and practice as accepted norms. The latter point of legitimacy is worthy of consideration if the concept is applied to the world of inter-agency working. It could be argued that every professional organisation has its own experience of hierarchy and cultures of discipline and control; the experiences of inter-agency power may be 'played out' in the context of the child protection conference where professional disciplines may be recognised in terms of their legitimate authority and professional expertise, with galvanised and unchallenged assumptions as to who in fact is more entitled to have the final say about decisions regarding the child and the process of protection.

Galinsky et al. (2008: 1450) state that 'one of the chief mechanisms of influence in social life is power' and this is the second type of power Payne (2000: 144) presents; that of 'social power'. He alludes to how this power is derived from the conventions and expectations about 'social institutions, social status and organisations' (p.144) and most importantly, a fear of an organisations' power and a subsequent distrust of their potential use of power. This concept may also be translated to the experiences of staff within their organisations of employment; the fear of breaching client confidentiality as opposed to sharing information about a parent who may be neglecting their child. The subject of sharing information is just one example of professional anxieties in child protection work (Powell and Uppal, 2012) and fears of getting it wrong remain an emotional 'hot potato'. Galinsky et al. (2008: 1451) reflect that power can impose on and limit people in their thinking and behaviours, but they also argue that power can be liberating, and reduce the impact of barriers (such as fear) in being more effective as an individual. The authors comment that 'power, it could also be said, is the capacity to be uninfluenced by others'. This point is interesting if we adapt the 'uninfluenced' disposition to the early childhood practitioner. The strength of this self-assurance is admirable, but I do add the cautionary note of the need for a mindfulness of healthy practice which should include the qualities of open-mindedness, humility and the ability to listen meaningfully to others, especially children, in terms of advocating their interests. The merit of the uninfluenced practitioner is when in their advocacy for the child, they are undaunted and uncompromised by the positions of assumed or real power held by other professionals in their communications and professional discussions. This point is conveyed by Payne (2000: 145) as he writes:

> Different kinds of power may be mistaken or misunderstood. For example, someone with expert power may assume that this also gives them high legitimate power. Others may think this too; where people take power, others often allow them to.

The positions of power held by or assumed by individuals in their relationships and communications between colleagues within and beyond their organisations, can be well established and may have a negative impact on others. However, the dynamics and status of powerful positions can be rightfully challenged, or must be challenged, particularly when the welfare of vulnerable children is at stake. Payne's comments may provoke an alternative position to a practitioner; that is to be assertive, to become empowered rather than overpowered and willing to verbalise your professional opinion.

Shoo fly don't bother me!

Here I make a timely return to the position of the fly, whose common experience and response from humans ranges from annoyance to disgust. The fly can be seen as the contaminant, an unwanted factor which alludes to the often quoted 'fly in the ointment' idiom at times of division within teams and organisations when there is conflict and vying for positions of power, authority or simply to be heard. The emotions of professional challenge as mentioned previously are valid in their need for consideration and reflection as to their impact on effectively sound professional inter-agency working. The professional who is assertive may be viewed as powerful, aggressive, expert, at risk of damaging professional relationships, persistent or bothersome. If this is the experience or expectation of professional challenge then perhaps it is understandable how it may be seen as difficult or threatening, and perhaps makes the prospect of discussion unpalatable or prone to procrastination.

Ames' (2008: 1541) commentary on the behaviour of assertive individuals relates to how 'people base their action not only on what they want but on what they expect their behaviour will achieve'. The early childhood practitioner as described in the short narrative above may be seen to exemplify some of these traits of assertive behaviour; she is the 'fly in the ointment' at this child protection conference as she is challenging the probable unanimity of the child protection conference's decision. She is confident in her assertion of her professional opinion of the child's needs and wishes; she is sensitive to the dynamics of political and social power within this professional meeting; she is uninfluenced by the legitimacy of power and expertise held or assumed by others; she is respectful in her challenge and she upholds her professional value in articulating her own professional voice in promoting the child's voice. So it is important to think again about those situations or individuals we might avoid or dislike because of how they behave and how what they have to say causes professional dissonance. Reflect on your own stand on this matter and how you would assert your viewpoint with a colleague, possibly and necessarily, having to be the fly in the ointment.

Professional transactions and enabling professional assertiveness

Davies and Ward (2012) emphasise the two key themes of professional accountability and challenge that have been strongly highlighted in the previously mentioned Laming Reports (2003, 2009); there is specific mention of the promotion of a culture across agencies and professions which is devoid of a blaming approach. The emphasis is more focused on responsiveness, openness and improving the quality of service delivery. However, the experience of professional challenge within professional discussion is undoubtedly coloured by the evocation of emotions that is part of being human, as Fiehler (2002: 98) reflects:

> If different views, opinions and interests meet, if a diversity of opinion, a controversy, or a conflict is present, then for the participants, this is frequently connected with emotions, which manifest themselves in the interaction.

It should be apparent in this chapter that it is difficult to minimise or ignore the significance of emotion, positions of power or powerlessness and the articulation of professional knowledge within the professional challenging discussion. The arena of child protection will bear witness to countless past inter-disciplinary exchanges where the outcomes for the child – the child's voice pronounced through the professional voice speaking on their behalf – goes unheard or is silenced. If we return to the earlier reference to the politicisation of early childhood (Pascal, 2003), there is an urgency to critically consider this meaning in the behaviour of the professional assertive early childhood practitioner. Ames (2008: 1542) describes how the tendency of this behaviour is to 'stand up and speak out for their own interests [the child's] and concerns', the communication of this viewpoint being critical in the assertion of the needs of the child, based on a relationship and knowledge of their life and circumstances. I referred earlier to the early childhood profession as being a fledgling, but I do not suggest a novice position in the context of professionalism or expertise. There is a need perhaps to consider how the early childhood practitioner can claim and profess their expert knowledge about the child as an equal to other professionals, and to be more valued and respected for their opinions within professional discussions.

Cartney (2011: 13) writes about the need to 'name your expert knowledge and know-how' and this I suggest controversially, is an issue where the profession of early childhood (without a professional body or home in the UK) may continue to struggle, if other groups may be seen to be more powerful, expert or deserving of their authority. This position may be reversed if the movement of democracy and more assertive behaviour takes greater hold, and part of this change is how the practitioner conveys their expert knowledge in the inter-professional arena. Laming's (2003) reference to respectful challenge is poignant; the respectful disposition is a positive attribute and a strength in ensuring a positive outcome to a professionally challenging discussion.

Conclusion

This chapter has highlighted some of the key issues to be considered in light of the experiences and prospect of challenging professional discussions in the field of safeguarding and protecting children. When practitioners face the need for professional challenge they may acknowledge their emotions, but have assurance in the legitimacy of their role in advocating for the needs of a child and sharing their professional knowledge of the child. It is important to recognise that this is the assumed professional intention of others at the meeting table, but I am suggesting that there are times when the more expert insight of the early years practitioner and their voice does need to be heard and listened to by others within their own expert roles. This instance of professional challenge should not be seen as an isolated event but as an integral part of the respectful assertive behaviour of the professional being of the practitioner who promotes and listens meaningfully to the voice of the child in its many forms. Nowhere perhaps, does this have greater impact and power than in safeguarding and protecting young children.

Critical Learning Activity

The chapter has focused primarily on the perspective of the early years practitioner asserting their professional voice within the context of inter-professional discussions in safeguarding and protecting children. Please read the chapter again and consider the perspective of the social worker. The social worker has a key role in assessing and managing the safety and welfare of a child, and should benefit from the shared information about the child and their family by other professionals and disciplines.

(Continued)

(Continued)

Reflect on the following questions and discuss your responses with your peers in study and practice.

- Why is child protection work and assessing the needs of children likely to evoke emotions in professionals working with children and their families? How should practitioners manage their emotions without compromising the effectiveness of their role? (See Richards (2012) about the role of professional supervision in supporting staff and safeguarding children in practice.)
- How do you see yourself as being professionally assertive? Consider how your developing knowledge and professional experience can enable you to develop this skill for ongoing practice and developing expertise.
- How do you see the politicisation of early childhood in promoting a more pronounced culture of professional voices in advocating for the needs of children?

Further reading

Brandon, M., Sidebotham, P., Bailey, S., Belderson, P., Hawley, C., Ellis, C. and Megson, M. (2012) *New Learning from Serious Case Reviews: A Two Year Report for 2009–2011*, Research report DFE-RR226. London: Department for Education. The report offers some key messages to a multi-professional audience on the issues to be addressed for improved safeguarding and child protection practice.

Powell, J. and Uppal, E.L. (2012) Safeguarding Babies and Young Children: *A Guide for Early Years Professionals*. Maidenhead: Open University Press. This helpful book for early years practitioners provides a good understanding of the key principles of effective safeguarding practice, in addition to highlighting the necessary skills for professional responses and inter-agency working.

Reed, M. and Canning, N. (2012) *Implementing Quality Improvement and Change in the Early Years*. London: SAGE. This book emphasises the importance of reflective practice and its impact on improving the quality of services for children and their families, with a wide range of pertinent themes to develop students' knowledge and understanding in their professional competence.

References

Ames, D.R. (2008) 'Assertiveness expectancies: how hard people push depends on the consequences they predict', *Journal of Personality and Social Psychology*, 95 (60): 1541–1557.

Cartney, P. (2011) 'Consolidating practice with children and families', in C. Cocker and L. Allain (eds), *Advanced Social Work with Children and Families*. Exeter: Learning Matters. pp. 8–25.

Davies, C. and Ward, H. (2012) *Safeguarding Children across Services: Messages from Research*. London: Jessica Kingsley Publishers.

Department for Education (DfE) (2012) *Development Matters in the Early Years Foundation Stage* (EYFS). London: Department of Education.

Feng, J.Y., Fetzer, S., Chen, Y.W., Yeh, L. and Huang, M.C. (2010) 'Multidisciplinary collaboration reporting child abuse: A grounded study', *International Journal of Nursing Studies*, 47: 1483–1490.

Fiehler, R. (2002) 'How to do emotions with words: emotionality in conversations', in S.R. Fussell (ed.), *The Verbal Communication of Emotions, Interdisciplinary Perspectives*. New Jersey: Lawrence Erlbaum Associates.

Galinsky, A.D., Magee, J.C., Gruenfeld, D.H., Whitson, J.A. and Liljenquist, K.A. (2008) 'Power reduces the press of the situation: implications for creativity, conformity, and dissonance', *Journal of Personality and Social Psychology,* 95 (6): 1450–1466.

Hingley-Jones, H. and Allain, L. (2011) 'Safeguarding children: the complexities of contemporary practice and the importance of working with emotions', in C. Cocker and L. Allain (eds), *Advanced Social Work with Children and Families*. Exeter: Learning Matters. pp. 43–57.

Lansdown, G. (2011) 'Children's welfare and children's rights', in L. O' Dell and S. Leverett (eds), *Working with Children and Young People*. Milton Keynes: Palgrave Macmillan. pp. 143–156.

Laming, Lord (2003) *The Victoria Climbié Inquiry*. London: The Stationery Office.

Laming, Lord (2009) *The Protection of Children in England: A Progress Report*. London: The Stationery Office.

Pascal, C. (2003) 'Effective early learning: an act of practical theory', *European Early Childhood Education Research Journal,* 11 (2): 7–28.

Payne, M. (2000) *Teamwork in Multiprofessional Care*. Basingstoke: Palgrave.

Powell, J. and Uppal, E.L. (2012) *Safeguarding Babies and Young Children: A Guide for Early Years Professionals*. Maidenhead: Open University Press.

Radford, J. (2010) *Serious Case Review. In Respect of the Death of a Child. Case number 14.* Birmingham Safeguarding Children Board. Available at: www.lscbbirminghm.org.uk/downloads (accessed 27 February 2013).

Richards, C.M. (2010) 'Safeguarding children: every child matters so everybody matters!', in M. Reed and N. Canning (eds), *Reflective Practice in the Early Years*. London: SAGE. pp. 69–82.

Richards, C.M. (2012) 'Quality matters because quality protects', in M. Reed and N. Canning (eds), *Implementing Quality Improvement and Change in the Early Years*. London: SAGE. pp. 125–139.

Thompson, N. and Pascal, J. (2012) 'Developing critically reflective practice', *Reflective Practice,* 13 (2): 311–325.

Want to learn more about this chapter?

Visit the companion website at **https://study.sagepub.com/reedandwalker** to access podcasts from the author and additional reading to further help you with your studies.

14

The language of special educational needs: learning from the past to build the future

Caroline Jones

Chapter overview

The aim of this chapter is to illustrate the way that policy, practice, attitudes and actions have changed and are indeed still changing about the way we perceive children's needs. This is done via a critical examination of the changing nature of the language, labels and terms used by professional groups to define and describe children who are perceived as somehow different from the majority of their peers and assigned the label: 'a child with special educational needs'. The chapter draws on the author's autobiographical experiences to illustrate attitudes to inclusion and argues these are not value-neutral but embedded in unique and changing private and public contexts. It situates the current position with regards to inclusion and support for children against a background of social, cultural, historical and political change, and in so doing revisits key historical concepts and highlights shifts in professional and public attitudes. In particular the way special education was seen as the primary response to children with special educational needs (SEN), and the change that had led to 'integration' into mainstream settings. More recently, the drive towards 'inclusion' which accepts the importance of providing a positive learning environment and the way education should be meeting the diverse needs of all children. The author asserts how the gap between political rhetoric and practice is significant as the current definition of SEN has only served to perpetuate inequalities. The chapter argues that any reforms are therefore based on outdated philosophies, definitions and concepts and that there is a need to reshape professional and political thinking by learning from the past.

Introduction

It is widely accepted that schools and early years settings are expected to be inclusive of children described as having special educational needs. Indeed, striving towards inclusive practice is no longer an option for those working with children and young people but is considered a social and professional responsibility. This contemporary perspective has been influenced by various changing, and sometimes competing, ideologies. Over the cycle of a century, values, attitudes and beliefs relating to special educational needs have been influenced by attitudes, language, labels and legislation. Overtly, at least, there appears to have been a shift from a narrow focus on labelling and decisions about where children with additional needs should be educated – including the 'integration' of individual children into existing learning environments – to more radical interpretations that focus on the provision of education that best meets the diverse learning needs of all children regardless of difference. These broader understandings have been encapsulated in the ideology of 'inclusion'. However, as Nutbrown and Clough with Atherton (2013: 4) point out, definitions of inclusion vary from person to person. They suggest:

> Inclusion is not the exclusive property of any one domain, be that political, academic, professional, cultural or otherwise, and how it is defined differs uniquely from person to person. Each version is made up uniquely of a cultural confection of experiences, beliefs, ideologies, hopes, loves, disappointments, passions, fears, of hierarchies of tolerance, thresholds to our empathies and boundaries to our sympathies.

This is an important view, as it tells us inclusion to some extent depends on a person's own values, beliefs and autobiographical or personal heritage. Almost everyone is defined and affected in different ways by their life experiences, with some people facing conflicting insights, beliefs, needs, hopes and voices (Rix, 2003). Indeed, this chapter reflects my own autobiographical experiences which are inextricably linked with public, socio-cultural historical and political changes in childhood, and education and society at national, international and global levels. I shall therefore be revisiting my own professional heritage and using language and educational terms in the chapter which were acceptable, if not appropriate, in their time, and will be seen today as offensive. Please forgive their use, which is purely to underline key points and I hope graphically illustrate historical and social change.

From ESN to SEN: An autobiographical lens

As a child in the early 1960s, attending my local primary school, I do not recall any children who were significantly different from me or the rest of the children in my class. There were no children with physical disabilities or ascribed labels such as 'dyslexia' or 'autism'. Attending a selective secondary girls' school, it is hardly surprising my peers all seemed similar in ability. So, in 1976, aged 18, when I embarked on a Bachelor of Education Degree at University to become a teacher, I was still in total ignorance of children with special educational needs or particular physical or sensory disabilities. I was unaware that 1978 was to be, arguably, the most significant year in the history of 'special educational needs' (SEN) in England and Wales (which I shall say more about later) and the year which shaped the future direction of policy and of my own professional life and personal values. Two events ignited my interest: first, an inspirational visiting speaker Masud Hoghugi, author of *Troubled and Troublesome* (Hoghugi, 1978), talking about his research and experience with children whom he described as 'severely disordered'; second, when engaged in practice placement as a student teacher where a young lad told me his friend, Colin, was going to a school for 'nutters and dumbos'. I was surprised to hear this and intrigued by his description. I found that Colin had a condition known as epilepsy and was transferring to a special school designated for (remember this was 1978) the physically handicapped. As I had never been inside a special school or even met a handicapped person, I arranged to visit this school and two other local special schools; one a residential school for children with severe and complex conditions, which were then described as severely educationally subnormal, abbreviated to ESN, (S); and the other for children described as educationally subnormal (moderate), abbreviated to ESN (M). I immediately felt that these were the children I wanted to teach and, as a consequence, worked as a volunteer in the ESN (S) school and became aware of how 'integration' of children into mainstream – that time called ordinary – schools was developing. I was totally convinced that children were better off in special schools than ordinary schools – a view based on the fact that special schools had more resources, for example sensory rooms and hydrotherapy pools, and also the trained human resources to meet the children's needs. On qualifying in 1980, I took up a teaching post in a hospital school for the 'severely subnormal' (SSN) catering for children described as having severe and complex mental and physical handicaps. Some children were educated on the hospital ward and others resided in the hospital but were taught in the special school located on the hospital site, which had a special room for the 'hyperactive' children. Eventually, the school closed and I moved into a mainstream primary school post as a 'remedial' teacher. This consisted largely of taking the 'bottom' group out of their classes into a tiny glass box-shaped room, usually to hear them read. This principle continued when I joined another school with the difference being the children were now supported at a table in the corridor, but still withdrawn from their 'normal' classes.

By 1994, I became a Special Educational Needs Co-ordinator, abbreviated to SENCO and was responsible for implementing a new *Code of Practice on the Identification and Assessment of Special Educational Needs* (DfEE, 1994). This involved identifying and assessing children with 'special educational needs', and liaising with parents, teachers and other agencies to implement a five-staged graduated model of assessment of the children. I therefore assessed and categorised children as SEN and wrote individual education plans (IEPs). It was about this time that I noticed new official labels were emerging to describe particular conditions with little reference to needs, notably, dyslexia and autism. As a teacher, and by this time a parent, I still believed in the traditional separatist system of 'special' and 'mainstream' schools, but I also supported what was then referred to as 'integration' – the placement of children in mainstream education – wherever possible and if that was what parents wanted. I then opened a home-based nursery and developed a small chain of private nursery provision on mainstream school sites, working with families and agencies to include numerous children who would normally have attended segregated provision. In the early nineties I completed a post-graduate degree in Education and as part of my research developed a case study of a boy with visual impairment, chosen as an example of successful integration. The study concluded that on closer observation, he was actually completely segregated from his teacher and his peers and totally dependent on a classroom assistant who was employed to aid his education. I began to question my beliefs in integration and recognise the gap between political rhetoric and the reality of integration. I progressed to a PhD, spending four years conducting case study research on early identification and assessment of SEN in mainstream schools, using the evolving notion of inclusion as an underpinning theoretical framework. I became aware that the complex interactions between policy, provision and practice were a key influence on the professional language, values and attitudes towards children perceived as having special educational needs and that the term itself was nebulous. In 2001 I took up a part-time post at a leading University lecturing on special educational needs and inclusion and wrote a book *Supporting Inclusion in the Early Years* (Jones, 2004). As an academic I developed a deep level of knowledge, expertise, understanding and commitment to children's rights. I felt that the perpetuation of segregated special schools and specialised educational units attached to mainstream schools was not the way forward and if barriers were removed, an inclusive framework was achievable. Therefore, as we arrived at the new millennium, my views, values and beliefs had changed. I felt that as many children as possible should be educated in local early years provision and primary schools.

In 2006 my first grandson was born. By the age of two it was becoming clear he had some significant communication difficulties. He received some speech therapy and completed the year in a mainstream nursery. Other than expressive language he was making good progress. On entering reception class, he was placed on the SEN register, at Early Years Action, in line with the staged assessment procedures of the revised SEN Code of Practice (DfES, 2001). He was withdrawn from his class and provided with some individualised support but made very little progress and following a review it was agreed that the school could not meet his needs. He was 'diagnosed' with 'severe verbal dyspraxia' and referred, by the school SENCO, to a special language unit in a mainstream school some 10 miles away from his home. I recall the initial feeling of intense disappointment that he was required to leave all his friends and that he would be seen as special because he would go to school by taxi, let alone the issue that he would have a long day for a 4 year-old. However, on visiting the Unit, it was clear, by looking at the other children, the size of the groups and the support available – as well as the way some social access to the mainstream school was arranged – this was a place where he would belong and be given the support he needed. Following a multidisciplinary assessment, he was given a Statement of Special Educational Needs. He has subsequently made good progress, spending more and more time in the mainstream school but still able to access specialist language support. He is thriving in the school which has a clear inclusive culture of supporting each child.

So, what have I learnt? Have my views been refined? I now feel it is not *where* a child is educated, but the *quality* of teaching and learning that determines whether each child is enabled to reach their potential. I am more aware of the complex series of interactions that are in play between 'public' systems and structures and 'private' or personal experiences. Moreover, that individual practitioners are working within a changing context and that current social values, attitudes and beliefs and ultimately practices are inextricably linked with the bigger picture as well as their own professional and personal contexts. My own journey has shown the way political initiatives and educational practice has changed not only in terms of the language we use to describe children with additional needs but in terms of changing attitudes. Inclusive education is now firmly established as the main policy imperative with respect to children who are described as having special educational needs or disabilities. In the last four decades, unprecedented changes appear to have taken place, in relation to the idea of inclusion and inclusive practice. But questions remain. What is the relationship between the idea of 'integration' and its successor, 'inclusion', and how have changes been reflected in policy and practice? Is the phrase 'special educational needs' helpful in promoting positive attitudes to children's differences? If all children are unique then why are some described as 'special'? I suggest these questions are best explored by looking back in order to adopt a reflective and questioning approach to one's own position. Only then is it possible to look forward and develop a shared understanding of what is meant by inclusion, and how inclusive practices can emerge and potential barriers be removed.

The four Ls: Language, labels, legislation and literature

We have moved forward, but the question still remains, is this enough? The literature surrounding SEN is still unclear in terms of its stance on inclusion or integration. A literature review from Winter and O'Raw (2010) outlines the key concepts relating to the principles of inclusive education and descriptors of inclusive education in practice. It suggests that inclusion has many definitions and interpretations. It involves a close examination of what goes on including an examination of societal shifts. In terms of professional development of teachers, a review of peer reviewed articles by Waitoller and Artiles (2013) again revealed no clear definition and suggested that some studies have defined inclusive education as related only to ability differences. Another group defined inclusive education as concerned with changing the curriculum to take into account gender and cultural differences but overlooked ability differences. A third group of studies defined inclusive education as a process of overcoming barriers to participation and learning for all students. In terms of policy formation the work of Pijl and Frissen (2009) provides a review of various academic positions and indicates how we should think carefully about the choices policymakers ask of teachers and parents.

My autobiographical lens identified how a number of formal and informal labels have been assigned in attempting to categorise children perceived as different from the majority of their peers. These labels were least about defining needs and more to do with the type of special school or provision children should attend. A critical question is whether this strategy created a group of children considered as 'ordinary or normal' and another group regarded as 'special or different'. Did a medical model of diagnosis, treatment and cure pervade educational thinking? Were staged models of assessment leading to what provision was available, rather than exploring how needs could be met? Did we just take the initials ESN and replace these with 'enlightened' descriptors such as SEN? Do the new terms have in reality the same meaning, purpose and consequence, or has a fundamental change taken place? Has a century of changing policies and legislation resulted in more inclusive language, labels and attitudes? To answer these questions it is necessary to understand how social, political and educational definitions have changed. When you do this I ask you to consider my paraphrasing of the words written by Rick Warren (2007): children have been the product of the past; they do not have to be the prisoners of it.

The past

Early official reference to dividing children into educational groups can be traced to 1899, when the Elementary Education Act (Defective and Epileptic Children) was passed.

Although there had been some provision in institutions such as 'asylums for idiots' or homes for the 'crippled', the Act heralded the first statutory requirement for local authorities to provide special schools or classes for certain groups of children. It distinguished two clinical categories of children – those who were 'mentally defective' and those who were not.

Definition 1 (Elementary Education Act, 1899)

'Mental defectives' were described as those who:

not being imbecile, and not being merely dull or backward are by reason of mental defect, incapable of receiving proper benefit from instruction in the ordinary public elementary schools, but are not incapable by reason of such defect of receiving benefit from instruction in special classes or schools... (Elementary Education Act, 1899, cited in DES, 1964: 2)

This indicated that some children's needs may not be met in the mainstream school, but these children could still learn if education was provided in a segregated class or school. This requirement for local authorities to make separate provision for certain groups was extended in 1921 to include Blind, Deaf, Defective and Epileptic children. The 'defect' was clearly located within the child, an individual deficit certified by a school medical officer. Here we find the origins of an approach later referred to as the 'medical model', where educational failure or difficulty in learning were viewed as

> a medical problem, belonging to the individual concerned, which needs treating, curing or at least ameliorating. It is fundamental to the philosophy of segregation which separates young children from each other on the basis of their medical diagnoses, and then designs a curriculum which is aimed at 'normalising' the child as far as possible. (Mason, 1992: 223)

Children were commonly classified by measurement of intelligence or an intelligence quotient (IQ) which measured the ratio of the mental age to the chronological age. Labels were assigned to the various scores below the average of 100. Those scoring 85–100 were known as 'retarded', those with an IQ of 85–70 were termed 'dull' (approx 15%), whilst those scoring 70–50 were described as 'feeble-minded' or 'mentally defective' (1.5%), and viewed as the lowest intelligence level that could be educated in a school. Children with IQs of below 50 were deemed ineducable (0.4%).

The next key milestone was the 'Butler Act' or Education Act of 1944 which reaffirmed the duty of local authorities' medical officers to ascertain which children had a 'disability of mind or body' that called for special educational treatment (HMSO 1944, Section 34). It was followed by an attempt to move away from a sharp classification based on deficiency and remove the stigma of being referred to as defective in some way. The Act was coupled with the *Handicapped Pupils and School Health Service Regulations* (1945) which depicted 11 categories of handicap: blind, partially sighted, deaf, partially deaf, delicate, diabetic, educationally subnormal, epileptic, maladjusted, physically handicapped and those with speech defects. The term educationally subnormal was widely welcomed as enlightened compared to mentally defective.

The Act endorsed the view that children had problems due to medical categories of handicap that could be diagnosed, and reinforced the dominance of the medical model, failing to acknowledge that a child's educational needs may stem from external circumstances. Changes stemming directly from government policies combined to create a set of experiences and responses from educational settings and those who work in them. In 1953 ESN pupils were described as,

> those who by reason of limited ability, or other conditions, resulting in educational retardation, require some specialised form of education, wholly or partly in substitution for the education given in ordinary school. (The Ministry of Education (1953) cited in Williams, 1970: 11)

This suggests that children would not necessarily spend the whole of the time in specialist provision, but could be educated for part of the time in an ordinary school environment. Significantly, it refers to 'other conditions', appearing to acknowledge that external factors may have a part to play. Until then, the idea that educational failure may not stem solely from individual deficit but might, in part, be due to interactions between children and their social or educational environment had been muted and largely ignored. Robertson (1950: 2) argues that 'the backward child is partly born, partly made by the conditions under which he is taught', a point developed later in this chapter. This shift in direction to a view that social and environmental factors could contribute to educational failure was later referred to as the 'social model', taking account of the quality of teaching and other external factors rather than the traditional view that special needs emanated solely from within a child.

It was not until the Education Act (Handicapped Children) 1970 that no child was deemed ineducable. This Act abolished the system 'for classifying children suffering from a disability of mind as children unsuitable for education at school' and transferred responsibility for the thousands of children, formerly considered incapable of learning but capable of receiving training, from Health Authorities to Educational Authorities.

Four years on, the late Baroness Thatcher of Kesteven, then Margaret Thatcher, Secretary of State for Education, commissioned a committee to review educational provision for handicapped children and young people in England, Scotland and Wales. This review, chaired by Dame Mary Warnock and commonly referred to as The Warnock Report, was published in 1978 and represented the first official application of the language of social justice to this hitherto marginalised group (DES, 1978). The Report intended to set out a framework for the redirection of traditional systems based on rigid categories to a more responsive and flexible arrangement. Overtly, at least, it represented a radical change and brought SEN into the frontline of education policymaking. The Government's response was the 1981 Education Act which, subject to certain conditions, called for integration wherever possible, but still focused on the child adapting to the mainstream environment rather than adapting the environment to meet a wider range of needs. The Act signalled a shift in thinking from the diagnosis of disability in order to isolate, to the graduated school-based assessment of children on a continuum of need in order to make appropriate provision; local authorities providing for those requiring special educational provision through a statement of special educational needs.

A legal definition of 'special educational needs' was provided:

Education Act 1981

For the purposes of this Act a child has 'special educational needs' if he has a learning difficulty which calls for special educational provision to be made for him.

… a child has a 'learning difficulty' [if]

(a) he has a significantly greater difficulty in learning than the majority of children of his age; or

(b) he has a disability which either prevents or hinders him from making use of educational facilities of a kind generally provided in schools, within the area of the local authority concerned, for children of his age; or

(c) he is under the age of five years and is, or would be if special educational provision were not made for him, likely to fall within paragraph (a) or (b) when over that age.

The 1981 Act, which actually came into force in schools in 1983, called for 'integration' wherever possible, subject to certain conditions. During the late 1980s and 1990s, the issue of integration was beginning to be regarded as related to social and political values rather than being a point of educational debate. Successive changes stemming directly from government policies combined to create a set of experiences and responses from educational settings and those who work in them.

The 1981 Act was replaced by the 1993 Education Act (and later repealed and consolidated into the 1996 Education Act) which introduced the role of the SENCO and called for an SEN Code of Practice. The *Code of Practice on the Identification and Assessment of Special Educational Needs* (1994) retained the definition of SEN from 1981 and referred to eight official categories:

- Learning difficulties;
- Specific learning difficulties;
- Emotional and behavioural difficulties;
- Physical disabilities;
- Sensory impairment/hearing;
- Sensory impairment/visual;
- Speech and language difficulties;
- Medical conditions.

Each of these also incorporated sub-categories, specific learning difficulties (SLD) – for example Dyslexia, Dyspraxia, Dyscalculia and Attention Deficit Disorder with or without hyperactivity (ADD/ADHD), Dysphasia, Speech and Language delay and/or deficit. Riddick (2012) identifies that some labels include disorder, deficit or impairment in the title whereas others do not. She points to the need to monitor the impact of labels on the attitudes of those they come into contact with and on a child's identity, self-efficacy, performance and well-being. A child can end up with a string of labels that 'parcels the child out into separate processes and fails to understand the overarching reasons for their difficulties/differences' (2012: 32). She concludes that labels can have positive, negative and sometimes ambiguous outcomes (Riddick, 2012: 34).

The 1996 Act was later amended by the Special Educational Needs & Disability Act (SENDA) (2001) which reinforced the Government's commitment to the inclusion of children with SEN in mainstream schools (TSO, 2001). A revised version of the Code of Practice came into force, which included a new section on early years education. SEN was grouped into four areas:

- Communication and interaction;
- Cognition and learning;
- Behavioural, emotional and social development;
- Sensory and/or physical. (DfES, 2001: 1.3)

In the last ten years there has subsequently been little change. The first decade of this century was dominated by the *Every Child Matters* agenda (TSO, 2003). The emphasis moved towards attention being focused on how teachers can be enabled to respond to the diverse needs of all pupils rather than focus on special needs. The Office for Standards in Education Children's Services and Skills (Ofsted), who are responsible for the inspection of standards within early years settings and schools in England in 2010 concluded that too many children are labelled as SEN when in fact better quality teaching that caters for a wider range of needs would avoid the need for a label (Ofsted, 2010). The change of government in 2010 resulted in a renewed focus on special educational needs with the publication of the Green Paper *Support and Aspiration: A New Approach to Special Educational Needs and Disability* (DfE, 2012) which set out plans for 'radically reforming' the current system. The implications of the proposals for 'radical change' have been published in a *Draft Revised Code of Practice* (DfE and DH, 2013) which will replace the 2001 Code from 2014. In spite of claiming to be radical the changes listed are in fact limited. The definition of SEN, now over 40 years old, remains virtually unchanged.

(2013 1.8) Revised Draft Code of Practice

A child or young person has SEN 'if they have a learning difficulty or disability which calls for special educational provision to be made for them'.

A child of compulsory school age or a young person has a learning difficulty or disability if they:

(a) have a significantly greater difficulty in learning than the majority of others of the same age; or

(b) have a disability which prevents or hinders them from making use of educational facilities of a kind generally provided for others of the same age in mainstream schools or mainstream post-16 institutions.

A child under compulsory school age has special educational needs if they fall within the definition at (a) or (b) above or would so do if special educational provision was not made for them. (Clause 20, Children and Families Bill: 9)

The definition of disability in the Equality Act (2010) includes children with long term health conditions such as asthma, diabetes, epilepsy and cancer. The Code points out that children and young people with such conditions do not necessarily have SEN, but there is often a significant overlap between disabled children and young people and those with SEN. Children and young people may therefore be covered by both SEN and disability legislation.

Conclusion

This chapter has shown that current policies, practices and attitudes do not occur within a vacuum but are influenced by past events, thoughts and actions. It has highlighted the impact of language, labels and legislation on values and attitudes to difference. It suggests that the current official definition of SEN, like its predecessors, has only served to perpetuate inequalities. Although some progress has been made, the gap between political rhetoric and practice is significant. There is a need for all of those involved in education – politicians, practitioners, teachers, the voluntary sector and the myriad agencies that support children and families – to engage in a critical review of the underlying values and purposes of education. Reed and Walker in the introduction to this book make a case that quality early education is only of quality if it is available to all. I suggest that we need to learn from the past and recognise the right of *all* children to a quality of care and education which enables them to reach their full potential.

Critical Learning Activity

This chapter provides a snapshot of policy and practice from in the main, England, and cannot predict the impact of planned policy changes for other nations. However, it has illustrated how looking back may help to look forward.

- Can you chart the way language, terminology, attitudes and practice has changed within your own nation? Does any of what you have read in this chapter resonate with experiences in your own context?
- Reflect on how the chapter has influenced your values and beliefs in relation to developing quality ECEC.
- Being aware of change is an important part of leading practice. How will you (as part of your own learning and professional development) continue to update yourself professionally about the changing legislative landscape that supports inclusive practice within your own country?

Further reading

European Agency for Development in Special Needs Education (2012) *Special Needs Education Country Data 2012*. Odense, Denmark: European Agency for Development in Special Needs Education. Available from: www.european-agency.org/sites/default/files/sne-country-data-2012_SNE-Country-Data2012.pdf. This report suggests there are 212,990 pupils who have special educational needs and of these 111,390 are educated in settings described as inclusive. Therefore it can be argued progress is being made, but again this tells us little about the quality of what is provided.

Pijl, S.J. and Frissen, P.H.A. (2009) 'What policymakers can do to make education inclusive', *Educational Management Administration & Leadership,* 37 (3): 366–377.

Waitoller, F.R. and Artiles, A.J. (2013) 'A decade of professional development research for inclusive education. A critical review and notes for a research program', *Review of Educational Research*, 83 (3): 319–356.

Warren, R. (2007) *The Purpose Driven Life: What on Earth Am I Here for?* Grand Rapids, MI: Zondervan.

Winter, E. and O'Raw, P. (2010*) Literature Review of the Principles and Practices Relating to Inclusive Education for Children with Special Educational Needs*. ICEP Europe in conjunction with the 2007–2009 NCSE Consultative Forum. Available from: www.ncse.ie/uploads/1/ncse_inclusion.pdf (accessed 29 May 2014).

References

Department of Education and Science (DES) (1964) *Slow Learners at School*, DES Education Pamphlet No 46. London: HMSO.

Department of Education and Science (DES) (1978) *Special Educational Needs Report of the Committee of Enquiry into the Education of Handicapped Children* (The Warnock Report). London: HMSO.

Department for Education (DfE) (2012) *Green Paper, Support and Aspiration: A New Approach to Special Educational Needs and Disability*. London: HMSO.

Department for Education (DfE) and Department of Health (DH) (2013) *Draft Special Educational Needs (SEN) Code of Practice and Regulations*. Available at: https://www.gov.uk/government/consultations/special-educational-needs-sen-code-of-practice-and-regulations (accessed 16 January 2014).

Department for Education and Employment (DfEE) (1994) *Code of Practice on the Identification and Assessment of Special Educational Needs*. London: DfEE.

Department for Education and Skills (DfES) (2001) *Special Educational Needs Code of Practice*. London: DfES.

HMSO (1944) The Education Act. London: HMSO.

Hoghugi, M. (1978) *Troubled and Troublesome, Coping with Severely Disordered Children*. London: Burnett.

Jones, C. (2004) *Supporting Inclusion in the Early Years*. Maidenhead: Open University Press.

Mason, M. (1992) 'The integration alliance: background and manifesto', in T. Booth, V. Swann, M. Masterton and P. Potts (eds), *Policies for Diversity in Education*. London: Routledge.

Nutbrown, C, and Clough, P. with Atherton, F. (2013) *Inclusion in the Early Years*, 2nd edn. London: SAGE.

Ofsted (2010) *The Special Educational Needs and Disability Review*. Available at: www.ofsted.gov.uk/resources/special-educational-needs-and-disability-review (accessed 29 May 2014).

Pijl, S.J. and Frissen, P.H.A. (2009) 'What policymakers can do to make education inclusive', *Educational Management Administration & Leadership,* 37 (3): 366–377.

Riddick, B. (2012) 'Labelling learners with "SEND": the good, the bad and the ugly', in D. Armstrong and G. Squires (eds), *Contemporary Issues in Special Educational Needs.* Maidenhead: Open University Press/McGraw Hill.

Rix, J. (2003) 'A parent's wish list', in M. Nind, J. Rix, K. Sheehy and K. Simmons (eds), *Inclusive Education: Diverse Perspectives in London.* London: David Fulton. p. 74.

Robertson, R.K. (1950) *The Treatment of the Backward Child.* London: Methuen.

The Stationery Office (TSO) (2001) *Special Educational Needs and Disability Act.* London: The Stationery Office.

The Stationery Office (TSO) (2003) *Every Child Matters,* Cm 5860. Norwich: TSO.

Waitoller, F.R. and Artiles, A.J. (2013) 'A decade of professional development research for inclusive education. A critical review and notes for a research program', *Review of Educational Research,* 83 (3): 319–356.

Warren, R. (2007) *The Purpose Driven Life: What on Earth Am I Here for?* Grand Rapids, MI: Zondervan.

Williams, A.A. (1970) *Basic Subjects for the Slow Learner.* London: Methuen.

Winter, E. and O'Raw, P. (2010) *Literature Review of the Principles and Practices relating to Inclusive Education for Children with Special Educational Needs.* ICEP Europe in conjunction with the 2007–2009 NCSE Consultative Forum. Available from: www.ncse.ie/uploads/1/ncse_inclusion.pdf (accessed 29 May 2014).

Want to learn more about this chapter?

Visit the companion website at **https://study.sagepub.com/reedandwalker** to access podcasts from the author and additional reading to further help you with your studies.

15

Supporting children with complex health needs and life-limiting conditions and their families

Erica Brown

Chapter overview

This chapter aims to provide readers with an insight into some of the factors which early years practitioners need to take into account if the holistic needs of children with complex health needs and life-limited and life-threatening conditions and their families are to be met. The discussion acknowledges that family ideals of parenting are challenged from the point of diagnosis through to the child's death. The importance of professional partnerships in achieving child-centred and family-centred care and support is discussed. Children's developmental understanding of death is described together with their emotional responses to their illness. Finally, it is argued that professional competence in caring for this vulnerable group of children is an evolving process, dependent on self-reflection and self-awareness, so that individuals are able to develop the resilience necessary to become partners in the palliative care journey.

Introduction

Amongst the most traumatic events a family can experience is when a child's life is threatened. Children are not supposed to die, but they do. Diagnosis of a life-limiting or life-threatening health condition is a turning point for families; the world will never be the same again. The stated vision in *Better Care: Better Lives* (Department of Health, 2008) was that: 'Every child with a life-limiting or life-threatening condition will have equitable access to high-quality, family centred, sustainable care and support.' National and local governments in the UK have embarked on reforms aimed at improving and integrating health, education and social services for all children and their families. Effective partnership working has been a core principle (HM Treasury and Department for Education and Skills, 2007). End of life care (palliative care) originated around 460BCE in Greek medicine practised by physicians such as Hippocrates. Children's palliative care embraces a philosophy that attends to the holistic needs of the child and their family. Improvements in technology and medicine mean that children with life-threatening or life-limiting conditions are surviving longer (Hewitt-Taylor, 2009) and as a result many children with a diagnosis of a life-limiting or life-threatening condition will access palliative care services for many years.

Children's life-limiting conditions have been described in four main groups (ACT and RCPCH, 2003):

- conditions which are a threat to life because although curative treatment is available it may not be successful in every case, e.g. irreversible organ failure and cancer;
- conditions for which treatment may lengthen life expectancy but for which no cure is known, e.g. muscular dystrophy and cystic fibrosis;
- conditions which are progressive and for which there are no curative options and treatment is palliative, e.g. mucopolysaccharidosis and Batten disease;
- conditions that involve severe neurological disabilities and deterioration may be rapid and unpredictable, e.g. cerebral palsy or brain damage.

Figures for the numbers of children in the UK who have a diagnosis of a life-threatening or life-limiting condition vary enormously. Notwithstanding, a study by Fraser and colleagues (2012) estimated the number of life-limited children in the UK to be approximately 40,000.

Diagnosis

At diagnosis, families enter a world previously unknown to them where parental ideals of nurturing their children are challenged. Research suggests how parents are told affects both the way they adjust and the well-being of their child (Brown, 2007). Gascoigne (1995) purports parents rarely come to terms with the fact that their child will die. Brown (2012) describes parental emotions as:

Disillusionment – parents' hopes for their child's future are shattered;
Aloneness – bonding and relationships may be more difficult for parents to establish with their child;
Inequality – parents' perceived unjustness of the diagnosis may lead to a feeling of inequality in relation to other families;

Insignificance – having a life-limited child may shatter parents' perceptions of rewarding parenthood;

Past orientation – parents may focus on the past and look back on the time before diagnosis as one that was more secure.

The sick child

Children look to their family for support. Typically young children mirror the coping strategies shown by their parents. The rights of children to be involved in decisions made on their behalf have been recognised (UNESCO, 1991; ACT and RCPCH, 2003; Coad et al., 2012). Adults may however wish to protect their child from information about their illness (Lester et al., 2002). However, Brown's study (2007) revealed that children may be very knowledgeable about their illness and, providing they are supported by understanding adults, they are likely to voice preferences about the care they receive.

Children's understanding of death

Because children mature at different rates, their understanding of death may vary. Knowledge comes through experience. Few young children understand the permanence of death, believing that 'dead' means being asleep. They think in literal terms, so euphemisms and metaphors may be confusing.

By about seven years old children begin to understand death as permanent and something that can happen to anyone, including themselves. Therefore, they may show signs of fear. Where families are members of faith communities, children's understanding of what happens after death will reflect the teachings and beliefs of the community.

Some researchers (for example, Brown, 2007) conclude that although children may not have a conceptual understanding of their illness, most are aware that something is physically wrong with their body. Bluebond-Langner (2000) says children who are life-limited have a more mature understanding of death than their healthy peers. First, the child understands they are seriously ill and then they gradually move towards a realisation of acute, chronic and fatal sickness. It is important to recognise, however, that these phases are not clear-cut.

The impact of illness on the child

The impact of life-limiting illness on the everyday life of a child is difficult to evaluate fully. However, they experience a number of events, which are unlikely to be experienced to the same extent by their 'healthy' peer group. These include:

- repeated GP, clinic and hospital visits and possible admission to hospital;
- repeated absences from school;
- long term treatment/palliative care;
- distress and discomfort of medical procedures and possible side-effects of treatment;
- chronic or continual episodes of pain;
- restricted social interaction or social isolation from their peer group.

Infant

Serious illness in the first year of a baby's life may alter the development of the child's self-awareness. Parents usually find this particularly distressing because they are unable to offer the baby reassurance. Where possible, parents should remain the main carers of their child and continue familiar tasks such as bathing and feeding if their child is admitted to hospital.

Toddler

During the toddler stage, the major developmental tasks include gaining a sense of autonomy and self-control, factors that may be severely jeopardised when a small child is very ill. The most frightening aspects of life-limited illness are likely to include separation anxiety and trauma if invasive procedures have to be carried out. Toddlers are likely to be very aware of parental anxiety. They may regress in previously mastered skills including toilet training and speech. Many will withdraw from primary carers and become easily agitated and angry. It is extremely important to maintain familiar routines as far as possible, and to encourage parents to be consistent in their expectations of their child's behaviour.

Early years

In the early years, the major developmental tasks are mastering skills such as walking, talking, toilet training and being separated from primary carers. Many young children are able to think about 'bad' things and they may assume that their illness is a punishment for something they have done wrong.

Typically, children react angrily to the impact of their illness (Brown, 2012). This may include breaking toys, lashing out or biting people, and refusing to co-operate. Because the child's security is derived from routines, it is extremely important to maintain these as far as possible and to be consistent in approaches to behaviour management.

Impact on the family

For many parents, bringing up a child with a complex health condition is a life-long responsibility. Rodriguez and King's (2009) study highlights parents' continuous adjustment throughout the trajectory of the child's illness. Everyone in the family is likely to be affected because the predictability of the family's future is put at risk. Many families have a chaotic lifestyle 'holding on' to the normal routines of life while being aware that their child might have a medical crisis. In spite of this, most families do adapt, but this is dependent on well co-ordinated, easily accessible service provision (Department of Health, 2004).

Family members are interdependent. Therefore, anything that affects one member will affect the family as a whole. Grandparents often have to cope with their own emotional anguish and the grief of their adult child (Brown, 2007). Despite years of parenting experience, there is little that a grandparent can do to make things better. When grandparents are involved, it is not unusual for them to be in almost daily face-to-face contact with at least some members of the life-limited child's family. In some cases grandparents become primary carers (Together for Short Lives, 2012).

Although the sick child is often referred to as 'the victim of illness' (Brown, 2007), brothers and sisters are partners in the same experience. Siblings are likely to experience a unique loss of their own, as they grow up in an environment that may be far from normal. They may feel on the periphery of what is happening. Some may experience a change of role in the family and a change in status, and it is not unusual for them to experience anticipatory grief before their brother or sister dies. The sibling may have been the sick child's closest friend and for young children who have not formed friendships with their peer group, the anticipated loss of their brother or sister means that they will lose the only friend they have (Brown and Arens, 2005).

Research has largely focused on the affect of the child's illness on mothers. Not surprisingly mothers are likely to exhibit higher levels of stress than mothers of healthy children. Fathers' involvement is often overlooked. Affleck and colleagues' (1991) study of parents found that while mothers reported more distress, fathers also experienced acute anguish although they were reluctant to express their distress outwardly.

Adapting to life-limited illness

Strategies families adopt for dealing with any crisis are generally an indicator of how they cope with their child's illness. Most parents will experience:

Numbness – on hearing the news of the child's prognosis. This may be accompanied by feelings of shock, disbelief and denial;

Yearning – for the normality of life before the news was heard which may be accompanied by acute feelings of searching, crying, reminiscing, anger and guilt;

Hopelessness and despair – this may be accompanied by feelings of loneliness, helplessness, depression and anxiety.

Parents need to be encouraged and empowered to develop strategies which are best for them. The challenge for professionals is in helping parents develop tactics which will enable the strategies to work (Contro et al., 2004). Brown (2007) has described some distinct phases in how parents cope:

Crisis phase – pre-diagnosis/diagnosis and coming to terms with the implications of the illness;

Chronic phase – when the family learns to cope with the day-to-day demands of the illness whilst maintaining a sense of 'normality';

End of life phase – where the family adapts to the progression of the illness and the child's eventual death, followed by a period of mourning and adjustment to the loss.

Parents rarely 'come to terms' with their child's inevitable death. Many live their lives hoping that the diagnosis was wrong and it may well be that this hope sustains them.

Families often have to face questions and painful decisions. The importance of assessing children within the context of the family has been well documented (Department of Health, 2004). The ACT Charter (2005) suggests that each child should receive an individual Care Plan which is reviewed at regular intervals and that where possible, the child and the family are active participants in deciding on the Care Plan. Key workers have a pivotal role in meeting holistic family needs (ACT, 2005; DfES, 2005) and negotiating access to a multidisciplinary children's team with knowledge about the whole range of relevant support services.

Professionals are likely to come from a wide range of services and each will have their preferred way of working, organisational structures and professional development programmes. This can result in what Jassal and Sims (2006: 154) term as 'different ideologies, cultures and attitudes'. Furthermore, Taylor (2000) identified that differences may create barriers and inhibit meaningful discussion with families.

Education

All children have a right to education (UNESCO, 1991). However, many parents report that they have to overcome hurdles so their child is able to enjoy equal opportunities. In some cases, barriers are likely to prevent their child realising their full potential (Brown, 2012). Factors which impact on educational opportunities include negative attitudes, lack of staff confidence and skills, and confusion over funding responsibility.

The Disability Discrimination Act 2001 calls for settings to make reasonable adjustments to prevent pupils with special needs (including a child with complex health needs) from being at a disadvantage and improved access to the curriculum. Many early years settings believe themselves to be inclusive, though not all have the skills and resources for effective provision.

Life-limiting illness may interfere with the attainment of normal educational tasks. Eiser (2000) believes restricted social experiences and hospitalisation may interfere with the attainment of normative goals. However, there are very few conclusive research findings concerning the impact of life-limiting illness on children's academic performance.

Ensuring that all children have access to a broad and balanced curriculum relevant to their individual needs is an ongoing challenge. It requires regular review of curriculum content, differentiated teaching approaches, appropriate accommodation, expert management, adequate resources and increased staffing.

Professional challenges

The relationship between professionals and the child's parents has been well documented (Coad and Shaw, 2008; Coad et al., 2014). In order to offer excellent care, professionals need to make sure that the child is able to 'live well' and 'die well' (Together for Short Lives, 2012). There is extensive literature concerning the way in which parents are first given bad news about their child's health (Rodriguez and King, 2009; Brown, 2011). Breaking bad news has been considered one of the most complex and challenging tasks for professionals (Price et al., 2006). Twycross and Wilcock (2001) assert that 'when and how to tell' is central to the process of breaking bad news. Therefore, the need for good communication that prepares parents has been identified as an important aspect of holistic family support (ACT, 2004; Midson and Carter, 2010). It is recommended that written information is used to support face-to-face discussions (ACT, 2004; Department of Health, 2004). Swallow and Jacoby's 2001 study revealed good communication is often the criteria against which families make judgements about the quality of the care they receive. It should be remembered however that cultures differ in the perception of what constitutes appropriate care (Leininger and McFarland, 2002). Although staff training in cultural competence is a recurrent recommendation in the literature (Badger et al., 2009) there is little by way of suggestion as to the components of professional development. Competence is an evolving process that depends on self-reflection, self-awareness and acceptance of differences (Brown, 2007). Many of the resources used for professional training purposes aim to give participants a rudiment of knowledge about religious beliefs and practices and inevitably this is open to relying on stereotypes.

It is easy for families and children to become isolated amidst the complexities of policies and protocols, legal requirements and health and safety regulations. Therefore it is imperative that health agencies, local authorities and early years settings work closely to ensure that children with complex health needs or life-threatening or life-limiting conditions receive the support they need. *Effective collaboration should:*

- Draw on the expertise and knowledge of staff across and within agencies;
- Promote continuity and ensure that all agencies concerned have shared governance and shared 'ownership';

- Ensure that roles and responsibilities are clearly defined;
- Empower parents in their understanding of the entitlement and level of support available to their child.

Although parents and carers have responsibility for their child's health, they are under no obligation in law to tell a setting about their child's medical condition. The setting therefore needs to take a proactive role, asking about the individual needs of children and promoting an ethos where parents feel comfortable to disclose information. Each early years setting should have a policy in place on supporting children with complex health needs. Generally the policy should demonstrate the commitment of the setting towards the inclusion of children with complex health needs, outline staff roles and responsibilities and provide families with information about what they can expect from the setting and what the setting can expect from the family. The policy may be included in the setting's Health and Safety Policy or Inclusion Policy. However it must be in line with the policy of the employer, most usually the local authority.

Although families may share some experiences in common, life-limited and life-threatened children and their families are not a homogenous group. Care needs to be matched to each child and to each family member and care plans need to be reviewed frequently, taking into account every stage of the child's illness trajectory from diagnosis onwards.

Families may encounter a wide range of challenges, including the psycho-social challenges imposed on them by families anticipating their child's death. Caring demands utilising a repertoire of skills and matching them to individual situations.

National and European legislation requires that people receive holistic, culturally appropriate and sensitive care (Brown and White, 2008). How people understand concepts such as 'health' and 'disease' arises from a complex interaction between personal experiences and cultural lifestyles which may include factors such as language, family values and faith (Gatrad and Sheikh, 2002). Phrases such as 'chronic childhood illness', 'disability' and 'palliative care' are likely to be perceived differently. For example, there is no word in the Urdu language to describe cognitive or physical disability (Gatrad and Sheikh, 2002). Gray (2002) recommends that family support workers should share the same language as family members and that written information is used to support face-to-face discussions.

All staff should be culturally sensitive and understand that practices and attitudes are constantly changing as individuals absorb the cultural mores of the communities in which they are living, whilst retaining some of their inherited values, attitudes and practices, a process known as acculturation (Brown and White, 2008). Professionals need skills, confidence and information to find out what each family wants and organisational structures which are sufficiently flexible to enable them to provide it. Families seldom mind if carers ask about what is important to them, as long as the subject is approached in a sensitive and respectful way.

Staff stress

Children and families will be cared for by a wide range of professionals, who themselves need to be supported. The role of caregiving is complex and working with vulnerable people carries risk (Brown, 2011). When professionals are constantly engaged in stressful work, symptoms of cumulative stress may develop. Nash (2011) describes this as 'depletion of the spirit'. People who give care need to receive care. Owen (2000) believes that valuing staff for what they do, and communicating this to them, is likely to act as a buffer against stress, especially where this is in the form of positive feedback and encouragement.

There is no single way to support life-limited children and their families. Yet there are avenues open to all of us. Keep travelling alongside families and listen to the words they use, and be aware of the ways they choose to communicate. Pace yourself and be sensitive to peoples' needs but do not intrude. Care, but do not lose sight of the emotional price which **you** pay for your own commitment. Seek solace, guidance and comfort for yourself. But most importantly, trust the children and the families with whom you work to be your guides.

Critical Learning Activity

This chapter has focused on the impact of a diagnosis of life-limiting or serious illness on a child's and a child's family's well-being. It has argued that family ideals of parenting are challenged and that professionals will need to draw on a shared repertoire of knowledge and skills if they are to help children achieve their right to education.

Read some of the texts cited in the further reading section and critically reflect on how your practice might contribute to meeting individual children's and family needs. Consider how theories of child development and child attachment provide an insight into this vulnerable group of adults and children.

Further reading

Ahmad, W. (2000) *Ethnicity, Disability and Chronic Illness*. Bucks: Oxford University Press.

Baggerly, J. and Abugideiri, S. (2010) 'Grief counselling for Muslim pre-school and elementary school children', *Journal of Multicultural Counselling and Development*, 38 (1): 112–124.

Brown, E. (2009) *Supporting Bereaved Children in the Primary School*. London: Help the Hospices.

Buglass, E. (2010) 'Grief and bereavement theories', *Nursing Standard*, 24 (41): 44–47.

Coad, J. and Houston, R. (2007) *Voices of Children and Young People. Involving Children and Young People in the Decision-making Processes. A Review of the Literature*. London: Action for Sick Children.

Jassal, S. and Sims, J. (2006) 'Working as a team', in A. Goldman, R. Hain and S. Liben (eds), *Oxford Book of Palliative Care for Children*. Oxford: Oxford University Press. pp. 89–91.

McCleod, S. (2009) *Attachment Theory*. Available at: www.simplypsychology.org/attachment (accessed 12 January 2013).
Stroebe, M.S. (2002) 'Paving the way: From early attachment theory to contemporary bereavement research', *Mortality*, 7: 127–138.

References

Affleck, G., Tennen, H. and Rowe, J. (1991) *Infants in Crisis: How Parents Cope with Newborn Intensive Care and its Aftermath*. New York: Springer.

Association for Children's Palliative Care (ACT) (2004) *The Transition Care Pathway. A Framework for the Development of Integrated Multi-Agency Care Pathways for Young People with Life-threatening and Life-limiting Conditions*. ACT: Bristol.

Association for Children's Palliative Care (ACT) (2005) *The ACT Charter*. Bristol: ACT.

Association for Children with Life-threatening or Terminal Conditions and their Families (ACT) and Royal College of Paediatrics and Child Health (RCPCH) (2003) *A Guide to the Development of Children's Palliative Care Services*, 2nd edn. Bristol: ACT and RCPCH.

Badger, F., Pumphrey, R., Clark, L., Clifford, C., Gill, P., Greenfield, S. and Jackson, K. (2009) 'The role of ethnicity in end of life care in the UK: a literature review', *Diversity in Health and Care*, 6 (1): 23–29.

Bluebond-Langner, M. (2000) *In the Shadow of Illness: Parents and Siblings of Chronically Ill Children*. New Jersey: Princetown University Press.

Brown, E. (2007) *Supporting the Child and the Family in Paediatric Palliative Care*. London: Jessica Kingsley.

Brown, E. (2011) *Life Changes – Loss, Change and Bereavement for Children Aged 5–11 Years*. Manchester: Lions/Tacade.

Brown, E. and Arens, G. (2005) *Siblings Project – Listening to Brothers and Sisters*. Birmingham: Acorns Children's Hospice Trust.

Brown, E. and White, K. (2008) 'The transition from paediatric palliative care to adult services', in E. Brown, R. Gatrad and A. Sheikh, *Palliative Care for South Asians: Muslims, Hindus and Sikhs*. London: Quay Books. pp. 131–145.

Coad, J. and Shaw, K. (2008) 'Is children's choice in health care rhetoric or reality? A scoping review', *Journal of Advanced Nursing*, 64 (4): 318–327.

Coad, J., Patel, R. and Murray, S. (2014) 'Communication barriers for palliative staff first disclosing diagnosis to children and their families: a literature review', *Death Studies*, 38 (1–5): 302–7.

Coad, J., Houston, R., Widdas, D. and Brown, E. (2012) 'Giving children a voice on making decisions on care and services: how involved are children and young people receiving palliative or end of life care?' *International Journal of Palliative Nursing*.

Contro, N., Larson, J., Schofield, S., Sourkes, B. and Cohen, H. (2004) 'Hospital staff and family perspectives regarding quality of pediatric palliative care', *Pediatrics*, 114 (5): 1248–1252.

Department for Education and Skills (DfES) (2005) *Professional Guidance for Children with Additional Needs*. London: Department for Education and Skills.

Department of Health (2004) *National Service Framework for Children, Young People and Maternity Services*. London: Department of Health.

Department of Health (2008) *Better Care: Better Lives – Improving Outcomes and Experiences for Children, Young People and their Families Living with Life-limiting and Life-threatening Conditions*. London: Department of Health.

Eiser, C. (2000) 'The psychological impact of chronic illness on children's development', in A. Closs (ed.), *The Education of Children with Medical Conditions*. London: David Fulton.

Fraser, L.K., Miller, M., Hain, R., Norman, P., Aldridge, J., McKinney, P.A. and Parslow, R.C. (2012) 'Rising national prevalence of life-limiting conditions in children in England', *Pediatrics*, 129 (4): e923–e929.

Gascoigne, E. (1995) *Working with Parents as Partners in SEN: Home and School – A Working Alliance*. London: David Fulton.

Gatrad, R. and Sheikh, A. (2002) 'Palliative care for Muslims and issues after death', *International Journal of Palliative Nursing*, 8 (12): 594–597.

Gray, T. (2002) 'Working with families in Tower Hamlets: an evaluation of the Family Welfare Association's Family Support Services', *Health and Social Care in the Community*, 10: 112–122.

Hewitt-Taylor, J. (2009) 'Children with complex continuing health needs and access to facilities', *Nursing Standard*, 23 (31): 35–41.

HM Treasury and Department for Education and Skills (2007) *Aiming High for Disabled Children*. London: HM Treasury and Department for Education and Skills.

Jassal, S. and Sims, J. (2006) 'Working as a team', in A. Goldman, R. Hain and S. Liben (eds), *Oxford Textbook of Palliative Care for Children*. Oxford: Oxford University Press. p. 518.

Leininger, M. and McFarland, M. (2002) *Trans-cultural Nursing: Concepts, Theories, Research and Practice*, 3rd edn. New York: McGraw Hill.

Lester, P., Chesney, M. and Cooke, M. (2002) 'Diagnostic disclosure to HIV infected children', *Journal of Child Psychology and Psychiatry*, 7 (1): 85–99.

Midson, R. and Carter, B. (2010) 'Addressing end of life care issues in a tertiary treatment centre: lessons learned from surveying parents' experiences', *Journal of Child Healthcare*, 14(1): 52–66.

Nash, P. (2011) *Supporting Dying Children and their Families: A Handbook for Christian Ministry*. London: SPCK.

Owen, R. (2000) 'Relieving stress in palliative care staff', *Palliative Care Today*, 9 (1): 4–5.

Price, J., McNeilly, P. and Surgenor, M. (2006) 'Breaking bad news to parents: the children's nurse's role', *International Journal of Palliative Nursing*, 12 (3): 115–20.

Rodriguez, A. and King, N. (2009) 'The lived experience of parenting a child with a life-limiting condition: a focus on the mental health realm', *Palliative Support Care*, 7 (1): 7–12.

Swallow, V. and Jacoby, A. (2001) 'Mothers' evolving relationships with doctors and nurses during the chronic childhood illness trajectory', *Journal of Advanced Nursing*, 36 (6): 755–764.

Taylor, C. (2000) 'The partnership myth? Examining current options', *Journal of Child Health Care*, 2 (2): 72–75.

Together for Short Lives (2012) *The BIG Study. Together for Short Lives*. Available at: www.togetherforshortlives.org.uk (accessed 10 January 2013).

Twycross, A. and Wilcock, A. (2001) *Symptom Management in Advanced Cancer*. Abingdon: Radcliffe Medical Press.

UNESCO (1991) *United Nations Convention on the Rights of the Child*. Geneva: UNESCO.

Want to learn more about this chapter?

Visit the companion website at **https://study.sagepub.com/reedandwalker** to access podcasts from the author and additional reading to further help you with your studies.

Section 4
POLICY AND PRACTICE

This section is intended to draw attention to the significant impact parents and professionals have in promoting and supporting children's learning. The chapters from Martin Needham and Diane Jackson, and Jo Bleach illustrate the way there has been a seminal shift in thinking away from perceiving parents as the recipients of professional knowledge towards a desire to engage in a purposeful collaborative way of working with parents. Their chapters place the parent and child at the centre of what we do as professionals. This point is forcefully made in other chapters which explore the influences that have fuelled a challenging debate about what constitutes an effective early education curriculum. For example, the chapters from Siân Wyn Siencyn, Derval Carey-Jenkins and Sandra Hesterman illustrate the way to carefully examine national policy with regard to the curriculum as well as the need to critically appraise approaches to learning and what values underpin the debate on what actually constitutes an ECEC curriculum. In particular, whether we engage with a learning approach which emphasises developmental outcomes for children's education and well-being, or an approach which views the different social and cultural contexts the child inhabits as being of prime importance. Of course, making such a statement can oversimplify the issues involved and this is used only for illustrative purposes. We also recognise the chapters are unable to expose every debate. However, we do feel they will enhance your studies and direct you towards wider learning.

The chapters also illustrate a contemporary feature of educational debate about ECEC. This was touched upon in the introduction to the book when the editors discussed what is meant by quality ECEC provision. An important point about determining quality is to decide whether spending considerable time developing quality actually means there is an impact on the well-being of children and families. Therefore, when we consider policy formation, leadership, curriculum design and working with parents we must also consider how these can reinforce positive impacts on children's learning and development. We suggest there is a need to think beyond curriculum debates (though there is a distinct need to understand what this means) and need for a deeper consideration of individual and local approaches. This point is reinforced in the chapter by Derval Carey-Jenkins who asks us to look carefully at whose curriculum we are describing when we consider the needs of children and by Sandra Hesterman who examines the needs of a particular region in one continent and asks if it is possible to design and deliver policy without carefully examining training, attitudes and the process of implementation. Likewise there is a need to carefully examine how and why practitioners collaborate with parents and the impact this can have on children's lives.

In practice this means practitioners understanding and actively participating in the design and implementation of the curriculum and considering how leadership strengthens any potential impact upon practice. This includes what has already been explored in Section 3 which considered inter-professional collaboration and the professional responsibility of practitioners today. As they do this they will form communities of practice (Wenger, 1998). This is seen when they work and collaborate with others and see themselves finding collective solutions, raising questions and developing their own independent learning and leadership styles. They will be representing what LaRocco and Bruns (2013: 33) see as typifying authentic leadership – exercising influence to reach shared goals, engaging in continuous learning, building and forging relationships, and modelling behaviour they want others to display. They are doing what Ebbeck and Waniganayake (2003) argue is learning from advances in theory and research across disciplines. They also need to look closely at the leadership approaches suggested within a detailed paper exploring an investigation of early childhood leadership by Aubrey and colleagues (2013) which we recommend that you read and is available on the companion website to this book (https://study.sagepub.com/reedandwalker).

Therefore, ask yourself: is leadership a construct that means those in charge tell and others follow or is leadership a professional responsibility that involves influencing others by having a clear understanding of wide ranging issues associated with ECEC? It is probably becoming obvious that we see leadership as influential (McDowall Clark and Baylis, 2012) and also as 'leading through inquiry'. This means developing interrogative skills in practice that have purpose and are broadly similar to those articulated in the introduction to Section 1 in this book when considering a positive engagement when on practice placement as a student. There is more about this in the introduction to Section 5 and the chapters by Carla Solvason and Mike Gasper.

We conclude the introduction to this section by again suggesting how the chapters do not 'stand-alone' – there are important interconnected features between chapters and this sections. They all underpin the value of developing quality provision which involves understanding what constitutes quality, the importance of understanding 'impact', the importance of policy design and the need for policies to be made real in practice by ECEC leaders. Indeed, we see being a purposeful leader as emerging through enhanced knowledge and practice. Therefore, mid-way through this book we ask you to look forward and back to reflect upon these points (below) about leadership and ask is it something which can easily be taught, or is it an integral part of being a professional? Leading practice means understanding not only what leadership looks like, but what quality looks like, and its impact on children and families. Remember:

- understanding what quality looks like is an integral part of leading practice;
- the ability to engage in reflective practice is an important facet of leadership;
- developing a clear purpose and direction and clearly conveying this to others is an essential part of being a leader;
- understanding the value of engaging in an ongoing debate about the way we perceive child development is another ingredient of leadership;
- valuing diversity in all its forms is an essential component of leading and managing practice;
- the need to critically examine how children learn and what influences the curriculum they follow is of central importance to a leader;
- understanding, valuing and implementing policies and practice that supports parental collaboration is an important facet of leadership;
- Developing quality experiences for children and families is underpinned by the knowledge, skills and practice of the leader.

Considering these points may prompt you to consider the important interrelationship and interconnectedness between knowledge, skills and understanding when implementing major policy decisions and having to critically examine and carefully consider how to implement curriculum design.

References

Aubrey, C., Godfrey, R., and Harris, A. (2013) 'How do they manage? An investigation of early childhood leadership', *Educational Management Administration Leadership*, 41 (1): 5–29.

Ebbeck, M. and Waniganayake, M. (2003) *Early Childhood Professionals: Leading Today and Tomorrow*. Sydney: MacLennan and Petty.

LaRocco, D. and Bruns, D. (2013) 'It's not the "what", it's the "how": four key behaviors for authentic leadership in early intervention', *Young Exceptional Children*, 16: 33.

McDowall Clark, R. and Baylis, S. (2012) '"Go softly ...": the reality of "leading practice" in early years settings', in M.Reed and N. Canning (eds), *Implementing Quality Improvement and Change in the Early Years*. London: Sage.

Wenger, E. (1998) *Communities of Practice: Learning, Meaning and Identity*. Cambridge: Cambridge University Press.

16

Whose curriculum is it anyway?

Derval Carey-Jenkins

Chapter overview

This chapter explores the way it is possible to look critically at the design and development of the curriculum. It is intended to stimulate arguments and in turn prompt questions rather than simply attempting to form easy solutions. It is based on the premise that examining our own experiences as practitioners and learners may help us to uncover our most deeply embedded allegiances and motivations as teachers and also challenge assumptions (Brookfield, 1995). It explores the multiple factors that can inform the design and development of early years curriculum frameworks but it does not intend to define what the curriculum should contain or the way children should be educated, encouraged to learn or observed in practice. These are aspects which are developed in other chapters in this book and you will find that each nation has their own well developed views on what should be included in terms of curriculum content. Instead, it concentrates on the way the curriculum is forged and influenced by a multiplicity of features – some are easily visible such as specific goals or targets and an emphasis on literacy or mathematical learning. Others are less visible features such as political ideology, personal values and belief systems. It requires, therefore, a need to view the way the curriculum should be influenced by considering the views of all involved in the learning process including the perspective of parents and the child. In doing so, the chapter offers a model through which a practitioner can explore and interrogate the way the curriculum they teach on a day-to-day basis has been shaped and influenced and asks the question – whose curriculum is it anyway?

Introduction

I lead a University Primary Post Graduate Certificate in Education course and have to ensure that programmes are designed so that trainees are equipped to meet the professional teaching standards (DfE, 2012a). These standards require dedication, enthusiasm and a thorough knowledge of early education. They also require reflection and the ability to challenge perceptions and develop an understanding of the complexities involved in deciding upon what is taught and how it is taught. In effect a clear understanding of the nature and purpose of curriculum. Practitioners need an understanding that the curriculum is not fixed; it shifts, moves, and takes shape according to a range of factors, for example the increased politicisation of education policy and practice. Prior to 1996 there was little political intervention with regard to early years education. However in order to reflect changes that were taking place in primary education, particularly defined by an intensification of standards, targets, inspection regimes and a results driven culture, the government introduced a framework for an early years curriculum: *Desirable Outcomes for Children's Learning on Entering Compulsory Education* (SCAA, 1996). This framework focused on specific and measurable goals that children were expected to achieve. Subsequent changes to early years provision have continued to focus on measureable outcomes linked to an even more performance, target driven, 'schoolification' of provision, most recently demonstrated by the revised Early Years Foundation stage (DfE, 2012b). Therefore, it is important for trainee practitioners and indeed more established practitioners, not only to understand the historical and political impact of this on curriculum provision but to challenge and critically examine it in light of what we, as early years practitioners, know is an educationally and pedagogically sound basis for early years learning. So, for example, we need to ask ourselves: What are the factors that are influencing such change? Are these based upon sound academic thinking and research? To what extent have professionals and parents been consulted and has there been a careful evaluation of what has gone before? What can we learn from our national and international colleagues who are leading the way in early years practice, for example in Australia and Scandinavia? All are questions which may well contain sound and valid prescriptions for change, but there are additional questions we should be asking to perhaps identify a more sophisticated range of factors.

I suggest we start with two, the first of which is perhaps obvious. It is to ask if any proposed or active curriculum is rooted in and informed by key theoretical principles and values with the child at the centre of the learning process. To ensure a balanced view can be achieved, it is important to consider and arrive at some consensus around what constitutes a high quality and appropriate early years curriculum. Therefore it may be useful to consider some important factors. These might be considered as *non-negotiables*. The use of this terminology might be seen as potentially closing down the opportunity for criticality and creativity but for the purpose of the chapter, it is intended to promote discussion and challenge thinking.

These important factors should focus on principles and values that underpin high quality practice.

- the role of the adult in scaffolding learning;
- the emphasis on children's active engagement;
- the emphasis on the social environment;
- the importance of what is present in the curriculum setting;
- partnership with parents.

If we believe that early childhood education is the foundation for future success, continued and lifelong learning, then we need an effective and appropriate early years curriculum that creates equity for all and recognises the distinctive needs of younger learners. Both here, in the United States and across the globe there has been significant research into effective early learning and best practice including the Effective Provision of Pre-school Education (EPPE) (Sylva et al., 2010), the Effective Pre-school Curricula and Teaching Strategies (Klein and Knitzer, 2006) and the Starting Strong project (OECD, 2001, 2006).

Klein and Knitzer's (2006) main research focus was lessons from research and practice about the role of intentional curriculum and professional development and support for teachers in closing the achievement gap in early literacy and mathematics for low-income pre-school-age children in Columbia. The report identified key features of an effective early years curriculum. It should be:

- Fluid;
- Responsive;
- Meaningful;
- Research informed;
- Contextualised;

and

- Recognise the impact of home in the early years;
- Identify the societal and community barriers that may/do exist.

Sylva and colleagues (2010) identified key elements of effective pedagogy in the early years that were consistently observed in good practice settings including: instructional techniques and strategies and most importantly sustained, shared thinking. High quality settings enable learning to take place and provide a learning environment that demands an interactive process between teacher and learner.

Klein and Knitzer (2006:14) offer a different perspective but again recognise key features that can define high quality, effective early years practice.

> ## Characteristics of a high quality intentional curriculum
>
> - Research-based;
> - Emphasises teachers actively engaging with children;
> - Includes attention to social and regulatory skills;
> - Is responsive to cultural diversity and English language learners;
> - Is not teacher-proof;
> - Requires new ways to measure classroom quality, teacher effectiveness and student progress.

There is no shortage of wider reading in this area and further examples of this are recommended at the end of the chapter. What is critical, however, is that practitioners consider and reflect critically on these *non-negotiables,* challenge and consider them in light of the actuality of what happens in early years settings in terms of the received curriculum.

The second question is then how does the practitioner engage in reflective practice which supports the practitioner in developing and deepening professional practice (Gibbs, 1988; Kolb, 1984; Rolfe et al., 2001)? (Please see Chapter 2 for a deeper discussion of reflective practice.)

If practitioners now consider that there are two very important key questions that influence the curriculum – one relating to how the curriculum is designed, i.e. its content and theoretical base, the other relating to practitioners' capacity to reflect, challenge and consider how the curriculum designed is driven by the chapter title, i.e. whose curriculum is it anyway?

Both are critically reflective and through engaging with the process of reflection other questions may well be adduced through the evidence presented. Importantly, both are also related; each can be interrogated separately but in order to develop a balanced view we should not accept a 'received' content-based curriculum without challenging and considering what factors have influenced its content.

To enable the practitioner to critically respond to the questions raised, a toolkit model is proposed. This toolkit will allow the practitioner to systematically unpack, distil and contextualise a variety of learning perspectives. The 'tools' will enhance and direct reflection. One such tool is the use of four critical lenses (Brookfield, 1995) through which we view and reflect upon our practice, which as we look through them may change our perspective or view of the world and this is not a safe process. Indeed, it can be intellectually stimulating and challenging but it is also a hopeful activity, done in what Brookfield suggests is a spirit full of hope for the future, and asks us to engage in purposeful and challenging questioning. In this case, as we shall see, this means a careful study of the features which can drive forward the design of the curriculum or indeed act as a resisting force.

Brookfield (1995) suggests that it is through the process of critical and reflective practice that we develop and continually strive to be excellent practitioners. He proposes four lenses through which practitioners at any stage of their careers can develop critical thinking in practice and develop a broader context for their understanding.

Lens 1 – The autobiographical lens: through this personal, reflective lens, practitioners can consider their previous experiences including their education and training and importantly, consider their developing understanding of pedagogy and practice in their field.

Lens 2 – The students' eyes: through this lens practitioners put themselves at the heart of the learning experience and into the position of the learner. They can then consider the quality of learning that is directly experienced by the learner and reflect on, for example, the relevance, purpose and meaning of that curriculum.

> This is why, in my opinion, the most fundamental metacriterion for judging whether or not good teaching is happening is the extent to which teachers deliberately and systematically try to get inside students' heads and see classrooms and learning from their point of view. (Brookfield, 1995: 35)

Lens 3 – Our colleagues' experiences: through this lens practitioners can examine the extent to which they engage with the community of learners around them. This is particularly important for trainee practitioners as they seek support and guidance from experts around them as they develop their skills in planning and enabling high quality early learning experiences. It also enables us to consider and challenge assumptions with our workplace within the broader context of the organisation's core values and beliefs.

Lens 4 – Theoretical literature: through this lens practitioners can critically reflect on evidence-based practice. This includes engagement in personal research, for example University or College assignments. Crucially, it connects theory into practice and enables the practitioner to consider how theory, scholarly activity and wider reading and literature impact on our own personal, professional pedagogies. However, it also informs us of the complexities and challenges that can impact on how early years curricula are shaped.

> Studying theory can help us realise that what we thought were signs of our personal failings as teachers can actually be interpreted as the inevitable consequences of certain economic, social and political processes. (Brookfield, 1995: 36)

However, these lenses are not intended as fixed or unchanging but to highlight key elements of reflective practice (Merriam et al., 2007). By gaining 'multiple perspectives' we can reflect on the same (learning) situation, gain a holistic understanding of all the forces at play and bring some meaning making to them. Using these tools allows the practitioner to ask questions that may challenge orthodoxy and consider the conceptual and theoretical frameworks that underpin effective teaching and learning and subsequently how the curriculum supports that. Fundamentally practitioners need to recognise that as early educators we are the critical mediators through which learning happens and that the curriculum, therefore, is a tool at the hands of the practitioner (Klein and Knitzer, 2006). Overall, the aim is to reflect and develop a deeper understanding of how theory can and does engage with practice. It is also intended that by the end of the chapter, practitioners will, by applying a 'multiple perspectives' model, respond to the question 'why and how has this made me a better practitioner?'.

The process

Building on Brookfield's (1995) concept of lenses, I am proposing that, in order to truly understand all the different stakeholders' views that may be involved in the learning process, interrogating the design of the curriculum revolves around six perspectives. These are explored in no particular order and each is explained below, in terms of why it has been chosen as a particular feature for examination and then in relation to relevant education theory, teaching approaches or pedagogy, research evidence and policy. It is critical to acknowledge that no perspective can stand alone and be seen in isolation; although distinct, they are inextricably linked. Each has clear implications for professional practice. After each perspective is unpacked, they are explored in terms of how they interconnect and what issues and common features for critical analysis emerge. Each perspective also needs to be considered within the context of what constitutes a high quality early years curriculum. At the end of the chapter practitioners are then invited to consider, through engagement with a Critical Learning Activity, how this process might be applied in practice.

Below is an overview of each perspective.

Lens/perspectives	Key words
Moral	values, ethics, beliefs
Child's	voice, entitlement, experience
Political	policy, legislation, process
Parent/carer	parenting, society, partnership
Pedagogical	theory, research, integrity
Curriculum	international perspectives

The moral lens

Those of us who choose to enter into the education profession generally tend to do so because we have a passion and commitment to work with and on behalf of young learners. We are likely to have a core set of values that may well define the types of practitioners we become and we may indeed, consciously or unconsciously, reflect on the values that underpin our practice but also how those values affect what we do and how we respond. It is therefore difficult, if not impossible, to separate our day to day practice in our settings from the underpinning principles that drive us. Therefore the moral lens reflects on a variety of factors that include: equality and equity, inclusive practice, access and achievement for all. It is likely to be underpinned by a sense of moral purpose or moral imperatives that consider issues beyond what is happening at a local level to consider broader, wider societal aspects that lead to a better society for all (Fullan, 2001).

The child's lens

The child is the learner at the centre of what we do. An effective, high quality early years curriculum should therefore take account of key principles of curriculum design that reflect the child's needs in its broadest most holistic sense including academic, social and emotional needs. It should also listen to and respond to the child's voice. From a child's perspective it is critical that their voice is heard, not just listened to, so that children's rights as enshrined in the United Nations Convention on the Rights of the Child (UN General Assembly, 1989; Clark et al., 2005) are truly embedded and not just paid lip service to. It is critical for practitioners to question why the child's voice must be a key driver in curriculum design, for example – Why should we involve children in evaluating our practice? This theme resonates throughout this book and is featured in Chapter 23 by Victoria Cooper who explores the importance of recognising children's identity and in Chapter 20 by Sandra Hesterman who explores the five key aspects of the curriculum in Australia.

The political lens

Whether as professionals, students, parent/carers or practitioners it is important to ask the question, in light of proven educational research and theory, what is the legitimate role of government in education? As critical and reflective practitioners, we need to understand and accept that, ironically, change is a constant and can be a force for good; a journey, not a blueprint (Fullan, 2001).

However, we also need to recognise and challenge the extent to which political ideology (including differing political parties either in office or opposition) might force unnecessary change for the sake of political expediency. There have been some significant government initiatives in early years that have been widely praised including the expansion of daycare and nursery provision (Alexander, 2010). However there has also been widespread criticism of not only the increased politicisation of education but according to Ball (2012) the 'instrumentalisation' of education. Ball argues that successive governments, through their education policy agendas, appear to be restructuring existing models of education towards a much more market led, privatised patchwork of provision. This may well challenge or indeed threaten the core moral and ethical values and beliefs that we as practitioners hold dear. Another potential disjunction is the variety of provision that exists within the United Kingdom itself where there are four different early years curricula operating alongside each other: in England there is the Early Years Foundation Stage (EYFS) curriculum that precedes transition into Key Stage 1 and 2; but in Scotland there is the Curriculum for Excellence that is a continuous curriculum framework from 3–18. The picture is then further complicated when we consider the various international early years curricula, for example the new curriculum for Australia, the New Zealand Te Whāriki curriculum or the Finnish Kindergarten curriculum. Through this lens practitioners reflect on the extent to which political ideology drives and shapes policy; policy that is potentially uninformed by and contrary to educational research, theory and the views of education experts (Alexander, 2010) It could therefore be argued that as a result of the constant change agenda in the United Kingdom and the increasing politicisation of education over the past three decades, the core principles, purpose and pedagogy have been sacrificed to a high stakes, outcome-driven testing system. Anyon (1981, cited in Wyse et al., 2013) recognised the dangers of an enacted curriculum of basic skills, rules recognition and compliance.

The parent/carer lens

It may be that you are now starting to see the interconnectedness between each of the lenses and reflecting critically on the themes identified. Every home will in some way or other impact upon the values and belief systems that shape our behaviours and actions: parents/carers are no different. Traditionally there is very little preparation for what is probably the most important and responsible role that anyone could undertake, therefore parenting is often based on our own experiences of being parented. The quality and effectiveness of pre-school is a significant predictor of future success and stronger still is the impact of the home circumstances (Sammons et al., 2008). Therefore whether practitioner or policymaker, it is important to question and reflect on whether high quality early years provision can support all young learners (and their families) and mitigate against the potential barriers or inhibitors to learning that exist. Bronfenbrenner (1979) refers to ecological environments and immediate settings and challenges practitioners to look beyond single settings and to consider and reflect on the interrelationships that exist between different settings, for example home and school. He goes on to say that

> a child's ability to read in the primary grades may depend, no less, on how he is taught than on the existence and nature of ties between the school and the home. (1979: 3)

What is clear, however, is that research consistently reports that children who grow up in lower socio-economic groups end up with lower educational attainment. Goodman and Gregg (2010) reported that children from poor backgrounds face much less advantageous 'early childhood caring environments' than children from better off families. Therefore practitioners must consider this in order to create a space for dialogue and to seek opportunities for finding solutions to these complex problems. Many parents do, however, have a voice and it is usually those from higher socio-economic groups who are heard the most. The recent growth of online parenting forums – for example, netmums and mumsnet – has further strengthened this voice through discussion, debate and even political lobbying. These can be recognised as a particularly rich data source, as both a popular cultural representation of parenting and through enabling people to actively participate. The voice of the parents is also given a much higher priority in new legislation under the Children and Families Bill (DfE and DfBIS, 2013). Families will be given personal budgets so that they can choose the best 'expert' support to meet their child's own particular needs.

The pedagogic lens

Early historical models of early learning that put the child at the centre of education have been influenced and shaped by key educators such as Lev Vygotsky, Maria Montessori, Susan Isaacs and Friedrich Frobel, all of whose inspiration was drawn from philosophers such as the French philosopher Jean Jacques Rousseau (Wyse et al., 2013). Rousseau believed that children should be enabled to learn what they wish to learn when they are ready to do so, and stressed play enriched by unobtrusive guidance from a teacher/facilitator (Soler and Miller, 2003).

Vygotsky (1978) recognised the importance of the socio-cultural context of learning and the fact that children learn from interactions and conversations with adults and older peers. As a result of these interactions more sophisticated and effective mental processes are developed, which he refers to as **higher mental functions**. These interactions which require children to engage mental processes at levels not yet available to them, for example deliberate memorisation or focused attention. Higher mental functions play a key role, with scaffolded adult support, in the child's construction of his or her own mind, thus influencing new categories and processes. This leads to the formation of higher mental functions, for example focused attention, deliberate memorisation and logical thought (Bodrova and Leong, 2001).

This model of socially constructed learning continues to influence current provision today and echoes some key principles that should underpin an appropriate curriculum. The inherent danger in not recognising these key theories of learning may result in an early years curriculum framework that does not meet the needs of the diverse range of learning it is meant to serve and fails to respond to the key features introduced earlier in the chapter.

The curriculum lens

This chapter has outlined, in terms of content, what a desirable curriculum should look like and it has also considered the importance of viewing situations from multiple perspectives. Regardless of which nation practitioners are developing their professional identities in, the ability to understand, deconstruct and reflect on this content is critical. Through this final lens a practitioner can consider a range of factors that once considered, may provide a rationale for future curriculum planning; for example one that relates to quality for learning and social well-being. Considering this from an objectivist stance Mathers et al. (2012) would argue that many aspects of quality can in fact be 'agreed upon by all stakeholders'. This raises an interesting issue and questions whether it is possible to define quality at all considering the multiple perspectives that need to be considered. She also argues that this view fails to include the views of 'different stakeholders'. Dahlberg and Moss (2008) suggest a relativist approach arguing that quality should be 'defined locally, varying according to the social and cultural context and reflecting the multiple perspectives of all stakeholders' (2008: 22).

However if practitioners are to attempt to define quality, then Mathers and colleagues (2012) argue one mechanism is to consider structural process versus outcomes.

Conclusion

Having considered and reflected on all the key ideas developed and explored throughout this chapter from a practitioner perspective, there is no clear weighting that can be placed on any aspects of the curriculum that suggests one or the other is more or less valuable. However, from a different stakeholder perspective this may not be the case, for example, a political outcome or a specific parental outcome. The toolkit offers a systematic framework for critical and reflective practice for early years practitioners with a view to developing and deepening professional practice through challenge and discourse. It is intended that as a result of engagement with this chapter practitioners will be better placed to understand the complex range of factors involved and, importantly, are able to select each perspective to gain a more holistic understanding. The chapter also intends to offer practitioners the scope and space to consider their own role in early years practice and to identify the value base from which she/he will build a professional contribution to the field.

Critical Learning Activity

In light of your engagement with this chapter, consider you own nation's early years curriculum and now look at it through each of the lenses and complete the column entitled 'Implications for professional practice'.

Lens/perspective	Key words	Implications for professional practice
Moral	values, ethics, beliefs	
Child's	voice, entitlement, experience	
Political	policy, legislation, process	
Parent/carer	parenting, society, partnership	
Pedagogical	theory, research, integrity	
Curriculum	international perspectives	

Further reading

Cochran, M. (2011) 'International perspectives on early childhood education', *Educational Policy*, 25: 65.

Soler, J. and Miller, L. (2003) 'The struggle for early childhood curricula: a comparison of the English Foundation Stage Curriculum, Te Whariki and Reggio Emilia', *International Journal of Early Years Education*, 11 (1): 57–68.

References

Alexander, R. (ed.) (2010) *Children, Their World, Their Education: Final Report and Recommendations of the Cambridge Primary Review*. London: Routledge.

Anyon, J. (1981) 'Social class and school knowledge', *Curriculum Enquiry*, 15: 207–214.

Ball, S.J. (2012) 'The reluctant state and the beginning of the end of state education', *Journal of Education Administration and History*, 44 (2): 89–103.

Bodrova, E. and Leong, D.J. (2001) *Tools of the Mind: A Case Study of Implementing the Vygotsky Approach in American Early Childhood and Primary Classrooms*. Geneva: IBE.

Bronfenbrenner, U. (1979) *Bronfenbrenner, The Ecology of Human Development: Experiments by Nature and Design*. Cambridge, MA: Harvard University Press.

Brookfield, S. (1995) *Becoming a Critically Reflective Teacher*. San Francisco, CA: Jossey-Bass.

Clark, A., Kjorholt, A.T. and Moss, P. (2005) *Beyond Listening – Children's Perspectives on Early Childhood Services*. Bristol: Policy Press.

Dahlberg, G. and Moss, P. (2008) 'Beyond quality in early childhood education and care', *CESifo DICE report*, 6 (2): 21–26.

Department for Education (DfE) (2012a) *Teachers' Standards*. London: DfE.

Department for Education (DfE) (2012b) *Statutory Framework for the Early Years Foundation Stage 2012*. London: DfE.

Department for Education (DfE) and Department for Business, Innovation and Skills (DfBIS) (2013) *Children and Families Bill*. London: TSO.

Fullan, M. (2001) *Leading in a Culture of Change*. San Francisco, CA: Jossey Bass.

Gibbs, G. (1988) *Learning by Doing: A Guide to Teaching and Learning Methods*. Oxford: Further Education Unit, Oxford Polytechnic.

Goodman, A. and Gregg, P. (2010) *Poorer Children's Educational Attainment: How Important are Attitudes and Behaviours?* Report to the Joseph Rowntree Foundation.

Klein, L. and Knitzer, J. (2006) 'Effective preschool curricula and teaching strategies', *Pathways to Early School Success*, Issue Brief No. 2.

Kolb, D.A. (1984) *Experiential Learning: Experience as the Source of Learning and Development*. Englewood Cliffs, NJ: Prentice Hall.

Mathers, S., Singler, R. and Karemaker, A. (2012) *Improving Quality in the Early Years: A Comparison of Perspectives and Measures, Final Report*. London: Daycare Trust and Oxford: University of Oxford.

Merriam, S.B., Caffarella, R.S. and Baumgartner, L.M. (2007) *Learning in Adulthood: A Comprehensive Guide*, 3rd edn. San Francisco, CA: Jossey-Bass.

OECD (2001) *Starting Strong 1: Early Childhood Education and Care*. Paris: OECD.

OECD (2006) *Starting Strong 11: Early Childhood Education and Care*. Paris: OECD.

Rolfe, G., Freshwater, D. and Jasper, M. (2001) *Critical Reflection in Nursing and the Helping Professions: A User's Guide*. Basingstoke: Palgrave Macmillan.

Sammons, P., Sylva, K., Melhuish, E., Siraj-Blatchford, I. and Taggart, B. (2008) *Influences on Children's Cognitive and Social Development in Year 6 (EPPE 3–11)*. Nottingham: DCSF.

SCAA (1996) *Nursery Education: Desirable Outcomes for Children's Learning on Entering Compulsory Education*. London: SCAA and Department for Education and Employment.

Soler, J. and Miller, L. (2003) 'The struggle for early childhood curricula: A comparison of the English Foundation Stage Curriculum, Te Whariki and Reggio Emilia', *International Journal of Early Years Education*, 11: 57–67.

Sylva, K., Melhuish, E., Sammons, P., Siraj-Blatchford, I. and Taggart, B. (2010) *Evidence from the Effective Pre-School and Primary Education Project*. London: Routledge.

UN General Assembly (1989) *Convention on the Rights of the Child*, United Nations, Treaty Series, 1577: 3. Available at: www.refworld.org/docid/3ae6b38f0.html (accessed 23 December 2013).

Vygotsky, L. (1978) *Mind and Society: The Development of Higher Mental Processes*. Cambridge, MA: Harvard University Press.

Wyse, D., Baumfield, V., Egan, D., Hayward, L., Hulme, M., Menter, I., Gallagher, C., Leitch, R., Livingston, K. and Lingard, B. (2013) *Creating the Curriculum*. Oxford: Routledge.

Want to learn more about this chapter?

Visit the companion website at **https://study.sagepub.com/reedandwalker** to access podcasts from the author and additional reading to further help you with your studies.

17

Approaches to the early years curriculum: a critical view from Wales

Siân Wyn Siencyn

Chapter overview

This chapter will outline the narrative of change in Wales since devolution in 1999. It will consider the influences of those changes on policy and practice and how these reflect social and cultural values, for example the Welsh perspective on the UN Convention on the Rights of the Child and child citizenship. There will also be discussion of the Foundation Phase 3–7 and the philosophic and practice influences on its development, including its incorporation of aspects of other philosophies of childhood and key influences on this approach. The chapter will conclude with a discussion of some of the challenges Wales now faces.

Introduction

Wales is a small country on the western part of the British Isles with its own language and cultural identity which has, in recent years, taken a radical approach to children's early learning. It has been a journey of devolved powers since the establishment of the Welsh Assembly in 1999 and a major part of that narrative is Wales' own confident voice in its view of children. I have been part of that change through work with the National Assembly on advisory groups and as a University teacher working with students who will themselves be engaged with young children in this new way. There have been many influences on my own thinking that have steered my own journey of discovery in my relationship with small children – a journey which is an unending and challenging adventure.

Appleby and Andrews (2012) suggest that adults working with children and making decisions about their lives should challenge themselves. We should consider our own values and beliefs and be ready to challenge policy and practice.

Background

Approaches to understanding children have long been acknowledged to be part of a changing process (MacNaughton, 2005; Penn, 2005; Dahlberg and Moss, 2005). This socio-cultural lens of perceiving who children are and how children learn is reflected in public policy and political ideologies. With devolution in Wales and the establishment of the Welsh Assembly in 1999, there emerged a new paradigm in early years provision and one that was considered, at the time, to be almost revolutionary in its approach. Whilst England still struggled with the vocabulary of goals and outcomes, Wales began talking in a new language and articulating a new confidence. This new language included terms such as 'dispositions to learn', 'creative thinking' and 'children leading the learning'. The Wales voice had, however, been apparent from 1996 when the clear divergence of tone between Wales and England became apparent, particularly in the Desirable Outcomes for Children in England (SCAA, 1996) and the Desirable Outcomes for Children in Wales (ACAC, 1996). Siencyn and Thomas (2007: 149) note:

> ... with its focus on the learning child, its robust celebration of the value of play in children's learning and its opening with two lines of an *awdl*, the Desirable Outcomes in Wales was published to universal acclaim.

The acclaim was not so resounding for the document for England. When comparing both guidance documents, David (1998: 81) said:

> It would seem that being under five in England is to be less joyful, less celebrated, less imaginative, less romantic, more pressurised, more rigid ... than in Wales.

Wales has been, perhaps, more open and responsive to the developing understanding of children and childhood and its commitment to the UN Convention on the Rights of the Child more robustly established.

The UN Convention and the rights of children in Wales

One of the first actions of the new Welsh Assembly was to establish the office of the Commissioner for Children in Wales and we are proud to have been the first country in Britain to have a Children's Commissioner. The history behind this move is, however, one of national shame, as outlined in the Waterhouse report *Lost in Care* (Department of Health, 2000). Waterhouse highlighted the systematic and endemic abuse of children and young people in care homes in north Wales during the 1970s and that these young and vulnerable children were not heard, not listened to, and not believed by adults charged with their welfare. It was this shocking revelation that galvanised public opinion to act. By the time the National Assembly was established in 1999, we were ready to commit to the expectations of the UN Convention on the Rights of the Child. This commitment is articulated in the Welsh Government's *Seven Core Aims for Children and Young People*. The Government's own website highlights this in respect of education, sustainability, justice, health, housing, local government and a range of other jurisdictions. Indeed, it is difficult to find a public policy document which does not refer to these seven core aims.

The Welsh Assembly and Welsh Government's seven core aims for children and young people

Our seven core aims for children and young people summarise the UN Convention on the Rights of the Child (UNCRC) and form the basis for decisions on priorities and objectives nationally. They should also form the basis for decisions on strategy and service provision locally.

We have adopted the UNCRC as the basis of all our work for children and young people. This is expressed in seven core aims that all children and young people:

1. have a flying start in life;
2. have a comprehensive range of education and learning opportunities;
3. enjoy the best possible health and are free from abuse, victimisation and exploitation;
4. have access to play, leisure, sporting and cultural activities;
5. are listened to, treated with respect, and have their race and cultural identity recognised;
6. have a safe home and a community which supports physical and emotional well-being;
7. are not disadvantaged by poverty.

Source: http://wales.gov.uk/topics/childrenyoungpeople/rights/
sevencoreaims/?lang=en

One area of stark political difference between Wales and England is in the smacking debate. Sdim Curo Plant! Cymru/Children are Unbeatable! Wales, launched in 2000 as the Wales co-ordinating body for the lobby to change the law on smacking, has had significant support from the Welsh Government. In a plenary debate on 14 January 2004 National Assembly members voted in favour of a ban on smacking children by 41 votes to 9 and noted its 'regret' that the UK government continued to maintain 'reasonable chastisement'. In 2005 the Welsh Government funded Sdim Curo Plant! Cymru/Children are Unbeatable! Wales to develop a toolkit which would promote changes in attitudes to smacking children (see www.helpathandtoolkit.info). The UK's 2008 report to the UN Committee on the Rights of the Child stated:

> The Welsh Assembly Government has already committed itself to supporting a ban on physical punishment of children and has funded publication of a booklet called Help in Hand given to all new parents that advises on positive ways of dealing with behaviour and avoiding smacking. (UN Committee on the Rights of the Child, 2008)

This remains a non-devolved issue but not, perhaps, for long. With the increased devolution of legal jurisdictions, it will only be a matter of time before Wales is in a position to protect its children from this form of domestic abuse.

Another area of particular interest is in relation to powers of appeal. Parents in Wales and England have, since 1994, had the right to appeal to the Special Educational Needs Tribunal when they are unhappy with what local authorities and schools provide for their children. However, Wales has gone further with the implementation of the values of Article 12 of the UN Convention. After two years of discussion, debate and consultation, from March 2012 children living in two local authority pilot areas (Carmarthenshire and Wrexham) have been able to make their own appeal or claim under equality law. Once this pilot process is completed, it is expected that children throughout Wales will be able to make their own appeals.

This is an historic statement of Wales' view of children. They are citizens with their own rights to appeal to the Special Educational Needs Tribunal for Wales (SENTW) and this is not a right reliant on their parents. It is not, either, a right based on age and competence, it is a universal right for all children regardless of age and level of disability. The position in England is different. Although the Tribunal in England is moving towards the principle of a child's right to appeal, this is only for children over the age of 11 and only those children who are able to prove competence. This is a limited right, based on the Gillick test, which views children in terms of competence, age and maturity (Taylor, 2007). Having debated, both philosophically and legally, what is meant by 'competence', who decides what 'competence' looks like and all the other challenging questions, the children's citizenship argument prevailed in Wales. In SENTW's annual report (2012) the President summed it up the Education (Wales) Measure 2009, by suggesting that it was '*an important step towards increasing the participation of children in processes and matters that affect them*'.

This approach to children's rights, particularly in respect of the challenging area of the rights of young children with special educational needs or additional learning needs, proclaims that they belong to all children. These rights are implicit in what

Warnock (1998) calls 'personhood' and what is now commonly referred to as *agency* or a child's capacity to voice rational views about her/his life (Dockett et al., 2012; Moss, 2012).

The underpinning assumption is that all children have views about their world but that we, as adults with limited skills, are not always able to understand or decode children's ways of expressing their views. This lays the onus on us to find alternative ways of listening and is sometimes referred to as 'the pedagogy of listening' (Clark et al., 2005). It is an approach resonant of Reggio Emilia ideas about competent and powerful children (Rinaldi, 2005) and what Malagussi describes as children communicating through 'a hundred languages' (Edwards et al., 1998).

Critical Learning Activity

Wales has decided that even very young children are capable of expressing views about their own lives, about their likes, dislikes, fears and aspirations. Consider the challenges that adults face when trying to negotiate meaning and decode children's messages, particularly children with no oral language. Potter and Whittaker (2011) will make a good starting point for this discussion.

The Foundation Phase 3–7

In 2000, one of the first education initiatives of the newly elected Welsh Assembly was to commission an expert adviser to review the provision of three year-old children in Wales and to survey the research literature on current thinking regarding best practice. As a result of this review (Welsh Assembly Government, 2001), *The Learning Country: Foundation Phase 3–7* was introduced in February 2003 (WAG, 2003a) outlining a radical new approach to children's early learning. In line with the Welsh Assembly Government's commitment to evidence-based policy development, this new curriculum was rooted in the experiential evidence of other countries and in what was – and is – considered good practice in early childhood provision. The consultation document on the *Foundation Phase 3–7* (WAG, 2003a: 10) refers to these.

> Practice in Denmark, Germany, Reggio Emilia in Italy and New Zealand … shows how children can be encouraged to make decisions about their learning, to be independent and physically active in doing so. The High/Scope Perry Pre-School study in America also suggests that allowing children suitable opportunities to make decisions about the activities they undertake helps them to improve their social and interpersonal skills.

By reflecting on new thinking and constructing ideas of childhood influenced by a sociological discourse such as Bronfenbrenner's ecological model (1978), there emerges a view of the impact of public policy on child development. Siencyn (2008) argued that the Foundation Phase is, in itself, an example of this. It is an educational policy which has, at its core, a clear intention of steering children's dispositions to be creative, to be flexible and to be confident life-long learners.

It has been argued that another key impetus behind the Foundation Phase was increasing concern about child poverty, the link between poverty and educational attainment, levels of functional illiteracy in young adults and the link between these and youth offending and the challenges generally linked to social exclusion. Complex social and economic concerns led to the view, well-articulated in the Foundation Phase philosophy, that the sooner and more effectively early intervention was implemented the better it was for everyone.

There was also concern about the kinds of early learning experiences children in Wales were having. Formal pedagogical methods were criticised, even by Estyn (the School's Inspectorate for Wales). This concern is noted in the initial Foundation Phase documentation (WAG, 2003a: 6):

> Teachers introduce formal learning too soon, before some pupils are ready. Children are given too many tasks to do while sitting at tables rather than learning through well-structured play, practical activity and investigation.

Significantly, and particularly in view of more recent policy initiatives relating to early literacy, the Foundation Phase document refers to concern that *'an over emphasis on making children read and write, before they are ready to do so, can be counter productive'* (WAG, 2003a: 11).

Following a pilot stage, a comprehensive evaluation was undertaken and the first *Monitoring and Evaluation of the Effective Implementation of the Foundation Phase* (MEEIFP) report was published in 2006. The first findings were encouraging. It was noted, for example, that the emphasis on learning through play and active learning was almost universally welcomed as was the holistic and integrated approach to children's learning (Siraj-Blatchford et al., 2006: 3). There were the usual concerns about funding, particularly the commitment to adult:child ratios of 1:8 for children under 5 and 1:15 for children aged 5–7 years. It is interesting to note, particularly in light of current debates around ratios, that the MEEIFP report suggests that appropriate training of staff is more important than numbers of adults.

> Care should be taken to ensure that improving ratios does not take precedence over high quality training for staff working in schools and settings. Staff qualifications show a stronger relationship to quality of provision than ratios. (Siraj-Blatchford et al., 2006: 7)

The implication is that staff understanding of children's development and of children's learning processes together with staff skills as reflective observers is a more influential factor than numbers of adults alone.

The seven areas of learning

The Foundation Phase was, and remains, set firmly in a framework of areas of learning which is the model first outlined in the *Desirable Outcomes* (ACAC, 1996) documentation. These are Language, Literacy and Communication Skills, Mathematical Development, Personal and Social Development, Knowledge and Understanding of the World, Creative Development and Physical Development. The first draft of the Foundation Phase also identified an additional area of learning: Bilingualism and Multiculturalism. This led to a lively debate and considerable confusion about terminology, for example, the meaning and definition of bilingualism caused difficulties and involved complex issues from disciplines such as linguistics, psycholinguistics and the sociology of language. By 2008, Welsh Language Development was introduced as an area of learning in its own right thus ensuring that all children in Wales, including those in English medium provision, had a right to the Welsh language (WAG, 2008). This is resonant of the Te Whāriki early childhood curriculum of Aotearoa (New Zealand) which 'establishes ... the bicultural nature of curriculum for all early childhood services.' (See www.educate.ece.govt.nz/learning/curriculumAndLearning/TeWhariki/Foreword.aspx.)

Over the years, there has been a small but vocal lobby for the scrapping of the old areas of learning framework. I have, myself, questioned the value of the old system and have argued that, for example, mathematical development is as much socio-cultural and linguistic as it is anything else (Siencyn, 2010). Moving from the old framework would be consistent with Te Whāriki and its model of strands: Well-Being, Belonging, Contribution, Communication and Exploration.

The Foundation Phase documentation clearly emphasises the importance of the integrated nature of the areas of learning.

> All aspects of learning are interlinked for young children; they do not compartmentalise their learning and understanding into curriculum areas. The seven Areas of Learning are complementary. (WAG, 2008: 5)

This, of course, begs the question, why have areas of learning? A visitor to any early childhood setting in Wales could well see, for example, a mathematics corner and an early marking corner which, in essence, promotes the impression of separate areas.

The process and impact of the Foundation Phase is being rigorously monitored and the government is presented with regular reports from Estyn and from academic research. The Wales Institute for Social and Economic Research (see www.wiserd.ac.uk/foundationphase) is currently reviewing the Foundation Phase and its most recent reports are extensive and detailed. There is agreement, however, that the commitment to the Foundation Phase should be long term and that benefits are already being seen (Welsh Government, 2013).

> ⭐ **Reflection point**
>
> It is now commonplace to assert that there is no one definition or understanding of childhood. Moss (Dahlberg and Moss, 2005) and others refer to a 'multiplicity of childhoods'. How do you think the Foundation Phase in Wales, with its emphasis on play and outdoor learning, on promoting bilingualism and child-led learning will give children in Wales a different childhood to children in England?

Influences and evidence

The major influences on thinking in Wales are clearly articulated in the early childhood curriculum documentation: practice in Reggio Emilia (Italy), Scandinavia, and New Zealand have all been instrumental in crafting the Welsh vision. Children are seen, in principle at least, as being powerful and competent learners.

The New Zealand *Competent Children, Competent Learners* Project (1992–) with its wealth of research evidence has also been influential. Since 1992, the number of reports and research papers presenting findings has been significant (see www.nzcer.org.nz/default.php?products_id=134). The evidence base which underpinned Welsh policy in favour of a particular type of early childhood pedagogy was supported by the New Zealand research. Similarly, the Scandinavian tradition of Forest Schools and outdoor learning began to chime with the Welsh Government's robust commitment to sustainability, ethical eco awareness and concerns about the well-being of children who were thought to be increasingly alienated from nature and the outdoors.

Early bilingualism

One of the unique aspects of the Wales perspective is its experience of bilingualism. The Welsh Government has made an unequivocal commitment to the promotion of the Welsh language. *Iaith Pawb – Everyone's Language: a National Action Plan for a Bilingual Wales* (WAG, 2003b), *The Welsh Medium Education Strategy* (WAG, 2010a), *Iaith Fyw: Iaith Byw: A Strategy for the Welsh Language* (WAG, 2010b) and other key documents attest to this aspiration for a bilingual Wales.

Over the years, there has been a substantial body of international research in support of early bilingualism (Cummins, 1979; Siencyn, 1989, 1990, 1993; Bialystok, 2001; Baker, 2006) and, with it, lively debate on definitions (Baetens Beardsmore, 1986; Cummins, 2003; Baker, 2006). Siencyn and Richards (2010) summarise some of the contentions: At what point in the development of their second language can children be considered bilingual? What linguistic skills are needed to be bilingual? What does 'being fluent' mean? However, policy documents in Wales do not reflect this complexity. Indeed the Foundation Phase has opted for a definition that is startling in its simplicity

> Bilingualism is the ability to speak, read and write in two languages (WAG, 2008:11)

This definition ignores the young child's journey to functional bilingualism, a journey which does not include 'speaking, reading and writing' but more subtle areas such as non verbal responding, understanding and bilingual behaviours (Siencyn, 2010). However esoteric the linguistic debate, the Welsh government has accepted the evidence in favour of early bilingualism as opposed to learning a second language later on. This evidence has come, over many years, from a wide range of disciplines such as neuro-science and psycho-linguistics (Penfield and Roberts, 1959; Lenneberg, 1967; Harley, 1986; Gopnik, 2009). Others argue in favour of an early start from a phonological perspective (Siencyn, 1982; Bialystok, 2001; Flege et al., 2006). Kuhl argues this also:

> ... phonetic development follows the same principles for two languages that it does a single language. Bilingual infants learn through the exaggerated acoustic cues provided by infant-directed speech ... as do monolingual infants. (Kuhl, 2008: 232)

So here we return to the 'new' thinking that children are competent, powerful learners, with skills adults are only beginning to appreciate.

Challenges

Changes of government, and changes of ministers, usually lead to changes in policy and in focus. These changes impact on children's lives and on the rhetoric of public services. Bronfenbrenner (1978) highlighted this in his ecological model of human development with its intricate web of interacting systems.

There has a been a flurry of activity in Wales as a result of the OECD Programme for International Student Assessment (PISA) results for 2011 and 2013 which tested and compared Welsh pupils' skills in reading, maths and science with other countries. The results were disappointing for Wales and there have been responses ranging from a questioning of PISA methodologies, a concern about the pedagogy of some more successful countries to PISA panic. There has also been a return to the language of assessment and testing, of outcomes and measurement. Although the National Literacy and Numeracy Framework (LNF), as the government states, 'is part of the drive ... to raise standards and break the link between deprivation and educational attainment', there is increasing concern that the problems of Key Stage 3 and GCSE results are impacting on the learning experiences of children in the Foundation Phase. For those of us who have lobbied so long for a child centred, competent, long term approach, the prospect of a return to fast gains and short term results is making us nervous. The dangers implicit in the tension between children's rights and school performance, between a more unhurried approach to children's learning and the political imperative to improve educational attainment are creating a potentially hostile environment for the advocates of what was Wales' radical vision.

Perhaps the most significant challenge facing Wales is the impact of poverty on children's lives. Since devolution, the government has sought to systematise its approach to this entrenched problem. Significantly, one of the more recent general policy steers – *Building Resilient Communities* (WG, 2013) – has a photo of very young children on its cover. There is agreement that these are hard times and Siencyn (2010) maintains that when governments face economic crises '*children are in danger of bearing the brunt of stringent belt tightening*'. As the Welsh ministers state:

> We do not have control of either the benefits system or the key economic levers. If we did, we would be using them very differently. (Welsh Government, 2013b: 2)

Children in Wales are still, in important areas of their lives, dependent on the political ideologies and priorities of a government based, not in Cardiff, but in London.

Further reading

Siencyn, S.W. and Thomas, S. (2007) 'Early years provision in Wales', in M. Clark and T. Waller (eds), *Early Childhood Education and Care: Policy and Practice*. London: SAGE. pp. 135–166.

Siraj-Blatchford, I., Milton, E., Sylva, K.., Laugharne, J. and Charles, F. (2006) *Monitoring and Evaluation of the Effective Implementation of the Foundation Phase* (MEEIFP report). Cardiff: Welsh Assembly Government.

References

ACAC (1996) *The Desirable Outcomes for Children Learning Before Statutory School Age. Anlyniadau*. Cardiff: Awdurdod Cwricwlwm ac Asesu Cymru (Wales Curriculum and Assessment Authority).

Appleby, A. and Andrews, M. (2012) 'Reflective practice is the key to quality improvement', in M. Rees and N. Canning (eds), *Implementing Quality Improvement and Change in the Early Years*. London: SAGE.

Baetens Beardsmore, H. (1986) *Bilingualism: Basic Principles*. Clevedon: Multilingual Matters.

Baker, C. (2006) *Foundations of Bilingual Education and Bilingualism*. Clevedon: Multilingual Matters.

Bialystok, E. (2001) *Bilingualism in Development: Language, Literacy, and Cognition*. New York: Cambridge University Press.

Bronfenbrenner, U. (1978) *The Ecology of Human Development*. Cambridge, MA: Harvard University Press.

Clark, A., Kjorholt, A.T. and Moss, P. (eds) (2005) *Beyond Listening: Children's Perspectives on Early Childhood Services*. Bristol: Policy Press.

Cummins, J. (1979) 'Linguistic interdependence and the educational development of bilingual children', *Review of Educational Research* 49 (2): 222–251.

Cummins, J. (2003) 'Bilingual education: basic principles', in J.-M. Daelewe, A. Housen and L. Wei (eds), *Bilingualism: Beyond Basic Principles. Festschrift in Honour of Hugo Baetens Beardsmore*. Clevedon: Multilingual Matters. pp. 55–56.

Dahlberg, G. and Moss, P. (2005) *Ethics and Politics in Early Childhood Education*. Abingdon: Routledge Falmer.

David, T. (1998) 'Learning properly? Young children and the desirable outcomes', *Early Years*, 18 (2): 61–66.

Department of Health (2000) *Lost in Care – Report of the Tribunal of Inquiry into the Abuse of Children in Care in the Former County Council Areas of Gwynedd and Clwyd since 1974*. London: Department of Health/HMSO.

Dockett, S., Perry, B. and Kearney, E. (2012) 'Promoting children's informed assent in research participation', *International Journal of Qualitative Studies in Education*, 26 (12).

Edwards, C., Gandini, L., Forman, G. (1998) *The Hundred Languages of Children*. London: Ablex Publishing.

Flege, J., Birdsong, D., Bialystok, E., Mack, M., Sung, H. and Tsukada, K. (2006) 'Degree of foreign accent in English sentences produced by Korean children and adults', *Journal of Phonetics*, 34: 153–175.

Gopnik, A. (2009) *The Philosophical Baby*. London: Bodley Head.

Harley, B. (1986) *Age in Second Language Acquisition*. Clevedon: Multilingual Matters.

Kuhl, P.K. (2008) 'Linking infant speech perception to language acquisition: Phonetic learning predicts language growth', in P. McCardle, J. Colombo and L. Freund (eds), *Infant Pathways to Language: Methods, Models, and Research Directions*. Erlbaum: New York. pp. 213–243.

Lenneberg, E. (1967) *Biological Foundations of Language*. New York: Wiley.

MacNaughton, G. (2005) *Doing Foucault in Early Childhood Studies*. London: Routledge & Falmer Press.

Moss, P. (ed) (2012) *Early Childhood and Compulsory Education: Reconceptualising the Relationship*. Abingdon: Routledge.

Penfield, W. and Roberts, L. (1959) *Speech and Brain Mechanisms*. Princeton: Princeton University Press.

Penn, H. (2005) *Understanding Early Childhood: Issues and Controversies*. London: SAGE.

Potter, C. and Whittaker, C. (2011) 'What does "the voice of the child" mean for children with complex learning and communication impairments', in P. Jones and Walker (eds), *Children's Rights*. London: SAGE.

Rinaldi, C. (2005) *In Dialogue with Reggio Emilia: Listening, Researching and Learning*. Abingdon: Routledge.

School Curriculum Assessment Authority (SCAA) (1996) *Nursery Education: Desirable Outcomes for Children's Learning on Entering Compulsory Education*. London: SCAA and DfEE.

Siencyn, S.W. (1982) *Methodolegau cyflwyno'r Gymraeg fel ail iaith. [Methodologies of Introducing Welsh as a Second Languge]*. Cardiff: Mudiad Ysgolion Meithrin and Brussell: The European Cultural Foundation

Siencyn, S.W. (1989) 'Y Plentyn Dwyieithog' in *Y Plentyn Bach*. Cardiff: Open University.

Siencyn, S.W. (1990) *Think Twice: An Introduction to Early Bilingualism*. Caerdydd: Mudiad Ysgolion Meithrin.

Siencyn, S.W. (1993) *The Sound of Europe: An Introduction to European Plurilingualism*. Brussels: European Bureau for Lesser Used Languages and the European Commission.

Siencyn, S.W. (2008) 'Cyflwyniad i Astudiaethau Plentyndod' yn S.W. Siencyn (gol), *Y Plentyn Bach: Cyflwyniad i Astudiaethau Plentyndod Cynnar*. Caerfyrddin: Cyhoeddiadau Coleg y Drindod (Welsh medium publication). pp. 11–26.

Siencyn, S.W. (2010) 'The challenges of rural poverty for children in Wales', in M. Clark and S. Tucker (eds), *Early Childhoods in a Changing World*. London: Trentham Books. pp. 43–55.

Siencyn, S.W. and Richards, C. (2010) 'Iaith, Llythrennedd a Sgiliau Cyfathrebu yn y Cyfnod Sylfaen' yn S.W. Siencyn (ed.), *Y Cyfnod Sylfaen: Athroniaeth, Ymchwil ac Ymarfer*. Caerfyrddin: Cyhoeddiadau Coleg Prifysgol y Drindod (Welsh medium publication). pp. 153–176.

Siencyn, S.W. and Thomas, S. (2007) 'Early years provision in Wales', in M. Clark and T. Waller (eds), *Early Childhood Education and Care: Policy and Practice*. London: SAGE. pp. 135–166.

Siraj-Blatchford, I., Milton, E., Sylva, K., Laugharne, J. and Charles, F. (2006) *Monitoring and Evaluation of the Effective Implementation of the Foundation Phase* (MEEIFP report). Cardiff: Welsh Assembly Government.

Special Educational Needs Tribunal Annual Report 2011–12 (SENTW) (2012) Llandrindod: SENTW.

Taylor, R. (2007) 'Reversing the retreat from Gillick? R [Axon] v Secretary of State for Health', *Child and Family Law Quarterly*, 19 (1): 81–97.

UN Committee on the Rights of the Child (2008) Third and fourth periodic reports of the United Kingdom of Great Britain and Northern Ireland, 25 February, CRC/C/GBR/4.

Warnock, M. (1998) *An Intelligent Person's Guide to Ethics*. London: Duckworth Press.

Welsh Assembly Government (WAG) (2001) *Laying the Foundations: The Early Years Provision for Three Year Olds*. Interim Report of the under 16 Education Committee. Cardiff: WAG.

Welsh Assembly Government (2003a) *The Learning Country: Foundation Phase 3–7 Consultation Document*. Cardiff: WAG.

Welsh Assembly Government (2003b) *Iaith Pawb – A National Action Plan for a Bilingual Wales*. Cardiff: WAG.

Welsh Assembly Government (2008) *The Foundation Phase: Framework for Children's Learning for 3–7 Year Olds in Wales*. Cardiff: WAG.

Welsh Assembly Government (2010a) *The Welsh Medium Education Strategy*. Cardiff: WAG.

Welsh Assembly Government (2010b) *Iaith Fyw: Iaith Byw – A Strategy for the Welsh Language*. Cardiff: WAG.

Welsh Government (2013) *Building Resilient Communities: Taking Forward the Tackling Poverty Action Plan*. Cardiff: Welsh Government.

Want to learn more about this chapter?

Visit the companion website at **https://study.sagepub.com/reedandwalker** to access podcasts from the author and additional reading to further help you with your studies.

18

Parental involvement and partnership with parents: 'T'ain't what you do (it's the way that you do it)'

Martin Needham and Dianne Jackson

Chapter overview

Many aspects of professional practice in early education require individuals to make judgements about how to balance competing arguments. This chapter examines some of the choices that professionals working with parents need to consider when they frame these relationships. The chapter briefly outlines the work of Baumrind (1996) on parenting styles, which underpins many parenting programmes. The chapter suggests that Baumrind's model, which advocates a middle course between authoritarian and too permissive parenting styles, may be in tension with political pressure to deliver formalised parenting courses. The title of this chapter is taken from the popular song, originally written in 1933 (Oliver and Young, 1939). The lyric draws attention to the argument developed in this chapter; that the medium is the message and try as we might, with the best of intentions and the best planned resources, if we fail to connect with parents through respectful relationships little progress will be made.

Introduction

Postman and Weingartner (1969) were very influential early advocates for more active and learner-focused approaches to learning. In *Teaching as a Subversive Activity*, they argued that *the medium is the message*; meaning that the learning which makes the most lasting impression is that where there is some harmonisation between the content and style of delivery. 'It is not what you say to people that counts. It is what you have them do' (1969: 30). Postman and Weingartner pointed out that many schools used to test pupils' memories rather than promoting the development of serious question asking. In this chapter we consider the harmonisation of content and methods of delivery in groups where professionals offer support to parents.

There is a growing body of international research evidence that indicates that parents play a crucial role in enhancing educational outcomes for children (Sylva et al., 2010). There is far less evidence regarding the impact of early interventions where practitioners engage with parents (Cummings et al., 2012). Nevertheless the political commitment to early interventions with parents continues to gather momentum. This chapter draws on examples from Australia and England to illustrate some of the common issues arising internationally with regard to working with parents (see also Chapter 19 by Josephine Bleach and Chapter 17 Sian Wyn Siencyn on parenting support initiatives in Wales and Ireland).

In 2011 the UK coalition government made a commitment to increase access to parent support in England (DfE, 2011) initiating the 'CAN Parent' trial in 2012 (DfE, 2012). This policy continued to build upon the Sure Start early intervention initiatives of the previous labour administration (Needham, 2007). The evidence is compelling and many authors internationally report that providing strategies to support parents and children early in children's lives maximises developmental opportunities and enhances early childhood outcomes which extend into adulthood (see Shonkoff and Phillips, 2000; Ghate and Hazel, 2002; McCain and Mustard, 2002; PPEL, 2007).

To provide a further example, research conducted in Australia shows similar investment in prevention and early intervention strategies such as *Community for Children Plus* (Department of Families, Housing, Community Services and Indigenous Affairs, 2013) and *Pathways to Prevention* (Barnes et al., 2006). These strategies also aim to influence children's, parents' or families' behaviours in order to reduce the risk or ameliorate the effects of unfavourable social or physical environments. The goal of these programmes, both in the UK and Australia, is to effect change so that protective factors outweigh risk factors and build resilience. It is argued that preventative programmes and interventions that offer social support to parents and quality learning environments to children are protective for families (Jackson, 2010).

The content of parenting support initiatives

The most commonly occurring named parenting programmes in both Australia and England are Webster-Stratton's The Incredible Years and Triple P Parenting (Cummings et al., 2012). These programmes have been widely adopted because they have a track record of research evidence to indicate their effectiveness (Sanders et al., 2005; Siraj-Blatchford and Siraj-Blatchford, 2010). Both programmes include initial elements which are intended to be universally accessible with discussion sessions drawing on book- and video-based materials. These are aimed at improving mental well-being through improved home relationships which help children assimilate into educational processes. Triple P and The Incredible Years both seek to promote authoritative parenting styles which advocate the setting of clear predictable boundaries that are negotiated and discussed with children rather than imposed. These are considered to lead to a more positive sense of personal agency, self-control and self-confidence in the child (Sanders et al., 2005; Siraj-Blatchford and Siraj-Blatchford, 2010).

This idea of parenting styles is very pervasive in regard to supporting social and emotional development. The parenting style typology developed by Baumrind (1973) identified three key parenting styles, *authoritative, permissive* and *authoritarian. Indifferent* is a fourth identified path (Bornstein and Zlotnick, 2009). Baumrind describes authoritative parenting as an integrated approach to parenting which is neither too permissive in deferring too much to the child, nor too authoritarian, where the adult exerts too much control over the child (Baumrind, 1996).

> Within the authoritative model, behavioral compliance and psychological autonomy are not viewed as mutually exclusive but rather as interdependent objectives: children are encouraged to respond habitually in prosocial ways and to reason autonomously about moral problems, and to respect adult authorities and to learn how to think independently. (Baumrind, 1996: 405)

Bornstein and Zlotnick (2009) showed how these styles have been increasingly widely tested and found to be helpful in a range of contexts which suggest them to be influential in the toddler period in shaping the child's attitudes to social engagement and collaborative learning. Bornstein and colleagues (2011) give an overview of a cross-cultural study comparing authoritarian and progressive parenting styles in over 1000 families in 9 countries. This study suggests that in several contemporary cultural contexts around the world there is a trend towards more progressive parenting styles, particularly in China. They suggest that country differences in progressive and authoritarian attitudes articulate with societal encouragement of child agency. 'Parents who hold more authoritarian attitudes may encourage less agency in their children than parents who hold more progressive attitudes' (Bornstein et al., 2011: 229). However, they still report considerable variance in interpretation within and across countries, cultures and communities. Rogoff (2003) showed how cultural expectations mediate both children's and parents' ideas about what are fair and acceptable. The same events might lead to more consistently progressive responses in one culture compared to another. This reminds those working with families of the importance of developing relationships which explore such cultural differences rather than assuming shared perceptions.

In programmes with more educationally orientated objectives there is also considerable emphasis on developing autonomous and positive learning dispositions. Evidence from pre-school studies, which included parents, emphasise the value of sensitivity to children's learning needs and scaffolding their learning through playful activity and problem solving (Jordan, 2004). The High/Scope research study from the USA (Schweinhart et al., 2005) demonstrated the potential long term benefits of a model of pre-school education which is neither too formal or too laissez faire. What is often under-reported is that the High/Scope children's parents were also encouraged to support this pre-school programme during weekly 90 minute home visits. Sylva et al. (2010) show that such pre-school approaches to supporting children's learning are effective but highlight that a positive home learning environment has a greater predictive power with regard to education attainment. The benefits of sensitive support of child-led learning in combination with the idea of working together with parents are well documented (Evangelou et al., 2007; Whalley and the Pen Green Team, 2007; Rinaldi, 2008).

Decisions about the content of parenting sessions

As evidence of a parenting programme's effectiveness develops there is political pressure to repeat those formats that have been proven to work (Rhodes, 2009). This may, however, lead to tensions if practitioners feel there is a mismatch between the expectations in a prescribed parenting programme and the needs of the parents participating in their local community. Rhodes (2009) argues the Incredible Years programme has a potential draw back where a set format is imposed, because while such programmes have been refined in terms of content for targeted efficacy there will be some individuals and groups for whom a set format is less appropriate. Rhodes suggests that there is a need to collect evidence to evaluate more flexible programmes which could be facilitated through the consistent use of similar pre- and post-test materials. In the second half of this chapter examples from case study research are presented to illustrate why a more flexible approach might be considered.

An example from practice

The first part of this chapter demonstrates that while there is broad agreement on the thrust of activities with parents and young children, professionals delivering parent and toddler groups are sometimes faced with making difficult decisions on the balance of approaches to adopt: how much guidance to offer, how to offer guidance and whether to concentrate on supporting the parent or the child. The importance of offering support for the parents' self-esteem, emotional well-being and bonding with their child are clearly extremely important and connected issues (Jackson, 2006). The following case study examples illustrate practitioners recognising the tension between what they are learning about and what they are doing with particular groups of parents.

The first example is taken from a case study of an English parent and child group offering a ten week programme located within a dedicated Children's Centre. These sessions were intended to include planned group discussions of children's learning; the group is referred to here as Talktime.

In this case study excerpt the practitioners facilitating the group are discussing adapting the format and weekly discussion agenda of the group with their manager.

Practitioner D:	If you follow the programme exactly it is quite prescriptive – this [showing a folder] is just our training notes. I'll show you this activity is in the parents' folder, we have given the paper work out in the sessions but they (the parents) don't take it.
Practitioner B:	No if we're not following the activity in the talking time group I thought it was better to leave it.
Manager M:	It might be worth documenting the informal activity following what the parents are doing which is obviously very rich so it might be worth almost retrospectively documenting. I mean there has been a very real discussion about a dilemma perhaps if we became more aware of the informal stuff we would be reassured that we are doing it well and are more tuned in to the moment and this is still a Talktime under any other name and I am going to interact with it and go with it. And there might be a moment where it is appropriate to just summarise and you'd be using their knowledge, their shared knowledge.
Practitioner D:	I found when I did the programme training it was very structured and I liked the bit where they did the hello and goodbye because I like singing but I was discussing it with B and that didn't work here and we decided that we were going to follow what B had learned from conducting our last group and keep it very similar.
Practitioner B:	This is a different type of parent.
Practitioner D:	That is it. It's not been tailored to fit our parents, we are looking at the parents we have got and it is all coming from their interests rather than us saying this, this and this. If you look on here [points to planning] it has all completely changed because we are supposed to be talking about living with television this week and we haven't. And we are supposed to be talking about favourite stories next week but we won't. We'll be continuing this week's activity and because Cheryl (child) wanted to bath the baby we are going to bath the babies aren't we? Because that is what they are interested in.

In this review meeting the practitioners indicate their reservations that the formal structured discussion part of the session is not working in the way they would like. Interviews conducted with the parents as part of the case study showed that their purposes in attending the sessions were not primarily to learn about parenting but rather to find creative and socialising opportunities for their children and to a lesser extent for themselves. Needham (2010) and Needham and Jackson (2012) highlight the importance of acknowledging and exploring each other's purposes rather than risking tensions arising from feelings that one party is not meeting the expectations of the other.

Manager M's comments highlight that there is some anxiety with regards to deviation from the proven programme but she demonstrates a clear willingness to support the practitioners' professional judgement, particularly if this can be documented and evaluated. As the discussion continues the practitioners highlight their perceptions that a formal structure is not in tune with the parents' purposes. The practitioners encouraged parents to interact supportively to promote the children's learning, and they reflected this in what they did with the parents. The questions for discussion and ideas for developing activities were arrived at jointly with the parents. Discussions, rather than being hypothetical and themed for the group, were sought in personalised exchanges arising from the activity of the child or the parent's questions. This approach has the advantage of helping bridge the divide between theory and practice. It takes what might be abstract ideas and helps to make them visible in personally meaningful situations. It supports parents who are uncomfortable talking in the formality of a group circle or possibly uncomfortable with discussing their personal circumstances. It is not, however, without drawbacks; such sessions may lose structure and important topics may not arise. Omitting structured discussions may miss opportunities to form group bonds or to show the wisdom and diversity of the parents or to build the skills of asking questions of each other. Monitoring the outcomes of these changes on parents' attitudes, self-confidence as well as their satisfaction with the programme could provide helpful evidence and future reference points. As with many things in life, judgement is needed to get the balance right. The medium should match, and model, the message.

The style of parenting support

While there may be broad agreement on the core principles of practice, the personal dimensions of human interaction will always be more complicated. Different families have different routines and cultural outlooks on many aspects of behaviour that are taken for granted by practitioners. Many authors highlight the limited research evidence addressing the broader questions of why programmes appear to work, under what circumstances and for whom (Vandenbroeck et al., 2009; Jackson, 2010). Vandenbroeck and colleagues argue that practitioners need to be more aware of the specific cultural adaptations that parents have to make in realising their own unique family identities based on ever changing circumstances as their children grow up and their needs change. They urge practitioners to be flexible and responsive to what parents have to say about their own inherited and emergent values.

An example from practice

The second example is from case study research that examined supported playgroups in Australia (Jackson, 2010). Supported playgroups are early childhood, dual-focused groups facilitated by practitioners in which parents and young children participate together. In this excerpt one practitioner articulates her awareness of the importance of acceptance, respect and sensitivity.

There's always the risk that people will come and actually be harmed because the interactions are negative towards them, and they actually go away feeling less well off than when they came. So because of that risk, I think it's quite important to keep an eye on the overall dynamic, and make sure that that stays positive and moves towards even, I mean, I still think we've got a lot of growth to do in that area, being more consciously demonstrating strength-based parenting, so consciously embodying that philosophy ... we're trying to further that cultural change ... because I think the natural or enculturated way of adolescents interacting can be quite brutal and harsh. And they've just come from that ... it's how you deal with your own feelings about seeing parenting you're not that comfortable with ... and some people feel like, oh, I've just got to say something, or, I need to be nasty to that person to express that I don't like the fact they haven't changed that baby's nappy. And really it's not helpful, and it's good to just have support for the feelings you're having, which are just almost like loyalty to your own sense of what is right, but have some other ways to manage the interactions with that parent. Because as you know, if you are doing the wrong thing, if you feel judged as well, it doesn't really help you change. It just makes you feel more probably bad about yourself, which might be where the problem's coming from in the first place.

(Supported playgroup facilitator)

In this research emotional support was integral to the relationships developed by the group facilitators with parents, particularly in cases where parents were known not to have experienced nurturing relationships themselves. The facilitators expressed genuine care and respect for parents in their groups and built trusting relationships with them. Parents benefited greatly from this type of support which enhanced their ability to provide nurturing care to their children.

Further, there were many examples that demonstrated the technical qualities, i.e. the knowledge and skills, that the facilitators possessed as a direct result of their training and experience. The main technical aspects in this context were their expertise related to child development and the provision of early childhood learning experiences and their family work expertise. The facilitators' understanding of the local community and welfare service system and their professional knowledge of formal supports and referral pathways could also be considered part of the technical skill that they brought to their facilitation role. Participants spoke at length about the importance of all of these aspects to the process of facilitation.

Relational practices (Dunst and Trivette, 1996), also known as *help-giving traits* and attributions, were seen as vital to the facilitation role by all participants in this research. These attributes included the facilitators' interpersonal skills, active listening skills and their ability to be empathetic, caring and nurturing. It also included the facilitators' ability to view parents as capable and to recognise their parenting capacities. The extent to which facilitators demonstrated these traits and attributions was evidenced through the ways in which they developed meaningful relationships with parents and through their ability to engage in processes of ongoing reflection that informed their behaviour and practice.

Also highly important in this context was the use of participatory practices (Dunst and Trivette, 1996). These practices included facilitators acting on their beliefs about involving parents actively and meaningfully and seeking and paying attention to parent input into the types of activities that were presented. There was particular emphasis placed on providing a range of supports within mainstream, social environments that were based on what parents said they wanted. Based on these same beliefs, facilitators at times also engaged in processes that addressed particular issues and promoted positive relational growth amongst parents.

The real strength of facilitators' work within the case study groups lay in their ability to provide a holistic, family-centred approach to working with families. The ways in which they situated their professional expertise and beliefs in parents' capabilities within caring and respectful relationships, enabled truly supportive environments to be created.

Above all, because the facilitators combined relational and participatory practices rather than relying on technical knowledge alone, parents experienced psychological benefits from their participation (Dawson and Berry, 2002; Trivette and Dunst, 2007). Parents in this research experienced emotional support, decreased isolation and increased confidence in parenting, which are known to influence children's positive developmental outcomes and to assist in the reduction of abusive or neglectful behaviours by parents (Munford and Sanders 2006; Higgins and Katz, 2008).

Conclusion

The development of nurturing, trusting and supportive relationships within groups such as the ones described in this chapter is dependent on the engagement and ongoing participation of parents, often over lengthy periods of time. This aspect of service provision is problematic in cases where families' participation is time-limited by the funding specifications dictated by government departments. The current policies that govern the operation of most groups involving parents are based on the premise that the support of parents influences positive child development. However, these policies also need to take into account that the relationships on which this type of support is dependent take significant time to develop and that outcomes for children are likely to be based on the continuity of these relationships. This issue deserves serious consideration by policymakers, especially in areas where supported playgroups are used as a strategy to target vulnerable communities (Jackson, 2010).

In very practical terms, whether activities with parents are structured, not structured or a mixture of the two, can be negotiated in the specifics of the group context. Keeping some degree of flexibility will allow for genuine exchange of meaningful questions and supportive open dialogues. Often people don't know what they don't know and there are times when practitioners should lead and others where responding to an individual's issues will open up a topic for a whole group. Sometimes a formal turn-taking discussion group will encourage everyone to join in, while at other times this may be overwhelming. People often benefit from thinking spaces and returning flexibly to themes may help parents to talk about what they do know rather than what they do not. In short celebrate difference, be self-critical, evaluate carefully, *take it easy, then your jive will swing* (Oliver and Young, 1939).

Critical Learning Activity

Essential warm up: use your favoured search engine to find a video recording of 'T'ain't what you do'. Listen to the original version by Jimmy Lunceford or the Fun Boy Three/Bananarama version (you might wish to use percussion instruments and join in).

This chapter examines a number of ways to encourage collaboration and harmony between those in an early years setting and parents. It asks that we understand the difference between parental involvement and partnership. Can this be seen within your setting or any group that you are familiar with? Represent this in words or bullet points within two circles as seen from the viewpoint of the parent and the viewpoint of those in the setting. How might each see their purposes and relationships? Importantly, ask yourself if these viewpoints overlap or interrelate?

Further reading

Jackson, D. and Needham, M. (2014) *Engaging with Parents in Early Years Settings.* London: SAGE.

References

Barnes, J., Katz, I., Korbin, J.E. and O'Brien, M. (2006) *Children and Families in Community: Theory, Research, Policy and Practice.* England: John Wiley & Sons Ltd.

Baumrind, D. (1973) 'The development of instrumental competence through socialization', *Minnesota Symposium on Child Psychology,* 7: 3–46.

Baumrind, D. (1996) 'The discipline controversy revisited', *Family Relations,* 45 (4): 405–414.

Bornstein, M.H and Zlotnick, D. (2009) 'Parenting style and their effects', in B.B. Benson and M.H. Marshall (eds), *Social and Emotional Development in Infancy and Childhood.* Oxford: Elsevier.

Bornstein, M.H., Putnick, D. and Lansford, J. (2011) 'Parenting attributions and attitudes in cross-cultural perspective', *Parenting: Science AND Practice,* 11: 214–237.

Cummings, C., Laing, K., Law, J., Mclaughlin, J. and Papps, I. (2012) *Can Changing Aspirations and Attitudes Impact on Educational Attainment? A Review of Interventions.* York: Joseph Rowntree Foundation.

Dawson, K. and Berry, M. (2002) 'Engaging families in child welfare services: an evidenced-based approach to best practice', *Child Welfare,* 81 (2): 293–317.

Department for Education (DfE) (2011) *Supporting Families in the Foundation Years.* London: Department for Education.

Department for Education (DfE) (2012) *Parenting Class Trial Essential Evidence-based Principles.* London: Department for Education.

Department of Families, Housing, Community Services and Indigenous Affairs (2013) *Communities for Children.* Available at: http://agencysearch.australia.gov.au/search/search. cgi?profile=fahcsia_preview&collection=agencies&query=Communities+for+children&form= simple (accessed 28 May 2014).

Dunst, C. and Trivette, C. (1996) 'Empowerment, effective help giving practices and family-centred care', *Paediatric Nursing,* 22 (4): 334–337.

Evangelou, M., Brooks, G. and Smith, S. (2007) 'The birth to school study; evidence of the effectiveness of PEEP, an early intervention for children at risk of educational under-achievement', *Oxford Review of Education,* 33 (5): 581–609.

Ghate, D. and Hazel, N. (2002) *Parenting in Poor Environments: Stress, Support and Coping.* London: Policy Research Bureau.

Higgins, D. and Katz, I. (2008) 'Enhancing service systems for protecting children', *Family Matters,* (80): 43–51.

Jackson, D. (2006) 'Playgroups as protective environments for refugee children at risk of trauma', *Australian Journal of Early Childhood,* 31 (2): 1–6.

Jackson, D. (2010) *A Place to 'Be': Supported Playgroups – a Model of Relational, Social Support for Parents and Children.* University of Western Sydney.

Jordan, B. (2004) 'Scaffolding learning and co-constructing understandings', in A. Anning, J. Cullen and M. Fleer (eds), *Early Childhood Studies.* London: Paul Chapman Publishing.

McCain, M. and Mustard, F. (2002) *The Early Years Study Three Years Later. From Early Child Development to Human Development: Enabling Communities.* Toronto, Canada: The Founders' Network of the Canadian Institute for Advanced Research (CIAR).

Munford, R. and Sanders, J. (2006) *Strengths-based Social Work with Families.* Melbourne: Thomson.

Needham, M. (2007) 'Keeping people in the big picture: national policy and local solutions', in I. Siraj-Blatchford, K. Clarke and M. Needham (eds), *The Team Around the Child.* Stoke on Trent: Trentham.

Needham, M. (2010) *Learning to Learn in Supported Parent and Toddler Groups: A Sociocultural Investigation*. London University.

Needham, M. and Jackson, D. (2012) 'Stay and play or play and chat: comparing roles and purposes in case studies of English and Australian supported playgroups', *European Early Childhood Education Research Journal*. 20 (2): 163–176.

Oliver, J. and Young, J. (1939) *T'ain't What You Do (It's The Way That You Do It)*. Decca Records 78: 2310 edn. New York: Decca.

Parents as Partners in Early Learning (PPEL) (2007) *Parental Involvement – A Snapshot of Policy and Practice*. London: DCSF.

Postman, N. and Weingartner, C. (1969) *Teaching as a Subversive Activity*. Harmondsworth: Penguin.

Rhodes, H. (2009) *Knowing What You Do Works: Measuring your own Effectiveness with Families, Parents and Children: A Short Guide*. London: Family and Parenting Institute.

Rinaldi, C. (2008) *In Dialogue with Reggio Emilia: Listening, Researching and Learning*. London: Routledge.

Rogoff, B. (2003) *The Cultural Nature of Human Development*. Oxford: Oxford University Press.

Sanders, M.R., Ralph, A., Thompson, R., Sofronoff, K., Gardiner, P., Bidwell, K. and Dwyer, S. (2005) *Every Family: A Public Health Approach to Promoting Children's Wellbeing,* brief report. Brisbane, Australia: The University of Queensland.

Schweinhart, L.J., Montie, J., Xiang, Z., Barnett, W.S., Belfield, C.R. and Nores, M. (2005) *Lifetime Effects: The HighScope Perry Preschool Programme Study Through Age 40*. Ypsilanti, MI: High/Scope Press.

Shonkoff, J. and Phillips, D. (2000) *From Neurons to Neighborhoods*. Washington: National Academy Press.

Siraj-Blatchford, I. and Siraj-Blatchford, J. (2010) *Improving Children's Attainment Through a Better Quality of Family-Based Support for Early Learning*. London: Centre for Excellence and Outcomes in Children and Young People's Services.

Sylva, K., Melhuish, E., Sammons, P., Siraj-Blatchford, I. and Taggart, B. (2010) *Early Childhood Matters: Evidence from the Effective Pre-school and Primary Education Project*. London: Routledge.

Trivette, C.M. and Dunst, C.J. (2007) *Capacity-building Family-centred Helpgiving Practices*. Winterberry Research reports Vol 1, No 1. Ashville, NC: Winterberry Press.

Vandenbroeck, M., Grietroets, G. and Snoeck, A. (2009) 'Immigrant mothers crossing borders: nomadic identities and multiple belongings in early childhood education', *European Early Childhood Education Research Journal*, 17 (2): 203–216.

Whalley, M. and The Pen Green Team (2007) *Involving Parents in Their Children's Learning*, 2nd edn. London: SAGE.

Want to learn more about this chapter?

Visit the companion website at **https://study.sagepub.com/reedandwalker** to access podcasts from the author and additional reading to further help you with your studies.

19

Supporting parents

Josephine Bleach

Chapter overview

Central to young children's learning is high quality adult interactions and a challenging and stimulating learning environment, both at home and in early years services (ELI, 2012). This chapter suggests that the curriculum is something that is shared between parents and practitioners. Learning and teaching is not just exclusively service-based but is integrated in a holistic way across all aspects of a child's life. Partnership involves practitioners and parents working together to support each other to ensure that there is continuity and progression in children's learning experiences, with the learning environments, methodologies and adult interaction styles of both home and service complementing each other. To be effective, this form of partnership should be an integral part of the culture of early years services, where all staff are encouraged to take a positive and proactive approach to supporting parental involvement in their children's learning, both at home and in the service. The chapter begins with a definition of partnership, which prioritises parental engagement in learning and teaching. It then examines the professional qualities and skills required if practitioners are to develop positive capacity-building partnerships with parents. A process for partnership, which engages parents and practitioners in sharing their pedagogy, is described. Finally, collaborative learning opportunities for partnering parents as co-educators of their children are explored.

Introduction

Children's outcomes are a product of both home and Early Childhood Education and Care (ECEC) services (Sylva et al., 2011) with the quality of learning in the home interacting with the quality of the ECEC services in shaping children's development. High quality adult interactions and a challenging and stimulating learning environment, at home and in the services, are central to young children's learning (ELI, 2012). Quality ECEC services recognise that parents play a pivotal role in their children's learning from birth and that the home is the place where language, social skills, moral values and citizenship are taught (Macbeth, 1994). Working in partnership with parents to provide a learning environment in which young children can develop to their fullest potential is central to their practice. However, it is not easy for ECEC services to find ways to harness home-learning without challenging the established system or putting undue pressure on both staff and parents. Providing opportunities for a more participative role for parents is no guarantee that they will be taken up or used (Munn, 1998). Staff may be anxious about involving parents and may feel threatened, particularly when parents question their practice, authority and professional competence. As a result, contact with parents may be limited. These factors need to be addressed if ECEC services are to value and proactively support partnership with parents.

This chapter examines how ECEC practitioners and services can work in partnership with parents and engage them in supporting their children's learning and development, both at home and in the service. Much of its content is underpinned by the work of the Early Learning Initiative (ELI), National College of Ireland, which is a community-based educational initiative in the Dublin Docklands. Influenced by Bronfenbrenner (1979), it aims to enhance children's complex interactions with their immediate environment by providing educational support to children and their families over the course of the child's education. Acknowledging, respecting and utilising the expertise and experience within the local families and communities is part of our ethos.

In Ireland, as in other countries, parents are recognised as the primary educators of their children. Partnership with parents is a key element of national education policy at all levels of the Irish education system, including the early years. The context for quality practice in the early years in Ireland is provided in the following documents: *Síolta: The National Quality Framework for Early Childhood Education* (CECDE, 2006) and *Aistear: The Early Childhood Curriculum Framework* (NCCA, 2009). Both these documents encourage and promote effective partnerships between parents and ECEC practitioners as central to professional practice. The appointment of Ireland's first Minister for Children and Youth Affairs, Frances Fitzgerald, in 2011 emphasises the Irish Government's commitment, despite the economic crisis, to prioritise improving outcomes for children and supporting Irish families in bringing up their children. As implementing national policy is a key element of ELI's work, it supports both parents and ECEC services to implement both *Síolta* and *Aistear*, with much of the good practice highlighted in this chapter informed by these frameworks.

The chapter begins with a definition of partnership, which prioritises parental engagement in learning and teaching. It then examines the professional qualities and skills required if practitioners are to develop positive capacity-building partnerships with parents. A process for partnership, which engages parents and practitioners in sharing their pedagogy, is described. Finally, collaborative learning opportunities for partnering parents as co-educators of their children are explored. This chapter is one strand of a holistic approach to working with children and their families. Other strands are considered more fully within Section 3 of this book, while Chapter 18 provides another perspective on partnership and parental involvement, together with integrated working in practice.

What is partnership?

Family–school relationships are socially constructed and historically variable (Lareau, 1997) with partnership having different meanings, connotations and applications depending on who is using the term. Partnership, for the purposes of this chapter, is defined as the relationship between parents and ECEC services in supporting and planning for the best possible care and education for children both at home and in early years services (Bleach, 2010). It involves parents, families and practitioners working together in an atmosphere of mutual respect to benefit children with each recognising, respecting and valuing what the other does and says (NCCA, 2009). Partnership involves responsibility on both sides. Unlike collaboration, which can be an implicit, ad hoc arrangement focused on single discrete areas, partnership entails an explicit negotiated agreement between parents and practitioners to work together and support each other to achieve their overarching goals for the child.

Over the years, various models of partnership between ECEC settings and parents have been developed by researchers. Each emphasise different aspects of the roles and responsibilities of both parents and practitioners. Figure 19.1 incorporates the key elements of parental involvement in their children's learning as outlined in the research literature. Supported by open, caring, respectful relationships, it acknowledges how partnership involves 'processes of progressively more complex reciprocal interactions' (Bronfenbrenner and Morris, 1988: 797) between home, services and community.

At this stage, it is important to delineate between parental involvement in their children's learning, i.e. as educators, and parental involvement in ECEC services, i.e. as spectators and volunteers. With research highlighting the influence of the home learning environment on children's educational development (Melhuish, 2011), society's expectations of parents have increased with parents now required to do a lot of 'educational' work (David, 1993). This home curriculum consists of not only the social, cultural and intellectual development of children but the formulation and transmission

Open, caring, respectful relationships		
Collaboration with community organisations including networking by families		
Parental involvement in the home curriculum	**Parental involvement in ECEC services**	**Home–service communication**

• The basic responsibilities of families, including creating a positive home learning environment
• Parental involvement in learning activities at home
	• Parental involvement in services particularly as volunteers and audiences
	• Parental involvement in decision-making, governance and advocacy
		• The basic responsibilities of services towards families which primarily revolve around home–service communications. These include:
		  • Children's learning and progress
		  • Events and activities
		  • Policies and procedures

Figure19.1   Key categories of parental involvement, adapted from Bleach, 2010

of values, including children's attitudes towards education (Bourdieu, 1997). Parental involvement in ECEC and other services is just an extension of this role as 'parent educator'. This has implications for practice with ECEC practitioners required to understand and appreciate how children's learning is a shared responsibility with parents.

From the literature, two parental traits emerge as crucial for children's success in education. One is 'cultural capital' (Bourdieu, 1997), where parents have the knowledge and economic resources to make the best use of the education system and to compensate for any inadequacies it may have. The other is the parent having the self-confidence and ability to deal with system (Coleman, 1998). Being an effective advocate for your child, being able to mediate between the child and ECEC service and intervene when appropriate is an essential parenting skill. Some parents, due to their own low levels of educational attainment, may lack confidence in their ability to help their children while others may possess similar or superior educational skills and qualifications to the ECEC practitioners (Lareau, 1997). This has implications for the interactions between parents and ECEC practitioners.

Proactive approaches, which enable both practitioners and parents to find ways of sharing their knowledge, skills and expertise with each other, have been shown to increase parental involvement (Mena, 2011). They support the development of shared meaningful practices and theories (Wong, 2009), which enrich the learning environment both at home and in the service. They also help to ensure smooth transitions between home and services by providing the consistency, continuity and progression (Nutbrown, 2006) that children need to thrive. In addition, positive interactions are modelled for children with both parents and practitioners receiving mutual affirmation and support from each other for the work they do with children. As a result, children receive maximum benefit from the early years curriculum with the significant adults in their lives having a shared understanding of the principles of the early years curriculum, the learning goals of each of the partners and the approaches and methodologies they adopt.

Professional partnerships

Warm, respectful and positive relationships with parents have been identified as an important attribute of a professional ECEC practitioner. ECEC practitioners in the Docklands identified a professional as one who '*demonstrates by their words, actions and body language that they have an interest in the parents, families and their children*' (Bleach, 2011). The relationship each practitioner has with parents will be determined by their professional identity as well as the community and cultural contexts in which they operate. It will be influenced by the individual dispositions and emotions, day-to-day lives and relationships, and education (McGillivray, 2008) of both parents and practitioners. 'How' these relationships are fostered is more important than the particular partnership activities, if positive outcomes are to be achieved (Trivette et al., 2010). Parents will be more willing to engage with practitioners who are enthusiastic, caring, available, provide strong direction and can clearly articulate their views (Creech and Hallam, 2009). Perceptions of roles and definitions of education are critical, particularly when education was traditionally thought of as the sole responsibility of trained professionals.

For positive capacity-building relationships to work, practitioners must build on the strengths and resilience of parents. Parents may be educators, supporters, consumers and welfare recipients (Bleach, 2010) and will require differential support to meet the specific learning needs of their children. The degree of expertise and effort required of practitioners will depend on the skills, values and dispositions of individual parents. Some parents may require little or no encouragement to get involved, while others, particularly those who may have had a bad experience of the education system themselves and/or may be under enormous stress due to their life circumstances, will need more support.

How a practitioner engages with parents is important, with the ability to smile and be nice to parents an essential, if somewhat obvious, requirement. Practitioners need to understand where parents are coming from, i.e. their culture, values and life experiences; and take the time to reflect on what is behind their words and actions before rushing in to judge and sometimes condemn. For many parents, particularly when conflicts arise, the ECEC practitioner is the last straw in a very tough situation. Therefore, the default approach for the practitioner when dealing with parents should be to ask open questions, look at the issue from the parents' point of view and listen carefully to what the parents are saying. Identifying and encouraging win–win solutions are essential skills. In addition, if practitioners wish to ensure honest and open relationships with parents, they should apologise when necessary and be open to critical questioning of their teaching approaches.

Planning for partnership

Partnership does not just happen. It requires reflection, action, learning and change from both practitioners and parents. For practitioners, the ability to reflect on and evaluate one's practice (Moyles, 2001) is a key element of developing a professional identity. Community action research (Senge and Scharmer, 2001) is a powerful method, which ELI (2012) uses to develop the capacity of both practitioners and parents to work together to achieve practical outcomes (see Figure 19.2).

The aim is to change the participants' educational practices collectively, by thinking, acting and relating to one another differently (Kemmis, 2009). Encouraging participation and allowing everyone to 'amicably disagree' and 'comfortably inhabit a position of not knowing everything' (Frankham and Howes, 2006) is critical.

A good starting point for practitioners to develop their competencies in partnership with parents is to use the action–reflection cycle (McNiff, 2010). The first step could be to reflect on whether they perceive parents to be educators with an equal responsibility for children's learning, or supporters whose role is to ensure that their children adjust to the norms and values of the ECEC service. This will help them to decide

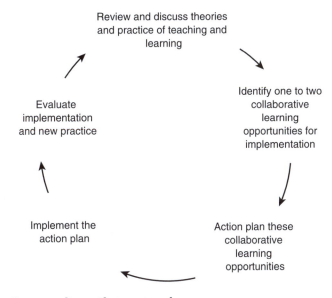

Figure 19.2 Community action research process

where to begin the process. Having thought about the outcomes they wish to achieve, they can then develop a process, which enables practitioners and parents to think about, articulate and discuss pedagogy together. To be effective, the practitioner needs to initiate this process by listening and talking to parents. The language used by practitioners, when engaging parents in these conversations, will be important as the meaning parents attach to words has a powerful influence on the way they respond. Care will be needed to ensure that parents understand what the practitioners are saying, particularly when professional terminology and technical terms are used. Helping parents understand and become familiar with the language of teaching and learning is a capacity-building activity for both parents and professionals. ECEC practitioners who do not have a clearly articulated pedagogical approach or a deep understanding of child development can find it more difficult to share their theories and practices with parents and may find the process challenges their professionalism (Whalley, 2001).

For this approach to work, parents and practitioners need to commit to working together to develop shared learning goals and opportunities, particularly around the key areas of language, cognitive development, literacy and numeracy. These goals should take both the needs of the child and the national curriculum into consideration. An action plan, which encompasses a variety of opportunities for regular, structured engagement with parents, is essential. These opportunities can be broken into the three key categories of parental involvement as outlined in Figure 19.1:

- Parental involvement in the home curriculum: Suggesting and/or providing activities that parents and children can do easily at home, which will promote a positive home learning environment, e.g. spotting shapes on the way home, playing games, reading books, drawing pictures together;
- Parental involvement in ECEC services: Inviting parents into the centre to attend events; observe, talk, read and play with children; prepare and help with activities;
- Home–service communication: Involving parents in the assessment processes; discussing with parents the principles and processes that underpin early years learning and teaching.

The plan should include informal and formal collaborative learning opportunities. Informal activities will consist of taking opportunities as they arise to talk positively to parents about their children's learning (see Table 19.1). Formal opportunities for engaging parents in their children's learning should be scheduled over the course of the year, with the practitioner ensuring that they enable and support the parents to get involved. Practitioners also need to understand that when working with real people within real social systems, things do not always go according to plan (McNiff, 2010). ELI has found that the quality of ongoing discussion and reflection during implementation is of greater importance than the initial plan. Not only does it improve future plans, but it helps to develop the capacity of and the relationships between the stakeholders. It teaches everyone that there are no experts, only a community of learners working together to improve the educational and life chances of children.

Table 19.1   Informal collaborative learning opportunities

Practitioner:	Hello. How are you?
Parent:	Great. How was he today?
Practitioner:	Grand. What did you enjoy today?
Child:	Water.
Practitioner:	Yes, you really enjoyed filling and emptying the containers at the water table and were able to tell me which ones were full and empty. I think he really understands that concept. What do you think?
Parent:	I agree. Last night, when he was having his bath, we had great fun emptying and filling the containers. We enjoyed your bath last night, didn't we? What did you like best?
Child:	Splash.
Parent:	Yes, you really enjoyed the splash the water made when you poured it into the bath. Every time he did this, he said, 'Splash'.
Practitioner:	Sounds like great fun. Tomorrow we are giving the children the experience of filling and emptying containers with lots of different materials, e.g. sand, flour, rice, blocks. We are also focusing on tidying up by encouraging the children to put the toys back in their original containers after they have played with them. I am hoping that they will learn about the concepts of shape, size and capacity by doing these activities. How do you think he will get on with this?
Parent:	I think he will enjoy it. I do encourage him to tidy up at home but sometimes it's easier to do it yourself. Since you are working on it here in the crèche, I will encourage him to do it at home. I like the idea of the rice and I might try giving him some at home to play with. He can use the tea set or anything else – maybe my saucepans – he loves playing with my saucepans and I will see how he gets on.
Practitioner:	That's wonderful. You're great. Let me know how you get on. Thanks for your support. See you both tomorrow.

Collaborative learning opportunities

Providing enjoyable and interesting opportunities for sharing pedagogy will help improve the quality of the children's learning environment and the adults' interactive styles. However, understanding the different roles parents and professionals play in children's lives is critical, if these opportunities are to be effective. The practitioner's role is that of a friendly guide rather an expert critic. They have no remit to tell parents how to rear their children or delegate to them the obligation to socialise their children to the rules of the ECEC service. The most effective approach is for the practitioner to give parents the space to talk about and reflect on their practices. Then, drawing on what the parents have said, the practitioner may discuss his or her own pedagogy.

Ending the contribution with an open question: 'What do you think?' gives the parents the opportunity to continue the discussion (see Table 19.1)).

The Docklands Early Numeracy Programme (ELI, 2012) is an example of how practitioners and parents can work together to support children's learning. Each term, play-based activities and events are developed to support children's learning in a particular area of Maths. Training sessions are provided for both practitioners and parents prior to implementation. As quality interactions (NCCA, 2009) extend not just a child's vocabulary, but also their cognitive, social and emotional development, the home-based activities are designed to encourage parents to have conversations with their children around a chosen numeracy topic. When, for example, the curriculum priority was 'Measures', children and parents discussed and explored the height, weight and capacity of different objects in the home environment. Opportunities are also provided for the parents to participate in centre-based activities. Parents found that the project helped them to understand what they could do at home to help their children improve their numeracy skills, while practitioners felt that it brought staff and parents together. To quote one participant, 'They really grasped the concept, reinforced at home and in school. Maths was great fun' (ELI, 2012: 29)

Parents have a wealth of information about their children and can make a valuable contribution to assessment practices in ECEC settings (NCCA, 2009). Learning stories, portfolios and displays can help the practitioner to keep parents informed of how their children are doing in the service, what they are learning and what is causing them difficulties. Explaining the links between the children's learning and the activities they are engaged in will be important. Parents should also have the opportunity of telling their own stories of children's learning with practitioners, encouraging them to observe how their children interact with and explore their home environment. Practitioners need to explain to parents how information from these observations is used to develop pedagogy. Involving parents in assessment practices builds their capacity and gives them the language, knowledge and skills to discuss their children with other professionals, thereby enabling smooth transitions for their children when they attend other services.

★   **Reflection point**

For many ECEC practitioners, working in partnership with parents to support children's learning in the way described in this chapter is new. For practitioners and parents to work effectively together, it will need to be embedded in the practices and policies of the early years services, with service managers actively encouraging all staff to engage parents in their children's learning, both at home and in the service.

However, changing practices within organisations is never a one-off or isolated event. It is a complex, analytical, political and cultural process of challenging and changing the core beliefs, structure and strategy of a community (Pettigrew, 1987). Successful change requires an emergent, evolutionary and educational process of engaging with others that needs to be sustained for significant periods of time (Herr and Anderson, 2005). Community action research supports the implementation of change in a way that enhances participants' capabilities, both individually and collectively, to produce results they care about (Senge and Scharmer, 2001). As it enables all those involved to create and share knowledge about what works, learn from each other's experience and find solutions to common problems (NCSL, 2002), it can be used to implement the approach to partnership described in this chapter.

Critical Learning Activity

Application for practice

- Having read this chapter on supporting parents, reflect on the various issues that arose in relation to partnership with parents. List the approaches that you think would work well for you as an ECEC practitioner and explain why. What are the challenges involved and how could you address them?
- Having re-read the section in this chapter on planning for partnership, devise an action plan to implement the strategies you have chosen. The learning opportunities, both home and centre-based, along with the relevant resources required to implement these opportunities, should be detailed.
- Having drawn up your plan, reflect on what you are hoping to achieve with this plan. Check that it is realistic considering the context in which you work and the time available to both you and the parents you work with. Revise your plan if necessary.
- Implement your plan. After each learning opportunity, ask the parents and children what they thought of the experience. Record their comments and your own reflections. What worked well? What did not work well and needs to be changed? Consider if you are still on track to achieve your goals and outcomes. If not, what changes are needed to both the plan and the next learning opportunity?

Further reading

Bleach, J. (2013) 'Improving educational aspirations and outcomes through community action research', *Educational Action Research Journal*, 21 (2).

National Council for Curriculum and Assessment (NCCA) (2009) *Aistear: The Early Childhood Curriculum Framework*. Dublin: NCCA.

References

Bleach, M.J. (2010) *Parental Involvement in Primary Education in Primary Education in Ireland*. Dublin: Liffey Press.

Bleach, M.J. (2011) 'Developing ECEC practitioners' sense of professionalism through reflective practice and on-going professional development', paper presented at the European Early Childhood Education Research Association 21st Annual Conference, Geneva.

Bourdieu, P. (1997) 'The forms of capital', in A.H. Hasley, H. Lauder, P. Brown and S. Wells (eds), *Education, Culture, Economy and Society*. Oxford: Oxford University Press.

Bronfenbrenner, U (1979) *The Ecology of Human Development: Experiments by Nature and Design*. Cambridge, MA: Harvard University Press.

Bronfenbrenner, U. and Morris, P.A. (1988) 'The ecology of developmental processes', in W. Damon and R.M. Lerner (eds), *Handbook of Child Psychology, Vol. 1: Theoretical Models of Human Development*, 6th edn. New York: Wiley. pp. 793–828.

Centre for Early Childhood Development and Education (CECDE) (2006) *Síolta: The National Quality Framework for Early Childhood Education*. Dublin: CECDE.

Coleman, P. (1998) *Parent, Student and Teacher Collaboration: The Power of Three*. London: Paul Chapman.

Creech, A. and Hallam, S. (2009) 'Interaction in instrumental learning: the influence of interpersonal dynamics on parents', *International Journal of Music Education*, 27 (2): 94–106.

David, M.E. (1993) *Parents, Gender and Education Reform*. Cambridge: Polity Press.

Early Learning Initiative (ELI) (2012) *Submission to the Joint Committee on Jobs, Social Protection and Education on Educational Disadvantage*. Dublin: National College of Ireland.

Frankham, J. and Howes, A. (2006) 'Talk as action in "collaborative action research": making and taking apart teacher/researcher relationships', *British Educational Research Journal*, 32 (4): 617–632.

Herr, K. and Anderson, L. (2005) *The Action Research Dissertation: A Guide for Students and Faculty*. London: SAGE.

Kemmis, S. (2009) 'Action research as a practice-based practice', *Educational Action Research*, 17 (3): 463–474.

Lareau, A. (1997) 'Social-class differences in family-school relationships: the importance of cultural capital', in A.H. Hasley, H. Lauder, P. Brown and A.M. Well (eds), *Education: Culture, Economy and Society*. Oxford: Oxford University Press.

Macbeth, A. (1994) 'Expectations about parents in education', in A. Macbeth and B. Ravn (eds), *Expectations about Parents in Education*. European Perspectives, Glasgow: European Parents' Association; Computing Services (University of Glasgow).

McGillivray, G. (2008) 'Nannies, nursery nurses and early years professionals: constructions of professional identity in the early years workforce in England', *European Early Childhood Education Research Journal*, 16 (2): 242–254.

McNiff, J. (2010) *Action Research for Professional Development. Concise Advice for New and Experienced Action Researchers*. Poole, Dorset: September Books.

Melhuish, E. (2011) *The Early Years and Later Development: Evidence and Social Policy*, presented at Growing Up in Ireland's Third Annual Research Conference, Dublin.

Mena, J.A. (2011) 'Latino parent home-based practices that bolster student academic persistence', *Hispanic Journal of Behavioral Sciences*, 33 (4): 490–506.

Moyles, J. (2001) 'Passion, paradox and professionalism in early years education', *Early Years*, 21 (2): 81–95.

Munn, P. (1998) 'Parental influence on school policy: some evidence from research', *Journal of Education Policy*, 13 (3): 379–394.

National College for School Leadership (NCSL) (2002) *Why Networked Learning Communities?* Nottingham: National College for School Leadership.

National Council for Curriculum and Assessment (NCCA) (2009) *Aistear: The Early Childhood Curriculum Framework*. Dublin: NCCA.

Nutbrown, C. (2006) *Threads of Thinking, Young Children Learning and the Role of Early Education*, 3rd edn. London: SAGE.

Pettigrew, A.M. (1987) 'Context and action in the transformation of the firm', *Journal of Management Sciences*, 24 (6): 649–670.

Senge, P. and Scharmer, O. (2001) 'Community action research: learning as a community of practitioners, consultants and researchers', in P. Reason and H. Bradbury (eds), *Handbook of Action Research, Participative Inquiry and Practice*. London: SAGE.

Sylva, K., Melhuish, E., Sammons, P., Siraj-Blatchford, I. and Taggart, B. (2011) 'Pre-school quality and educational outcomes at age 11: low quality has little benefit', *Journal of Early Childhood Research*, 9 (2): 109–124.

Trivette, C.M., Dunst, C.J. and Hamby, D.W. (2010) 'Influences of family-systems intervention practices on parent-child interactions and child development', *Topics in Early Childhood Special Education*, 30 (1): 3–19.

Whalley, M. (2001) *Involving Parents in their Children's Learning*. London: SAGE.

Wong, A.C.Y. (2009) 'Dialogue engagements: professional development using pedagogical documentation', *Canadian Children*, 34 (2): 25–30.

Want to learn more about this chapter?

Visit the companion website at **https://study.sagepub.com/reedandwalker** to access podcasts from the author and additional reading to further help you with your studies.

20

Policy into practice: implementing the Early Years Learning Framework for Australia from a Western Australian perspective

Sandra Hesterman

Chapter overview

This chapter provides a brief overview of contemporary Western Australian early childhood education during a period of reform. It describes, through the lens of a University lecturer, the complexities early childhood teachers experience as they try to implement Australia's first national *Early Years Learning Framework* (EYLF) in a policy environment of Australia's first national curriculum (for students aged 5–17 years) and an already overcrowded state-education early years curriculum. It also considers how the lack of practical support for teachers is crippling the crusade for nationally consistent, high quality experiences and programs in children's education. Finally the chapter examines some leadership and advocacy initiatives that can facilitate the early years reform agenda. In this chapter the term 'teacher' refers to those who have completed a University degree in early childhood education (ECE). The term 'educator', as identified in the EYLF, includes early childhood practitioners (working directly with children in early years settings) who do not have early childhood teacher/education University qualifications.

A national crusade to lift the standards in early childhood education

Australia is a vast country. The island continent has a land area of almost 7.7 million square kilometres, almost as great as that of the United States of America (excluding Alaska), about 50% greater than Europe (excluding the former USSR states) (Australian

Bureau of Statistics, 2009). Its multicultural, multiracial population, nearing 23 million, is spread across six states and two territories and has two levels of government – commonwealth/federal and state/territory. Whilst each state and territory has its own government and constitution, and has the power to make its own laws on certain matters, including education, the Commonwealth prevails in any conflict between state/territory law and commonwealth law (Australian Government, 2012).

Western Australia (WA), the largest, most isolated and least densely populated state, has developed its own distinct model of pre-school services. It leads the country in universal access to pre-school education, with 97.5% of 4 year-olds accessing 15 hours a week of funded 'school' education, and 100% of 5 year-olds eligible for full-time pre-school education in 2013 (Alderson and Martin, 2011). A national government crusade aspiring to reform ECE in a state that believed it had already 'lifted the standards' was destined to be challenging.

In 2008, the newly elected Labor government identified education as its most important economic policy issue, claiming that 'the future of ordinary people and their children was tied to educational success' (Gillard, 1998). The Australian public was promised an 'education revolution', including high quality ECE interventions, which would 'build the best education system in the world … to produce the most innovative, the most skilled and the best trained workforce in the world' (Rudd, 2007: 2).

Since the launch of its *Programme for International Student Assessment* (PISA) in 2000, the Organisation for Economic Co-operation and Development (OECD) has wielded considerable influence on Australian education policy. Perceived failings of its education system (as measured by PISA) have been instrumental in driving education reform with urgent haste, particularly in relation to early literacy and numeracy learning (Baird et al., 2011; Garrett, 2012). This sense of urgency is palpable – the Melbourne Graduate School of Education (2011: 7) notes that 'if Australia stands still it will fall behind and we can see this happening already'. The OECD, which conducts analysis on many aspects of ECE across many countries, has emphasised that 'the educational impact of early childhood education shows up clearly by age 15' (2009: 1). There is a persuasive argument that education systems should maximise learning opportunities for young children during early brain development; a case of 'use it or lose it' (OECD, 2009: 1). While Australian PISA performance has been relatively high, there is indication that students are 'flat-lining' in reading and mathematics with a level of underperformance greater than that of many similar countries (Melbourne Graduate School of Education, 2011).

To enshrine education reform in law, the Commonwealth Government will soon introduce legislation that clarifies its national plan for school improvement. While this massive reform is now underway, the finer details of how the Commonwealth Government will reach consensus with the states and territories on matters of ECE are not yet finalised.

A national vision for the early years

In late 2008, the Commonwealth Government held an *Australia 2020 Summit* to identify 'big ideas' that would enable Australia to maximise its wealth, excellence and
equity through productivity growth. The final summit report identified children's
development as central to the national productivity agenda. It was envisaged that
children's achievement of individual excellence (and having their learning and social
needs met) would enable Australia to secure a position in the top five schooling systems in the world by 2025, with predictions of a stronger economy and a more
prosperous future (Department of Prime Minister and Cabinet, 2008). Delivery of a
national school curriculum and national universal access to high-quality education for
early childhood development was pledged. Development of a common learning
framework to meet early childhood and schooling needs was also deemed necessary.
The Victorian Curriculum and Assessment Authority (2008) provided the following
example to illustrate differences in ECE provision:

> Expectations for a 5 year-old might be vastly different in different systems. For example,
> the 5 year-old child can be included in an early childhood curriculum document for birth
> to 5 years which caters for their characteristics and dispositions for learning while at the
> same time the 5 year-old child can have a set of expectations in terms of 'areas of learn-
> ing' or subjects with a set of learning outcomes if in their first year of primary school.
> (2008: 1)

Whilst education is a state responsibility, in recent years 'the Commonwealth government involvement in schooling has increased so greatly that it is now referred
to as a "shared" responsibility, where programs, spending, and intergovernmental
relations are highly interrelated, and complex and contested' (Hinz, 2010: 1). WA
retains constitutional control over education but the federal government is exercising its political might to ensure change occurs at the state level on national terms,
in exchange for increased funding and grants for specific purposes (Steketee, 2010).
The recent establishment of two governing bodies to oversee the quality of ECE
across the nation illustrates the new wave of federalism occurring in Australian
education:

1. The Australian Curriculum, Assessment and Reporting Authority (ACARA), a
   national independent statutory authority, is responsible for the development of a
   national curriculum kindergarten to Year 12, a national assessment program, and
   a national data collection and reporting program; and
2. The Australian Children's Education and Care Quality Authority (ACECQA), a
   national independent statutory authority, monitors the consistent application of
   the Education and Care Services National Law across all states and territories
   including the implementation of the *Early Years Learning Framework* (Department
   of Education and Early Childhood Development (DEEWR), 2011).

The Melbourne Graduate School of Education notes that 'there has been a lot of discussion in Australia about curriculum and *what* should be taught in schools, but less debate about *how* it is taught' (2011: 59). Whilst the EYLF (DEEWR, 2009) was designed to provide guidance to early childhood teachers on this issue, it ultimately depends on a shared vision between the Commonwealth and states/territories.

Early Years Learning Framework for Australia

Hard on the heels of the *Summit 2020*, the EYLF was developed and distributed to Early Childhood Education and Care (ECEC) centres across Australia. The framework would be an integral part of the *National Quality Framework* (NQF) (DEEWR, 2011) for ECEC, with the first of its seven quality areas directed to *Educational Program and Practice*. The framework aligns with the United Nations Convention on the Rights of the Child (United Nations General Assembly, 1989), and the Council of Australian Governments' vision that, 'All children have the best start in life to create a better future for themselves and for the nation' (DEEWR, 2009: 5). It also provides detail on ECE pedagogy, principles and practice to support achievement of five broad, observable learning outcomes for children aged 0–5 years:

1. Children have a strong sense of identity.
2. Children are connected with and contribute to their world.
3. Children have a strong sense of well-being.
4. Children are confident and involved learners.
5. Children are effective communicators.

Special consideration was given to how the document could be distinctively Australian; to celebrate Australia's multiculturalism and recognise that 'childhood is experienced in multiple ways, in differing circumstances' (Victorian Department of Education and Early Childhood Development, 2008: 2). Hence, the EYLF was designed to empower teachers (and educators) to use their professional judgement on how they approach each child's learning, being mindful that:

• Each child will progress towards the outcomes in different and equally meaningful ways;
• Learning is not always predictable and linear; and
• Educators will plan with each child and the outcomes in mind (adapted from DEEWR, 2009: 19).

The case for ECE reform is founded on extensive research evidence that supporting children in the pre-school years greatly increases their chances of successful transitions to school, achievement of better learning outcomes, and social and emotional well-being (WA Department of Education and Training, 2010). The Commonwealth Government aims to provide a 'comprehensive, cohesive and mandated curriculum framework' for early childhood services (both education and care) (Moore, 2008: 4). From an insider's perspective, however, there were many 'decision points and dilemmas' encountered when the framework was being developed (Sumsion et al., 2009). Articulating a collective vision for Australian ECE within a mere 12-month period resulted in political compromise, particularly for children aged 6–8 years who would not be covered by the new framework. In the case of WA, where ECE and childcare have traditionally been overseen by separate departments (namely education, health and community services), the mandate to unify early childhood services through the NQF would result in additional challenges.

In the absence of WA curriculum guidelines for the 0–3 age group and the transfer of kindergarten and pre-primary programs into the public/state education system (in the late 1990s), with 'more formalised curriculum structures and culture of the compulsory years [adopted] in the precompulsory school years' (Kronemann, 2001: 2), there has been a 'patchwork of provision', with 'many children missing out on quality early childhood programs' (Moore, 2008: 4). Ongoing tension between WA state-government ministers with seemingly divorced agendas led to a 'digging in of heels' regarding changes in ECE, contributing to confusion about how to move forward with the NQS at state level. Complexity was further heightened when, in 2012, the WA Director General of Education advised teachers that the NQF (hence the EYLF) would not be mandated in its early years classrooms.

The promise of a meaningful revolution to lift standards of education through play-based learning and holistic teaching approaches is thus slipping away. WA ECE teachers are largely left to lead sole crusades in a revolution costing $6.5 billion but providing them with no support to unravel the essence of the EYLF.

Early childhood education in Western Australia

During the first decade of the twenty-first century, WA early childhood teachers focused on teaching content in eight state-curriculum learning areas and supporting children's development in cognitive, social, emotional, physical, creative and linguistic domains (WA Curriculum Council, 1998). Despite state level demands for academic curriculum push-down in ECE, the majority of teachers aimed to implement a play-based and integrated curriculum to facilitate learning and development. These holistic approaches were consistent with approaches pre-service teachers were taught during their ECE University studies. However, as ECE has moved under the auspices of primary school administration, demands for pedagogical uniformity, teaching the three Rs, early intervention and primary school program integration have increased, resulting in less time for quality play. There is also a keen focus on children aged 4–5 (kindergarten and pre-primary) to better prepare them for National Assessment Program – Literacy and Numeracy (NAPLAN) testing. The Western Australian Primary Principals' Association (2011) has also produced its own resources to map the *Australian Curriculum Mathematics and English* for this age group. While most members do not have ECE qualifications, they have actively promoted their guidelines for best practice in the ECE 0–8 context.

Following two years of silence on the Commonwealth Government's early years reform agenda and on EYLF implementation, the WA Department of Education (2011) published a document, *Early Years of Schooling,* to clarify its position on ECE. State-school teachers were told what they already knew: that there was 'a lack of clarity among early childhood educators and school leaders about what constitutes high quality early childhood curriculum, pedagogy and assessment', and 'that practice in the early years is inconsistent across schools, with no clear guiding vision and expectations' (O'Neill, 2011: 2). On reviewing the document, teachers were confused further when presented with a diagram showing an arbitrary (hence divisive) line drawn between the applicability of the EYLF to kindergarten (children aged 4 years) and the Australian Curriculum for children aged 5–8 years. Teachers were also subsequently advised that:

> While early years' teachers may have specific expertise in early childhood development and learning, it is the responsibility of each principal to ensure there is continuity in the learning program across Kindergarten, Pre-primary, Year 1 and Year 2, and that the school operates with one cohesive whole-school plan.

> In some schools, Kindergarten and Pre-primary teachers in particular operate in isolation from the rest of the school, often with a quite different educational philosophy and practice. This can result in a disconnection between teaching programs in those years and subsequent years.

> All teachers share responsibility for the performance of all students in the school, and school leaders are responsible for making sure all staff operate as a team. This means, for example, that all early years' teachers need to be familiar with Year 3 literacy and numeracy requirements and understand their role in preparing students for the demands of future years. (O'Neill, 2011: 4)

While WA leads the nation in universal *access* to pre-school education, this is not the same as providing nationally consistent, high quality ECE. Recent NAPLAN results showed that WA Year 3 results are below the national average (O'Neill, 2011). Government expectations that early childhood teachers will integrate Australian Curriculum priorities while maintaining state-education curriculum initiatives have resulted in WA teachers feeling overwhelmed, particularly when reading Department of Education rhetoric that they must raise their expectations of what children can achieve in the first years at school. In the absence of state level policy guidelines regarding the EYLF and its practical implications for ECE teachers, play-based learning has not been a key characteristic of universal access, and WA remains fragmented in its ECE provision and content:

1. Children aged birth to three years receive their child-centred, play-based education guided by the EYLF through childcare providers (largely Long Day-care Centres);
2. The education of children aged four and five years attending non-government schools and Long Day-care Centres is guided by the EYLF;
3. The EYLF is not mandated for children aged four and five years attending state-school based ECE; and
4. The EYLF may have some pedagogical significance for teachers overseeing the education of children aged six to eight years with little emphasis on the natural processes of learning through play.

Different curricula and languages, working to different concepts of program quality, with different cultures of program delivery, viewing each other with some suspicion, and not self-identifying as a unified workforce/profession now characterise WA ECE (Cahill, 2012). While there is frustration at the lack of leadership from the education sector, a small number of teachers are accessing online forums to support each other as they trial EYLF implementation in the belief that they should be following the same guidelines as the rest of the country (Early Childhood Australia, 2012b). Failure to provide teachers with ECE state-leadership and EYLF professional development during 2010–2011, followed by ad hoc and minimal support in 2012, has crippled early crusade efforts for nationally consistent and high quality early childhood programs in WA.

A University perspective

Following the release of the country's first EYLF, there was widespread expectation that the ECE traditions of play-based learning and holistic teaching approaches would be returned and strengthened, and that the framework would 'inspire conversations, improve communication and provide a common language about young children's learning among children themselves, their families, the broader community, early childhood educators and other professionals' (DEEWR, 2009: 8). The realisation that in the foreseeable future the EYLF would not be instrumental in WA ECE reform was met with great disappointment.

During their practicum at state schools (2009–2012), the majority of pre-service teachers did not observe the EYLF in practice. Despite the publication of an Early Childhood Australia (ECA) and ACARA position paper *Foundations for Learning: Relationships between the Early Years Learning Framework and the Australian Curriculum* (ECA and ACARA, 2011), which confirmed that the education approaches espoused by the EYLF would continue to be appropriate in ECE, the Australian curriculum national assessment program, national data collection and the reporting program dominate ECE pedagogy and practice. As the majority of WA ECE teachers do not integrate the EYLF into their programs, there is limited role modelling of 'walking the talk' for University students. Limited communication between the Department of Education and academics also impedes conversations essential to supporting the national reform agenda.

The need for leadership and advocacy work to promote the EYLF in schools is necessary if WA children are to share in their ECE entitlements.

Leadership and advocacy

Pedagogical debate on play versus formal learning is well documented (Miller and Hevey, 2012), but there is little research published that documents the experience of ECE professionals when raising issues and asking for change to make a difference to children's lives (ECA, 2012a). Wanting to reframe early childhood leadership in the context of current reform, Stamopoulos claims that the role of the ECE teacher is more than teaching children:

> Rather, it is to lead with intent, mentor and advocate in their work context, in partnership with children and families, within community settings and is a response to federal and state educational initiatives targeting children from birth to age eight years. (2012: 42)

Leaders are defined as 'early childhood professionals who share a reciprocal process to pursue changes that lead to a desired future' (Stamopoulos, 2012: 42). Leadership in ECE involves networking with interested and like-minded others to connect with the profession and discuss advocacy goals both inside and outside the workplace. ECA, citing Smale's (2009) research on early childhood professionals' perceptions and experiences of advocacy for children's well-being has identified a range of advocacy initiatives that teachers can engage in to promote change. These include: communicating with interested parties and professionals; requesting and supporting the advocacy of stakeholders and discussing advocacy goals with professionals; documenting children's competencies and engaging the media; supporting the training of advocates; sharing information with wider networks of colleagues; and receiving support and resources from other early childhood organisations.

In 2012, University lecturers on ECE regularly emphasised the need for pre-service teachers to join organisations that voice 'children's rights and needs to other community groups or politicians … those people who can help advance the cause' of implementing EYLF in WA schools (ECA, 2012a: 1). As previously mentioned, some teachers are accessing online forums to seek practical support in using the EYLF. Others have established book clubs to transform their practice in the absence of departmental professional learning. Early evidence of these leadership and advocacy initiatives among network groups confirms there is empowerment through involvement.

Conclusion

While 0–8 years is the 'official' definition of the early childhood period (hence an early years education associated with holistic teaching approaches and play-based learning), this entitlement cannot be assumed in WA. This chapter has examined some of the complexities that underpin diversity in ECE pedagogical considerations and practice. The lesson learned from the WA experience is that when putting policy into practice, such as implementing the EYLF, pre-service and new graduate teachers cannot rely on a national reform agenda or education systems to ensure quality ECE experiences. Neither can they assume that experienced teachers will demonstrate high quality teaching and leadership in implementing the EYLF. To strengthen ECE in WA, it is recommended that teachers' professional lives be characterised by:

1. *Belonging* to an advocacy networking group (which includes families and community members) that can assist them in developing high quality leadership skills in ECE;
2. *Being* more innovative, responsive and accountable to the rights of the child to strengthen ECE in their school; and
3. *Becoming* aware of the requirements of the National Quality Agenda Education and Care to facilitate effective implementation of the EYLF in their ECE program.

Ultimately it is each teacher's responsibility to make a difference to children in their care during 'school' life. Stamopoulos believes that 'if leadership is to be reframed, it must have a basis of professional knowledge, professional identity, an interpretative frame and relational trust' (2012: 47). Each of these qualities is embedded in the above list of recommended action.

The WA Director General's *Focus 2013: Direction for Schools* (O'Neill, 2012) identifies strengthening ECE as a priority. However, there is no provision in the state budget (2012–2013) for expenditure on teachers' professional development on the NQS (including the EYLF). Neither is there inclusion of the EYLF in the 2013 Western Australian Primary Principals' Association's *Professional Learning Services* for teachers. Despite continued calls from the wider education community for 'WA political parties to commit to monitoring the impact of implementation of the EYLF in particular in the area of pedagogy ("structured play-based" pedagogy versus formal learning), with particular attention to aspects of mental health and wellbeing', there is continued silence at the state level (State School Teachers' Union of Western Australia, 2012). It remains to be seen whether the Commonwealth Government will intervene in matters of state education to maximise opportunities for all children to achieve the EYLF outcomes, or whether teachers (against the odds) will continue their own crusade of 'lifting the standards' in ECE tradition.

Further reading

Department of Education, Employment and Workplace (DEEWR) (2009) *The Early Years Learning Framework for Australia*. Available at: https://education.gov.au/early-years-learning-framework.

Early Childhood Australia and Australian Curriculum, Assessment and Reporting Authority (2011) *Foundations for Learning: Relationships between the Early Years Learning Framework and the Australian Curriculum*. Available at: www.earlychildhoodaustralia.org.au/pdf/ECA_ACARA_Foundations_Paper/ECA_ACARA_Foundations_Paper_FINAL.pdf.

References

Alderson, A. and Martin, M. (2011) *Report on the Feasibility Study into the Provision of Preschool in Childcare Settings*. East Perth: Department of Education.

Australian Bureau of Statistics (2009) Available at: www.abs.gov.au/ausstats (accessed 25 May 2014).

Australian Government (2012) *Your Connection with Government*. Available at: http://australia.gov.au/about-australia (accessed 25 May 2014).

Baird, J., Issacs, T., Johnson, S., Stobart, G., Yu, G., Sprague, T. and Daugherty, R. (2011) *Policy Effects of PISA*. Available at: http://research-information.bristol.ac.uk/files/14590358/Baird_et_al._2011.pdf (accessed 25 May 2014).

Cahill, R. (2012) *Preschool within Schools: Same Direction, Different Pathway*, paper presented at Early Childhood Australia National Conference, Perth, Western Australia.

Department of Education, Employment and Workplace (DEEWR) (2009) *The Early Years Learning Framework for Australia*. Available at: http://education.gov.au/early-years-learning-framework (accessed 25 May 2014).

Department of Education, Employment and Workplace (DEEWR) (2011) *National Quality Framework for Early Childhood Education and Care – Legislation, Standards and Progress*. Available at: www.acecqa.gov.au/national-quality-framework (accessed 25 May 2014).

Department of Prime Minister and Cabinet (2008) *Australia 2020 Summit: Final Report*. Available at: www.preschoolmatters.act.gov.au/the-early-years-learning-framework (accessed 25 May 2014).

Early Childhood Australia (ECA) (2012a) *Advocacy to Promote Children's Wellbeing and Rights*. Available at: www.earlychildhoodaustralia.org.au/every_child_magazine/every_child_index/advocacy_to_promote_childrens_wellbeing_and_rights.html (accessed 25 May 2014).

Early Childhood Australia (ECA) (2012b) *EYLF in WA Kindergarten Setting*. Available at: http://forums.earlychildhoodaustralia.org.au/showthread.php?443-EYLF-in-WA- (accessed 25 May 2014).

Early Childhood Australia (ECA) and Australian Curriculum, Assessment and Reporting Authority (ACARA) (2011) *Foundations for Learning: Relationships between the Early Years Learning Framework and the Australian Curriculum*. Available at: www.earlychildhoodaustralia.org.au/pdf/ECA_ACARA_Foundations_Paper/ECA_ACARA_Foundations_Paper_FINAL.pdf (accessed 25 May 2014).

Garrett, P. (2012) *Aussie Schools Flatline in Global Education Tests*. Available at: www.abc.net.au/news/2012–12–11/aussie-schools-flatline-in-international-education-tests/4422532 (accessed 25 May 2014).

Gillard, J. (1998) *Maiden Speech in the House of Representatives*. Available at: http://australian-politics.com/1998/11/11/julia-gillard-maiden-speech.html (accessed 25 May 2014).

Hinz, B. (2010) *Australian Federalism and School Funding Arrangements: An Examination of Competing Models and Recurrent Critiques*, paper presented at Canadian Political Science Association Annual Conference, Montreal, Canada.

Kronemann, M. (2001) *The Western Australian Model of Preschool Education*. Perth: AEU.

Melbourne Graduate School of Education (2011) *Schooling Challenges and Opportunities: A Report for the Review of Funding for Schooling Panel*. Melbourne: The University of Melbourne.

Miller, L. and Hevey, D. (eds) (2012) *Policy Issues in the Early Years*. London: SAGE.

Moore, T. (2008) *Towards an Early Years Learning Framework for Australia*. Available at: www.rch.org.au/uploadedFiles/Main/Content/ccch/TM_WP4-TowardsAnEarlyYearsLearningFramework_2_.pdf.

O'Neill, S. (2011) *The Early Years of Schooling*. East Perth: Western Australian Department of Education.

O'Neill, S. (2012) *Focus 2013: Direction for Schools*. East Perth: Western Australian Department of Education.

Organisation for Economic Co-operation and Development (OECD) (2009) *Investing in High Quality Early Childhood Education and Care (ECEC)*. Available at: www.oecd.org/education/preschoolandschool/48980282.pdf.

Rudd, K. (2007) 'Rudd unveils new education policy', *The 7.30 Report*, 23 January (with Kerry O'Brien), transcript. Sydney: Australian Broadcasting Corporation. Available at: www.abc.net.au/7.30/content/2007/s1832341.htm (accessed 30 January 2007).

Smale, S. (2009) *Early Childhood Professionals' Perceptions and Experiences of Advocacy for Children's Wellbeing*, Master of Teaching (Early Childhood) thesis, Melbourne University.

Stamopoulos, E. (2012) 'Reframing early childhood leadership', *Australasian Journal of Early Childhood*, 37 (2): 43–48.

State School Teachers' Union of Western Australia (2012) *Putting Kids First*. Available at: www.sstuwa.org.au/component/content/article/532-sstuwa-information/sstuwa-campaigns/putting-kids-first/9066-list-of-recommendations.

Steketee, M. (2010) *Federalism is a Dead Idea. So What Now?* Available at: www.theaustralian.com.au/national-affairs/opinion/federalism-is-a-dead-idea-so-what-now/story-e6frgd0x-1225857322222 (accessed 25 May 2014).

Sumsion, J., Barnes, S., Cheeseman, S., Harrison, L., Kennedy, A. and Stonehouse, A. (2009) *Insider Perspectives on Developing Belonging, Being and Becoming: The Early Years Learning Framework for Australia*. Available at: researchoutput.csu.edu.au/dtl_publish/24/14198.html.

United Nations General Assembly (1989) *The Convention on the Rights of the Child*, adopted by the General Assembly of the United Nations, 20 November.

Victorian Curriculum and Assessment Authority (2008) *Analysis of Curriculum/Learning Frameworks for the Early Years (Birth to Age 8)*. Melbourne: Victorian Curriculum and Assessment Authority.

Victorian Department of Education and Early Childhood Development (2008) *A Research Paper to Inform the Development of An Early Years Learning Framework for Australia*. Melbourne: Office for Children and Early Childhood Development, Department of Education and Early Childhood Development.

WA Department of Education (2011) *Early Years of Schooling*. Available at: www.education.wa.edu.au/home/redirect?oid=SiteProxy-id-14755380 (accessed 21 June 2014).

Western Australian Curriculum Council (1998) *Curriculum Framework for Kindergarten to Year 12 Education in Western Australia*. Osborne Park: The Council.

Western Australian Department of Education and Training (2010) *The Best Possible Start*. East Perth: School Matters.

Western Australian Primary Principals' Association (2011) *Quality Leadership, Quality Schools Online Shop*. Available at: www.wappa.asn.au/general/online-shop.html.

Western Australian Primary Principals' Association (2013) *Professional Learning Services*. Western Australia: WAPPA.

Want to learn more about this chapter?

Visit the companion website at **https://study.sagepub.com/reedandwalker** to access podcasts from the author and additional reading to further help you with your studies.

Section 5

PROFESSIONAL ROLES AND RESPONSIBILITIES

Early Education Practitioners are actively encouraged to explore and develop their role. They are now required to, respond to individual family needs and have a wide knowledge of child development, and critically examine their own professional world. Such training allows those who may not have previously engaged in higher education to access University courses and use work-based expertise to link theory with practice, in effect starting a cycle whereby telling someone they have valuable experience and expertise makes the person want to consider the theoretical perspectives which underpin their practice. An interaction which Knowles (1990) recognised and defined as the term 'andragogy'. He asserted it was the learners' involvement in the process, through interacting in the decisions about what they wanted to learn and underpinning their self-motivation that gave momentum to learning. The process is therefore more self-directed and autonomous.

Students today are therefore involved in this learning journey and co-construct their learning alongside their peers. Not necessarily 'student peers' but also those colleagues involved in practice – a point that is made in this section when considering professional practice today in Chapter 21 by Mike Gasper and one that is the focus of Chapter 25 by Carla Solvason on practice-based research. Both authors suggest this involves a transmission of knowledge and a level of perception about what is taught and learnt (Jarvis, 2002). This helps to draw a line between a traditional pedagogical (teaching) approach and this more interactive form. This involves both teacher and taught seeing the purpose of what interacts between them, which we can call andragogy. In this way, practitioners are not solely *acquiring* knowledge but also *constructing* a purposeful knowledge base within the learning and work environment. This allows the learner to go beyond accepting the values presented before them and explore the practice environments – such as the identity of the children they work with as exposed in Chapter 23 by Victoria Cooper. They are then starting to develop what we know as heutagogy, a term coined by Hase and Kenyon (2000). It is concerned with self-determined learning and in particular (for tutors and students) considering what conditions are necessary for self-determined learning to take place. In essence, allowing students to learn how to learn. It can be argued that work-based inquiry is a means of facilitating such an approach as is an interrogation of such important and complex issues as policy design and development, as articulated in Chapter 20 by Sandra Hesterman. Her views help us to understand the driving forces which attempt to move forward a national educational and economic agenda and consider the tensions between national goals versus local cultural values and actions. This tells us that policy is much more complex than a simple series of 'top down' strategies that are then enacted on the ground.

In the same way this section underpins the danger of seeing professionalism as a simple top down process of training and professionalising the workforce. Collaborative working is exposed in Chapter 22 by Alison Nicholas who recognises the importance of engaging with others as a means to elicit views on what is happening and what works on the ground (Reed, 2008). Practitioners are no longer expected to passively look at what is going on and act more as an active agent of collaboration with others, in which case they are demonstrating personal and professional qualities or what are increasingly known as professional dispositions; a term coined by Rike and Sharp (2008) when considering the qualities of young early years teachers. In the context of this book and this section they may be something like:

- the ability to provide a warm, caring and purposeful way of effectively working with children, young people and families;
- being adept at sharing information with other professionals;
- seeing the value of being part of multi-agency working;
- the ability to be curious about a child's development, recognising their individuality and identity and wanting to improve practice from the ground up;
- seeing the research process as ethical – doing no harm to anyone involved and safeguarding the welfare of the child;
- seeing professionalism as something which allows a reflection on practice and embracing change;
- viewing policy design and development with an open mindset that encourages a critical perspective on what is needed, its importance and its value to children.

It could be argued such descriptors are no more than can be expected of any sound ECEC practitioner or leader. That may well be the case, but look again at the descriptors. Consider the level of professional thought and actions required and consider the level of responsibility that has to be taken on board. A responsibility wider than day-to-day practice but impacting on practice. A responsibility to compare and contrast the practice of others and learn from others, consider what works and why and ask what can be done to extend and improve what goes on. To examine personal and professional values and have an ethical understanding of why and how their actions may impact on children and families. To do this honestly and reflect and learn from the process. To then form communities of practice (Wenger, 1998; Wenger et al., 2002) and do this by working with others and seeing themselves finding solutions or raising questions and developing their own independent learning styles. What a set of tasks, what a set of responsibilities, but one that has its own opportunities and rewards because what you do matters to children and parents – you are the future of our developing professionalism.

Finally, as you read through this section ask yourself some questions based on the work of Jacobson (1998):

- To what extent should a practice-based researcher see their role not as 'the' investigator but 'facilitating' an investigation with others?
- To what extent should a practice-based researcher see their role as not only utilising instruments to investigate practice but see themselves as a powerful instrument to investigate practice?
- To what extent are you moving away from accepting views which unpack meanings associated with educational experience and considering your actions on, in and for practice?
- To what extent do the chapters tell you something about your actions and children, their identity and the integrity of critically examining what you are learning about them?
- Should a professional working in the field of ECEC recognise theory in action?

References

Hase, S. and Kenyon, C. (2000) *From Andragogy to Heutagogy*. Melbourne, Australia: ultiBASE.

Jacobson, W. (1998) 'Defining the quality of practitioner research', *Adult Education Quarterly*, 48: 125.

Jarvis, P. (2002) *Adults and Continuing Education*, 2nd edn. London: Routledge.

Knowles, M.S. (1990) *The Adult Learner: A Neglected Species*. Houston: Gulf Publishing Company.

Reed, M. (2008) 'Professional development through reflective practice' in A. Paige-Smith and A. Craft (eds), *Developing Reflective Practice in Early Years*. Maidenhead: Open University Press pp. 160–169.

Rike, C. and Sharp, L.K. (2008) 'Assessing pre-service teachers' dispositions: a critical dimension of professional preparation', *Childhood Education*, 84 (3): 150–153.

Wenger, E. (1998) *Communities of Practice: Learning, Meaning and Identity*. Cambridge: Cambridge University Press.

Wenger, E., McDermott, R. and Snyder, W. (2002) *Cultivating Communities of Practice*. Cambridge, MA: Harvard Business School Press.

21

Professional practice and early childhood today

Michael Gasper

Chapter overview

This chapter explores several factors influencing the aims, focus and direction of Early Childhood Education and Care (ECEC) professionals in their day-to-day work. Consideration is given to the values, aims and principles which have traditionally guided and underpinned ECEC practice (principled practice), set against the fluctuating and changing social, political and cultural demands shaping and re-shaping the context in which ECEC professionals strive to achieve the best they can for children and families. While citing emerging contradictions the chapter provides reflections on the challenges and opportunities these present.

Introduction

Since the late 1990s there has been an increasing understanding of the need to see both theory and practice of early childhood development in holistic terms, rather than as separate, compartmentalised areas. Professionals from a wide range of backgrounds including health (which itself embodies a complexity of disciplines), childcare, education and social care have come to regard increased professional co-operation and multi-agency working as the most efficient and effective way of providing support for young children, their families and their communities. The growth in the number of reference and text books exploring and promoting multi-agency working published since 2000 indicates the development in understanding its value in theory and practice and demonstrates research informing and working towards improving practice. These two principles – the value of multi-agency working and of research-led improvement to practice – are the foundations on which this chapter is grounded.

What is a modern early years professional?

In this chapter, ECEC encapsulates a professional response to children up to the age of 8 years. However, what is meant by 'professional' is more complex and less easy to define. In other contexts 'professional' refers only to those with a qualification or specific expertise, but in early years there is a greater understanding of the value and importance of the qualities individuals demonstrate in practice, with or without formal qualifications. There is also a distinct emphasis on 'principled practice', that is, value-based practice grounded in ethics, from which principles are derived recognising the needs of the child and parents as central, with the 'professional' as a facilitating partner. When combined with theoretical knowledge and an understanding of a child's physical, social and emotional, spiritual and intellectual development, these qualities produce the optimum professional, dedicated to best practice and the constant development and improvement of ECEC. An example of the recognition of the value of both academic knowledge and positive attributes is the National Professional Qualification in Integrated Centre Leadership (NPQICL). This unique leadership development programme developed by the National College for Teaching and Leadership, which ran from 2004 to 2014, uses an experiential approach balancing the theory and practice of the process of leadership as well as the outcomes.

NPQICL

This postgraduate-level programme evolved from the recognition that early years leaders lacked distinctive leadership training relevant to the field. The first version provided separate pathways for existing graduates, with an approach based on independent study, and those without a formal qualification – of which there were many – with a facilitated programme using an experiential approach. At the first review the National College acknowledged the feedback from participants which highlighted the mutual benefits felt by all when they had been able to meet and dialogue together. The revised version provided for two forms of entry application to a single, facilitated experiential programme. The subsequent changes to the programme treated all participants as equals, once they had satisfied the entry requirements. Having facilitated in different areas and for different providers over a seven year period, the value of professional exchange, interaction and dialogue has been manifest. The creation of Leadership Learning Groups to explore concepts outside the face-to-face sessions further enhanced professional support, exchange and development.

Why ECEC? During the 1990s the Conservative Government introduced initiatives targeted at health and education inviting local authorities to identify and apply for funding of 'Action Zones' (Ofsted, 2003). These were conceived as separate entities, but in practice professionals from different disciplines often found themselves working in more than one zone and recognised the overlap between their services. At the same time, the voice of early years had become an effective force influencing Westminster and local politics so that with the advent of New Labour, these emerging trends were transformed into a policy of co-operation. Education, social care and health overlapped and were actively encouraged professionals to work towards greater co-operation. This has been especially important in developing best practice in safeguarding (see Chapters 11 and 16).

Characteristics of a modern early years professional

A significant feature of ECEC is its attraction for people from a variety of backgrounds. These include education, health, social care, community development, private, voluntary and independent practice and the wider world of commerce, service and manufacturing industries. Each of these backgrounds provides the individual with a unique perspective and is a rich resource for teams to explore and appreciate. However, this can only happen if there is active encouragement of attitudes which promote open dialogue, value contributions from all, and are free from constraints of traditional hierarchy. The diverse backgrounds and qualifications among ECEC professionals, combined with formal qualification, extend knowledge and understanding and strengthen attributes underpinning communities of practice, considered in Chapter 3. What characterises ECEC professionals is revealed by their 'key attributes and attitudes', including what unites and contributes to a team's 'aliveness' (Wenger et al., 2002: 50). I propose the following key attributes of practitioners I have observed over 40 years: seeing themselves as servants, identifying and serving the needs of children, families and communities; willing to actively understand other perspectives (Covey, 2004: 236ff); open in terms of what they know or don't know, what they agree or disagree with; adaptable in recognising conflicting pressures and willing to consider new approaches which may be unconventional or require fresh protocols and working agreements, as in Schön's 'professional pluralism' (Schön, 2011: 17); willing to share good practice; being reflective listeners, attentive, actively using deep listening and using what has been learnt from the past in planning future action (Schön, 2011: 350); being non-judgemental, able to de-personalise issues and to look beyond the obvious; having a strong sense of values, based around identifying and meeting the needs of children and their parents. These attributes promote more efficient partnership and positive working relationships. More efficient because they encourage awareness of each person's skills and knowledge and confidence to put them to best use, and more positive working relationships, because each person's contribution is valued and encouraged.

These attitudes and attributes are tools enabling and encouraging modern ECEC professionals to contribute confidently, to know when they need to ask and to do so, to work alongside colleagues from other agencies, respecting their skills and knowledge, but willing to contribute when they can, and respectfully challenging when necessary, rather than keeping their own counsel. Equally important is confidence in *not knowing*: understanding their limitations and accepting themselves as 'imperfect leaders' (Taylor, 2007) yet 'comfortable in their skin' while seeking to extend and develop their knowledge and understanding to enrich individual and team practice. This is fundamental in underpinning personal confidence, and developing a whole-team approach to practice which fosters similar attributes in the children and adults who are served.

How does theory support these characteristics?

Laurence Stenhouse, who died in 1980, had a major impact on the development of a school curriculum that took more account of process, summarised as follows:

> Underpinning this view of the educational process was an epistemology that situated all 'knowledge' as provisional, and from it emerged Stenhouse's 'process model' of curriculum design (1975) to counterbalance the 'objectives model' implied by a transmission view of education, and the concept of 'the teacher as a researcher' implied by the need to discern conditions that allow pupils to accept responsibility for their own learning. (British Educational Research Association annual conference 2012 email to members 31 July 2012)

These three aspects, the *provisional* nature of knowledge, the importance of the *process* of learning, and the *practitioner as researcher,* remain of paramount importance to all those involved in ECEC (see also Chapter 16). The pace of change requires all involved to understand ethical implications and to have secure values, shared with colleagues, upon which clear aims are based, and from which overarching principles are devised to guide practice. The kind of knowledge, skills and understanding required by practitioners navigating the shifting sands of change need a sound base but must also be flexible and adaptable. My involvement with ECEC has shown me that practitioners who are open to challenge and confident enough to risk creative approaches are less likely to become fixed in comfort zones or frightened by change. Whether challenges come from their immediate colleagues or from partners sharing their prime focus of the child, the family and the local community, practitioners open to challenge and unafraid of change will be more confident to move beyond the known, tried and tested, thereby developing through their own 'Zone of Proximal Development' (Vygotstky, 1978). Practitioner attitudes, dispositions, personal and shared confidence are critical factors influencing successful and effective practice (Goleman, 1999: 68–72; Covey, 2004: 75–78). Understanding the inevitability and necessity of change means practitioners can embrace research findings aimed at improving their understanding of child, family and community needs to guide and develop change, and which in turn stimulates improvement of existing practice and current 'provisional' knowledge.

The debate over the primacy of outcomes or process is not new. I trained as a teacher between 1969 and 1972 at a time when there was a significant shift in methodology away from didactic approaches focused on imparting knowledge. In the 1970s the Nuffield Foundation, supported by Government, developed a Secondary Science curriculum encouraging practical enquiry and discovery learning. The professional was a companion on a journey ready to listen, challenge, support or direct as necessary. This spoke to me as a new professional as I learnt more about how learning takes place, focusing on progressively younger ages. It reinforced the importance of experiential learning and interactive, practical enquiry. The critical importance of interaction between parents and babies during their first six months of life in establishing attachment bonding is well documented (Bowlby, 1953: 91; Edmond and Price, 2012: 119ff.; see also Chapter 14). The value of 'play' in early childhood in extending physical and mental capacities also depends on a high level of practical experience and appropriate challenge (Fabian and Mould, 2009: 25; Bruce, 2010: 314ff.). Approaches recognising early years as 'not merely a time when children are prepared and trained for adult life' (Bruce, 2010: 55) owe a great deal to Froebel, Montessori and Steiner who saw childhood as an important stage 'in its own right' (Bruce, 2010: 55). This child-centred, process-focused model, combined with critical observation of each child's progress and assessment of their continuing development needs, is promoted by settings such as Pen Green in England and those in Reggio Emilia in Italy. It tends to be more common in pre-schools than in schools themselves, although some continue to promote 'discovery' approaches. Professionals see themselves as servants whose task it is to develop creative environments for children to explore. As Bruner put it:

> Mastery of the fundamental ideas of a field involves not only the grasping of general principles, but also the development of an attitude toward learning and enquiry … towards the possibility of solving problems on one's own … (Bruner, 1977 in Bruce, 1987: 49)

This requires more than simply presenting facts (see Edmond and Price, 2012: 39).

ECEC is dynamic and constantly changing: practitioners will be encouraged to extend whatever grounding in theories they have of learning and knowledge of emotional, physical, psychological, social and spiritual development, as they progress to enable children to start strong.

How do these characteristics affect practice?

In the last two decades ECEC professionals have found themselves in a context of perpetual flux. Initially the emphasis was on improving quality and qualifications with financial support provided. The Welsh National Assembly began to develop its own distinctive plan (see Chapter 17), as did Northern Ireland and Scotland. Under New Labour, Northern Ireland developed regional multi-agency co-ordinating groups while Scotland and Wales focused on improving interprofessional co-ordination and raising professional standards. All three now have developing strategies which emphasise multi-agency co-ordination focused on addressing issues of child poverty and a more professional, graduate workforce (see Welsh Government, 2013; Education Scotland, 2014; nidirect, 2014). In England, however, shrinking economies and national reductions in funding have limited professional development, enforcing re-structuring at local level and causing an almost universal shift to re-organise children's centres into 'locality' models: larger grouping of centres, often joining less effective with more effective centres, under a single leader with the Office for Standards in Education Children's Services and Skills (Ofsted) inspection framework re-structured to reflect this. This is echoed by the grouping of small schools in rural areas under one Headteacher due to the post-2008 reductions in funding. The withdrawal or reduction of public money and emphasis on commissioned services has increased provision of ECEC by private, independent or voluntary agencies. Financial and organisational pressures have forced reductions in services, increasing tension between the emphasis on targeted services, reinforced by Ofsted target expectations, and universal services, which frequently provide first point of contact with new families. This false distinction between 'targeted' and 'universal' exemplifies the dilemmas facing practitioners, who find themselves powerless to influence critical decisions. While increased funding for places for two year-olds, and for 'troubled families' has been provided, there remains an overall reduction in capacity to provide a wide range of ECEC services, the most recent report on Children's Centres (House of Commons Education Committee, 2013) re-emphasising the core purpose of centres focusing on those in greatest need. An unseen effect of the reduction of staff resulting from the re-shaping of local authorities means there are already fewer people left in practice and decision making positions with a sufficient knowledge of ECEC to make considered decisions, informed by knowledge of practice rather than expediency.

Private nursery provision is still popular but affordability is a mounting concern – the growing gap between those who can and cannot afford it increasing the negative pressures on families with young children. Pressures on schools to show improvement in performance remain, judged by narrow outcome measures and in consequence undervaluing *process* including child-centred, play-based approaches. The diminished ability of families on reduced means to adequately support their children in extra-curricular and homework activities is another hidden consequence of local level re-structuring. ECEC practice is challenged with maintaining the highest quality stand-ards, meeting reaching targets including those families deemed 'troubled', tracking development to show value for money and providing evidence of effectiveness which will help to develop payment by results, balancing the resourcing of targeted and universal services, all on significantly reduced budgets.

While there are many settings in which the approaches, attitudes and attributes discussed above are encouraged and work well, good practice can be constrained by external expectations and demands. Government policy to significantly reduce the funding of local authorities and to fundamentally change their role so they become commissioners and overseers rather than direct providers of services will adversely affect ECEC providers increasing emphasis on private provision has positive and negative aspects: positive because innovative partnerships can provide alternative sources of funding and open new initiatives; negative because good quality practice can be lost for lack of funding and sectors can be hostages to fortune in an open market where large corporations can quickly consume areas of provision, immune from external audit and quality control, as witnessed in parts of the USA and Australia.

Difficulties arise when systems and practice, or those operating within them, become narrow or constrained and cease to encourage development in all key areas. It is a small step that shifts the balance from a child-centred, developmentally appropriate curriculum and environment to one focused on meeting externally imposed demands. These may be well intentioned: the demand for evidence of success is no bad thing in itself, but if it becomes the main priority dominating all else, it shifts the balance nega-tively. Whatever the setting – daycare, private pre-school provision, nurseries or the early years of school – leaders committed to a single philosophy or method or who are only interested in statistical proof of success, risk losing sight of the reason their setting exists. Inspection regimes which focus unduly on outcomes alone, with insufficient regard to process, are unhelpful and push settings and practitioners away from key aspects of interaction with children and families. Negative attitudes of other profession-als towards those with EYT qualification negatively affect team building (Hadfield et al., 2012). Quality measures tied to narrow definitions of success also risk missing the point. All these tend to disempower the early years workforce, families and children. An early conclusion in the Sure Start National Evaluation noted:

> In addition, where partners have put the interests and needs of families … before the interests of their own agency or organisation, and listened and responded to parents' views, has also been a key determinant for a successful partnership (Ball, 2002)

This remains equally true in all areas of early years provision. The challenge for practitioners is to hold fast to their values and principles and maintain high quality practice. All too often enforced change includes fixed timescales, which don't allow meaningful consultation, imposed by administrators also under pressure to complete actions to strict timescales, with limited consideration of consequences. Too often it is the ECEC workforce which has been treated as the piñata of policy review, to be beaten and broken before providing hidden treasures. Employers find themselves unable to use the best practice which their workforce recognises and adopts, no longer listening or inclusive, imposing change. This is de-motivating and disempowering. How can practitioners overcome the worst effects?

What is the value of reflective practice and practitioner research?

The notion of knowledge being provisional brings to mind Socrates' use of dialogue among a small group of his students to arrive at new understandings of knowledge and which are very much based in the 'present' for those involved. I suspect that the dialogues were not always unstructured; that they built on previous dialogues, gradually extending and deepening understandings. Tina Bruce argues that:

> Informed reflection, within the context of a developmentally appropriate curriculum and an understanding of how children think and learn, will help you to recognise and value your strengths, identify the areas in need of future development and establish priorities for action to move your practice forward. (Bruce, 2010)

Bruce stresses the additional value of this process when it involves others. Sharing reflections on practice with colleagues and through professional journaling has become more valued. The notion of the 'reflective practitioner' (Schön, 2011) promoted the value to practitioners of stepping back and reflecting on what has happened, identifying what has gone well and what can be improved to inform future planning and practice. This 'reflection on action' then translates into 'reflection in action' (Schön, 2011).

Reflective practice involves the active engagement of a professional with the people and situations around them (see Chapters 2, 3 and 4 for a deeper exploration). It involves the professional working at different levels of engagement simultaneously as they talk and actively listen, attuning themselves to the emotional and practical circumstances of those around them, whether colleagues or clients. The reflective process sees the professional constantly questioning what they see, hear and feel, sharing the insights this provides with their colleagues. It requires constant adjustment and challenging of assumptions, searching for deeper meanings, for what is not being said as much as what is, and helps the professional to consider why this may be so.

Reflective journals become a 'critical friend': a means of recording what professionals believe they have seen, heard and understood, enabling them to analyse, challenge and clarify their thoughts. The physical act of writing is helpful here because it employs different mental processes and can unlock new pathways into understanding. The process of reflection enables the professional to better understand what they are dealing with and to arrive at a balanced view of how they might appropriately help the individual, the situation or themselves to move forward positively. It can also help them to comprehend what is within their skill, resources and working remit to deal with and what is not or where they will have to seek advice or help.

After struggling with the negative attitude and abrasive attitude of a member of their team, the team leader took time to reflect and consider what the real issue might be. By setting emotional responses aside and de-personalising, the focus became fixed on 'difficult' actions rather than a 'difficult' person. The leader began to understand the team member's perspective, the responses they had given and those of other team members. This became the first step in positively identifying the real issues and addressing them, rather than simply being reactive and inadvertently contributing to the negative spiral. Reflection provided time and space and was the first step in resolving the issue and establishing a positive and more trusting relationship between the leader and the team and the team members and each other.

Research is in many ways closely linked to reflective practice. Both involve questioning, summarising and critical analysis, identifying key questions and finding the most appropriate way of exploring them further, and are intended to improve practice. However, research still retains a certain mystique and can be viewed as a discourse whose applicability lies beyond the remit of everyday practice. This view is changing and practitioner research is becoming more accessible. There are now more introductory texts which define methodology and set out clearly different research methods and their uses, de-mystifying the process. Essentially the research method will depend on what you want to explore or find out but practitioner research tends to be 'action research' (McNiff, 2010). This approach recognises and celebrates the involvement of the researcher in the process, questioning the researcher's perspective and interpretation of what is observed or recorded in order to inform and improve everyday practice. It is rigorous, grounded in the principle that professionals want to know what is going on in their practice, what is working well and what can be improved further. The process actively involves others, whether professionals or not. The value of practitioner research and reflective practice lies in the desire of practitioners to constantly improve; to benefit those they serve.

> ## Parents trained as volunteers and partners in collecting data
>
> Family Workers in a Children's Centre wanted to explore how parents and children saw the services they were being offered: how did they value the services they were using; what did they like and why; what was missing; what could be improved? They decided to use parent volunteers to help and working with their local College, arranged for the parents' training and the research to be accredited. The staff and setting were able to gather useful information about the quality of the services on offer, possible improvements and new services to explore. The parents were able to gain credits towards a Level 2 award and boosted their self confidence, going on to achieve Level 3 qualifications.

The example above illustrates how reflective practice can make significant changes using an inclusive process, enabling parents to actively contribute as equal partners in the research. It can provide a pathway towards achieving qualifications and raise self-esteem for partners, thereby benefiting all involved.

However this process depends on professionals using open and inclusive approaches, modelling and encouraging a creative, developmental ethos, rather than being constrained by systems which are inflexible, including the limitations imposed by their own comfort zones. Professionals need to fight for systems which *serve* principled practice rather than dictate, which encourage freedom rather than constraint. It is essential that early years professionals actively engage and ensure their voice is heard.

Key emerging issues and themes

Tensions between imposed targeted tasks and creative, child-centred processes

The political desire for quick, quantitative data risks undervaluing the qualitative benefits which reveal the real impact of services on individuals. The process of change is gradual as witnessed by the international successes of the first decade of the new millennium. Assessment and accountability require the right kind of rigour, focus, emphasis and time: developing balanced accountability, which includes where people have started from as well as where they finish, is essential for a true picture to emerge.

Understanding the processes of child development and learning will require child-centred professionals with a better understanding of both if realistic targets are to be set.

The need for joined up working: multi-agency collaboration

The case for multi-agency collaboration has been successfully made (Wenger et al., 2002; Aubrey, 2008; Siraj-Blatchford et al., 2009; Gasper, 2010; DfE, 2012). The challenge in an era of rapid change and economic downturn is to ensure knowledge and wisdom from previous decades is used to plan and inform structures underpinning future practice. This is a severe test: both nationally and internationally, reductions threaten to leave fewer people with knowledge and understanding of ECEC best practice and the possibility of externally imposed, narrowly focused targets. ECEC services are likely to become 'leaner', more tightly focused, and less able to be delivered collaboratively as organisations look inwards, with accountability in conflict with their knowledge of local and individual needs.

Regulation

Economic constraints will need creative approaches, for example, the commissioning out of services. A high degree of responsibility for identifying and meeting local and individual needs and maintaining high quality practice will rest on those providing commissioned services. Regulating at local level will rest with a reduced workforce led by organisations which may have limited knowledge of the field and may be focused on financial detail and specific contractual obligations rather than quality or best practice: those commissioning services need a clear standard of quality, based on local needs, and not to rely on providers themselves for quality control. Could this mean increased self-assessment or practitioner research with researchers working in collaboration with early years professionals?

What kind of attributes does this call for in those working in the field?

New early years professionals and those providing commissioned services need to embody the characteristics defined earlier. These are:

- having a strong commitment and sense of service to the needs of children, families and communities;
- willingness to actively understand and engage with other perspectives;
- seeking to engage with and include all professional colleagues;
- openness in terms of what they know or don't know, what they agree or disagree with;

- adaptability in recognising conflicting pressures and being willing to consider new approaches which may be unconventional or require fresh protocols and working agreements;
- being reflective listeners, attentive, actively using deep listening and using past experience in considering action in future; non-judgemental, able to de-personalise issues and to look beyond the obvious; optimistic even in the face of difficult times;
- aware of each person's skills and knowledge and seeking to put them to best use.

Critical Learning Activity

What 'skills' and 'qualities' do you think would underpin being a 'new early years professional'? In particular when are these transferred into practice? Some examples are set out below to act as a stimulus for discussion and reflection as part of a student study group or online student community or for personal study. What do you think?

- Interprofessional, inter-agency or integrated practice is an integral part of any professional role within the ECEC arena. This is a strong assertion and one that has a profound implication for practice. Do you agree this is an essential component of demonstrating professional quality?
- Do you:
  - have a professional conviction when describing what you do?
  - embed values and ideas about the way children should be taught and learn into what you do as a practitioner?
  - show persistence – find alternative approaches, not giving up, even if it means starting again?

- Are you able to:
  - ask for support if you need it? In particular can you discuss how to find solutions for any challenges with co-workers and those from other agencies?
  - engage in ongoing training?
  - manage your professional time which is precious and find a balance between administration duties and working with children?
  - understand and articulate what inhibits and what enables your role?
  - take time to observe and recognise how others lead and manage?
  - understand the patterns and predictability of events which have an impact on children and families?
  - take time to consider, reflect and explain your actions?
  - understand the distinction between leading change and responding to change?
  - show people from different professional agencies you value what they do?
  - work out how best to communicate with other professionals?
  - take time to consult with other professionals to find tools, materials and resources needed for a particular project or idea?
  - articulate and share the values and beliefs which underline the way your setting operates?

Further reading

Brock, A. (2013) 'Building a model of early years' professionalism from practitioners' perspectives', *Journal of Early Childhood Research*, 11: 27.

References

Aubrey, C. (2008) *Leading and Managing in the Early Years*. London: SAGE.

Ball, M. (2002) *Getting Sure Start Started*: London. DFE, p.7. Available at: www.ness.bbk.ac.uk/implementation/documents/159.pdf (accessed July 2013).

Bowlby, J. (1953) *Childcare and the Growth of Love,* London: Penguin, in Bruce, T. (ed) (2010) *Early Childhood: A Guide for Students,* London: SAGE, p.91.

British Educational Research Association (2012) *Reviewing the Implications of the Work of Lawrence Stenhouse in Emerging Education Policy Contexts, with Special Reference to the UK* www.bera.ac.uk. (accessed 02 August 2012).

Bruce, T. (ed) (2010) *Early Childhood: A Guide for Students*, 2nd edn. London. SAGE, p.55; 314 *ff.*

Bruner, J. (1977) in Bruce, T. (1987) *Early Childhood Education*. Sevenoaks. Hodder and Staughton, p 49.

Cole, M., John-Steiner, V., Scribner, S. and Souberman E. (eds) Vygotsky, L. (1978) *Mind in Society*. London: Harvard.

Covey, S.R. (2004) *The 7 Habits of Highly Effective People: Powerful Lessons in Personal Change*. London: Simon and Schuster.

Department For Education (2012, DfE) *Foundations For Quality: the Independent Review of Early Education and Childcare Qualifications* - Nutbrown Review. Ref: DFE-00068. Available at: www.gov.uk/government/collections/nutbrown-review (accessed 30 June 2012).

Edmond, N. and Price, M. (2012) *Integrated Working with Children and Young People*: London: SAGE.

Education Scotland (2014) *Early Years*. Available at: www.educationscotland.gov.uk/earlyyears/.

Fabian, H. and Mould, C. (eds) (2009) *Development and Learning for Very Young Children*. London: SAGE, p.25.

Gasper, M. (2010) *Multi-agency Working in the Early Years: Challenges and Opportunities*. London. SAGE.

Goleman, D. (1999) *Working With Emotional Intelligence*: London: Bloomsbury.

Hadfield, M., Jopling, M., Needham, M., Waller, T., Coleyshaw, L., Emira, M. and Royle, K. (2012) *Longitudinal Study of Early Years Professional Status: An Exploration of Progress, Leadership and Impact,* final report. CeDARE: University of Wolverhampton.

House of Commons Education Committee (2013) *Foundation Years: Sure Start Children's Centres*. London: The Stationery Office.

McNiff, J. (2010) *Action Research for Professional Development: Concise Advice for New (and Experienced) Action Researchers*: Poole: September Books.

nidirect (2014) *Sure Start Services*. Available at: www.nidirect.gov.uk/index/information-and-services/parents/preschool-development-and-learning/sure-start-services.htm.

Ofsted (2003) *Excellence in Cities and Education Action Zones: Management and Impact*. HMI 1399. London: Ofsted.

Schön, D. (2011) *The Reflective Practitioner: How Professionals Think In Action*. Farnham:Ashgate.

Siraj-Blatchford, I., Clarke, K. and Needham, M. (eds) (2009) *The Team Around the Child: Multiagency Working in the Early Years*. Stoke on Trent: Trentham Books.

Stenhouse, L. (1975) *An Introduction To Curriculum Research and Development*. London: Heinemann.

Taylor, D.H. (2007) *The Imperfect Leader: A Story About Discovering the Not So Secret Secrets of Transformational Leadership*. Bloomington, Indiana: Author House.

Vygotsky, L.S. (1978) *Mind in Society* (M. Cole and S. Scribner, eds). Cambridge: Harvard University Press.

Welsh Government (2013) *Building a Brighter Future: Early Years and Childcare Plan*. Available at:wales.gov.uk/topics/educationandskills/publications/guidance/building-a-brighter-future/?lang=e (accessed 25 May 2014).

Wenger, E., McDermott, R.A. and Snyder, W. (2002) *Cultivating Communities of Practice: A Guide to Managing Knowledge*. Boston, MA: Harvard Business School Press.

Want to learn more about this chapter?

Visit the companion website at **https://study.sagepub.com/reedandwalker** to access podcasts from the author and additional reading to further help you with your studies.

22

Integrated working in practice: why don't professionals talk to each other?

Alison Nicholas

Chapter overview

This chapter could not have been written without the collaboration of others. It models a collaborative approach to the complex subject of integrated working through asking the reader to consider the approaches different professionals have to the issues raised by a case study. It exposes some of the different perspectives held by professionals and parents and discusses how these can help or hinder effective practice.

Introduction

As a children's centre manager I work collaboratively with up to 35 agencies, some of which I see on a regular basis and others less frequently. This means I have to collaborate with a number of different agencies and learn different professional languages. I need to understand how each profession works with families and highlight not only differences but ways we can work together (Ranade, 1998). Children's centres are multi-agency settings that draw upon the services of many disciplines to deliver services to families with children under the age of five. This can often mean that professionals from different agencies are actually based in the centre or deliver a specific service as a 'drop-in' service. I have asked these professionals to join me in exploring a case study which highlights some of the ways in which we work together effectively and some which despite our close proximity lead to misunderstandings that hinder achieving the best outcome for children and families.

There is no easy answer to ensuring the success of collaborative working. Indeeed, Claire M. Richards, in Chapter 13 of this book, suggests that we know more about what goes wrong than what works well. She suggests that poor inter-agency communication is a major feature of child protection tragedies, borne out by UK experience and evidence from public inquiries, which examined the deaths of Victoria Climbié (Laming, 2003), Peter Connelly (Laming, 2009) and Kyra Ishaq (Radford, 2010).

Before we look more closely at this, let's define what we mean by integrated working.

Integrated working

Integrated working is the process of ensuring everyone who is involved in supporting children, young people and families works together to put them at the centre of decision making to meet their needs and improve their lives. This means practitioners having the confidence to challenge situations by looking beyond their immediate role and being assertive about what is required to remedy poor outcomes for the child or young person (CWDC, 2010). Being that competent professional who can navigate the complexities of working in an integrated way requires confidence, skills and the reflective ability to work openly with professional partners. This places considerable responsibilities upon the shoulders of practitioners. They are asked to work in partnership with parents, share information and ensure they understand the driving forces which promote integrated working, and protect and safeguard the child and do this by forging what are called communities of practice (Wenger et al., 2002; Wenger, 2010) – in effect, developing positive networks of communication between professional groups at a local level. In addition, they need to adhere to prescribed and co-ordinated strategies which ask practitioners to work together in order to protect vulnerable children. For example, in England strategies such as the Common Assessment Framework (CAF) (CWDC, 2007) and Early Help (DfE, 2013) have been developed to improve the effectiveness of multi-agency working by establishing common processes for assessment and information-sharing to assist the monitoring of vulnerable children. Early intervention through working with children and their families as soon as a problem arises is more successful than reacting later when an issue may become more entrenched (Siraj-Blatchford and Siraj-Blatchford, 2009).

What do we mean by integrated professional working?

This is sometimes described as joined-up working, joint working, multi-agency working, cross-agency working, multidisciplinary working, or cross-boundary working, as well as co-ordinated and partnership working. It is perhaps no wonder with such a plethora of labels that practitioners and parents may be confused about the nature of working together. Such labelling gives the impression that services work together, but these descriptors fail to show how services are engaged in collaborative working which starts to move towards a sharing of skills, experience and professional understanding (Reed, 2010). We may be able to hide behind such titles but how do these ensure that professionals actually talk to each other? This is a view recognised by the Australian Institute of Family Studies who advocate a need for professionals to forge interdependent connections, develop opportunities for frequent communication between agencies and who encourage a letting go of individual professional agendas (ARACY 2009, 2010). This also involves cross training, easily accessed shared data, joint case management and cost sharing between services which need to underline a defined purpose for those involved.

Does integrated working make a difference?

In terms of early intervention for vulnerable children and families the call for integrated working is clear. Field (2010) asked for more effective integration and co-ordination of services. His report gives examples of good practice and underpins the need for professionals to work together to improve quality. In terms of models of working, Atkinson et al. (2007) examined existing research reports to consider the impact, possible facilitators and challenges as well as their implications for good practice. They reported that in terms of the impact of multi-agency working there was an improvement to services and an increased understanding and trust between agencies. In addition, when there was active collaboration between professionals the result was more emphasis on a proactive focus on preventing problems via earlier referral and intervention. Relationships improved, as did communication, but there were some conflicting messages about whether multi-agency working resulted in an increased or reduced workload for the professionals involved. As for direct evidence of the impact on families, this was sparse. However, when there was collaboration there appeared to be a greater focus on preventing problems occurring with earlier referral and intervention. A report exploring costs and outcomes of inter-agency training for safeguarding children (Carpenter et al., 2010) revealed that although inter-agency training was mandated by the government, participation was varied. There were concerns about the low participation of some professions taking the opportunity to attend specialist courses to update their knowledge and skills. There were, however, substantial and significant gains in knowledge and in self-confidence regarding safeguarding policies and procedures and the opportunity to learn together was valued. Importantly, it suggested that government relies on the goodwill of professional and personal relationships to make this happen. This once again reminds us about the important role the early years service provides and the volume of time and energy they give to this.

So is inter-agency, inter-professional or partnership working seen as valuable? The short answer appears to be 'yes', particularly in ways that are of benefit to professionals, children and families. Conversely, there is evidence that when we do not work together there can be tragic consequences. Richards (2010) confronts this issue and explains the need for continued vigilance and the importance of working together in order to protect children. Percy-Smith (2005, 2006) also argues that partnership working is indeed valuable and again raises the point that it provides a collective energy that might not exist when we act alone. However, there needs to be care about not blurring roles and clear levels of expectation between different agencies and professionals. Commentators such as Gasper (2010) and Trodd and Chivers (2011) provide a comprehensive view of partnership working and there are international comparisons regarding integrated services and professional collaboration (OECD, 2006). These all represent positive aspects of professional collaboration as well as indicating the barriers. For example, how professionals need to ensure that the volume of agencies involved with a family do not foster professional dependency and perhaps marginalise even further vulnerable families who come to rely on services.

Quality of provision

A detailed report, *Evaluating the Early Impact of Integrated Children's Services* (Lord et al., 2008), suggests that professionals ask themselves questions about what they do which focus on improving quality of provision. For example, is there a clear purpose for what action is taken? Who takes responsibility for what goes on? What were the outcomes? These questions are important because they go to the very heart of integrated professional working, namely the quality of practice, which ia a point that Siraj- Blatchford and Siraj-Blatchford (2009) considered when they explored effective practice in integrating early years services. They suggest it is the *quality* rather than the *type* of integration that matters in terms of improving outcomes for children. It therefore appears that there is more to integrated professional working than a type of working, or identifying different ways of working; it is about placing the child at the centre, sharing information, and having a value system that sees integrated working as important and stops maintaining professional hierarchies at the expense of safeguarding children.

CASE STUDY

Join me in looking at a case study considering how practice 'looks' from differing professional standpoints or landscapes. This is a snapshot intended to illustrate, explore and debate issues surrounding integrated working. It has no easy answers.

I shall report the voices of different agencies who were asked to consider the case study. The professionals within each agency were asked to look at the situation from their perspective and to say what action should be taken to support the family and secure the best outcomes for the child. This replicates the questions posed above focusing on improving the quality of provision. To begin with, we could argue that participation in the exercise itself demonstrates a willingness for agencies to actually work together and use their expertise to help shape the understanding of those in training.

Firstly, read the picture of practice:

Hannah, who attends the local children's centre with her son Jack aged two and a half, had an informal conversation with Satvinda, the Family Support Worker, at the setting. Hannah is worried about Jack who attends the centre nursery three days a week as well as a weekly Stay and Play session. He is showing some unusual behaviour, for example being very quiet and unlike his usual boisterous self.

Satvinda spends time each week in the nursery and has formal and informal meetings with staff and parents. She has developed a very trusting and positive relationship with all her colleagues and parents.

Jack's key worker at the nursery tells her that Hannah does not work and her partner is about to lose his job. The situation is putting a strain on their relationship and they are arguing frequently. The police were called out by neighbours a fortnight ago. The neighbours have complained to the housing association and yesterday the local Housing Officer visited the family home.

During the visit the Housing Officer, John, reported to the nursery with Hannah's permission that she finds her young son's noisy playing irritating. She states that the nursery Jack attends have said that they think he may be 'a little behind' the other children and does not seem to be talking much. She feels overwhelmed and no longer able to cope and says she just needs to 'get away from it all'.

The Housing Officer is concerned about Hannah's emotional health and the impact this may have on Jack.

Many professionals may look from a distance as though they are working well together. It is easy to make the presumption that professionals are prepared to cross difficult terrain, but we have to remember that some have differing professional viewpoints, differing structures, practices and work cultures. We also must remember that within different organisations there are power imbalances, professional hierarchies and different roles and responsibilities.

Although responses to the case study were dependent on the professional's individual role within the agency, they were reflective and recognised the personal skills needed to work in an integrated way with other professionals. Many of the agencies had similar boundaries and a shared understanding of the process and need for signposting to more appropriate services for particular specialist support. Agencies crossed over in terms of boundaries, solutions were child-centred and family-led and there was commonality of language in certain areas. Agencies discussed what they were able to contribute to the family as a 'stand-alone' organisation. Discussion about roles both as an individual practitioner and as a representative of their agency demonstrated that they understood their inherent roles and where they were placed in terms of safeguarding and responsibility to the family. For example, a male worker from a domestic abuse support service stated that both parents would be supported around domestic abuse and that they would concentrate on safeguarding and highlighting inconsistencies in behaviour to support future information sharing. A volunteer's main area of work was around advice on debt management but they saw their role as significant in signposting the mother and child for support around health and well-being.

The responses to the case study from the agencies identified three key themes:

1. Collective support for children and families – shared policy and emphasis

Each professional's first consideration was whether the family met the criteria for accessing their services and the appropriateness of the services for the family. It was also essential to discover if there was a need to involve social care at this stage. Professionals recognised that the remit of social care is around protection and in this particular case felt that the family did not meet the threshold for social care as Jack was not in need of protection at this stage. Thresholds have been developed based on a scale of need in order to promote early identification of concerns by universal services. Thresholds refer to the level of services, categorised in tiers, available to all children and families and determining the different stages of need. Children and young people can access services from different tiers at different times in accordance with their changing needs, whilst continuing to receive universal services throughout their childhood. In this case study, the current needs of the family can be met by universal services. No concerns were raised between agencies about the shared understanding of the roles of their services. Knowledge about services on offer to families in any local area is key for professionals: having a shared understanding of agencies' protocols and criteria enables practitioners to seek the right help from the right agency at the right time. Shared understanding comes from spending time with other agencies, often through joint training, attending conferences together and making time as a professional to be open and honest and approachable to other agencies. Some areas of work have a joined up approach to working with families and communities as they are based in the same building and increasingly agencies are now sharing budgets and working towards common aims and goals. For example a Children's Centre has a target to work with children who have speech difficulties, as do Speech and Language therapists. Therefore Children's Centres host clinics for therapists to meet children and their own families in their own communities.

2. Working together purposefully

Professionals recognised the importance and functions of other agencies and that working in isolation with the family meant that services would not be co-ordinated and the family would not be supported in the areas they identified. Early help was a common denominator and all felt that this process would enable the family to come together with the agencies to discuss concerns and draw up practical solutions. Professionals recognise that this process ensures that services will be co-ordinated and this in turn will avoid duplication; there will be a shared responsibility; communication is more concise; and it is less likely that there will be mixed messages. It also ensures that a smoother transition for the family could be made if a referral to social care was necessary.

Case study respondents commented on the time constraints and the responsibility of being the lead in the early help process but recognised the positive outcomes for the family and child. There needs to be care about not blurring roles and clear levels of expectation between different agencies and professionals. Professionals identified that a successful process is dependent on all agencies being responsible for carrying out the support identified and the recommendations made. When this does not take place it leads to conflict and a lack of trust. Another key factor identified was consistency, with the same people being present at each meeting. This enables good communication and does not hinder the recommendations being carried out and responsibilities being met.

3. Communicating effectively and using a shared language

When discussing early help, professionals used identical language. This is an effective measure of integrated working and is considered successful by parents too. Feedback demonstrates that parents find it useful for everyone to come together in one meeting although it must be noted that they found it initially intimidating to meet with several different agencies at once and that having an advocate in the meetings is imperative.

The professionals contributing to the case study detailed the qualities needed to engage effectively with other services. Personal qualities such as approachability, trustworthiness, honesty and integrity are often appreciated by parents who have received early intervention support. A professional can invest in integrated working and have the organisational structure in place to support inter-agency working with a solid understanding of the legislation underpinning practice, yet this may still not be enough. It is important to recognise that the personal qualities the professional has will have a significant bearing on how children, families and professionals interact with that professional and inevitably impact on how progress is made. For example if a family builds a trusting relationship with a professional they are more likely to be honest about the level of support they need and whether the strategies put in place are working for them. Effective communication skills, the ability to collaborate, relate to experience, share and reflect, to be understanding, to empower, to be open, honest and to empathise with the family is needed when supporting families and children (McInnes, 2007).

Many of the professionals commented that knowing other professionals certainly helped 'cement' positive relationships and working in the same locations, even if for a small amount of time, created the foundation for trust between different agencies. In an increasing climate where many professionals are hired on a temporary basis the turnover of staff has increased and therefore professionals need to forge good strong relationships more quickly. Services are also increasingly becoming 'project based' with budgets allocated for services in a specific time span; consequently services have an increasing need to be target driven. Professionals need to balance these constraints with the needs of children, families and communities and an understanding of the needs of other professionals.

What about families?

Three families were asked to share their viewpoints. Lord and colleagues (2008) suggest that parents and carers value a number of elements of integrated services, such as early identification and intervention and easier access to services. They found that parents recognise the value of joined-up inter-agency activity and that listening to parents' views was an important attribute for all professionals.

Families commenting on the case study felt that the most important factor was that they were listened to by agencies and that they were part of the support as opposed to work just being done 'unto them'. There was a recognition that it became difficult if they worked with each organisation in isolation as it meant that they had to 'tell their story' on numerous occasions to different professionals. Families also identified the need for different agencies to work together well and shared the view that it was easy to see when one organisation does not work in an integrated way with others. This was particularly pertinent for families who have been involved in the early help process. This relies on recommendations being carried out and from one meeting to the next it quickly becomes apparent when one agency does not meet its responsibilities. Families viewed the accountability of agencies as one of the key strengths of early help.

What does this mean in practice?

Practitioners have to liaise with other early years settings, safeguard children's welfare, develop interprofessional assessment and understand the importance of collaborative working. They have to lead and manage the process on the ground which means understanding and translating these expectations into actions that can be understood at a local level. This requires an ability to respond and understand duties associated with regulation and inspection, which means having a clear idea of who to work with and forging ways of making this happen. It also means understanding the professional landscape, because this has changed and continues to evolve. Many agencies and individuals play a part in supporting families, from health visitors to pre-school settings; from social workers to integrated workers. The skill of integrated working lies in observing and identifying issues and finding solutions with families that prevent these developing into problems.

Professionals who participated in the case study accepted that the impact of integrated working is varied and making it work is difficult, especially within a complex and changing landscape of professional practice. A practitioner, leader or supervisor must deal with differing professional viewpoints and perspectives as well as professional hierarchies, structures and practices. They have to consider work cultures including their own 'stereotypes' of what other practitioners look like, and overcome a lack of trust: factors that we know hinder progress (Fitzgerald and Kay, 2008). Recognising and dealing with trust is also important, and this issue is a consequence of a history of organisations not working together, not sharing information and having very different internal organisational polices. To this we could add insufficient funds, ring fenced budgets, organisations with short term contracts, complex geographical boundaries, lack of time, multiple initiatives/targets, and problems in recruiting and retaining staff. This is not to be pessimistic or give up on the notion of what 'integrated quality' looks like. It is only to recognise that organisational difficulties, different forms of leadership and different organisational cultures often dominate our professional landscape. Therefore, quality must be dependent on understanding the different complexities involved and a consideration of what personal and professional dispositions it is possible to bring to bear. It also means developing the qualities necessary to engage in integrated working. The benefits of working together are profound and negate the difficulties surrounding integrated work. Positives include a co-ordinated approach, not duplicating services, families telling the story once, the most appropriate services being in place to meet the needs of the child, strategies being in place with the right professional support, early identification of emerging issues, less chance of families 'dropping through the net', seamless services within realistic timescales, easier access to a wider range of specialist services, easier and smoother referral processes between agencies, appropriate information sharing and progress, and how celebration of positive outcomes can be shared.

Conclusion

This chapter has been the culmination of working in an integrated way. As an author I have engaged with different people along the journey. I have needed to seek permission from my employer to contribute to this book, to negotiate with the publishers and editors on the workings of the chapter, and seek the opinions of parents and different professionals from a wide range of organisations. I have also integrated Figure 2.1 from Chapter 2 in the Critical Learning Activity in order to model an integrated approach to learning. The chapter therefore mirrors the experience of working and supporting families as an individual professional. Just as I did not have all the answers to write this chapter, as a professional supporting families I do not have all the professional expertise to provide all the support a family would need. I end by revisiting an earlier point. Integrated working should be seen as about placing the child at the centre, sharing information, and having a value system that sees integrated working as important and stops maintaining professional hierarchies at the expense of safeguarding children.

Critical Learning Activity

Having read the chapter, consider your position with regard to integrated/collaborative work with other professionals. Look at Figure 2.1 in Chapter 2 (Hanson and Appleby). Re-read their views, and look at their 'Evolutionary critical reflection' diagram. This offers a more systematic evaluation as it focuses attention on your own thinking, the views of colleagues, perspectives from other students and a consideration of theoretical/research-based evidence. Does it sharpen your views? Does the socio-cultural lens operate in this context? Does this help to reflect (wider than the here and now), reframe (reorganise, so as to be meaningful to you), act upon (in terms of reading more, finding out more or talking to other professionals) and revisit (think again) about integrated working?

Further reading

Davies, C. and Ward, H. (2012) *Safeguarding Children across Services, Messages from Research*. London: Jessica Kingsley Publishers.
Fitzgerald, D. and Kay, J. (2008) *Working Together in Children's Services*. Abingdon: David Fulton.
Gasper, M (2010) *Multi-agency Working in the Early Years*. London: SAGE.

References

Atkinson, M., Lamont, E. and Jones, M. (2007) *Multiagency Working and its Implication for Practice: A Review of the Literature*. Reading: CfBT Education Trust.
Australian Research Alliance for Children and Youth (ARACY) (2009) *Improving the Wellbeing of Children and Young People by Advancing Collaboration and Evidence Based Action*.

Available at: www.aracy.org.au/search?command=search&search_terms=conference+ 2009&search_order=Relevance (accessed 27 November 2013).

Australian Research Alliance for Children and Youth (ARACY) (2010) Key elements of collabora-tion (Fact Sheet 5). Available at: www.aracy.org.au/search?command=search&search_ terms=conference+2009&search_order=Relevance (accessed 20 May 2014).

Carpenter, J., Hackett, S., Patsios, D. and Szilassy, E. (2010) *Outcomes of Interagency Training to Safeguard Children: Final Report to the Department for Children, Schools and Families and the Department of Health*. Nottingham: DCSF and University of Bristol.

Children's Workforce Development Council (CWDC) (2007) *Common Assessment Framework for Children and Young People: Practitioners Guide*. Leeds: CWDC.

Children's Workforce Development Council (CWDC) (2010) *The Common Core of Skills and Knowledge*. Leeds: CWDC.

Department for Education (DfE) (2013) *Working Together to Safeguard Children*. Available at: www.education.gov.uk/aboutdfe/statutory/g00213160/working-together-to-safeguard-children (accessed 27 November 2013).

Field, F. (2010) *The Foundation Years: Preventing Poor Children Becoming Poor Adults*. London: The Stationery Office.

Fitzgerald, D. and Kay, J. (2008) *Working Together in Children's Services*. Abingdon: David Fulton.

Gasper, M (2010) *Multi-agency Working in the Early Years*. London: SAGE.

Laming, H. (2003) *The Victoria Climbie Inquiry: Report of an Inquiry by Lord Laming*. London: HMSO. Available at: www.gov.uk/government/uploads/system/uploads/attachment_data/ file/273183/5730.pdf (accessed 27 November 2013).

Laming, H. (2009) *The Protection of Children in England: A Progress Report*. London: HMSO.

Lord, P., Kinder, K., Wilkin, A., Atkinson, M. and Harland, J. (2008) *Evaluating the Early Impact of Integrated Children's Services: Round 1 Final Report*. Slough: NFER.

McInnes, K. (2007) *A Practitioner's Guide to Interagency Working in Children's Centres: A Review of the Literature*. London: Barnardo's Policy and Research Unit.

OECD (2006) *Starting Strong II: Early Childhood Education and Care*. Available at: www.oecd.org/ edu/school/startingstrongiiearlychildhoodeducationandcare.htm (accessed 27 November 2013).

Percy-Smith, J. (2005) *Definitions and Models: What Works in Strategic Partnerships for Children*. London: Barnardo's Policy and Research Unit.

Percy-Smith, J. (2006) 'What works in strategic partnerships for children: a research review', *Children and Society*, 20 (4): 313–323.

Radford, J. (2010) *Serious Case Review. In respect of the death of a child*, Case number 14. Birmingham Safeguarding Children Board. Available at: www.lscbbirminghm.org.uk/downloads (accessed 27 November 2013).

Ranade, W. (1998) *Making Sense of Multi-agency Groups*. Newcastle: Sustainable Cities Research, Institute University of Northumbria.

Reed, M. (2010) 'Children's centres and children's services?', in M. Reed and N. Canning (eds), *Reflective Practice in the Early Years*. London: SAGE.

Richards, C.M. (2010) 'Safeguarding children: Every Child Matters so everybody matters', in M. Reed and N. Canning (eds), *Implementing Quality Improvement and Change in the Early Years*. London: SAGE.

Siraj-Blatchford, I. and Siraj-Blatchford, J. (2009) *Improving Development Outcomes for Children through Effective Practice in Integrating Early Years Services*, C4EO Early Years Knowledge Review 3. London: Centre for Excellence and Outcomes in Children and Young People's Services. Available at: http://socialwelfare.bl.uk/subject-areas/services-client-groups/children-young-people/c4eo/125780c4eo_effective_practice_kr_3.pdf (accessed 18 November 2013).

Trodd, L. and Chivers, L. (2011) *Inter-professional Working in Practice*. Berkshire: McGraw-Hill.

Wenger, E. (2010) *Landscapes of Practice*, a series of workshops held at the Practice-based Professional Learning Centre for Excellence in Teaching and Learning. Milton Keynes: Open University.

Wenger, E., McDermott, R. and Snyder, W. (2002) *Cultivating Communities of Practice*. Cambridge, MA: Harvard Business School Press.

Want to learn more about this chapter?

Visit the companion website at **https://study.sagepub.com/reedandwalker** to access podcasts from the author and additional reading to further help you with your studies.

23

Children's developing identity

Victoria Cooper

Chapter overview

This chapter shares the findings from a participatory study designed to explore children's identity. The findings illustrate 'picture making' through art and photography as a method which facilitates reflective time and space within the research process and encourages children to talk about different aspects of *self*. These findings are discussed in relation to early childhood professional practice and demonstrate how listening to children using multi-modal instruments provides opportunities for practitioners to consider the diversity of identity development across home and school contexts and enables children to share their views.

Introduction

Children convey aspects of their identity using a range of social markers, including their age, gender and ethnicity, family and group membership. This is a dynamic process in which children negotiate, construct and re-construct multiple identities. Identity is not fixed or singular, but multi-faceted and reflects a range of social, cultural and political influences. Yet focusing on these markers alone may not reveal the richness of children's sense of *self*. It is important to appreciate the distinctive ways in which children express their identity through friendship, play and many forms of social interaction, for example, methods such as photography, art and map-making, in order to provide them with opportunities to communicate their views using methods they enjoy and can use independently. This is of particular interest to me as a researcher at the Open University where I use children's pictures as an instrument for exploring childhood. I shall therefore share with you some aspects of that research which suggest ways of listening to children which reveal insights about the way they learn and see the world.

Identity

Identity is a key foundation for children's social and emotional development and it may be valuable to consider the work of Cooper and Collins (2009) who consider how identity is related to feelings of security and self-worth. Research continues to explore the association between identity, resilience development and mental health (Burns and Rapee, 2006). This process is important for anyone working with children because identity and feelings of well-being are firmly linked to life experiences.

As researchers and practitioners interested in working with children it is important to reflect on how we view and understand childhood. It is easy to misinterpret how children feel about themselves, or to overlook characteristics of their developing identity. Working with children, identifying and supporting their needs are primary objectives for educators, researchers and practitioners in the field of early childhood education, as Durand (2010: 839) indicates:

> If the goal of education is to truly serve *all* children and families in ways that are authentic and meaningful, it is imperative that, as early childhood professionals, we begin to broaden our knowledge about children's development, and the lenses we use to view children's developmental trajectories.

Durand draws attention to two central themes; how professionals identify the needs of children and their families and how these needs are effectively met. The vast majority of developmental theories about childhood have relied on adult interpretations. Children's own stories about *self* have been shared, but they are frequently 'told' stories (Brooks, 2006). Researchers have argued that it is important to reflect on how people make sense of their own lives (Cooper, 2013).

Children's right to be listened to, have their voices heard and taken into account is fundamental to recent developments designed to capture children's views through participatory research. Not only does this recognise children's competency in being able to contribute to research (Christensen and Prout, 2005), but re-positions them as pivotal within the research process (Clark, 2011). This reflects a children's rights perspective in which children are valued and acknowledges how research about children must build upon approaches which consult with children.

The example which follows provides a case study of my own participatory research undertaken with a small group of 12 children aged between 4 and 6 years. This research is part of a much larger ongoing ethnographic study of 210 children and young people since 2011. The research combines a number of small projects across education and care settings (including primary and secondary schools, as well as youth clubs and after school groups) in Gloucestershire. The principal focus of the research is to explore different ways of engaging with children and young people, including the analysis of different data collection instruments, as a means to examine childhood and youth identity.

Participatory research

This participatory research project was carried out at a local after-school club and utilised four primary data collection instruments: focus group discussions, observations, children's photographic pictures and free drawings. The research started with a focus group discussion. We met weekly and I observed and talked with the children individually, in friendship pairs, in groups and as a whole research group. The ethical considerations of the study were discussed and all the participants were impressed of their right to withdraw at any time, the confidential nature of the work and the importance of anonymity. Consent was provided by each participant and participant caretaker. All participant names have been changed.

A sub-text for my own reflection on the research process was the different approaches I could employ. For example, I could have observed children within a particular social context and interviewed them about different aspects of their developing identity. However, I have employed these approaches in the past and recognise problems viewing children's experience primarily through an adult lens. The work of Clark (2011) and Stephenson (2009) attempted to overcome this issue. Both authors describe how many interesting insights about children often sit outside the research agenda or are overlooked by the use of particular data collection instruments. It was important for me to try and develop an approach in which children could have some level of control and freedom to express their own views.

Developments within the sociology of education have witnessed an expansion in research methodologies to embrace participatory approaches, in which creative multi-modal tools, such as images, map-making, photographs and pictures are used to work with children in ways which respond to children's interests and strengths (Clark, 2011). These facilitate opportunities for children to reflect on how they communicate important messages about their lives and which does not rely solely on 'talk'.

The project therefore integrated 'picture making' (drawings and photographic pictures) as instruments which are flexible and which children can use independently – a 'reflective method' as Liebenberg (2009: 444) describes, where the researcher and participant can discuss images created by participants, which 'situates participants as authorities on their lives, better at controlling research content'.

A research case study

As a research group we began with an introductory focus on 'who am I?'. Each child drew a picture of themselves. This provided a starting point to situate each child within the research group and confirm cohort details, such as age, gender and ethnicity.

Bernie and Duncan illustrate how the children used pictures and drawings to communicate aspects of their developing identity. I use the pictures and accompanying narratives to try and build what some of the older children called 'personality pictures', in which the children were invited to draw and take pictures as a means to tell me and share with the research group features of their identity.

Who am I?

Bernie (aged six) took an interesting approach in introducing himself through his drawing (see Picture 23.1). On first glance you can see that Bernie has drawn himself, as a boy (and a house), alongside other objects, including a car, oven and fridge. When I asked Bernie about his drawing he talks about himself 'as a boy', who is six and has 'brown hair', and also about when he 'grows up'. The following exchange with myself (R) illustrates how Bernie chooses to talk about how he wants to be an inventor.

Picture 23.1

B: It's me. I am a house here. It's my home. I could invent a home like me. I would live next door to Simon. I want to be an inventor when I grow up. Well and sort of a designer. I am going to design a house which looks like me (pointing to his picture) and I am going to design a car with wheels on the bottom, at the side and on the top (points and laughs) and an oven which cooks meals all by itself.

R: I would like one of those …

B: I can make you one.

R: How will the cooker know what to cook?

B: You just have to think about what you want and it will cook it for you. You might have to wear something on your head. To get your thoughts.

This extract illustrates how Bernie used his picture to convey a range of themes about himself, including his hopes, sense of place, significant others, as well as the 'things' he found interesting and might invent in the future.

In contrast, Duncan (aged four) describes his picture about himself (Picture 23.2) and his cousin's dog 'Bubba', and in doing so, introduced different themes, most notably, his relationships with others;

Bubba is a brown dog. He's been ill at the vets when we saw him on Saturday. My picture is me and Oscar's dog. I have a hamster called Fluffy. It's not my hamster but my brother's.

Picture 23.2

Whilst talking about his picture, Duncan shifted from talking about himself, his friends and family and then in a similar way to Bernie, his likes and thoughts about the future:

D: It's me. I am four. I have one brother. And Bubba.

R: Who is Bubba?

D: Its Oscar's dog. My cousin. He's new. I don't have a dog, but we do have a hamster called Fluffy.

R: Do you?

D: My Dad would like a dog when we have got all our grass. I can then play on the grass.

R: Do you like playing on the grass?

D: I like drawing. I am good at drawing with felt pens. I will be an artist I think.

Children typically use social markers such as age, gender, friends, family, ethnicity and hobbies to convey aspects of who they are. Sometimes an aspect of identity is clearly signalled by appearance. When considering a child's developing identity it is necessary to reflect on how a child projects an image but also their subjective aware-ness of *self*. It is interesting to see how Duncan and Bernie use a variety of social makers to build up a picture of who they are, with references to place, friends and family.

This response can be set within the research work of Bronfenbrenner in his eco-logical systems theory (1979). He argues for the importance of understanding child development within social and cultural systems. This recognises how children relate within social *micro-systems* such as home and nursery and how these sys-tems interact as *meso-systems* to influence social behaviour. The child is not passive within this process, but an active agent who in turn influences the social systems within which they are placed. Understanding children therefore warrants a holistic process in which practitioners can explore children's sense of *self* across various contexts and so acknowledge the wider influences of friends, family, community and culture.

This view provided the stimulus to use photography as the primary data collection instrument; designed to broaden the research focus to include a more holistic explora-tion of the child across various contexts, including school, home and with the aim of incorporating 'other' significant people such as family and friends. Children were given a digital camera to use at the after-school club and at home independently. They took photographs for ten minutes each day. Whilst each child's parent/carer supervised the activity the children were free to take photographs of things which they felt reflected 'all about me'. At the end of the week, the cameras were collected and the photo-graphs were stored.

All about me

During this study each child was invited to 'talk me through' each of their pictures. This reflected my interest in how children construct meaning and communicate their views within a research process rather than focusing on the pictures and drawings as a research product. Narrative evolved as an essential feature of our discussions as the children talked about what their pictures meant to them.

They were encouraged to select their favourites. I then merged a selection of pictures into a series of photographs (see Pictures 23.3–23.5). We then used these pictures to talk in more detail and to build up 'personality pictures', as one older member (Liam, aged six) of our research group describes:

> The pictures can tell all about the things you do and your friends. It's a good way of finding out about you. The things that other people might not know.

CASE STUDY 1

Identity and 'other'

Bernie selected a range of photographs which signposted to other people, such as friends, family members or pets. Bernie talked freely about each picture which also provided him with an opportunity to introduce important people within his life, such as his mum, cousin, pet hamster and his cousin's dog.

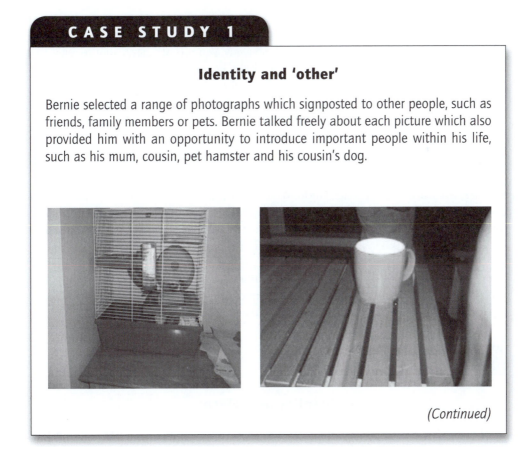

(Continued)

(Continued)

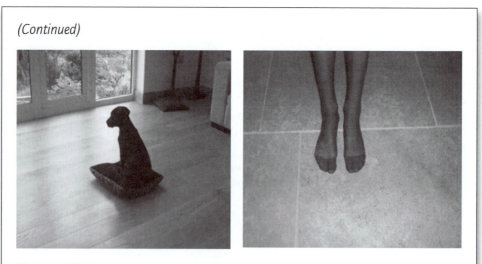

Pictures 23.3

My hamster has red eyes and is a girl. So is my Mum. That's her favourite red cup for tea. My cousin is a girl. Molly. That's her feet and her dog. My best friend Simon is a boy, like me and he has a dog and we battle a lot. He likes it a bit better than me. We play it at school. He can be very silly sometimes. He's leaving school. Moving to Scotland. I think I will need more friends when he's gone. I like to be popular.

Bernie's reference to his friend Simon, his type of play and desire to be popular indicates how children move in and out of different social contexts which are important factors which shape their experiences. This is a point that resonates with social identity theory: Tajfel (1981) examined how children take on personal identities as distinctive individuals, as well as social identities, which may reflect group membership. There is also the work of Holloway and Valentine (2000) who explored the impact of social dynamics on children's developing identity and the fluidity of this process, with a particular emphasis on the significance of place.

CASE STUDY 2

Identity and place

Duncan selected his photographs and was keen to talk about his 'home' and most importantly, his 'bedroom'.

Pictures 23.4

My room I share with my brother Dan. It's messy always [laughs]. My mum tidies it up. I have a football duvet. The car. It travels you quicker. We go to grandad's in it. If I walked to grandma's it would take for ages. It would take so long we would be dead [laughs]. You can see my house here [pointing]. The window. The toilet's in there. We have new grass. Nearly new. You can't walk on it yet can you? I will play on my scooter and my bike then.

Duncan uses his picture to reflect on a variety of important people within his life, including his mum, grandma and grandpa as well as referencing a number of places, including his home and spaces within his home, such as his bedroom and his garden, as well as places he travels to, such as his grandparents' home. Children's developing identity represents how they feel and project their sense of *self* in place and time.

An interesting feature of the all the children's photographs was pictures taken of material 'things', such as Duncan's picture of his family car, to position important artefacts, routines and places, as well as special toys and achievements.

CASE STUDY 3

Identity and 'things'

Bernie took many pictures of different artefacts in his own home and outside. Many of the objects included toys, everyday artefacts and his 'special things'.

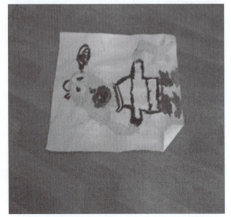

Pictures 23.5

In the following extract, Bernie talks about some of the *things* he has photographed:

I like my 3 DS. It's my favourite thing. I play on it all the time at home. I like the computer. It's my dad's but I have my own account. I go on Amazon. I am good on the computer. Do you know that's Homer Simpson. I painted that. I love the Simpson's. When I get my own. I can't have a room of my own yet. Cos. Well, it will be a Simpson room I think. And at night I always have my night time water. See. My name's on it. It helps me sleep. I know it's time for bedtime.

It is interesting how Bernie had selected artefacts to signpost an array of features not only about himself and the things he likes, but also his achievements and pleasures as well as the everyday routines within his social life, such as bed and leisure time. Some authors (Horton and Kraftl, 2006; Jones, 2008) suggest that materialism has been a largely neglected aspect of childhood research yet provides rich insight into children's everyday social life and developing identity.

The case studies illustrate how the insights gained come from the actual research process rather than the pictures as an end product. As a meaning making activity, 'picture making' provided many opportunities for each child to reflect and present a distinct feature of their developing identity as they chose it and not as an adult version. The children were able to raise themes and issues which they deemed important and which I, as an adult researcher, may not have considered.

★ Reflection point

As a research exercise, the discussion of each set of photographs was time consuming but well worth the effort. It allowed me to work in partnership with the children, be guided by them and establish a relationship where we could talk and share ideas. The children were all very different in how they talked about their photographs. It is a shame that these pictures cannot fully convey the affective dimension within this research process, including the laughter, joy and pride as the children talk about their pictures and photographs. For example, Duncan's laughter when describing his 'messy' bedroom and Bernie's pride and joy in talking about the picture of Homer Simpson he painted. Age was a factor which appeared

(Continued)

> *(Continued)*
>
> to influence the nature and length of individual discussion times. The younger children, aged four, were easily distracted. Despite this, the discussion times provided rich opportunities for me to listen to the children; to engage with different aspects of their lives reflected in their pictures and to gain some insight into the things which they liked, disliked and the fine nuances about their lives which often sit outside conventional research agendas.

It is important to acknowledge that images are not 'records of reality' (Liebenberg, 2009: 445), but can be used to represent experience. Meanings always depend on when, how and where the images were constructed, by whom and in how the images are interpreted in one way or another. The emphasis upon meaning making here is important for a number of reasons. Not only does this acknowledge research as a process in which knowledge is produced, but recognises children's role in contributing to this process. In this sense, data is not extracted by the researcher to be represented elsewhere, but that research as a process is able to capture how meaning is constructed. The use of 'picture making' is valuable here as a tool which children can control, direct and so provide a means through which to witness how they choose to share their sense of *self*.

How children express their identity can vary according to social circumstances within any given situation. There are aspects of *self* which may be regarded as enduring – ethnic origin for example – whilst there are other features which are quite different and evolve over time and place (Kelleher and Leavey, 2004). This research examines the complexity of identity development which encompasses a host of important factors, including friends and family as well as material *things* which make reference to features of children's play, achievements and social interaction. Identity is not fixed or pre-determined and can change over time and space as children move in and out of social contexts, such as home, garden, bedroom and school. The core of this research addresses how children choose to communicate 'who I am' and 'all about me' rather than selecting a research approach in which adults attempt to construct another's sense of *self*.

Implications for professional practice

The value of addressing children's experiences has increasingly been the focus within education, health and social care professional contexts. Clark (2011) has developed the essence of 'listening' within the Mosaic approach, which recognises how children can use multi-modal instruments, such as map-making, photography and art as a means to voice their views.

Engaging with and listening to the views of children involves more than just acknowledging what children tell us verbally; it includes the rich multi-modal experiences that constitute children's lives and so reflects how they play, interact with friends and family, their experiences at school and outside of school as well as their likes and dislikes. A multi-modal approach acknowledges how meanings are not solely dependent upon 'talk' but recognises that communication is negotiated through combinations of 'modes' including gesture and movement as well as through words and through different media, such as picture making.

Listening to children using a range of senses is central to early year's professional practice and encourages practitioners to take stock of the diverse ways in which children communicate features of their emerging identity. Getting to know and understand children means being responsive to these diverse modes of communication as well as the rich array of factors which influence identity development.

Children draw upon their sense of place, significant others as well as material 'things' to convey their sense of *self* and provide opportunities to witness the layers of rich social experiences that make up social life. Understanding identity formation involves building up an in-depth picture of the *whole child* (Cooper and Collins, 2009). In order to understand children, practitioners must venture to consider both the individual child and how he or she interacts and experiences social life within a distinct social dynamic (Bronfenbrenner, 1979).

Conclusion

The essence of this investigation rests upon research as a meaning making exercise in which the process facilitates opportunities to talk, reflect and take time to listen to children. Children's drawings and photographic pictures are flexible instruments which enable children to reflect and draw upon experiences 'outside' and 'within' a given research context.

This investigation provides one example of research which engages with children. It is by no means recommended as the best way, but has attempted to demonstrate the different approaches children use to impart aspects of their developing sense of *self* and the diverse ways in which professionals can work in partnership with them. This is important in so many ways; not only does working with children respect and value what they have to say but it acknowledges that there are many ways to listen. It is important also to consider how research *with* and not *on* children can provide opportunities to address diverse needs, which is central to developing supportive environments for all children.

Critical Learning Activity

In this chapter I have discussed research as a process and attempted to impart the value of meaning making within research practice. So often the evaluation of research focuses on the end product rather than addressing many important features within the investigative process. This Critical Learning Activity encourages you to address the research process and the important questions that need to be considered when evaluating any research.

This activity sets out a critical template and encourages you to ask a range of *what*, *how* and *why* questions which are important when designing as well as when evaluating research, such as:

- *What* are the purposes of this research?
- *What* can this type of investigation achieve?
- *How* has the study been designed to meet its objectives?
- *Why* is the research important?

This type of questioning allows careful consideration of how a study has been designed and the methods and data collection instruments that have been used to satisfy the research objective. The results of any investigation can then be examined critically and within the context in which they have been generated.

The diagram below provides an overview of the critical process for any researcher or anyone interested in engaging with research literature. It provides a series of questions which allow you to evaluate the process as much as the findings. Use this template now and address each question in relation to this research example.

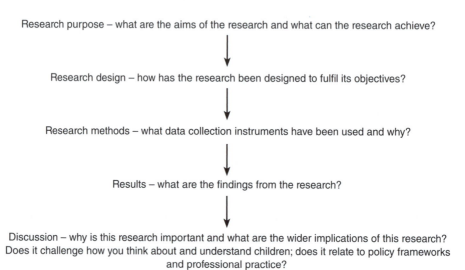

Research purpose – what are the aims of the research and what can the research achieve?

↓

Research design – how has the research been designed to fulfil its objectives?

↓

Research methods – what data collection instruments have been used and why?

↓

Results – what are the findings from the research?

↓

Discussion – why is this research important and what are the wider implications of this research? Does it challenge how you think about and understand children; does it relate to policy frameworks and professional practice?

Further reading

Barron, I. (2013) 'Finding a voice: a figured worlds approach to theorizing young children's identities', *Journal of Early Childhood Research*, 1476718X2463912, first published online 5 February.

Schnoor, O. (2012) 'Early childhood studies as vocal studies: examining the social practices of "giving voice to children's voices" in a crèche', *Childhood*, 20: 458.

References

Bronfenbrenner, U. (1979) *The Ecology of Human Development*. Cambridge, MA: Harvard University Press.

Brooks, L. (2006) *The Story of Childhood: Growing up in Modern Britain*. London: Bloomsbury.

Burns, J.R. and Rapee, R.M. (2006) 'Adolescent mental health literacy: young people's knowledge of depression and help seeking', *Journal of Adolescence*, 29 (2): 225–239.

Christensen, P. and Prout, A. (2005) 'Anthropological and sociological perspectives on the study of children', in S. Greene and D. Hogan (eds), *Researching Children's Experiences: Approaches and Methods*. London: SAGE. pp. 42–60.

Clark, A. (2011) 'Multi-modal map making with young children: exploring ethnographic and participatory methods', *Qualitative Research*, 11 (3): 311–330.

Cooper, V.L. (2013) 'Designing research for different purposes', in A. Clark, R. Flewitt, M. Hammersley and M. Robb (eds), *Understanding Research with Children and Young People*. London: SAGE.

Cooper, V.L. and Collins, J. (2009) 'Children and identity', in J. Collins and P. Foley (eds), *Promoting Children's Wellbeing: Policy and Practice*. Bristol: The Policy Press.

Durand, T.M. (2010) 'Celebrating diversity in early care and education settings: moving beyond the margins', *Early Child Development and Care*, 180 (7): 835–848.

Holloway, S. and Valentine, G. (eds) (2000) *Children's Geographies: Playing, Living, Learning*. London: Routledge.

Horton, J. and Kraftl, P. (2006) 'What else? Some more ways of thinking and doing "children's geographies"', *Children's Geographies*, 4 (1): 69–95.

Jones, O. (2008) '"True geography [ ] quickly forgotten, giving away to an adult-imagined universe". Approaching the otherness of childhood', *Children's Geographies*, 6 (2): 195–212.

Kelleher, D. and Leavey, G. (eds) (2004) *Identity and Health*. London: Taylor & Francis.

Liebenberg, L. (2009) 'The visual image as discussion point: increasing validity in boundary crossing research', *Qualitative Research*, 9: 441–467.

Stephenson, A. (2009) 'Horses in the sandpit: photography, prolonged involvement and "stepping back" as strategies for listening to children's voices', *Early Child Development and Care*, 179 (2): 131–141.

Tajfel, H. (1981) *Human Groups and Social Categories*. Cambridge: Cambridge University Press.

Want to learn more about this chapter?

Visit the companion website at **https://study.sagepub.com/reedandwalker** to access podcasts from the author and additional reading to further help you with your studies.

24

Assessment: a critical companion to early childhood pedagogy

Alma Fleet, Catherine Patterson and Janet Robertson

Chapter overview

This chapter explores a view of assessment in the early years which values children's perspectives and everyday experiences as well as the insight of thoughtful educators. It offers examples of narratives that clarify the role of the educator's 'gaze' in authentic assessment contexts and demonstrates that analysis of ordinary events can contribute to meeting the requirements of accountability frameworks. Reported from an Australian context, the examples of reflective practice have implications for educators working in a wide range of children's services.

Introduction

People working with young children and their families are known variously by such terms as early years practitioners, childcare workers, and University qualified early childhood teachers. For the purposes of clarity in this chapter, differences in experience, country of origin or tertiary qualification will be put to one side in favour of the term 'educator'. While those who have themselves been 'assessed' for their level of qualification – whether in schools, Colleges or Universities – wish to be credited for their achievements, limits in available space and the vagaries of language make the use of a generic term necessary.

This opening brings us to the focus of this chapter: What do we mean by assessment in the early years? This is a deeply complex arena which invites wide reading and discussion rather than automatic acceptance of any singular approach. This chapter will offer an overview of interpretations of this term and several narratives that illustrate authentic approaches to understanding and recording children's growth and learning.

★ **Reflection point**

As you read this chapter, try to develop your own definition of 'assessment'. What does the term include? Consider how a narrow approach to defining the term can limit opportunities for children to experience interesting, relationship-rich early childhood settings.

Rethinking

Internationally, attention is being drawn to assessment in the context of accountability-oriented policies. Narrow approaches can become mechanical and almost medical in tone, while authentic approaches offer rich insight to families and educators (Grisham-Brown et al., 2006; Fleet and Patterson, 2011; Swaffield, 2011). Any attempt to revise, rethink or energise curriculum and pedagogy must consider these challenges within the context of assessment, while noting the importance of assessment FOR learning as well as outcomes-based assessment OF learning (Hargreaves, 2010).

James notes that:

> ... the word 'assessment' has its roots in the Latin verb *ad sedere* meaning 'to sit beside', a notion somewhat removed from familiar images of examination halls with students writing silently at separated desks. In recent years, the notion that assessment might have something important to do with the teacher sitting beside the student (literally or metaphorically), and gaining an understanding of what the student knows and can do in order to help them move on in their learning, has begun to gain new ground. (2010: 161)

This interpretation of assessment suggests a formative approach where early childhood educators use their observations to build on children's knowledge, skills, dispositions, questions or concerns. Current practices of effective assessment go beyond the traditional idea of collecting data to measure children against developmental norms. Rather, educators think deeply about their observations to understand what they have observed, then use what they understand 'to enrich and extend children's learning' (Cheeseman, 2012: 1). According to Arthur and colleagues:

> … contemporary images of children as competent and capable with diverse strengths and interests have challenged educators to look critically at traditional approaches to observation and consider broader approaches to observing, analysing and documenting children's learning. (2012: 286)

While 'assessment' may have negative connotations for the reader as a result of personal experiences as a child or adult learner, the assessment of young children's learning is a significant element of early childhood teachers' work. In this chapter we invite readers to consider their understanding of assessment and its role in early childhood education. We draw on real-life examples of the documentation of children's learning to illustrate key concepts of assessment. These ideas are influenced by practices from Reggio Emilia (pedagogical documentation) and New Zealand (learning stories). The narratives may include observations of children, snippets of conversations, photographs of children engaged in learning, and samples of children's work (including photographs of block building and constructions), along with representations in various media (including painting, clay and drawings). Families are invited to make a contribution to these 'voices' of children and educators. Through thoughtful analysis of this diverse 'data', early childhood practitioners identify essential insights into the learning processes of young children. In this way, 'assessment is occurring alongside learning' (DEEWR, 2010: 37).

This documenting of 'the learner-in-action' (Carr, 2001: 141) makes children's learning visible for children, parents, teachers and communities (Giuduci et al., 2001). Unlike traditional observations which were often for the teacher's eyes only, newer approaches involve staff working collaboratively with colleagues, children and families to create records of learning and assessment. As well as spring-boarding planning, engaging children and families as active participants in assessment 'helps educators to make better sense of what they have observed and supports learning for both children and adults' (DEEWR, 2009: 17). These multiple perspectives embedded in a collaborative approach 'give all participants a voice in documentation and assessment' (Arthur et al., 2012: 289).

Assessment is also essential for accountability purposes. As Stacey notes:

> Regardless of the kind of setting teachers work in, they are accountable to others for showing what children are doing, how they are developing, what interests them, who their friends are, and what they are learning. (2009: 109)

As part of the National Quality Standard in Australia, early childhood educators are obliged to demonstrate how 'each child's learning and development is assessed as part of an ongoing cycle of planning, documenting and evaluation' (ACECQA, 2011: 32). It is important, therefore, that key stakeholders, including bureaucrats and local administrators are aware of the learning that is happening in early childhood centres. The rich and meaningful information in documentation readily draws attention to unexpected revelations about children's theories of their world, and over time it shows how children have 'engaged with increasingly complex ideas and participated in increasingly sophisticated learning experiences' (DEEWR, 2009: 17). The following example highlights the importance of thoughtfulness in approaching assessment and the need to move beyond simplistic assumptions about the focus of learning experiences.

Janet speaks: It's about the water

Many years ago as a novice teacher, I planned a traditional experience with four year-olds about floating and sinking. We sat around a tank of water and experimented with an assortment of objects; I would authoritatively state, 'It's floating', 'It's sinking', labelling each action. The next day, to see if my message had 'stuck', I repeated the event, asking each child to tell me what was happening. They easily read my intentions, and correctly labelled objects as 'sinking' or 'floating'. One child, however, looked me directly in the eye and said '**It's wet**'.

The summative 'post-test' assessment of the 'it's wet' child, in its narrowest definition, was that he did not grasp the concept of floating and sinking. But we all know that he knows a whole lot more than that. The rock was indeed wet. As you might have guessed, he was a clever child, quick-witted and funny, who 'read' beyond the educational cultural mores of giving the teacher the answer she wants. I knew that he knew it would sink and indeed had sunk. *He was adding to the concept of sinking, giving another idea for the group to consider*. The formative assessment for my learning would be that I needed to look at my teaching practices, and 'mine' the 'it's wet' concept for the range of possibilities it presented me.

Fortunately I was able to reflect on my single-minded teaching plan, and realise that I had indeed not allowed scope for a wider discussion and meaning making about floating and sinking. For example, could this action be described without water, such as floating in the air? If I had situated myself as a less authoritative 'know-it-all', I might have admitted then, as I admit to you now, that I still don't understand why heavy metal ships don't sink … My floating and sinking lesson plan was narrow and uninformed, and the summative assessment of it was that I failed. The 'it's wet' chap on the other hand, passed with flying colours, illustrating how I 'ignored the rich interplay of supportive interactions that stimulate and enable learning'. (Hatherly and Richardson, 2007: 54)

This reflection not only reminds us to value the child's perspective and to include the incorporation of the child's 'voice' in curriculum planning; it also foregrounds the importance of reflective practice, of the educator being honest with herself and others about the learning that takes place when she (or he) is thoughtful about assessment processes.

Recognising the policy context

Contemporary assessment practices in Australia are guided by the national Early Years Learning Framework (EYLF), which states that:

Assessment for children's learning refers to a process of gathering and analysing information as evidence about what children know, can do and understand. It is part of an ongoing cycle that includes planning, documenting and evaluating children's learning. (DEEWR, 2009: 17)

This positive conception implies a shift in focus towards the recognition of social and cultural contexts of learning, rather than a deficit framework of measuring what a child does not yet know. The Educators Guide for the EYLF also states that:

In order to be assessed, children need to have had opportunities to learn any knowledge, skill or disposition, either through prior experience, intentional teaching, modelling or planned for through the curriculum and learning environment. (DEEWR, 2010: 38)

Here focused opportunity is seen as the key for children's learning.

Janet's example of documentation described above reflects the philosophies presented in the EYLF. It shows assessment as part of an ongoing curriculum decision-making cycle in which there is clear evidence of 'what children know, can do and understand' (DEEWR, 2009: 17). This 'credit-based (rather than deficit-based)' approach to assessment takes a holistic view of learning (Wood and Attfield, 2005: 187), and sees children as 'searching for meaning, with a right to hope, to be considered competent and strong and to be valued' (Rinaldi, 2006: 64).

The Early Years Learning Framework (DEEWR, 2010) reminds us that children demonstrate their learning in diverse ways. Therefore documentation intended to support assessment and contribute to teacher planning should reveal greater complexity than can be provided in traditional approaches to assessment. Authentic assessment as portrayed in the analytic narratives shared here provides that complexity.

The following story has a focus on inclusion as a social justice issue, but also highlights the importance of considering assessment over time, rather than in single snap-shot moments.

Janet speaks: The ones with no eyes can't play

Several children were choosing Duplo® figures as the players for a game of table soccer. Several of these figures were rather well loved and their facial features erased by time and wear. These were put on the sidelines, as one child said, *The ones with no eyes can't play*. We interrupted this notion that people who are blind cannot play, by introducing the knowledge that players who were blind used a ball with a bell inside. The children considered that provocation and altered their play.

Months later Serena, while creating the rules for another game and remembering this interlude, said, W*ell, how can the blind people play? Maybe we could tie a bell to it.*

Learning takes time. It was only by chance we witnessed Serena's generalisation of the idea that fairness and inclusion crosses game codes.

Another aspect of the consideration of time concerns relationships – the time for children to know each other and the materials available to them, and the time for educators to know families and build points of connection with them. In this light, consider Janet's following narrative.

Janet speaks: The tiger

For several days I observed Adam and Jeremy (both just two years-old) reading an illustrated Birthday Cake book. They sat legs outstretched, to prop the book up, in various places in the room, heads together. Occasional outbursts of laughter and shouts punctuated the game. I was prompted to listen to what was happening after seeing them engage with the book in the midst of a bustling space, where children moving to and fro had to step over them. Their game persisted despite these interruptions. I realised this was something vital to them.

The next day I placed the book on a table in the foyer and invited the boys to read it again. Immediately they resumed their tryst, ignoring my presence. As they flipped through the pages they narrated to each other what they were seeing, labelling the pictures, 'pool, shoe, number three' and so on. It was only on the second run through of the book, as their page turning was inexact, that I was aware that they were hunting a particular cake image. 'Where tiger?' asked Adam, 'yeah where?' agreed Jeremy. At this point it is important to know that the book has over a hundred pages. Each time they reached the end, they returned to the beginning, labelling what they saw with each turned page.

When they reached the animal cakes (wedged between numeral cakes and theme cakes) their labelling became louder, and the page turning more frantic. It was on the fourth run through that they came upon the tiger cake. 'Yeah tiger, tiger' they shout, laughing and looking at each other, slapping the page with gusto. After a few minutes of adoration, they slam the book shut, look once again at each other and say in unison 'Again?' Which indeed they do, and in three more searches find the tiger cake once more. They work together for about 20 minutes, amicably turn taking, and engaging in a joint enterprise.

That evening when chatting to Adam's mother she divulged that Adam's 1st birthday cake was one she had made from that book and it was the tiger cake; Jeremy had been a guest at the party. Aside from the literacy knowledge the boys demonstrated, and their ability to turn take and have delight in each other's company in a sophisticated relationship (beyond the notion of parallel play), dispositions of tenacity and persistence were being evidenced.

This approach to working thoughtfully through narrative helps us understand things about these children we wouldn't know through checklists, domain-based mini-observations, or commercially constrained computer records.

A further example of this is evident in Carr and colleagues' unfolding understanding of a two year-old refugee child's fondness for the centre's rocking horse in the context of the family's history as donkey traders. Narrative information was able to be shared between the educator and members of the family, collated to pass on to the next centre with the need to get to know a transient young child quickly (Carr et al., 2001: 34–35). Equity and social justice have important places in the consideration of approaches to assessment (see for example, Fleet et al., 2012).

Some readers may be tempted to assume that these insights can only be gained when children are old enough to express themselves verbally, or to draw, write or build their interpretations of the surrounding environment. This is not the case, as the informed educator will 'see' interesting aspects in children's play, explorations and interactions which can be analysed from the perspective of 'assessment' as well as shared with families and other educators as valuable moments within the day's experiences. Thoughtful narratives can highlight curiosity and early thinking as well as infants' urges to connect with people and their surrounding environments.

Janet speaks: Claire and the box

> Claire, 15 months, has ambled up to the low outdoor table, to a basket of large gumnuts (woody fruit of the eucalyptus tree). As she goes to place it on the table, it slips and some gumnuts tumble to the floor and into a nearby large fruit box. She looks around questioningly, and I encourage her to pick them up, which she does, starting with the ones on the floor. Each gumnut is collected singly and popped into the basket, often without her looking, as she uses her fingers to find the basket edge, while her head is bent scanning and looking for more. Several have fallen away from the table, and she persists in finding them all. She straightens, and spies the few which had fallen into the box. She lets go of the table, squats down, reaches in and grasps the closest, transferring it to the basket, once again not looking where it is, but using her fingers as a guide. The other gumnuts were too far for her to reach so she stands and begins to try and put her leg into the box, with the aim of getting into it. As it is cardboard, it shifts position, so she quickly holds the table for support. She uses the box's lightness to her advantage and scuffs it closer with a kick of her leg, then attempts to pull the other leg over. The cuff of her pant snags on the edge and the box folds inwards. She pauses, reaches down with her hand and pulls the edge toward her, releasing the foot, which reaches its partner, so she is now fully inside. Now in the box, she stands and looks down, scanning where the gumnuts are. She hunkers down and collects the three from the right. She then stands, turns around, squats down again and gets the remaining nuts. She smiles, looks around, smiles at me, then sits inside the box and rocks gently with her hands on the sides. I know from past observations she is playing 'row, row, row your boat'.

Using the Australian regulatory assessment tool, the Early Years Learning Framework (DEEWR, 2009), I can note the following about Claire's ability to

- scan the situation and complete the task without help ('persist when faced with challenges', Outcome 1, p. 22);
- invent a new game referencing previous musical knowledge ('make connections between experiences', Outcome 4, p. 36);

- discover and understand the space around her, and her interaction with it ('try out strategies that were effective to solve problems in one situation in a new context', Outcome 4, p. 36).

Furthermore as a teacher–researcher, I marvel at her spatial awareness skills, as she navigates her way through a minefield of obstacles, fitting her body into spaces and shapes novel to her experience. This willingness to explore space is exciting, as she self-assesses what her body can do by trial and error. I like to call this physical deliberation, a kinaesthetic aesthetic.

Janet speaks: Sarah

Nine months-old Sarah crawls towards the home corner kitchen bench in a determined manner. Each cupboard is stocked with supplies; pans and lids in the left, kitchen utensils in the middle and empty food packets in the right. Once there, she pulls herself up, holding onto the stainless steel edge. Before her are three cupboard doors, partially obscured by her body. She steps to the right and opens the left hand door, bending down to peer inside. Straightening, she steps to the left and opens the middle cupboard. Again she bends to peer inside, while holding onto the edge for support. This time the look is longer; she squats down, reaches inside and pulls out a spatula. Standing she drops it into the sink (into which she can only see by being on tip toes). Turning to her right she opens the last door and after giving inside a cursory look, shuts it and returns to the middle cupboard. Hunkering down in front of the open door, she rummages about, making a delightful clatter. After a few moments she straightens up with a bowl in her hand. Grasping the wooden end of the spatula, she bangs the spatula on the bowl, making more noise. She looks about and sees me watching, gives me a smile and nod, bangs more and waits to see my response. I too smile and together we listen to her noise. Breaking off our joint gaze she gets back to business, using the spatula in the bowl.

For assessment purposes, I can easily tick off (assess) her physical competencies, her persistence and planning skills, as well as her concentration. However the really big questions are these: I wonder *when* it was she learnt about moving away from doors so that they can be opened, and *when* did she make an internal inventory about what is usually kept in these particular cupboards?

What do we see in these narratives? A thinking educator. What do we learn about these children? We have a nine months-old child playing with kitchen cupboards. We can choose to see her simply as 'happily occupied' or with a richer perspective, our assessment gaze can be 'seeing thinking' and valuing her use of memory as a tool to organise her play. We also have a 15 months-old box organiser. In being thoughtful about her play we have evidence that, barely a year old, she is pre-planning her activity and problem-solving as issues arise.

As Drummond has noted,

When educators assess children's learning, their intention is to find out, to make sense of what they discover and to use what has been learnt to facilitate ongoing learning. In this way, assessment becomes part of the day to day process of teaching and learning. It is an integral rather than separate activity in the curriculum development process. (2003: 14)

With informed analysis of children engaging with each other and the environment, data are generated that can contribute to further curriculum decisions. In the cases above, both girls could be offered the time and space for other opportunities to engage with these materials, as they are fruitful sources for thinking and experimentation.

Sharing responsibility for assessment

In addition to valuing children's perspectives and engaging families in conversations that lead to understandings about children, staff members benefit from a shared orientation to assessment. A team approach to assessment can be evolved over time. There will be different staff who value and recognise ('see') different things, relating in different ways to each of the children, contributing to varying books/formats/ records. This variation has implications for the individual staff member, for children and for the programme. Considering these opportunities can be a worthwhile focus for any staff group, as is shown in Janet's story below.

Janet speaks: Team assessment

Over the years, various forms of team or 'adult assessments' have been undertaken in our setting. Recently we have – as a school – focused on a particular area, using an action research methodology. One year it was 'What is assessment?'; another year 'What is our knowledge of mathematics in early childhood?' Another was 'What is the role of an iPad in an early childhood program?' At times when reviewing our reflective program documents, we have noticed a silence, an absence which needs our attention. Recently we realised that we had a strong focus on puzzles in the older room. Quite rightly we were celebrating the achievement of these four and five year-olds who were completing 500 piece jigsaws. However, it was apparent that pretend play as a focus for our observation and writing was marginalised. Studying our archive documents (records of pedagogical documentation) enabled us to redirect our 'gaze' and externalised thinking to the importance of writing and thinking about pretend play as a pedagogical emphasis.

Conclusion

So where does this discussion leave us? Assessment is about more than measurement or policy outcomes. It is a thinking process related to teaching intentionally which has the potential to highlight inclusion, thinking, creativity, family and linguistic diversity, the building of relationships and social justice issues. It has ethical constraints and both individual and community responsibilities.

Swaffield has written that '… assessment and its issues cross national boundaries. Indeed, there is much to be learned from practice developed in other countries and the way that educators elsewhere have responded to policy challenges' (2008: xii). It is hoped that these Australian examples resonate with people elsewhere.

Critical activity

Think of a child you know. Watch (or remember) a short event (an exploration or interaction) which demonstrated that child's curiosity, inventiveness or problem-solving. Write a narrative in the style of the vignettes in this chapter. From the perspective of assessing this child's growth and learning, what have you learned about this child?

Further reading

Carr, M. (2001) *Assessment in Early Childhood Settings: Learning Stories.* London: Paul Chapman Publishing.

Dahlberg, G., Moss, P. and Pence, A. (2007) *Beyond Quality in Early Childhood Education Care: Languages of Evaluation,* 2nd edn (1st edn, 1999). London: Routledge.

Early Childhood Australia (2014) *National Quality Standards Professional Learning Program.* Available at: www.earlychildhoodaustralia.org.au/nqsplp/.

New Zealand Ministry of Education (2009) *Te Whāriki.* Available at: www.educate.ece.govt.nz/learning/ curriculumAndLearning/ (accessed 19 May 2014).

References

Arthur, L., Beecher, B., Death, E., Dockett, S. and Farmer, S. (eds) (2012) *Programming and Planning in Early Childhood Settings,* 5th edn (1st edn, 1993). Melbourne: Cengage Learning.

Australian Children's Education and Care Quality Authority (ACECQA) (2011) *Guide to the National Quality Standard.* Sydney: ACECQA.

Carr, M. (2001) *Assessment in Early Childhood Settings: Learning Stories.* London: Paul Chapman and Thousand Oaks, CA: SAGE.

Carr, M., Cowie, B., Gerrity, R., Jones, C., Lee, W. and Pohio, L. (2001) 'Democratic learning and teaching communities in early childhood: can assessment play a role?', in S. Webber and L. Mitchell (eds), *Early Childhood Education for a Democratic Society: Conference Proceedings.* Wellington, New Zealand: New Zealand Council for Educational Research. Available at: www. nzcer.org.nz/system/files/ece-democratic-society.pdf (accessed 4 February 2013).

Cheeseman, S. (2012) 'Gathering and analysing information to inform curriculum decision making', *NQSPLP e-newsletter,* 39. Available at: www.earlychildhoodaustralia.org.au/nqs-plp/wp-content/uploads/2012/07/NQS_PLP_E-Newsletter_No39.pdf (accessed 4 February 2013).

Department of Education, Employment and Workplace Relations (DEEWR) (2009) *Belonging, Being and Becoming: The Early Years Learning Framework for Australia.* Canberra: Commonwealth of Australia. Available at: http://deewr.gov.au/early-years-learning-framework (accessed 19 May 2014).

Department of Education, Employment and Workplace Relations (DEEWR) (2010) *Educators Belonging, Being and Becoming: Educators' Guide to the Early Years Learning Framework for Australia.* Canberra: Commonwealth of Australia.

Drummond, M.-J. (2003) *Assessing Children's Learning,* 2nd edn (1st edn, 1993). London: David Fulton.

Fleet, A. and Patterson, C. (2011) *Seeing Assessment as a Stepping Stone: Thinking in the Context of the EYLF.* Canberra: Early Childhood Australia.

Fleet, A., Patterson, C. and Robertson, J. (2012) *Conversations: Behind Early Childhood Pedagogical Documentation.* Sydney: Pademelon Press.

Giuduci, C., Rinaldi, C. and Krechevsky, M. (eds) (2001) *Making Children's Learning Visible: Children as Individual and Group Learners.* Reggio Emilia: Reggio Children.

Grisham-Brown, J., Hallam, R. and Brookshire, R. (2006) 'Using authentic assessment to evidence children's progress toward early learning standards', *Early Childhood Education Journal,* 34 (1): 45–51.

Hargreaves, E. (2010) 'Assessment for learning? Thinking outside the (black) box', *Cambridge Journal of Education,* 35 (2): 213–224. Available at: http://dx.doi.org/10.1080/03057640500146880 (accessed 4 February 2013).

Hatherly, A. and Richardson, C. (2007) 'Building connections: assessment and evaluation revisited', in L. Keesing-Styles and H. Hedges (eds), *Theorising Early Childhood Practice: Emerging Dialogues.* Sydney: Pademelon Press. pp. 51–70.

James, M. (2010) 'Educational assessment: overview', in E. Baker, B. McGaw and P. Peterson (eds), *International Encyclopedia of Education,* Vol. 3, 3rd edn. Oxford: Elsevier. pp. 161–171.

Rinaldi, C. (2006) *In dialogue with Reggio Emilia: Listening, Researching and Learning.* London: Routledge.

Stacey, S. (2009) *Emergent Curriculum in Early Childhood Settings: From Theory to Practice.* Minnesota: Redleaf Press.

Swaffield, S. (ed.) (2008) *Unlocking Assessment: Understanding for Reflection and Application.* Oxon: Routledge.

Swaffield, S. (2011) 'Getting to the heart of authentic assessment for learning', *Assessment in Education: Principles, Policy & Practice,* 18 (4): 433–449.

Wood, E. and Attfield, J. (2005) *Play, Learning and the Early Childhood Curriculum,* 2nd edn (1st edn, 1996). London: Paul Chapman Publishing.

Want to learn more about this chapter?

Visit the companion website at **https://study.sagepub.com/reedandwalker** to access podcasts from the author and additional reading to further help you with your studies.

25

The responsibility of the practice-based researcher

Carla Solvason

Chapter overview

In this chapter we look at the responsibility that the practice-based researcher has to show respect and sensitivity toward the settings in which they work. This chapter takes that responsibility beyond permissions to consideration of character, relationships, openness and trust. However mindful the researcher is, their study will impact upon the setting in some way – how can they strive to ensure that their 'research footprint' is a positive one?

Introduction

In its most traditional form academic research has been a somewhat selfish activity. Researchers have, for want of a better term, 'used' participants as a means of gathering data. They have then utilised this data to make new claims to knowledge and to demonstrate their prowess as a researcher. But where does that leave those that they have researched with, or more traditionally 'on'? The absence of any chapter about feeding back or disseminating findings to research respondents in so many research handbooks (there are plenty about sharing research with an academic audience) demonstrates a neglectful lack of recognition of those who have provided the ways and means for the research to be carried out. As Coady (2001: 65) comments, even the most altruistic of intentions when embarking on research can become lost when an element of that study involves the researcher 'furthering their career and status

… [then] the good of the research subject can be forgotten'. In the quest for new knowledge we can forget to value the sources of that knowledge. The only way that we can begin to remedy this within early years research is to shift our focus; so that the aim of data collection is not only to do 'good research', but that we embrace, as Bloor (2010) describes it, *the researcher's obligation to bring about good*.

Carefully making an impact

Inevitably all research, even that with the best of intentions, will leave a mark; there is a researcher 'footprint'. The situated cultures in which we carry out our studies will have changed in sometimes a considerable, but most times an almost imperceptible way, as a result of our research. But the certainty is that there will be change. To exemplify this McNiff (2010) uses the analogy of a garden. She says that if we plant even one new flower in our garden it will alter the biosphere in some (albeit minute) way. This garden is like the public spheres in which we live, work and research. Because of the certainty of our actions causing a reaction we have a responsibility as researchers to make sure that the impact is a positive one. If we have reached a point within our professional development where we are carrying out research activity, then we are becoming leaders in the creation of knowledge, and as such our aim should be to encourage and to inspire, never to judge, never to blame.

Of course I am not suggesting that all research that we carry out should create a significant impact upon the thoughts and processes within the setting. It is a rare and privileged researcher that can bring about such profound alterations through their work. The reality of practice-based research is that much of it will create a new range of questions that need to be pursued; this is a far more customary result than actually reaching conclusive 'solutions'. And it may be that the setting does choose to pursue some of these questions, or it may be that they believe that they are fine just as they are, thank you very much. An impact in terms of the results of the data is not what I am referring to here. The point that I wish to emphasise is that through the very process of interacting with the setting in order to fulfil your curiosity, by speaking with practitioners, parents and children, by scrutinising documents, perhaps observing practice, you are expecting the setting, if only in some small way, to 'open up' to you. They are allowing their actions to not only be observed but critically analysed and for that analysis to be recorded. By doing this they put themselves in a very vulnerable position. It is important to remember this when settings appear reluctant to support our research endeavours. What we need to consider is how we can reassure them that they are in safe hands.

As those that we are researching with are showing a willingness to place themselves in a position where, potentially, fault could be found with their practice, it is our responsibility as researchers to act with humility and sensitivity. We need to demonstrate, through our words and actions, a sincere intent to help build and to support, not to demean. MacNaughton et al. (2001: 5) describe how 'Research … challenges habitual ways of doing things, and provides reasons to modify, refocus or change'. Our responsibility as practice-based researchers is to reassure settings that our aim is to find ways to make that which is good even better, to support their endeavours; it is not to find that which is 'wrong' and tell them how to put it right.

Many times when discussing practitioner research with colleagues and students I have referred to Stern's (2011) reminder that as researchers we are in a privileged and powerful position to potentially cast judgements on others (see also Walker and Solvason, 2014). Stern makes the point that as researchers we can produce research that is 'vicious' or 'virtuous'. Now it is unlikely that any researcher will purposefully set out to produce a study that will be damaging, but sometimes researchers do explore an area because they believe that they have seen things that are not being done 'correctly'. This is often carried out naively, especially by new researchers who are prone to take what McNiff (2011) refers to as the 'balcony' approach to research. This approach involves the researcher looking 'down' on others from their privileged position of theoretical knowledge. As a result the focus becomes those behaviours that do not fit the ideologies of espoused theory and results are inevitably negative. The setting and practitioners become the 'subjects' of this type of research as opposed to research partners involved in developing practice.

Rather than this focus upon the negative, practitioner research should be about increasing our own knowledge through better understanding the experiences and motivations of others. If, having viewed a situation we conclude that we would have done things very differently, then it is important that we learn about the values and motivations of those involved. We need to better understand why it was that they behaved in the way that they did. Difference does not need to be a criticism, simply because you would have responded in a dissimilar way. Stern (2011) emphasises that purely because we hold information that could be seen as defamatory it does not mean that that information needs to be told. It is not human to behave in a way that is faultless. Instead we need to remember our responsibility as researchers and leaders of practice to support and nurture, rather than to undermine. In this paragraph I refer in general terms to practices, processes and interactions; I do not refer to any actions which may cause concerns of a safeguarding nature. In such situations all other formalities become moot – any actions causing potential or actual risk or harm to a child should be reported through the systems established within that context.

Walker and Solvason (2014) encourage practice-based researchers to see themselves not as 'investigators' but as 'facilitators' of an investigation. We should see ourselves as working with the setting to discover ways of improving the child's experience.

There is a humility which should be central to research, whereby the researcher aims to learn from and alongside those with whom she is researching. Our primary aim should be to improve our own practice; to consider our own actions (Walker and Solvason, 2014). Pring (2004) lists the qualities of respect, humility, modesty and kindness as being vital in our approach to research. Costley and colleagues (2010: 43) refer to this as a 'caring' approach that 'reframe[s] the research project as a mutual activity which has personal consequences'. The type of interpretive approach that practitioner research usually takes involves people, relationships and emotions. It involves working with people who may have very strong feelings about their setting, their parents, their children; it involves researching alongside people who may have spent many hours and sometimes many years developing their setting into what it is. Their emotional investment should not be taken lightly.

The stance taken at the outset of research sets the tone for building purposeful research relationships. Sometimes promoting openness to change can be tricky, but this is a central element of reflective practice. How can settings possibly be open to change if those researching them are not? McNiff (2010: 106) suggests that the knowledge that we hold (and which can sometimes dominate a study in a rather heavy-handed way) should be held 'lightly' because 'what you know today may change tomorrow. Always remember that you may, after all, be mistaken.' It is always disheartening to read a study where the overriding aim is to prove that the researcher was 'right'. Openness to new ideas and a reflective stance which is open to change are vital when carrying out research. Palmer (1998: 108) used the wonderful phrase, 'Humility is the only lens through which great things can be seen …'. If we already have the answers then what would be the point of inconveniencing others with our research?

Beginning with the end

It is really important that we keep the ideas above to the forefront when we frame our research and that we do not become so focused on the process of 'collecting data' that we overlook the individuals that we are collecting that data from. What will we be requesting from the individuals within the setting in order for us to gain the data which we require? In considering that question we need to also consider whether our relationships with individuals in the setting are already established or whether we need to gain the trust of those that are new to us. How will we be able to assure the setting that our aims are positive? Being able to inform all of those that we wish to research with of our intentions is vital if research partners are to feel comfortable with the research process. Increasingly I have swayed students towards the appreciative enquiry approach, for a number of reasons; I hope that those reasons will become evident when you have reflected upon the activity below:

★   **Reflection point**

Put yourself in the position of a nursery manager who regularly has students within the setting. Two students present their research ideas to you – what would be your initial response to each? How would the comments make an impact upon you emotionally? Which would you most willingly support?

Kerry: I would like to investigate your practitioners' views about using the outdoors as a learning area because I don't think that they are using it enough. I'd like to find out what is stopping them from using the outside and help them with information about how beneficial the outdoors is in order to encourage them to use it more.

James: I would like to explore the ways in which your practitioners use the outside area as this is an area in which I have little experience. I'd like to see how practitioners use the outdoors to promote learning, and whether this approach could be used more, across all subject areas.

The two projects above actually have exactly the same aims, only Kerry has taken the traditional approach to research which assumes that there is a problem that needs to be solved. There is a strong temptation when you are new to research to want to find out if something is being done 'properly', and if it is not, to put it right. This is caused by our media-fed views of research which imagines it as something akin to detective work. Unfortunately this approach also has undertones of 'them against us', which you see reading between the lines of Kerry's proposal. The suggestion is that she knows better and needs to share her superior knowledge with those in the setting. Silverman (2000: 198) provides a wonderful description of this approach (and I make no apologies for making regular reference to it), he says:

> Under the remit of divine orthodoxy, the social scientist is transformed into philosopher-king (or queen) who can always see through people's claims and know better than they do.

This approach starts with the assumption that people are mistaken. It assumes that things 'out there', in terms of others' understanding and their practices, need to be improved. It does not focus upon the change and development of the practitioner who is carrying out the research. James wants to look at the same topic, but he has switched the primary focus to his own improvement, with further improvements in practice as a desired by-product. Although both have the same desired endpoint (increasing the use of the outside area to support learning) one research project is posed in a far more positive way than the other.

James' is a more humble approach. The aim of James' approach is to learn from the knowledge and experience of others. This is sometimes referred to as Appreciative

Enquiry (Cooperrider, 2005) and it looks for the positives which already exist in practice. It reflects upon those positives and investigates what it is that makes them work – thus enabling them to be built upon. So James will be looking at what is already done well within the setting, with the aim of learning from it and potentially expanding upon it. Research should not only be about 'avoiding harm' whilst we extract the evidence that we require, but it is about 'discovering how to make a positive difference' (Munford et al., 2008: 64). What better way for students to do that than exploring the essence of successful approaches and considering how to replicate that?

Another positive approach to research is McNiff's (2010) Action Research approach. She focuses all of the change and development upon the individual. The focus of this type of research is individual self-improvement. It acknowledges an area that the researcher would like to improve upon and sets about gaining the knowledge needed in order to do that. With McNiff's approach any wider change comes about as a by-product of the improved understanding and practice of the researcher themselves. They do not expect others to change; instead they lead by positive example.

And this all leads us towards 'the end': what and how will we feed back to the people that we have gained the data from? Walker and Solvason (2014: 123) state that:

> … the actions from your research may occur at the end but the process of dissemination starts at the beginning. This consideration will help to authenticate your research by giving credence to your motivation in carrying out the research and establishing your values to the reader and the participants.

If we consider any impact that our research findings could have on the participants from the outset then this should, theoretically at least, prevent us from asking any inappropriate research questions. This should help us to formulate an approach that is not only beneficial to us in terms of improving our practice, but will also be beneficial to the setting. Kerry was, rather heavy-handedly, looking to improve practice within the setting, but she had not really considered the feelings of the individuals that she would be working with, or their emotional investment in the practices and processes that were already in existence.

Mindfulness of the setting culture

By carrying out research in settings we are delving into the existing culture, or the 'set of beliefs and unspoken rules, based on history and tradition, which affects how individuals act and interact with one another' (Solvason, 2005: 86). The way that we act, the questions that we ask, will all impact upon that public space. By aiming to improve our own practice we can, potentially, have a positive impact upon those around us, without needing to make recommendations, or tell others what to do. As a practice-based research study is predominantly about your personal development, making recommendations may not always be appropriate. More often consideration of how you might modify your own future practice is far more appropriate than suggesting that others modify theirs. McNiff (2010: 132) says that 'If you can make your action enquiry public, and produce an account to show how you tried to improve one small aspect of your work, you stand some hope of influencing the thinking of someone somewhere…'. If you disseminate your own findings to your colleagues, or others with whom you share your working sphere, then there is the possibility that your discoveries could influence the thinking of others and bring about change for the better.

Ultimately it is important that practitioner–researchers remember that they are working with *people* and not *settings*. Because of this it is important that we move beyond the procedural approach to ethics, which includes cover letters and permissions, to one which considers our relationships with, our position and impact upon, those settings with which we are researching. Banks (2009: 59) suggests that we move away from the concept of professional ethics and towards the concept of ethics within our professional lives. Or that we move from the abstracted area of study to the reality of lived experiences, and that we do this by 'broadening the scope of focus from codes, conduct and cases to include commitment, character and context'. If we have been employed by our research setting for a while these things will already be familiar to us; the challenge will be to stand back and consider them objectively, but if we are new to the setting it is important to spend some time familiarising ourselves with it.

McNiff and Whitehead (2010: 66) suggest the consideration of a range of questions before carrying out your research, such as: how supportive will your colleagues be, what type of help you may (or may not) receive and the nature of the manager or equivalent. These types of questions will help you to assess what McNiff and Whitehead refer to as the *cultural climate* of the setting. The existing culture within the setting should have a direct impact upon the data that you deem it appropriate to collect and the methods that you choose to use in order to do that. Prosser (1999: 13) describes culture as 'a unifying theme that provides meaning, direction and mobilisation' and says that this theme is solidified in terms of 'artefacts and behavioural norms, and sustained implicitly by jargon, metaphors and rites'. If we are outsiders coming to a setting (as many undergraduate students carrying out placements are) then it is very important that we take the time to ascertain an understanding of the setting culture and to work appropriately within it, rather than imposing ourselves upon it in a heavy-handed way. We need to consider not only the data that we wish to collect, but how that can be collected in a way that is congruent with the culture of the setting and which will cause minimum disturbance. In some cases that will involve providing explicit reassurance to individuals who may be wary about the nature of the work (Cohen et al., 2007). This need to reassure those that you are working with had a profound effect upon my own large scale research project, where it took a whole year of being present on site before a slot was found to tell the staff as a whole the actual purpose of my work. As a result I constantly met with barriers to my data collection, based upon suspicion and the fact that I might be seeking fault. Even after the time was found for me to clarify the aims of the project many staff needed individual assurance about what would happen to the data that I collected from them. In observing them or in collating their views we have ownership of a small part of those that we have researched with. We have a responsibility to let them know what has become of that information.

We have a responsibility to feed back

Mac Naughton et al. (2001: 3) state that:

> The best research will always involve close, ongoing collaboration between those who plan the research, those who carry it out, those who participate in it and those for whom the results have an impact.

You need to consider what the setting can reasonably expect from you as a sign of your appreciation for them enabling you to carry out your research. When I first began to mark Independent Studies I did not expect to see any type of dissemination of results mentioned. I now see this as central to the researcher's partnership with the setting – what I 'know' has changed. This brings me back to the opening comments of this chapter, where I stated that traditionally settings have simply been utilised as a means of collecting data. Such an approach does not ring true with Pring's (2004) concept of virtuous research or with Banks' (2009) drive away from ethical procedures towards the embodiment of professional ethics. It is misaligned with McNiff's (2010) vision of research having a fruitful (if subtle) impact upon the culture of the research context and with Munford et al.'s (2008) assertion that research should make a positive difference. We have a duty to share our discoveries with the research partners that helped us to create them and it is only by doing this that we have potential to generate change for improvement.

There is no set approach to sharing our findings with settings; the approach will alter according to context. Just as your initial ideas for your research should be discussed with the setting at the outset, your ideas for dissemination should also. Your feedback may take the form of ideas shared in a staff meeting, a written report for governors or an information leaflet for parents. It may be that your options are limited and your only means of sharing your new understanding is by demonstrating improved practice, and that is fine. As an early years professional you have a duty to share your findings as a thank you to those that shared their time, their physical space, their experience and their wisdom. Remember that the ultimate aim of all early years research is that the quality of the experience of the child is improved; your findings, however modest, could help others to reflect on ways to do that.

How can we strive to ensure that our approaches to research embody sensitivity towards others, humility and respect? Munford et al. suggest that critical reflection is (2008: 63) 'an essential component of effective research practice'. Although not often recognised within literature, research and reflection are inextricably linked. If reflection is central to high quality practice then it seems entirely logical that it should also be central to high quality research. We are used to the phrase 'reflective practice' but not to 'reflective research' – although one is simply a more formalised version of the other. Central to the concept of reflection is that we recognise the multiplicity of viewpoints that exist and how we act and interact within these in our social spheres (Brookfield, 1995, and Luft and Ingham, 1955 explore these concepts). We cannot carry out ethical, sensitive and worthwhile research without consideration of the thoughts and feelings of others. Whether planning our research, carrying out our research or considering the data that we have collected, we need to be mindful of the impact that our research could have upon those that we are researching with. Our responsibility towards others is embedded in every step of our research and is a world away from the superficiality of ethical forms and procedures that are often seen as representing 'ethical research'.

Critical Learning Activity

There are a number of points within this discussion where I have used words and phrases such as 'professional' and 'leaders of thought' in relation to the early years practitioner–researcher. I would argue that an effective early years practitioner embodies professionalism and leadership and is also an active researcher (as illustrated by figure 25.1). What are your views on this? Can each of these character traits be present independently or are they interlinked?

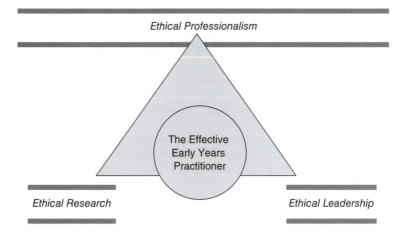

Figure 25.1   Ethical professionalism

Further reading

McNiff, J. (2010) *Action Research for Professional Development*. Dorset: September Books.
Walker, R. and Solvason, C. (2014) *Success with your Early Years Research Project*. London: SAGE.

References

Banks, S. (2009) 'From professional ethics to ethics in professional life: implications for learning, teaching and study', *Ethics and Social Welfare*, 3 (1): 55–63.

Bloor, M. (2010) 'The researcher's obligation to bring about good', *Qualitative Social Work*, 9 (11): 17–20.

Brookfield, S. (1995) *Becoming a Critically Reflective Teacher*. San Francisco, CA: Jossey-Bass.

Coady, M. (2001) 'Ethics in early childhood research', in G. Mac Naughton, S.A. Rolfe and I. Siraj-Blatchford (eds), *Doing Early Childhood Research: International Perspectives on Theory and Practice*. Buckingham: Open University Press.

Cohen, L., Manion, L. and Morrison, K. (2007) *Research Methods in Education*, 6th edn. London: Routledge Falmer.

Cooperrider, D. (2005) *Appreciative Inquiry: A Positive Revolution in Change*. California: Berrett-Koehler.

Costley, C., Elliott, G. and Gibbs, P. (2010) *Doing Work-Based Research: Approaches to Enquiry for Insider Researchers*. London: SAGE.

Luft, J. and Ingham, H. (1955) *The Johari Window, a Graphic Model of Interpersonal Awareness*, proceedings of the Western Training Laboratory in Group Development, UCLA, Los Angeles.

Mac Naughton, G., Rolfe, S.A. and Siraj-Blatchford, I. (2001) *Doing Early Childhood Research*. Buckingham: OUP.

McNiff, J. (2010) *Action Research for Professional Development*. Dorset: September Books.

McNiff, J. (2011) *Exploring Practice Based Research*, paper presented at the BECERA Annual Conference, Birmingham.

McNiff, J. and Whitehead, J. (2010) *You and Your Action Research Project*. Oxon: Routledge.

Munford, R., Sanders, J., Mirfin, B., Conder, V. and Conder, J. (2008) 'Ethics and research: searching for ethical practice in research', *Ethics and Social Welfare*, 2 (1): 50–66.

Palmer, P.J. (1998) *The Courage to Teach: Exploring the Inner Landscape of a Teacher's Life*. San Francisco, CA: Jossey-Bass.

Pring, R. (2004) *Philosophy of Education: Aims, Theory, Common Sense and Research*. London: Continuum.

Prosser, J. (ed.) (1999) *School Culture*. London: Paul Chapman.

Silverman, D. (2000) *Doing Qualitative Research: A Practical Handbook*. London: SAGE.

Solvason, C. (2005) 'Investigating specialist school ethos … or do you mean culture?', *Educational Studies*, 31 (1): 85–94.

Stern, J. (2011) *From Negative Ethics to Positive Virtues in Inquiry*, paper presented at the Value and Virtue conference, 1–2 June, York St John University.

Walker, R. and Solvason, C. (2014) *Success with your Early Years Research Project*. London: SAGE.

Want to learn more about this chapter?

Visit the companion website at **https://study.sagepub.com/reedandwalker** to access podcasts from the author and additional reading to further help you with your studies.

Index